Conceptualising China through translation

Manchester University Press

ALTERNATIVE SINOLOGY

Series editors: Richard Madsen and Zheng Yangwen

This series provides a dedicated outlet for monographs and possibly edited volumes that take alternative views on contemporary or historical China; use alternative research methodologies to achieve unique outcomes; focus on otherwise understudied or marginalised aspects of China, Chineseness, or the Chinese state and the Chinese cultural diaspora; or generally attempt to unsettle the status quo in Chinese studies, broadly construed. There has never been a better time to embark on such a series, as both China and the academic disciplines engaged in studying it seem ready for change.

Previously published

The advocacy trap   Stephen Noakes

Communists constructing capitalism: State, market, and the Party in China's financial reform   Julian Gruin

Conceptualising China through translation

James St. André

MANCHESTER UNIVERSITY PRESS

Published by Manchester University Press
Oxford Road, Manchester M13 9PL

www.manchesteruniversitypress.co.uk

British Library Cataloguing-in-Publication Data
A catalogue record for this book is available from the British Library

ISBN 978 1 5261 5732 4 hardback
ISBN 978 1 5261 9573 9 paperback

First published 2023
Paperback published 2026

EU authorised representative for GPSR:
Easy Access System Europe – Mustamäe tee 50,
10621 Tallinn, Estonia
gpsr.requests@easproject.com

Typeset by Newgen Publishing UK

Contents

Tables

Series editors' foreword

The study of China has in recent decades seen an explosion as many universities began to offer modules ranging from Chinese history, politics, and sociology to urban, cultural, and Diaspora studies. This is welcome news; the field grows when the world is hungry for knowledge about China. Chinese studies as a result have moved further away from the interdisciplinary tradition of sinology towards more discipline-based teaching and research. This is significant because it has helped integrate the once-marginalised Chinese subjects into firmly established academic disciplines; practitioners should learn and grow within their own fields. This has also, however, compartmentalised Chinese studies as China scholars communicate much less with each other than before since they now teach and research in different departments; the study of China has lost some of its exceptionalism and former sheen.

Alternative Sinology calls for a more nuanced way forward. China scholars can firmly ground themselves in their own perspective fields; they still have the advantage of sinology, the more holistic approach. The combination of disciplinary and area studies can help us innovate and lead. Now is an exciting time to take the study of China to new heights as the country has seen unprecedented change and offers us both hindsight and new observations. Alternative Sinology challenges China scholars. It calls on them to think creatively and unsettle the status quo by using new and alternative materials and methods to dissect China. It encourages them to take on understudied and marginalised aspects of China at a time when the field is growing and expanding rapidly. The case of China can promote the field and strengthen the individual discipline as well.

Richard Madsen and Zheng Yangwen

Acknowledgements

Part of the research for this project was made possible by funds provided by the Hong Kong Research Grants Council, General Research Fund Project #14603115. The author also acknowledges the generous support of the Faculty of Arts Publication Fund, The Chinese University of Hong Kong, in covering part of the publication costs.

Introduction: setting the terms

In 2010, the Chinese writer Yu Hua published a collection of essays entitled 十個詞彙裡的中國, which appeared first in a French translation as *La Chine en dix mots*, then in Chinese in Taiwan, and finally in English as *China in Ten Words* in 2011. I stumbled upon this work just as I was finishing up an article on the vagaries of the phrase 'to lose face' in English, a calque from Chinese which had then spawned the phrase 'to save face'. I had discovered in my research that this pair of expressions in English were widely perceived to be the 'key' to understanding the uniqueness of China in the late nineteenth and early twentieth century, only later to morph into a universal category in sociology and sociolinguistics to explain the basis for politeness in all cultures (St. André 2013). The conflation of these two events set me thinking about who decides what are the key terms to understand China, how they decide, and what happens to these terms over time, both in Chinese and in English.

This study posits that when two cultures meet, there are often a tightly limited set of terms that are theorised as key concepts to explain what is different or unique about one or both cultures. Neither the list of concepts nor the meaning of each concept is fixed; they may change as they travel in time and space and between languages. Such a process is not necessarily one-way, but rather may be back and forth between two languages, or in various circuitous routes among several languages. Moreover, it is not just the Other who is liable to such reductive description through keywords; the Self may also participate in, or even initiate, such a process.

The question of how terms and concepts change over time is not a new one, and initially I drew inspiration from two essays on travelling theory, one by Edward Said and one by J. Hillis Miller. Said (1983) conceptualises a four-fold process, wherein a theory starts from a given location, travels to another culture, encounters conditions of resistance or acceptance, and is thereby adapted for use in the new culture. Miller (1996) uses the story of Ruth from the Old Testament to think about the possibility of the theory having some agency in the process (where Ruth is the theory). Both essays emphasise the perils involved when theory travels: Said worries that theory will become codified and institutionalised, thereby losing its revolutionary potential, while for Miller the danger is that theory will be promiscuous when it travels (in his reading, Ruth's main agency lies in her decision to sleep with Boaz) and/or be misunderstood by the host culture. While these models both provide interesting insights, in both cases I was dissatisfied, first by Said's insistence on a one-way, passive process, and second by Miller's gendered politics that reads the theory as promiscuous female in danger of infecting others, while at the same time wanting to reserve a patriarchal dominion over his theory that he denies to literary authors over their literary creations, which the critic is free to interpret as he wills.

Once I started looking, I quickly discovered that key concepts as an explanation for what is essential or at least different about China or the Chinese are everywhere, and new ones are proposed on a regular basis. Most recently Lake (2018) has proposed the concept 'leftover women' (*shengnü* 剩女) to explain an important and unique element of Chinese culture that has emerged in the past thirty years, the understanding of which is crucial to understanding contemporary China. After claiming that women's roles in China had remained the same for 'five thousand years' (13), she posits that:

> China's 'left-over women' are the ultimate linchpin to the country's rise and development. They are broadcasting a cultural shift so massive that it defines not only contemporary China, but also the single greatest demographic movement of our era across the world. (Lake 2018, 14)[1]

Lake certainly pulls no punches in her claims, from the five thousand years of unchanging China to the exaggerated notion that this single concept is the key to understanding events that are reshaping the entire world.

Although the concepts used to understand China are often related in some fashion to Chinese culture, this is not always the case. In the 2018 edition of the Australia National University's annual *China Story Yearbook 2018: Power*, they chose the concept 'power' as the theme, and featured articles on political power, soft power, cultural power, financial power, military power, girl power, and several others (Golley *et al* 2019). This concept is not specifically linked to China or Chinese culture, and in fact the concept chosen for 2019, 'dreams' (Golley *et al* 2020), has arguably traditionally been more closely associated with the United States.

Moreover, the use of key concepts is by no means limited to China; almost any country may find itself explained by one or more key concepts.

Japan offers at least three good examples: *bushidō*, *miyabi*, and *mujō*. Benesch (2014, 2) discusses the belief that *bushidō*, the 'way of the samurai' or honour code, was a key factor in explaining Japan's modern success in everything from the economy to baseball. She cites Nitobe Inazō, *Bushido: The Soul of Japan* (1899) as one of the first works to stake a claim for the term's centrality in Japanese society. In the 1960s, Yukio Mishima proposed that *miyabi* (courtly elegance) was the soul of Japanese culture and flowed from the emperor; therefore, defending the emperor was defending the core of Japanese identity (Nathan 2019, 29). More recently, in the wake of the Fukushima disaster, Haruki Murakami, in an interview in *The Asia-Pacific Journal*, has advanced the term *mujō* to explain how Japanese are able to live on the brink of disaster: 'This concept of mujō has been *seared deeply into the Japanese spirit*, forming a *national mindset* that has continued on almost without change since ancient times' (Murakami 2011, 2; my emphasis). The italicised passages link Murakami's understanding of Japan with Lake's understanding of China: the terms are connected with nation, and with a sense of timeless essence. This explanation has been picked up by others: 'To explain Japan, the authors also cite Murakami Haruki's use of the word *mujō*, a Buddhist concept that means that everything is ephemeral and nothing is immutable or eternal, something that has been burned into the spirit of the Japanese people' (Glosserman and Snyder 2015, 801).

Most such works tend to pick one or at most a handful of terms to explain a foreign culture. Working closer to home, Raymond Williams in his *Keywords* (1985) set out to cast a wider net, engaging with over one hundred interlocking concepts that would illuminate various areas of culture and society in his native Britain.[2] His example has been followed by Bennett *et al* (2005). That follow-up study is illuminating in how, whether through the passage of time or the difference in individual choice, which words are identified as 'key' may change: 96 of the 146 keywords in Bennett, or over 65 per cent, are not found in Williams's study.

Taking a wider view, the linguist Anna Wierzbicka (1997) has devoted an entire book to a handful of key concepts that are either unique to a particular country or that, by the variation in shades of meaning in different languages, enable her to explain differences between cultures in different parts of the world. A conference at Leicester, 'Key Cultural Texts in Translation' (April 2014), based on an AHRC-funded project, expressly took their cue from Gallie's notion of essentially contested concepts. Their list of Western key cultural concepts consisted of ten terms: 'childhood, adulthood (and the relations between them), citizenship, freedom and personal identity (and the relations between them), nationhood, foreignness, democracy, dictatorship (and other political "states") and the sacred'.[3]

Several of these terms come from the political realm, and there is a rich tradition of writing about key concepts in political theory. Williams (1985) and Bennett *et al* (2005) both contain a high percentage of words related to politics, as a comparison with the more recent *Politics: The*

Key Concepts (Harrison *et al* 2015) shows.[4] In Germany, the discipline of *begriffsgeschichte*, or history of concepts, has resulted in two massive reference works, one on concepts in German, begun in the 1960s, and another on key concepts in French, begun in 1982 (Richter 1987). As Richter (1986) points out, these works concentrate on political and social terms, and deal with translation at least to the extent that the terms they index are, like Williams's keywords, often derived from Greek, Latin, or Arabic roots, and include sensitivity to change over time, with the period of 1750–1850 seen as a watershed for the development of the modern sense of most of these terms in German.

For individual terms there is also a rich tradition of writing. Liberty/ freedom, to take just one example (these are usually treated as synonymous, although some writers such as Pitkin [1988] take pains to distinguish between them), is one of the most written-about in the English tradition (see among others Mill 1859; Berlin 1958; McCloskey 1965; Skinner 1998). This is a good example of where the Self is involved in the construction of its own identity, for quite a lot of the research in this area is done by British and American authors describing their own culture.

More recently, the intersection of begriffsgeschichte, translation studies, and historical studies of social and political thought were brought together in Burke and Richter (2012), a collection of essays that looks at the movement of ideas both within Europe and between Europe and Asia. There is also the project on philosophical terms in European languages under the direction of Barbara Cassin, which resulted in the *Vocabulaire Européen des Philosophes: Dictionnaire des Intraduisibles* (Cassin 2004).

Finally, I would like to note the increased attention being paid to concepts in the humanities, not necessarily to understand individual cultures, but rather to understand the difference between approaches to analysis, and how concepts may change as they travel through both time and space.

Jonathan Culler (2002) traces the development of the notion of performativity from Austin's speech acts to Butler's gender as performance. Along the way, one of the key authors is Derrida and another is Paul de Man, but the issue of translation never arises. In a sense, Culler is showing how concepts evolve within a particular tradition (mainly Anglo-American) but the presence of Derrida already points to the less-than-airtight nature of that system.

Mieke Bal (2002, 24–25) details how concepts shift in meaning as they move from one discipline to another, for example hybridity, which moves from biology as a concept with negative associations of sterility, only to migrate into postcolonial studies, where it is celebrated. Other terms may experience a going-out and then return movement, as in her example of focalisation moving from optics into art history, then to literary studies, and finally back again to art history (36–37). With all this movement and shifting that she sees, she hesitates between saying that intersubjectivity (complete agreement about a concept) can never be achieved, and wanting to build at least some consensus within the humanities on how and what concepts mean (11–12), because for her, 'interdisciplinarity in the humanities, necessary, exciting, serious, must seek its heuristic and methodological basis in *concepts* rather than *methods*' (5).

Drawing on these approaches, this study looks back to four key concepts that I will demonstrate have travelled back and forth between Chinese and English over centuries.[5] The concepts are filial piety and *xiao* (孝), geomancy and *fengshui* (風水), face and *mianzi/lian* (面子/臉), and connections and *guanxi* (關係). In each case, I will trace how the concepts changed and developed interlingually, from the earliest period of contact to the present.

The relation between language and thought: words, terms, concepts

Many of the works consulted for this book use an array of terms, including keywords, key terms, and key concepts in ways that, when brought together, could sometimes be confusing or contradictory. Before I proceed any further, I would like to make clear what terms I use and why. In order to do so, however, I must first explore the rather vexed question of the relationship between words, terms, and concepts.[6]

In philosophy, 'concept' refers to an indeterminate abstract thing that is variously theorised as being an image or representation in the mind, an ability, or a sense. It has traditionally been delimited by definition, but more recent understandings have sought to use a prototype model (for example, 'apple' as prototypical of the concept 'fruit' in English), a theoretical model (concepts are part of an interrelated scientific systemic understanding that can be learned), or a referential model (like proper nouns, they are essentially tags that point to something) (Margolis and Laurence 2014). Concepts can be fairly simple. 'Bachelor' is often used as an example, especially by those who embrace a definitional approach, where the concept consists of two components that are both necessary: it denotes a *man* who is *unmarried*. It seems that concepts are what words get translated into in the mind and thus are fundamental to thought processes.

Outside of philosophy, not many theorists are concerned with simple concepts such as 'bachelor'. Rather, they use 'concept' to refer to ideas that are complex, often rather nebulous, and subject to debate or contestation. Wierzbicka (1997) looks at a small number of concepts such as 'friend' which, while certainly common, are not as easy to define as bachelor and have a number of different shades of meaning in different languages. Others use 'concept' to denote ideas that are in the domain of specialist knowledge. Bal, for example, says that 'text' is both a *word* 'from everyday language' in common use and also a specialist *concept* in the fields of semiotics, anthropology, art history, and film studies (Bal 2002, 26). Here the meaning of a word in 'everyday language' is specifically excluded from enjoying the status of concept.

Philosophical definitions of concept are generally too broad to be of use to me (although there are important insights to be gained regarding how we can theorise what concepts are and how they work), while Bal's specialist knowledge model is too narrow. Thus I follow Wierzbicka and, to a lesser extent, Williams and Richter, not because I do not believe words like 'bachelor' can be considered concepts, or because I do not believe that certain words are used in different ways by different groups, but rather because the concepts that interest me cross over between specialist and general use and show a relatively high degree of complexity, uncertainty, and variability. Indeed, in his introduction Williams (1985, 14) states that the simultaneous use of a term in both general and specialist domains is one of the main criteria for inclusion in his list. Moreover, Wierzbicka is one of the few writers who has tackled the problem of the 'same' concept in different languages, and shown how even a simple term like 'friend', which is often treated as a universal, has a degree of difference from concepts in other languages that are too often treated simply as different labels for the Anglo-Saxon concept of friend. There remain problems with Wierzbicka's work (to which I will return later), but her point is well taken that concepts that many people believe to be fairly standard across languages may in fact, upon closer examination, turn out to be different, sometimes in surprising ways.

Wierzbicka's work raises the possibility that no concepts are universal to human experience, because each language develops concepts in different ways. This would seem to lead to a linguistic relativism reminiscent of the Sapir-Whorf hypothesis, with speakers of different languages locked into different mindsets. However, I do not think that she is trying to argue this. Rather, she is pointing out that we cannot assume that because we think the concept of friendship must be universal to all cultures, our *particular* definition of friendship is a universal. Rather, we need to compare how different cultures define friend, mate, *ami*, *pengyou* 朋友, et cetera. Then we have three choices: either strip the concept down to its bare essentials (what they all share in common), build up a composite, or embrace pluralism. Failure to do one of these three results in a sort of cultural hegemony that, in today's anglo-centric world, would result in English concepts being defined as the standard against which concepts in other languages are judged.

The flip side of Wierzbicka's project is to argue that cultures are different, and so therefore concepts are going to be different and, in fact, if we select the right concepts and study them carefully, we can better understand what makes a culture unique. Here she is right in line with Yu Hua and the long tradition of writings about China and many other countries, cultures, or ethnic groups that zero in on a few key terms to explain why that group is different. Her discussion of the Australian term 'mate' as a near synonym for 'friend' that yet reveals important differences between American and Australian culture is a case in point (Wierzbicka 1997, 101–11).

If I am talking about certain terms in different languages to denote concepts, am I taking issue with Wierzbicka and implying that concepts float free of language? Certainly some people believe this to be true. An article by Podger and Chan (2015), 'The Concept of "Merit" in Australia, China and Taiwan', blithely ignores the question of translation, never mentioning once the Chinese terms circulating in China and Taiwan that supposedly are equivalent to 'merit' in English. This is all the more interesting because their conclusion is that 'merit' means different things in different cultures.[7] The researchers do not seem to be aware of the work by Wierzbicka and others.

A more interesting case is advanced by Margolis and Laurence (2014), who cite research on the ability of birds to do things like understand the relative perishability of different food items and prioritise retrieval of stored food based on that information and also on whether another bird or animal observed them caching it. This suggests that some animals are capable of developing concepts (food types; perishability; danger of discovery; location) and integrating them into survival strategies.[8] If animals are capable of developing such concepts without the use of language, then humans should also be capable of using concepts independently from language.

However, there seems to be strong evidence that when humans think about the types of complex and variable concepts that concern me in this book, they do so through language, and certainly when they talk or write about them, they are using language. So I will assume that the concepts discussed in this book are, or can be expressed as, verbal structures. Although this may seem to tie concepts to individual languages, I would argue that this would be to neglect the experience of an important subgroup of both populations: multilinguals. In other words, rather than think of linguistic systems as airtight compartments that remain forever separate, concepts may be made up of experiences in more than one language. Therefore, when I want to indicate that I am talking about a word in a particular language, rather than the concept, I will use the term 'term', as in 'the term fengshui enters into the English language quite early, although in a rather bewildering variety of spellings'.

Some concepts are considered as broadly applicable in many different cultures, even if they are slightly different in each, while other concepts are thought to be more culturally specific, tied to one particular group or time period. The use of the term 'key' in front of the word concept often signals both that the concept is important, and also that the reason the concept is important is that it is culturally specific. This study, while challenging the notion of universal concepts, conceives of an international, interlingual situation where concepts may overlap between languages but seldom (if ever) coincide completely.[9] Moreover, there may be important differences within one language or even one culture concerning the meaning of a particular concept. Here I am following Gallie's (1956) notion of essentially contested concepts, and departing from Wierzbicka, who seems to believe in a rule of one culture—one nation—one concept.[10] Culturally contested concepts are open in the sense that they admit of modification. More importantly for my work, 'recognition of a given concept as essentially contested implies recognition of rival uses of it ... as not only logically possible and humanly "likely", but as of permanent potential critical value to one's own use or interpretation of the concept in question' (Gallie 1956, 193). Part of the reason such concepts are contested is that they relate to values of a group or subgroup.

In early China, a good example of an essentially contested concept is the term *dao* (道 way, path), to which A. C. Graham devotes an entire book, *Disputers of the Tao* (1989). In it, he argues that in early China different schools of thought had different interpretations of what dao meant, and that as a key concept used by all major schools of thought in this period, a careful consideration of how the different schools used it reveals much about the differences between their standpoints and worldviews.

Since this book is written in English, I will use the English terms to refer to concepts; if I intend to refer to just the English term, I will specify that by using 'term' as in 'the (key) term "filial piety"'. When I want to refer specifically to the term in Chinese I will use a romanised version of the term and, if I wish to restrict my discussion to the concept of filial piety in Chinese, again, I will specify that, as in 'the concept of filial piety in China underwent a radical change in the early twentieth century'. This does not mean that I endorse the view that the English term is a supersign determining the meaning of the concept in other languages.

'Keyword' in this study refers specifically to the words typed into a search engine, as in the phrase 'perform a keyword search for "geomancy" in the database Early English Books Online'. While these keywords will often be words that are used in English to refer to a key concept regarding Chinese culture, they could also be any other word in either English or Chinese. The process of extracting relevant data from large corpora through keyword searches is an art in itself, as Spedding (2011) has shown, and in some cases I have performed keyword searches for a variety of terms more or less closely related to one of the key concepts.

How concepts change

First, we note that concepts may change within a single language over time 'spontaneously', or in other words, with little or no identifiable outside influence. If I may take a simple example close to my home, consider the term 'Yankee'. Its earliest use was restricted to the denizens of New England, and was seemingly used derogatively first by Dutch settlers in New York and then by the British to refer to New England settlers (Quinion 2004). In New England itself the term was adopted and used in a neutral or positive sense, implying characteristics of 'conservatism, thrift, pertinacity or shrewdness' according to *Webster's Third New International Dictionary, Unabridged* (Gove 1993), and the sharp Yankee trader became a stock figure in early American folklore. By the time of the civil war, Yankee was extended to refer to anyone in the northern states, in contrast with Southerners, and then later became a general term to refer to any citizen of the United States; it is likely that the image of Uncle Sam evolved from caricatures of the Yankee (Botkin 1947, 4). In an ironic twist of fate, one of the two New York baseball teams took the name Yankees, and the rivalry between the Boston Red Sox and the New York Yankees means for many baseball fans that Yankee is no longer associated with New England at all, but rather has returned to New York, where it was first coined almost three centuries ago.

Yet even as this relatively simple example shows in its probable origins in the Dutch language, concepts often change as a result of interlingual contact and the role of translation. Moreover, once Yankee was used to denominate anyone from the United States, it travelled abroad and began to take on negative connotations once again, especially in its Spanish form *yanqui*, which in turn has migrated back into English (Gove 1993) and is associated with imperialism, occupation, invasion, crass consumerism, bullying, and right-wing ideology.[11] Of these characteristics, the only one that can be matched even tangentially to the early meaning of the term 'Yankee' is right-wing, which we may associate with the conservatism of nineteenth-century New England Yankees, although I would argue that the choice of 'conservatism' in the nineteenth century carries positive connotations, whereas the designation 'right-wing' has decidedly negative ones, so even here the match is not exact.

The second way in which concepts change over time, then, is through outside influence. In some cases, where there are two distinct groups both using the same language, such influence may be intralingual. But outside influence may also involve translation. In some cases, where a concept is in a specialist domain, the process of change may involve a combination of intralingual and interlingual transfers, as the work of Stengers (1987) in the sciences shows.

Theorists such as Eugene Nida (1959) have called upon translators not to violate the norms of the host language. If this were possible, then translators would merely be maintaining the status quo of languages, and their utterances would have no effect on the connotation or denotation of terms, other than to maintain and reinforce existing usage. They would thus become a conservative factor, actually retarding language change. However, in practice, translation rarely (if ever) achieves one hundred percent 'covertness', to use Juliane House's term for this phenomenon (1977). Therefore translation plays a crucial role, both by introducing new concepts (such as fengshui being introduced into English from Chinese), and by modifying the connotations and sometimes the denotation of existing concepts.

Finally, the role of multilingual speakers should not be overlooked. They are, first of all, the people responsible for translation and interpretation. However, even when not actively translating or interpreting, anyone with competency in more than one language who uses a term in one language may base their understanding of that term on related terms in another language. The concept 'Yankee' as designated by the terms 'Yankee/yanqui' among bilingual English-Spanish speakers is a good example of this.

These are the purely mechanical means by which such change can be affected. Why such changes occur is, I think, highly contingent on a great number of specific historical, social, and cultural factors that must be examined individually. To the extent possible given existing resources, I have tried to do that in the following chapters when I consider individual terms.

Directionality

Traditionally, studies of how concepts change through translation have tended to focus on one-way transactions. Like diffusion studies in anthropology, the idea is that a concept is invented or evolves in one particular time and place, and then spreads out to others. This one-way view of the process is aided and abetted by a wide range of metaphors that are popularly used in translation studies, such as source and target language; the translator as following in the footsteps of the author; the act of translation as anthropophagy or incorporation; migration or transfer; refraction; submission; painting a portrait; and playing a musical score. All of these metaphors assume that translation is a one-way and irreversible process. Indeed, despite the fact that early translation studies relied heavily on communication theory, which is based on face-to-face, two-way dialogue, diagrams of translation in such works are of one-way processes beginning on the left-hand side and moving right (see for example Nida 1959, 18).

It is certainly true that in many cases concepts travel one way and can play an important role in cultural change, especially in the short term, and much fine work has been done in this regard. The fields of history of philosophy, intellectual history, and the history of ideas are full of examples. Bertrand Russell's *History of Western Philosophy* (1945) contains many examples of the development and spread of philosophic concepts, while *The Dictionary of the History of Ideas* (Weiner 1973–74) and the *New Dictionary of the History of Ideas* (Horowitz 2004) give good overviews of the extent of such studies in the history of ideas and intellectual history. In the German begriffsgeschichte tradition, the three magisterial reference works cited by Richter (1986) all contain multiple examples of concepts that began in some other language and then were imported into either German or French, and the essays collected in Burke and Richter (2012) also contain several examples, either of concepts travelling from Europe to Asia or vice versa. Other disciplines, such as anthropology, also have contributed to the discussion (Hanks 2014).

To take just a few examples from East Asia, the influx of both terminology and concepts into late imperial and Republican China has been the subject of numerous studies (notably Gao and Liu 1958; Masini 1993; Liu 1995; Lackner *et al* 2001; Huang 2008; Kurtz 2012). Similarly, studies on the importation of European terms and concepts into Japan, especially during and immediately after the Meiji Restoration, are also numerous (Abosch 1964; Iyenaga 1966; Hane 1969; Beasley 2000; Howland 2002; Howland 2012). Yoon Sun Yang (2017) has looked at the importation of ideas surrounding the modern subject into Korean.

Looking further afield, it is not difficult to find many such studies, often under the rubric 'knowledge transfer', dealing with either the exportation of European ideas to other parts of the world, or the importation of select ideas from abroad back to Europe. The papers presented at the conference 'Knowledge Translation on a Global Scale (Asia-Europe-the Americas, Sixteenth through Twentieth Centuries)' (2017) features papers on Europe-Paraguay (Boidin 2017; Brignon 2017), Europe-Peru (Llerena 2017), Europe-South Asia (Lefèvre 2017), and Europe-China (Klaising Chen 2017).

However, there has slowly been growing recognition that the situation is more complicated. While Williams was quite content to focus on Britain, even though he drew attention to the foreign origin of many of his terms and discussed those roots extensively, Bennett *et al* (2005, xix) signal in their introduction that they would have liked to adopt a cross-cultural approach for a few terms—liberalism, market, consumption, ideology, socialism (that last one 'in China today')—but that it proved to be beyond them.

Zhongshan Daxue Xixue Dongjian Wenxian Guan (2016) notes that, since translators may work in both directions between languages, they may draw upon their experience in one direction when looking for equivalences in the other direction. Specifically, they note that Christian missionaries were translating the Bible into Chinese while simultaneously translating Chinese classics into Latin, Spanish, French, Portuguese, Italian, German, and English. Gentzler (2017, 70) speaks of translation as not 'one-way directional flow of ideas ... [but rather] the *circulation* of texts, or better said, the *spiraling* flow of ideas' (his italics).

There are also a few earlier studies that at least implicitly recognise that concepts may develop interlingually. One excellent example is Koebner and Schmidt's *Imperialism: The Story and Significance of a Political Word* (1964). They trace the varied fortune of the term from the early nineteenth century through 1960. Their tale begins with the Napoleonic wars, when the British used it as a term of opprobrium against Napoleon's empire and it was linked to militarism, despotism, and a maniacal leader intent on territorial expansion. In this sense it was used against Disraeli by his opponents, only for the term to reverse its polarity and become a rallying cry for the success of the British empire in the second half of the nineteenth century. Up until this point the authors concentrate on the term in Britain, but starting from the Second Boer War (1899–1902), they bring in writings by peoples of other nations; first the Germans, then the French, the Americans, and finally African and Asian nationalists, so that by the end of World War I, a combination of writings and discussions results in a worldwide consensus emerging that 'imperialism rose to global eminence as the leading slogan of three world struggles, the struggle against capitalism, against Anglo-Saxon domination, and the struggle against white colonial power' (Koebner and Schmidt 1964, 279). In the course of this development, the authors mention specifically that certain key works in different languages were read by other important players, either in the original language or in translation, and that they then influenced how those subsequent thinkers conceptualised imperialism (265–78).

Other factors involved

When two or more cultures come into contact and exchange concepts or modify their use, political, historical, social, and economic factors play a large role in determining which cultures, and therefore which usages, are dominant. Such factors may also determine when external factors may be more important, or internal factors more important.

The evolution of the Chinese concept of *yi* (夷) is an excellent example. Originally *yi* was one of four terms used in Chinese to denote non-Han people living to the East, along with *man* (蠻 to the South), *di* (狄 to the North), and *rong* (戎 to the West). Yi gradually came to be used generally for anyone coming from outside of China, either on its own or sometimes combined with *man* to form a compound. Early translations of this term into English tended to use the term 'foreigner' as its equivalent, but at some point in the third decade of the nineteenth century, translators began using 'barbarian' with increasing frequency, which then was used as evidence that the Chinese were not treating the British with the respect they thought they deserved (Liu 1995), although there were some who continued to argue that yi was no more insulting than the word foreigner in English as late as the 1850s (see Thoms 1853). Eventually, at the end of the Second Opium War (1856–60), the British were able to impose as a condition of the Treaty of Tientsin that the Chinese were not allowed to use the term yi to refer to the British in any official Chinese document, and the term yi, to the extent that it is used today in Chinese to mean foreigners, does in fact usually have a negative connotation akin to 'barbarian' rather than just 'foreigner' (Liu 1995) (mostly in the compound adjective *manyi* 蠻夷, barbaric; the noun *niyi* 逆夷, barbarian invaders; and the phrase *rangyi* 攘夷, repel the barbarians). Thus military superiority on the part of the British (with help from the French and Americans) resulted in a decidedly one-sided process: the concepts of 'foreigner' and 'barbarian' in English probably changed very little through contact with yi, yet yi changed greatly.

The Japanese concept *bushidō* allows for an interesting comparison with the Chinese concept yi. According to Benesch (2014, 1–5), bushidō emerges in the late nineteenth century as an important concept; it is sometimes translated as 'way of the warrior' or 'way of the samurai', where the final syllable *dō* is the Chinese character dao, discussed earlier as an essentially contested concept in early China. Like yi, bushidō was heavily influenced by a British concept, in this case chivalry; yet it was not a direct military threat from Great Britain that influenced the conceptualisation, but rather admiration for a successful nation and their traditions that led Japanese writers to voluntarily choose to model bushidō to some extent upon the Victorian notion of chivalry.

As with foreigner and barbarian, the meaning of chivalry was not strongly affected by the exchange with the Japanese concept bushidō. However, in this case, rather than suppressing the foreign term, the British took over the Japanese term as a loanword to describe a unique characteristic of the Japanese. To the extent that the term exists and is used in English, its meaning is largely based on the (modern) definition in Japanese. So chivalry and bushidō come to be separate, if still related, concepts in both languages, where the meaning of chivalry in both languages relies heavily on the English concept, while the meaning of bushidō in both languages relies heavily on the modern Japanese term, which in turn was first influenced by the English concept of chivalry and then has developed subsequently in that language (Benesch 2014, 10).

Bushidō is also an interesting case because, like some of the concepts I consider in the chapters that follow, there are a cluster of terms related to it in both languages that overlap and compete with one another. In nineteenth-century Britain, the aristocratic chivalry is partially translated into the bourgeois gentlemanship, or the way of being a gentleman, and texts relating to the virtues of an English gentleman are important to the development of the concept of bushidō in Japan through the writings of Ozaki Yukio (Benesch 2014, 49–55). In Japanese, terms included '*budō* (the martial way), *shidō* (the way of the samurai/gentleman), *hōkōnin no michi* (the way of the retainer), *otoko no michi* (the way of masculinity), *heidō* (the way of the soldier), and many others' (4). Thus in both languages we have multiple terms that may be referring to one concept, or to concepts that overlap substantially. In English, 'chivalry' in the late nineteenth century is probably closer in meaning to 'the way of the gentleman' than it is to medieval concept(s) of chivalry; to a certain extent, advocates of gentlemanship had borrowed the cachet of chivalry in order to refine and promote their own concept.

Lydia Liu (1995) has proposed the concept of 'supersign' to describe the English concept 'barbarian' and explain how it was able to determine the meaning of a word in another language. While I certainly agree with her description of what happened to yi in Chinese due to it being equated with barbarian in English, I hesitate to embrace the concept of supersign because it seems to suggest that some concepts exist on some higher plane above language, or in some ill-defined third space. Moreover, it suggests that there is something intrinsic to the sign that allows this to happen, when in fact there is nothing special about the term 'barbarian/barbaric'; rather, it is the (temporary!) political and military superiority of the British that allows them to dictate the meaning of yi to the Chinese. The fate of yi, then, is an extreme example of how concepts can change through translation.

Although I argue that overlapping concepts in different languages may influence each other as they develop over time, I ultimately decided that it would be better to continue to treat the concepts separately in Chinese and in English. If we imagine a simple Venn diagram with two circles that overlap partially, what I will demonstrate is that the area of overlap between the concepts in the two languages is not fixed; at times they may overlap to such an extent that they are for all intents and purposes the same; at other times they may diverge sharply and share relatively little. Moreover, what elements of meaning they share may also change over time. Among my four pairs of concepts, filial piety and xiao may be said at the beginning to seem to Europeans to be synonymous; yet as time goes on, they first diverge and then come closer together, but when they come closer together in the modern period, it is because the original concept of filial piety in English has largely been evacuated and then filled with the definition of filial piety from Chinese. The concepts of geomancy and fengshui begin as radically different, but through the postulate of early translators that geomancy equals *dili* (地理), gradually the English term largely loses its original meaning and takes on the meaning of the Chinese concept of fengshui (which, I must hasten to point out, is not identical to the earlier concept of dili). Today few people are aware that geomancy originally referred to a divinatory practice from the Middle East; such knowledge is limited to a small number of specialist works. Likewise, in linguistics today, the question of whether face equals mianzi/lian is a hotly contested topic.

An area where one language does seem to dominate the discourse on how a concept is defined today is science. In *Scientific Babel* (2015), Gordin traces how English has increasingly become *the* language of science in the twentieth and twenty-first century (299–315). Thus native speakers of English can be monolingual scientists, but for the rest of the world, science is always to a greater or lesser extent experienced in translation. To the extent that science is thought of as a language containing concepts, many seem to believe that science is a universal language, because the concepts in it are based on observation of the natural world. This viewpoint is neatly encapsulated in the science fiction story 'Omnilingual' by H. Beam Piper. In it, archaeologists exploring ruins on Mars come across a Martian representation of the periodical table of elements. Since the periodical table represents universal constants regarding the composition of elements, the archaeologists are able to 'read' the table and thus begin to decipher the Martian language (Piper 1957).[12] The story ends with this epiphany, and readers do not see the Martian script in its entirety being understood, but it is clearly implied that, now that they have this 'key', the archaeologists and linguists of the team will quickly be able to do so.[13]

English as the lingua franca for science is, however, exceptional. For most other domains of knowledge, other languages continue to play a role. In some cases, such as traditional Chinese medicine (TCM), the dominant language is clearly still Chinese, not English, and discussions of TCM concepts are more likely to be arbitrated in Chinese than any other language.

However, in the modern era, few languages exist in isolation, and even within the field of TCM, where Chinese definitions are still generally considered authoritative, there is pressure to discuss TCM in Chinese using scientific terminology and concepts; given the dominance of English in determining the meaning of scientific concepts, this in turn means that English concepts begin to have an influence in the understanding of TCM concepts. Moreover, there have been increasing attempts to translate TCM into English as a way of establishing its legitimacy internationally, probably because English is the lingua franca of science, and TCM as a body of knowledge ultimately wants either to be considered scientific, or to challenge the universality of current scientific norms.[14]

My interest is not in any of these 'universal' concepts, but rather with a cluster of terms that all relate to the culture of one specific country: China.

There are many culturally specific terms that have crossed over into English from Chinese, either in translation, transliteration, or a mixture of the two (see Chan and Kwok 1985 for transliterated terms). Some of these terms, after a brief vogue, fell out of fashion; more of them never developed significantly beyond their original meaning in Chinese, and the English translation exerted little or no influence on the original Chinese term. There are also many more terms that have crossed over from English and other European languages into Chinese, but these have, by and large, not been centrally concerned with describing Chinese culture.

This study concentrates on four key concepts that enjoyed, for at least a period of time, a process of mutual interaction between the Chinese and the English terms. In some cases, two independent concepts in the two languages existed before interaction (xiao and filial piety); in other cases, a concept in Chinese was introduced into English ('to lose face' as a structural calque for *diu lian* 丟臉). For yet another term, both of these processes applied (fengshui is both borrowed from Chinese and also equated with a pre-existing term, geomancy). Finally, in one case, a late nineteenth-century coinage in Japanese borrowed into Chinese, and then again subsequently borrowed into English is involved (guanxi).

Along the way, we will also encounter some concepts that, while important for the development of a discourse about China, the Chinese, and Chineseness in English, changed relatively little due to interlingual interaction. A cluster of terms related to *fengshui* that demonstrate this include *qi* (氣 vital essence), *yinyang* (陰陽 yin and yang, dark and light, female and male, et cetera), and *wuxing* (五行 five elements or five phases). The first of these terms, qi, has been somewhat modified by exposure to Western scientific concepts of matter, in particular gas, air, and breath, while the latter two have been relatively unaffected.[15]

Guanxi, which is a late nineteenth-century loan from Japanese, is a bit trickier, but we will see that a whole cluster of terms in English, including nepotism, connections, favouritism, and old school ties, are involved, while in Chinese, pre-twentieth-century terms included *renqing* (人情 sometimes glossed as human relations or affective ties).

For the concept of face, first we have two terms in Chinese, lian and mianzi, along with a cluster of fairly set collocations with a limited number of verbs.[16] Fengshui, by contrast, has only the one term in Chinese in the modern period. In earlier periods the related term dili was also available (and is in fact older than fengshui), but dili today in Chinese has become the term for the modern concept of geography and is seldom associated with fengshui. This is an interesting example of the continued existence of a *term* but with a completely different *concept* now associated with it. In English we continue to have both fengshui and geomancy as competing terms, geomancy in English having largely lost its original meaning of a fortunetelling practice originating in the Middle East. Indeed, the terms are often used together interchangeably, as in the website for the Centre for Applied Feng Shui Research, whose web address is www.geomancy.net.

Filial piety became grouped together with three other concepts in Chinese, *zhong* (忠 loyalty), *jie* (潔 continence/chastity), *yi* (義 righteousness) to form the four virtues; it was also part of one of the 'five bonds' or 'five relationships', fuzi (父子 son to father), wherein the son was supposed to be xiao to the father. The other four bonds were *junchen* (君臣 subject to ruler; so again loyalty comes back), *fufu* (夫婦 wife to husband; wherein the wife must be chaste), *xiongdi* (兄弟 younger brother to elder brother; again, the younger was supposed to follow the elder) and *pengyou* (朋友 friend to friend). Of these, the one most closely related to filial piety was loyalty, and there are many examples where Confucianists struggled with the potential conflict between these two, as we will see in Chapter 1. In English, the term filial or filiality is sometimes used in place of filial piety, while other terms such as filial duty, duty, and dutiful, are sometimes used, and affectionate (or filial affection), or even loving, seems in places to be a close, but not exact synonym.

For all these concepts, there has also been historical development, with terminology changing over time. Thus the Jesuits seem to have first encountered the term dili, which they equated to geomancy; later dili was adopted as the translation for the English term 'geography' while the term fengshui in Chinese (already present at least as early as the eighteenth century) became the only term available for the set of practices relating to the proper situation of buildings and graves in relation to their natural surroundings.

Mianzi and lian, likewise, emerge at different times. Hu (1944) cites texts as early as the fourth century BCE that use the term *mian*, without the nominalising suffix *zi*, and posits that this was a southern term, while lian was a much later term that emerged in North China around the time of the Mongol invasion. The modern compound mianzi is seldom used before the Republican era, and yet now generally is the default term to discuss the concept of public social status in a wide variety of matters;

people are more likely to say that something is a matter of mianzi rather than say it is a matter of lian.

Filial piety has been more stable in Chinese, probably because it is such a central concept in Confucianism. However, in the modern period compound words have become increasingly common, and the single character xiao is less likely to be used by itself. The most common compound for xiao is *xiaojing* 孝敬, but there are also others like *xiaoshun* 孝順 that are fairly common and close in meaning. By itself *jing* means to respect, while *shun* means to follow, so in the first case more emphasis is placed on the child's attitude, while in the second case it is more on actions—obediently following parental wishes.

Thus when comparing concepts between Chinese and English, we run into the problem of the relationship between characters and words in Chinese. In the premodern era, three of the four concepts I am concerned with were expressed by words consisting of a single character, but in the modern period they may either be expressed by those single characters or by compound words that contain the character plus some other character that may be a near synonym or may extend the meaning in varying directions. The single characters are most likely to occur in set phrases and writing or formal language, such as newscasting or public speeches, while the compounds are today generally more common, especially in everyday conversation.

This all means that there is no one-to-one correspondence between either a single character or a single word in Chinese and any of these concepts, just as in English there are frequently near synonyms, such as liberty and freedom, fengshui and geomancy. At the risk of oversimplifying, I will use filial piety, face, fengshui and guanxi as labels for the four concepts, whether in English or Chinese, but will frequently have recourse to the development of different terms related to these concepts.

A (relatively) simple example would be the varying terms in English and Chinese for the study of all things relating to China and the Chinese. In English, the terms sinologist and sinology were coined in the nineteenth century at about the same time as the French terms sinologue and sinologie. The hallmark of sinology was its breadth of scope in terms of disciplines, including as it did linguistics and language acquisition as its base, but also history, literature, philosophy, and religion. The rise of the social sciences in the twentieth century, especially after World War II, however, led to sinology coming to be seen as rather old-fashioned. With the rise of Area Studies, the terms 'Chinese Studies' became more common, which emphasised a social sciences approach (politics, sociology, anthropology and still history) and a downplaying of language skills. It also led to the increasingly frequent 'housing' of academics who specialised in China in different disciplinary departments, leading to 'Chinese history' becoming a subset of historical studies rather than a subset of sinology for some practitioners. In the twenty-first century, 'China Studies' has emerged as a term for the study of all things relating to the country of China, specifically the People's Republic of China (PRC). In return, some scholars unhappy with this nation-centred approach have called for either a 'new sinology' (Barmé 2005) or sinophone studies (Shih 2004; Shih 2011). Alongside these rather broad umbrella terms, there are also constituent areas such as Chinese linguistics, Chinese literature, Chinese history, and Chinese philology. In Chinese, *hanxue* (漢學 Han studies) is often seen as a rough equivalent of sinology, as is sometimes *guoxue* (國學 national studies), while *zhongguo yanjiu* (中國研究 the study of China) is closer to China studies. Yet these are not exact equivalents, and the debates over which term is best cross over between the two languages in surprising ways.

Methodology

This study uses a mixed methodological approach, combining close reading of texts in their historical context along with various automated or semi-automated processes taken from what is now called digital humanities approaches. The main approach that I use is corpus studies, which at its most basic level simply means the maintenance and manipulation of texts and images in digital format. I have used a variety of corpora, both found (pre-existing, having been built by others) and custom-built. In some cases, I have searched through a corpus manually, meaning that I have looked at each occurrence of whatever I was searching for, the computer merely helping me to locate passages based on keyword searches. In other cases, I have used automated tools to compile statistical data, which I have manipulated in various ways using further digital humanities tools. Since the way that I use various corpora differs, rather than explain them all here, I will do so as and when appropriate in individual chapters.

Such methods are still relatively new and have certain limitations, which I have tried to take into account when drawing conclusions based on them. First, my study ranges over four centuries, two languages, and four continents; it must be acknowledged that there is great unevenness of the data available for different time periods, genres, and languages, with certain periods better represented than others. Early English Books Online (hereafter EEBO) has as its stated goal to digitise every book published from the earliest incunabula through the year 1700, and as of December 2018 claimed to have 132,600 titles in its collection.[17] Eighteenth Century Collections Online (hereafter ECCO) picks up where EEBO leaves off, and covers the period 1700–1800, again aiming to digitise everything printed commercially in the United Kingdom and much of what was printed in North America, with a count of 185,000 titles.[18] Thus a researcher with access to these two databases can search through 317,600 works published up to the year 1800. After that date and up until about 1920, coverage in English becomes spotty. For books, I have had to rely upon a combination of Googlebooks, HathiTrust, the Internet Archive, and Project Gutenberg, along with some specialised databases such as Nineteenth Century Collections Online: Asia and the West, and Western Books on China up to 1850 Online.

After 1920, an increasing percentage of books is still in copyright and therefore not easily available in digital format; after the lawsuit filed against Google, even though Google still holds texts in digital format, users are not allowed to read them, although snippets of text or single pages may show up in search results. The Internet Archive has, since at least 2018, gotten around this problem somewhat by allowing a single reader to 'borrow' books still protected by copyright for a period of time, just as a traditional circulating library does, but the text cannot be downloaded and so therefore cannot be compiled into a local corpus; they must be searched individually using the Internet Archive's own search engine.

There are also specialised databases for magazines and newspapers; I have mainly used three databases from ProQuest: Historical Newspapers, American Periodicals Series, and British Periodicals. Historical Newspapers contains over forty English-language newspapers covering both the nineteenth- and the twentieth-century. American Periodicals (1501 titles) cover earliest periodicals up to about 1900, while British Periodicals (493 titles) includes a selection of titles in the first half of the twentieth century. After this period, electronic versions of many magazines and newspapers are available through subscription services.

In terms of secondary material in English, what journals, and what years of what journals, are available for searching has been a relatively minor issue, but book-length studies (edited volumes and monographs) are unevenly available electronically.

Finally, in terms of the quality of the data (how accurately the texts have been digitised) and what sort of search functions are available, the databases mentioned above vary wildly. In 2018, I published the results of a study on the use of electronic corpora in translation studies, where I evaluated several of those just discussed (St. André 2018b). Briefly, only two of the databases (EEBO and Project Gutenberg) employ a robust system to ensure that texts are as close to being error-free as possible by manually checking every line of text. The other platforms all rely on conversion from image files (generally PDF format) to text file through an automated process of optical character recognition (OCR) software, which has a varying rate of error, especially for older texts; my study showed that on a text printed in 1769, the error rate (per word) was between 9.4 and 54.1 per cent. This means that search results may not be reliable, missing as many as half the occurrences of a key-word in a search. Searches on texts after about 1800, when the long *s* was abandoned and recognisably modern typefaces began to be used, are better, typically with an error rate between 2 and 10 per cent.

Turning to Chinese-language materials, similar problems present them-selves, along with others unique to Chinese. A study by Cao (2018) found that, although a higher percentage of digital materials that have been con-verted to text format have been manually keyed in because OCR software for Chinese characters lags behind that used for English in terms of accur-acy, many important databases for the nineteenth and first half of the twen-tieth centuries consist mainly of texts held in PDF format with little or no search functionality. Thus while many premodern texts are available in high-quality, fully searchable format, the early modern period is poorly served. For premodern Chinese texts I have relied on the Chinese Text Project; for modern books I have mainly used Apabi Reader.

Unless I was able to download entire texts and compile a local corpus, all searches had to be done using the proprietary search engines of each database, and these differ substantially in the use of stop words, wildcards, and Boolean operators. Finally, due to the constant changing nature of all digital platforms, search functions, and OCR reliability, a search carried out three years ago (or even three days ago, in some cases) is not replicable today, or would not yield the same results, due to changes in one or more of these factors.

Despite this rather long list of caveats, I still feel that digital methods are well suited to a study that aims to trace the development of concepts between Chinese and English. They allow, at the very least, the rapid loca-tion of many examples of the use of any and all terminology. Indeed, the main problem with this approach is the sometimes overwhelming number of hits, which it would be impossible to examine individually. For my study of filial piety, I looked at each individual entry in EEBO since there were not too many, but then for ECCO the hits rapidly multiplied and I adopted a dual approach: first, a representative sample of all works that contained the word filial, and then a selective approach, focusing on works whose titles or synopsis (when available) indicated that the content might be more cen-trally concerned with the concept of filial piety. When it came to Chinese-language sources, however, the sheer number of references to xiao made it completely impossible to ever begin to look at more than a fraction of examples, since xiao is such a central concept in Confucianism. Luckily, since it is such a central concept, there is a rich secondary literature on its growth and development, and I have drawn extensively on that material in my research. Indeed, just searching for articles on xiao in modern academic articles produces thousands of hits, and necessitated much care in the selection of the studies most directly relevant to my topic.

Based on this mixture of quantitative and qualitative data, the chapters that follow will trace the development of these four terms over an extended period of time. Each case begins at a different starting point, but all of them continue into the present.

In Chapter 1, I discuss the twin concepts of filial in English and xiao in Chinese. After noting their early, independent development, I tease out both commonalities and differences in these two concepts which, on the surface, seem quite similar, as both emphasise their 'natural' basis in father-son relations. After an initial period of contact where the two terms are seen as basically synonymous, differences emerge in the English discourse surrounding the translation of the term xiao, leading eventually to two terms, filial duty and filial piety, being the most commonly used binomes. Then finally in the twentieth-century consensus devolving upon the term 'filial piety' in English as, not a native English concept, but a translation of the Chinese concept xiao, which by the modern period is conceptualised as significantly different from natural feelings of a child towards parents, and believed to be holding China back from entering modernity. This new understanding of filial piety in English then impinges on the concept in China, where it is thoroughly debunked by many leading intellectuals and by the Chinese Communist Party, only to be resuscitated in the post-Mao era in the services of the state.

Chapter 2 looks at the concept of fengshui, or geomancy, as it is sometimes called in English. While xiao has been quite stable as a term in Chinese from a very early period, fengshui is of much more recent provenance, emerging sometime in the late Ming or early Qing dynasty. Previously, there had been a concept dili, associated mainly with the proper location of palaces and tombs of the ruling class; it was this term that the Jesuits chose to render as geomancy. Although the term dili subsequently fell into disuse and was re-assigned as a translation equivalent for the Western science of geography, the term geomancy has remained associated with the concept of fengshui in English to this day, side by side with the transliterated importation of fengshui. Unlike xiao, which was initially well received in English and indeed throughout Europe as a positive Chinese virtue, the practices of dili and fengshui were from almost the beginning associated with paganism, superstition, and magic, and therefore conceptualised in English as a blight on Chinese civilisation. Such a view of fengshui (not dili) was embraced by many members of the literati class in China even before the fall of the Qing dynasty in 1911 and accelerated during the May Fourth Movement. However, due to British scruples about interfering with native belief systems, fengshui became a powerful tool for local resistance to both Western incursions and government control, specifically the construction of telegraph lines, railroads, and other works. Fengshui's value and meaning, therefore, split along class lines in a way that xiao never did, and was practiced especially in the British colonies of Hong Kong and Singapore; to this day, the Hong Kong government has a fengshui fund to recompense villagers in the New Territories when a public works project is claimed to damage the fengshui of a village or an individual house or grave site. The persistence of fengshui practices outside of Mainland China after 1949 eventually led to it being adopted, now with positive connotations, in English-speaking countries, to the point that it can be used to describe local practices in American cities by people with little or no knowledge of Chinese culture. Unlike xiao, then, fengshui has undergone a positive makeover in English, while in Chinese, in modified form, it continues to be an important but localised (mainly southern and overseas) social practice.

Chapter 3, like Chapter 2, explores a concept that is imported into English from Chinese, this time through calquing. A word-for-word translation of an expression in Chinese, diu lian, enters pidgin English as 'to lose face' probably in the eighteenth century and then slowly becomes accepted as a regional expression, along with the phrase 'to save face', which is coined in English slightly later. As with filial piety, the concept of face undergoes heavy criticism, first in English in the nineteenth century, and then in Chinese in the early twentieth century. Unlike either filial piety or geomancy, however, face manages to escape its initially close ties with Chinese culture and become accepted as a general explanation of human social interaction. Under this guise it is adopted first by sociologists in the late 1950s and then sociolinguists in the 1970s, where it is awarded a special status as the cornerstone to polite behaviour in all societies, only to be attacked by Chinese and Japanese scholars as a now thoroughly Western concept, incapable of explaining social behaviour in East Asia. Finally, I show how face today remains both a general category in English and Chinese, with most English speakers completely unaware of its foreign origin, while in sociolinguistics it continues to act as a lightning rod of controversy in the debate over universal models of politeness theory, playing out stereotypical notions of Asian culture as group-oriented and shame-motivated, while Western culture is conceptualised as individual-oriented and guilt-motivated. At the same time, there are also attempts to distinguish two types of face in Chinese, based on the fact that there are two nouns that can be used in expressions relating to it (mianzi and lian), and that they have different collocations, especially the verbs used with them. This allows me to return to the issue of the relation between terms and concepts.

Chapter 4 looks at what is probably the most modern concept of the four, guanxi, which is a binome that emerges at the end of the Qing dynasty. Perhaps more than the other three terms, however, the concept of guanxi spreads out into nearby cognates in both Chinese and English. This chapter will show how debates in both Britain and the United States concerning patronage and corruption in government led to a wider discourse that guanxi and its related Chinese terms such as *zou houmen* (走後門 to use the back door) were inserted into and which conditioned the manner of its acceptance in the English-speaking world. The English reaction against it, in turn, predictably during the May Fourth Movement led to it being vilified; Lin Yutang, writing in the late 1930s, singled it out as one of the greatest evils of modern China. In English, besides being borrowed in transliterated form, it has also been translated by terms such as connections, pull, and social network.

Like face, guanxi has been adopted in English academic discourse, first in the social sciences and then in business management studies. It first arose to prominence in Chinese-speaking academic circles in Taiwan and Hong Kong, then was imported into English-language studies primarily through the work of Mayfair Yang, who brought this term to prominence as a way of explaining a whole facet of Chinese society that, she argued, had no real close analogues in American culture and that was traceable both to ancient Chinese culture and to the specific upheaval of the Cultural Revolution and authoritarian rule by the Chinese Communist Party. In these studies, guanxi is to a certain degree rehabilitated as a way of getting things done under difficult circumstances, an understandable but minor foible for individuals and a part of the cost of doing business in China for multinational companies. Guanxi thus inhabits a rather precarious position of 'business with Chinese characteristics', alongside such emergent concepts as *shanzhai* (山寨 knock-off) and *huyou* (忽悠 bamboozle),[19] where an emergent Chinese superpower becomes less apologetic for its modus operandi and the English-speaking world responds with seminars on how to negotiate alien business practices, thus reifying difference.

Finally, the conclusion pulls together the analysis in the four case-study chapters in order to argue that, despite various surface differences, they are all examples of a bi-directional interlingual practice. On the theoretical level, then, the project demonstrates the multifarious ways in which such interlingual practice may evolve, and the diverse pathways that it may follow. Yet the case studies also reveal that, in relation to Chinese culture specifically, such practices have enabled the development of a restricted number of concepts used to create a stereotypical image of China, both in Anglo-American culture and also in China itself.

Notes

1 An emphasis on thousands of years has been a popular way to characterise the age of a unified Chinese civilization at least since the blockbuster exhibit that toured several major cities in the United States between 1983 and 1986, 'China: 7000 Years of Discovery'. Thanks to the Museum of Science in Boston for furnishing information about that exhibit, which was at their venue from June through December 1985.

2 The work was first published in 1973, but I have used the second edition of 1985 in this study.

3 Malmkjaer (2018). A selection of papers from the conference was subsequently published in Malmkjaer, Şerban, and Louwagie (2018). The quotation, which appeared on the conference website, is reproduced on the first page of the introduction to that volume.

4 Of the 131 terms in Williams's work, 26 are found in Harrison, Little, and Lock, and there are several other terms in Williams, such as utilitarianism, which are also arguably political in orientation. For Bennett, Grossberg, and Morris the number is 35 out of 149, and again there are many that are not in Harrison, Little, and Lock yet are clearly of a political nature.

5 In computational linguistics, key concepts are terms that emerge from the application of various formulas onto nouns and noun phrases in (usually large) corpora on a given topic. Although I have used both English and Chinese corpora in my study, I have not used any of these methods to identify the key concepts, which emerged rather out of my extensive reading over the years and the identification of a small number of terms of particular interest to me because of cross-cultural interaction.

6 I prefer the term 'concept' to 'idea' mainly because I am more in sympathy with the programme of German begriffsgeschichte than the history of ideas in the English tradition. Begriffsgeschichte places emphasis on structural linguistics and the simultaneous use of semasiological analysis (all the meanings of a given word or concept) and onomasiological analysis (all the terms in a language for the same concept), and the embrace of both lexical semantics (the analysis of single words) and a semantics based on the broader semantic and linguistic field. See Richter (1986, 619–24) for a more detailed discussion of the relation between begriffsgeschichte and various related disciplines.

7 It is also an interesting article because one of the reasons that 'merit' differs from country to country is the presence in China of *guanxi*, one of the key concepts I discuss in this book.

8 The works in animal behaviour studies they cite (Clayton, Bussey, and Dickinson 2003; Emery, Dally, and Clayton 2004) do not themselves make the claim that birds have concepts. Margolis and Laurence are extrapolating from the research.

9 This is a point where I differ from Wierzbicka, who claims to have located sixty 'semantic primitives' (universals of language) that allow her to build up universal definitions of concepts (Wierzbicka 1997, 24–28).

10 This is most obvious in her discussion of terms in the English language, where she sometimes mixes examples from British, American, Canadian, and Australian English indiscriminately and at other times insists on sharp differences (when discussing the Australian concept 'mate').

11 Based on an examination of the twenty-seven occurrences of 'yanqui' in the Corpus of Contemporary American English, maintained by Brigham Young University and available at https://www.english-corpora.org/coca/. Hereafter cited as COCA. Search conducted 21 March 2019.

12 Some historians of science challenge this idea of science as a universal language. See for example Longino (1990).

13 The idea that knowing the Martian symbols for the atomic elements would allow humans to decipher Martian literature, philosophy, and history seems rather far-fetched, given that the characters cannot assume a common physiology, environment, biology, or social structure. The opposite view may be seen in the work of Willard Quine (1959), who posited that a linguist set down in the midst of a group speaking a language they were unfamiliar with would only be able to translate a very circumscribed number of basic concepts, and that knowledge of those concepts would not necessarily lead to the understanding of anything else.

14 Indeed, some scholars argue that the concept of TCM itself was invented in the twentieth century as a reaction to the introduction of Western-style medicine into China. See for example Andrews (2013).

15 The translation of the concept wuxing, has, however, changed over time to reflect a changing understanding by English speakers as to what the concept means. Briefly, the shift from the term 'five elements' to 'five phases' reflects a shift in understanding these from static objects, similar to the four elements in ancient Greek thought, to dynamic processes, linking them to the concept of change associated with the trigrams and hexagrams of the *Book of Changes*.

16 Hu (1944) claims that her list of five expressions that use lian and twelve that use mianzi is exhaustive.

17 https://eebo.chadwyck.com/about/about.htm. Accessed 4 April 2019.

18 https://www.gale.com/c/eighteenth-century-collections-online-part-i and https://www.gale.com/c/eighteenth-century-collections-online-part-ii. Accessed 4 April 2019.

19 These are two of the ten concepts featured in Yu Hua's *China in Ten Words*.

1

Filial piety

Introduction

Filial piety is the oldest of the four concepts and most fundamental to the development of Chinese civilisation, inextricably intertwined in many facets of law, custom, and religious observances for thousands of years. Although some concerted efforts were made to dethrone it from that central position in the twentieth century, it remains an important concept in China today, having made a comeback beginning in the 1990s. It also existed independently in English before exposure to Chinese culture; although it was never as important to Anglo-American culture as it was to the Chinese, there is plenty of evidence of a strong tradition extolling filial piety as a Christian virtue. Moreover, in both traditions its importance can be traced at least partially to a discourse concerning its relation to 'natural' feelings arising from the parent-child bond. This chapter is thus concerned with how two cultures, both with pre-existing concepts that are initially rooted in a discourse of nature, debate the meaning of these concepts interlingually and attempt to establish an equivalence across the linguistic and cultural gulf separating Anglo-American and Chinese culture.

The first section of this chapter will sketch the early, independent development of the two concepts of filial piety (English) and filial piety (Chinese), and compare their meaning prior to contact between the two. Since there has been extensive research on the concept of filial piety in Chinese culture, while its English counterpart has received relatively little treatment, this section relies mainly on secondary literature regarding the Chinese concept, whereas for the English concept a more exhaustive consideration of primary texts is necessary. This is followed by a discussion of how the Chinese concept was initially received in English from the seventeenth through the early twentieth century, exerting an increasing influence on the English concept and leading to a fundamental change in its meaning for Anglo-American readers. The third section will discuss how foreign (mostly English) conceptions of filial piety began to impact upon the Chinese concept in the nineteenth and early twentieth century. This will be followed by a section detailing how the Chinese concept changed rapidly during three key periods in the modern and contemporary periods: the May Fourth Movement, the early years of the PRC, and the post-Mao era. Finally, the last section documents the increasingly close identification between filial piety in Chinese and English in the modern era, even as the two terms point to slightly different concepts in the contemporary period.[1]

Early meaning of filial piety in China

The character *xiao* (孝) is quite old. Although there is disagreement about whether it occurs in oracle bone inscriptions, it is definitely found on cast bronze vessels dating back to the Shang dynasty (second millennium BCE) (Kinney 2004, 37n19). The early Chinese dictionary *Shuo wen jie zi* (說文解字 Explanation of written characters), compiled by Xu Shen (ca. 58–147 CE), defines it as '善事父母' (serving your parents respectfully) and gives as the etymology that this is a compound graph, the image of a son (*zi* 子) supporting an old man (*lao* 老) (Duan 1988, 402). The comprehensive modern *Hanyu da zidian* (漢語大字典 Unabridged dictionary of Chinese characters) lists eight distinct definitions, all attested in early texts, of which Xu Shen's definition is only the second (Hanyu Dazidian Bianji Weiyuan Hui 1987). The first is to offer sacrifices to the dead, the fourth is to be in mourning, and the fifth is mourning clothes. Kinney (2004, 37n19) notes that in the earliest sources from the Shang, 'the term does not refer to a child's care for living parents'; rather, there is a strong association with ritual observances around deceased parents and more remote ancestors. Even in later periods this basic meaning of the term persists; it is never just about taking care of parents while they are alive, but also continuing to serve them after they are dead. It is also about maintaining the continuity of the male line of succession; this link with the (dead) past is also evidenced indirectly in the third definition, 'to carry on the work/wishes of earlier generations' (能繼先人之志), and the sixth definition, 'to follow the example of; to model oneself on' (效法). The seventh definition is 'to nourish, support, or feed' (畜養); according to Knapp (1995, 197–200), in the earliest bronze inscriptions from the Western Zhou dynasty (1045–771 BCE), this refers to offerings of cooked food to deceased ancestors, not feeding one's living parents (Knapp 1995, 201–2).[2]

The history of *xiao*'s development up through the time before the arrival of the Jesuits in China has been well documented elsewhere (see Knapp 1995 for the early period and the essays in Chan and Tan 2004 for later developments). Here I will relate in brief its standing in Chinese culture and describe the main facets of this concept, up to about the year 1500CE.

It is worth stressing that xiao is first and foremost associated with male children and their relation to the male line of succession. This can be seen first by the fact that the bottom half of the character represents a son, not a daughter, and is tied up with the patrilineal nature of ancestor worship in Chinese culture, where the rites to the dead are supposed to be performed by male descendants. A woman could serve living parents, but she could not fulfil that duty prescribed for sacrifices to the dead. Also, normally upon marriage she left her parents' household to join her husband's family, whereupon her filial duties became centred around her husband's parents and, if living, grandparents. Neither the *Xiao jing* (孝經 *Classic of Filial Piety*) nor the *Lie nü zhuan* (烈女傳 Biographies of exemplary women) contain any examples of filial daughters, while the *Yuye nü jing* (玉耶女經 Scripture on young women) shows us the filial role of daughters-in-law rather than daughters (Lo 2004, 71; Tan 2004, 230).

Also, although a son could (and should) be filial to his mother, his primary duty was to his father and the male line, both past and future. If he was the son of a concubine, he owed filial duty first to his father, then to his father's legitimate wife, and then finally to his birth mother. This stress upon male succession was amply summed up by the early Confucian philosopher Mencius, who said 'Of the three ways of being unfilial, not producing a [male] successor is the worst' (不孝有三，無後為大) (both Chinese original and English translation from Legge 1895, 313).

Third, filial piety was, at least in the early period, mainly practiced by adults. Kinney (2004, 26 and 44–48) notes that the major traits outlined above (making sacrifices to the dead, supporting one's parents, carrying on in one's parents' way) are all tasks that young children would normally have been incapable of performing, and that tales of young children being celebrated for filial piety only begin to emerge in the Later Han dynasty (25–220CE). Kinney (115–16) also notes that there are tales of adults with limited resources choosing to abandon or kill their infant child in order to direct those resources to supporting either the child of a deceased brother or their living parents; these people were celebrated for their filial piety. One only has one set of parents, and one's deceased brother can no longer produce children, but one can always have more children at a later time. These admittedly extreme examples clearly show that filial piety is heavily concerned with the elderly and the continuity of patrilineal descent lines rather than emotional attachment between father and son.

Thus filial piety should clearly be distinguished from affection that a child might feel for birth parents. This is made more obvious when we consider that there are many examples of a son exhibiting filial behaviour towards a

parent who does not deserve it (Raphals 2004, 219). Confucianism sometimes tried to cover over this gap between filial piety and affection by stressing that filial piety was natural. Yet Confucius himself clearly states that
simply caring for parents was a bare minimum standard that even beasts
could observe:

> Zi You asked what filial piety was. The Master said, 'The filial piety nowadays
> means the support of one's parents. But dogs and horses likewise are able to
> do something in the way of support; —without reverence, what is there to
> distinguish the one support given from the other?'
>
> 子游問孝。子曰：「今之孝者，是謂能養。至於犬馬，皆能有養；不敬，何
> 以別乎」 (both Chinese original and translation from Legge 1893, 148)

So in fact, filial piety is a cultural practice regulated through rites or proper
behaviour (*li* 禮). Lisa Raphals (2004, 215) therefore argues that we need
to distinguish between filiality as a natural emotion and filiality as a virtue.
And indeed, many documents try to set out regulations for the observance
of filial piety, notably the *Book of Rites* (see Tan 2004, 227, 229, and 233
for some examples). Yet I would go further than Raphals or Tan, who both
propose to classify filial piety as a variant of love (one of the six basic emotions in early Chinese thought), and say that it is not necessarily linked to
emotion at all; rather, filial piety is about duty, and therefore the translation into English as filial piety or filial duty is in at least one sense appropriate. Moreover, if we understand filial piety as duty or service, Haines
(2008, 476) proposes that we can thereby understand how it is linked to
two other crucial concepts in Confucianism, *zhong* (忠 loyalty) and *ren*
(仁 benevolence), which he interprets as other types of duty or service.

Filial piety becomes one of the basic tenets of Confucianism and is
institutionalised after Confucianism was adopted as the state orthodoxy
during the Former Han dynasty (206BCE–9CE). It was even used as a cri-
terion for public office during both the Former Han and Later Han dynasties; Bielenstein (1980, 134–35) states that starting in 130BCE, two to
three hundred men who were *xiao lian* (孝廉 filial and incorruptible) were
recommended each year from each commandery and kingdom within the
empire for public office.

Filial piety takes its place beside loyalty, *jie* (節 chastity) and *yi* (義 righteousness), and although there is widespread belief that it yielded pride of
place to loyalty (see for example Lee 2004, 147–51), the state at least paid
lip service to filial piety as the foundation upon which loyalty was built (see
Nylan 1996, 2–4 on the many Chinese thinkers who saw a conflict between
filial piety and loyalty). One of the greatest challenges to the introduction
of Buddhism into China was the perceived conflict between filial piety and
the Buddhist practice of renouncing all one's earthly ties, often referred

to in Chinese as 'leaving the family' (*chu jia* 出家), including abstention from sex and therefore not producing offspring. This was partly resolved by stories of children reaching enlightenment and then saving their parents, as in the story *Mulian jiu mu* (目連救母 Mulian rescues his mother), where the eponymous hero descends into hell to find and save his mother's damned soul.

Filial piety also becomes enshrined in the legal code, where punishments for many crimes are dictated by the degree of kinship and the relative position in the family hierarchy between the criminal and the victim. The closer the kinship, the heavier the punishment if the criminal is of a junior generation, while the lighter the punishment if the criminal is senior; the heaviest punishments were reserved for children committing a crime against their parents.

In sum, filial piety is an integral part of Chinese religion, custom and law. Its primacy among the virtues was only ever challenged by loyalty to the ruler; but even this was more in practice than in theory, since the state often claimed that filial piety in the personal realm was the equivalent to, and preceded, loyalty.

Early English meaning of filial piety

The term filial is from the Latin *filialis* (having the characteristics of a son), derived from *filius* (son). Either by itself or in combination with other terms, it appears in a wide variety of texts. The earliest usage cited in the *Oxford English Dictionary* (OED) is from 1393. From 1533 to 1700, EEBO gives a total of 4445 hits in 2102 texts, beginning with the writing of Sir Thomas More, dated 1533.[3] Since EEBO shows each occurrence with a small amount of context, it is possible to examine collocations. Common collocations immediately following filial include:

- filial *fear*: (1562 hits) By far the most common collocation, this is usually directed towards God. Commentaries distinguished filial fear of God as being bound up with faith, as opposed to common fear focused purely on damnation;
- filial *obedience*: (412 hits) an early instance occurs in a discussion of whether parents have the power to force children into arranged marriages, to which the answer is no (Gibbon 1591);[4] the majority of identifiable cases are towards natural parents;
- filial *duties*: (346 hits) a large majority of identifiable cases are towards natural parents; these include 'decent burial' of parents after their death (Barrow 1591), so there is some attention in the English concept to filial duties continuing after death;

- filial *love*: (303 hits) like filial fear, this is often in relation to God. Examples include the first usage of the word filial in the database (More 1533). This is also the collocation in Langland's *Piers Plowman* from 1393 as cited in the *OED*;
- filial *affection*: (228 hits) like fear and love, affection is most often towards God;
- filial *reverence*: (166 hits) occurs quite early and by a narrow majority refers to God or the Church more often than parents;
- filial *respect*: (106 hits) a relative latecomer with the first example from 1612; the majority are towards parents or other authority figures;
- filial *confidence*: (92 hits) occurs quite early (1538); all instances are towards God;
- filial *relations*: (70 hits) another term overwhelming in relation to God or the Church;
- filial *awe*: (65 hits) the earliest example is a classical text how two brothers lack this quality, in a translation of Seneca (Seneca 1581); but later use of the term is overwhelmingly towards God;
- filial *portion*: (51 hits) this occurs exclusively in legal texts and does not indicate an attitude towards parents, but rather a son's inheritance rights;
- filial *subjection*: (48 hits) Thomas Morton, *Treatise on Threefold State of Man* (1596), contains an entire chapter on this topic in relation to God. The related term filial *submission* occurs (32) times.

In most of these examples, through context it is clear that there is an idea of natural feelings of a child towards a parent. Yet at the same time there is also a strong sense of 'filial' being religious in nature, partly because of its occurrence in many sermons; this religious sense is most clearly seen in a limited set of terms, which are overwhelmingly religious (fear, love, affection, confidence, relations, awe, and subjection). The analogy of 'God the Father' in Christianity leads easily to the idea that filial feelings are 'natural', or bestowed by God, and also due to him as the father of all. Furthermore, the Catholic Church is often referred to as the 'Mother Church', and expressions of filial duty to the Pope also occur. Except for love (and possibly courtesy), the emotions described are distancing (fear, awe, reverence) and entail obedience, subjection, and the necessity to perform duties or obligations to someone in a superior position. A handful of terms (obedience, duty, respect) collocate more strongly with secular contexts, mostly towards parents but also occasionally towards one's ruler or superior; such secular usage becomes more common as we move through the data chronologically.

'Piety' is usually glossed as a near synonym of 'duty' or 'dutiful'. Merriam-Webster defines it simply as '(a) fidelity to natural obligations: devoted loyalty to parents, family or race (b) dutifulness in religion: habitual reverence for God' (Gove 1993), while the *Oxford English Dictionary* reverses the order of those definitions, but gives substantially the same meaning, with citations from 1500 onwards. The term is so common that it is impossible to even begin to list all occurrences in the databases. As with filial, it is derived from a Latin term, *pietas*, which Lewis and Short (1879) define as

> that acts according to duty, dutiful; esp. that performs what is due to the gods and religion in general, to parents, kindred, teachers, country; pious, devout, conscientious, affectionate, tender, kind, good, grateful, respectful, loyal, patriotic, etc. (of persons and things) .... Of things having reference to religion: sacred, holy .... Of respectful, affectionate conduct towards parents, etc.

Notable here is that *pietas* and the English piety both seem, like filial, to be applicable mainly to God or to one's parents, with the Latin term having the additional sense of loyal or patriotic. That meaning is barely present in the early occurrences of filial.

The more specific term 'filial piety' (84 hits) emerges in this context of a nexus of compound terms involving the word 'filial' and 'piety', and is well attested in English before the term is applied to the Chinese in 1669. Of the eighty-four hits in the database, forty-four occur between 1590 and 1668 in thirty-one distinct texts, some of which were also reprinted.

Like the term 'filial' or 'piety' by itself, 'filial piety' is sometimes used in a religious context. Two clear examples are Hall (1608), which speaks of 'filial piety to the Church of God', and I. C. (1619), 'with the burning wings of filial piety and humble devotion for so many and those unspeakable gifts and graces'.

However, 'filial piety' is overwhelmingly linked to actual parent-child ties (thirty-six out of the forty-four examples found), rather than to God. Epicurus (1656) goes so far as to explicitly reject a religious meaning of the term, speaking of: 'Filiall Piety (not supernaturall Piety)'. So 'filial piety' is markedly more secular in tone overall than either 'filial' or 'piety' by itself, or 'filial' linked to other terms such as 'fear' and 'love', but is linked to a small cluster of terms as noted above: obedience, duty, and respect. The first recorded instance of the phrase 'filial piety' in the database is in Sir Philip Sydney, *The Countess of Pembroke's Arcadia* (1590), where a son, mistreated by his father, is nonetheless filial, unlike his bastard half-brother, who mistreats the father. In a similar vein, Thomas Heywood's *The Life of Merlin* (1641) describes a battle between King William and his rebellious son. Another son of his, Robert, hearing that his father had been unhorsed, 'in true filial piety he restored his Father, set him upon a fresh Horse, and delivered him from all danger'. Sir Richard Baker, in *Chronicle of the Kings of England* (1643), uses it twice, once in relation to Henry VIII, and once in speaking of Thomas More going to pay respects to his father at the King's Bench on his way to his own duties at Westminster.

Burton (1626) speaks of 'a princely mirror of filial piety' while a translation of Pliny the Younger (1645) speaks of the filial piety of a prince, and Starkey's *Royal and Other Innocent Bloud Crying Aloud to Heaven for Due Vengeance* (1660) links together 'true filiall Piety and Princely wisdom'. In these cases there are ties to statecraft, the personal virtue as manifested in a prince's behaviour towards his father having a direct effect on the ruling of the nation, but it is not used in the sense of the Latin *pietas* of a feeling of duty towards one's country, even though the discussion is in the political realm.

As we can also see from that last example, several are drawn from classical Greco-Roman sources, either directly through translation or by adaptation. Heywood's *Gynaikeion* (1624) takes most of its examples from classical antiquity. There are also Bolton's *Nero Caesar, or Monarchy Depraved* (1624), Greville's *Tragedy of that Famous Roman Oratour Marcus Tullius Cicero* (1651), Epicurus's *Morals* (1656), Virgil's *Aeneas* (1660), and Machiavelli's *Discourses upon the First Decade of T. Livius* (1663). These classical examples further dilute the association between filial piety and Christianity.

Filial piety in this time period may also apply to a son's feelings towards his mother, as in Coryate (1618), who speaks of a son's 'filial piety and officious respect' for his mother. The same example recurs in Taylor (1630).

There are two examples which are negative ones, that is, where someone is shown to lack filial piety. In Bolton (1624), Nero is said to have been motivated to kill his mother because of a 'concubinary love grown far more potent in him then [sic] filial piety'. Browne (1646) speaks of someone's conduct as 'an unsufferable affront unto filial piety'. So clearly people could lack filial piety, but filial piety itself always has positive associations in this period.

Early definitions in dictionaries from this period restrict the meaning of 'filial' to the conduct of sons. Here, for example, is the definition given in the *English Expositor Teaching the Interpretation of the Hardest Words Used in Our Language* (J. B. 1616): 'Filial. Of or belonging to a son.' Yet a significant number of texts after 1624 begin to speak of daughters exhibiting filial piety. Thomas Heywood in the *Gynaikeion* (1624) speaks of extraordinary examples of women's filial piety actually exceeding those of men. James Shirley also uses it in regard to daughters in two plays. In *The Bird in a Cage, a Comedy* (1633), the Duke praises his daughter for possessing filial piety towards him; in *A Pastoral Called the Arcadia* (1640) we hear of 'the daughter of our late good King/Lost to her filial piety'. Such usage becomes more common in the eighteenth century, as we will see below.

I have dwelt at length on the particular term filial piety because by the twentieth century this term comes to have a fixed and very particular meaning in relation to China. However, any discussion of the *concept* of filial piety in this time period also needs to pay attention to the cluster of other terms associated with filial, almost all of which can be seen as either other names for the same concept, or closely related concepts that, to some extent, determine the boundaries of filial piety.

First among these is filial duty. These two terms are close synonyms, and indeed many texts in later periods use the terms 'filial piety' and 'filial duty' interchangeably. Checking through the forty-three results up to 1668 reveals that filial duty is more likely to be associated with God than was filial piety, although this is still a minority use, with ten associated directly with God, while one discusses the filial duty due by princes to the Pope as Christ's representative on earth.

More interesting, however, is that in several cases filial duty is seen to be in conflict with other duties or emotions. In Baron's *Mirza a Tragedie, Really Acted in Persia* (1647) a prince on the eve of battle is summoned by his father the king, and agonises over whether to fulfil his filial duty or pursue honour on the battlefield; ultimately he decides to be filial and heed his father's summons, but only after his advisors suggest disguising another fighter as the prince so that it will appear that he is at the battle in case he cannot return in time. In *Three Treatises Concerning the Scotish Discipline* (R. B. G. 1661), filial duty acts as an important brake on abuse of power by a magistrate. Similarly, in Hall's *Cases of Conscience Practically Resolved* (1654), filial duty outweighs religious vows according to the rules of a monastic order. In *Theophania, or, Severall Modern Histories Represented by Way of Romance* (Sales 1655), one of the heroes Demetrius experiences a conflict between his love for Mariana and his filial duty to his father, who commands him to marry the queen of another state in order to cement a political alliance. Unable to decide what to do, Demetrius flees his father's domain. In all of these cases of conflicting duties, except possibly the last one, despite the fact that a conflict exists between filial and other duties, filial duty is seen as the primary one.

Yet there are two cases where filial duty is explicitly dethroned, and one where it is implicitly thrown into doubt. In Beaumont's *Psyche, or Loves Mysterie* (1648), the speaker rejects the idea that filial duty to his parents should compel him to do something contrary to the tenets of Christianity, because while his parents gave birth to his body, his soul comes from God. Thus the individual's duty is first and foremost to God and, by extension, the self, because in carrying out one's duty to God, one is ensuring that one's immortal soul will be saved. In Wilson's *History of Great Britain* (1653), filial duty also loses when it comes into conflict with self-preservation, since self-preservation is 'an adjunct of Nature, more powerful than Filial duty'. Finally, in Bramhall's *Replication to the Bishop of Chalcedon* (1656), the author argues that states are justified in making laws that, if someone breaks them even for good reason, such as filial duty, that person should be punished. While Bramhall does not explicitly say that people should not fulfil their filial duty in these cases, the fact that they should be punished regardless of the motivation implies it.

Unlike filial piety then, filial duty, especially a blind or absolute filial duty, may give rise to conflict with other values, and in some cases may be wrong. The idea that filial duty is just one of several conflicting duties will eventually spread to filial piety in the eighteenth century, which up until this point in time is unreservedly positive.

Following on from Bramhall, another notable development is that other examples continue to expand on the metaphor of the state as mother or the ruler as father of the people and therefore the people owing filial duty to them. Given the English Civil War and the Protectorate, we should not be surprised that a number of works published in the middle third of the seventeenth century would be concerned with the question of legitimate government, or that, in cases where the author is defending the 'natural' right of the sovereign over the people, some of them should draw upon the analogy of the *pater familias*. I found four texts that make this argument, all published after Hobbes's *Leviathan* (1651) (Parker 1651; Goslicki 1660; Philipps 1663; Waterhouse 1663). Hobbes's work itself does not use the term filial, but is certainly concerned with the relationship between parents and children as indicative of the relation between ruler and subject, and he speaks of the obedience, duty, and honour that a child owes to his parents, who are sovereign over their children until and unless they surrender that sovereignty to another as head of state.[5] *Leviathan* is thus an example of an important cultural text, widely seen as the founding of social contract theory of government, that engages with the *concept* of filial piety without naming it as such. Most importantly for us, Hobbes both equates filial duty with political duty, and at the same time subjugates the former to the latter, because once people have surrendered their sovereignty to the state, their children's primary duty is then also owed to the state, *not* to the parents. This, even though filial piety must exist prior to loyalty and thus in some sense be more fundamental.

If we turn to filial respect, one of the other two terms that, like filial piety, is more secular, we see good examples of how filial behaviour was extended by analogy to other spheres of behaviour. First, it is extended to the Pope who, as head of the Catholic Church, is a sort of father figure to sovereigns of various Christian nations (Walker 1684; Louis XIV 1688). Second, in the secular world it is explicitly linked to loyalty to the sovereign through the invocation of the fifth commandment, 'Honor thy father and mother' (Adams 1675). Indeed, Adams interprets the fifth commandment as providing justification for the maintenance of all hierarchical relationships, from elderly relatives (grandparents, uncles and aunts) to one's master and thus one's sovereign. We can clearly see some overlap in how filial piety functioned in a similar fashion in both English and Chinese.

Turning to the last term that is more secular, filial obedience, we discover that the question of whether filial obedience is natural or based on gratitude (nature or nurture) is bound up with the civil war and the Glorious Revolution. Many of the examples of filial obedience are related to the question of whether princes should be filial to the Pope, and whether subjects should be loyal to their prince regardless of his actions. In China, Mencius carefully circumvented this second problem by declaring that despots who were overthrown were not legitimate sovereigns (*jun* 君) but rather thieves (*zei* 賊), and that therefore the question of whether subjects should obey bad rulers was nonsensical (see Legge 1895, 35 for both Chinese and an English translation). But in England, most commentators who engaged with this question chose to build an argument starting from filial obedience as something that was the result of nurture, of how parents treated their children as they grew up (see for example Kennett 1689 and Saavedra Fjardo 1700). For these thinkers, making filial obedience dependent upon how children were treated by their parents allowed them to argue that subjects were not obliged to obey an unjust sovereign even though he remained a sovereign, thus attacking the idea of the divine right of kings.

Thus the link between loyalty and filial piety in England resulted in filial piety becoming more circumscribed, as philosophers and political theorists struggled to find justification for limiting the power of the sovereign. This never happened in China, where instead philosophers decreed that the mandate of Heaven would be withheld from unjust rulers, making them no longer proper rulers and therefore no longer entitled to the loyalty of the populace, not because loyalty was based on a mutual bond, but because loyalty was only due to someone who was a proper ruler in the first place.

Unlike duty, respect, and obedience, which are closely synonymous with piety, fear, which I noted was the most common collocation for filial in this early period (1562 hits in 323 records in the database), marks in some sense a sharp distinction between feelings due to one's parents and what is due to God. Filial fear is used almost exclusively in religious contexts, usually sermons, and refers to the emotion that should inspire our obedience to God. Of the 323 records in the database, only two were examples of filial fear directed at real parents (Brome 1659 and Woolley 1673); the rest are about man's fear of God, mainly sermons based on passages in the Old Testament and the Book of Revelation.

Finally, while filial affection is usually linked to real child-parent relations, filial love is more often directed towards God, with seventy-seven out of ninety-nine examples being of a religious nature.

Thus generally children are not encouraged to have strong emotions (fear, love) in regard to their parents; these are reserved instead for God. Children may need to respect and obey parents, but this is linked to the less extreme emotion of affection, which in turn is sometimes linked to parental affection and care. In some cases, especially with filial duty, there may actually be an antipathy between duty to one's parents and emotion.

In sum, filial piety in this period is perceived as both a classical and a Christian virtue practiced mainly in this world towards one's parents, but also sometimes towards God. Examples are drawn from different nations and different time periods, suggesting that it is both natural and universal, although its status as arising from nature is contested especially towards the end of the seventeenth century, when it is increasingly placed in a reciprocal relation with parental affection and care. All examples are positive; it is never a bad thing to be filial, but when the closely related term filial duty comes into conflict with other duties, it may have to take second place. Filial piety begins by being strongly marked as male-gendered (sons to fathers) but gradually becomes unisex, with both the practitioner as potentially female and also the object of such piety, with examples of daughter-father, daughter-mother, and son-mother relations as well as son-father.

Chinese and English filial piety compared

First, there are definite similarities between filial piety in the two traditions before they come into contact. They both are concerned almost exclusively with the relationship between a usually adult son and his father in the early period. Second, they are both conceptualised as universal and good; there should be no exceptions to filial piety, and it is never wrong to be filial. Third, although the concepts may have arisen out of ideas about natural feelings, both describe the role that society expected sons to play vis à vis their families. Only later, and to a limited extent (especially in China) were women seen as possible agents of filial piety. Both involved a sense of duty and respect, with emotion playing less of a role. In both cases, it is possible for filial piety to lead to better behaviour in other realms, for example making someone a better ruler.

However, important differences remain. To the extent that in China filial piety is related to religious beliefs, it is tied firmly to the family through veneration of ancestors, their maintenance, and mourning rites for parents, grandparents and beyond. Other religious belief systems in China, notably Daoism and Buddhism, struggle to reconcile filial piety with core concepts in their respective belief systems, and a lack of filial piety is one of the charges levelled against both religions by Confucian scholars. Conversely, in the English tradition, filial piety is easily incorporated into Christianity through the analogy that God is the Father of all men and therefore all men should be filial towards God. Chinese filial piety is likened, not to a religious virtue, but to a political one: loyalty to the ruler, who is 'the parent of the people' (*min zhi fumu* 民之父母; see Legge 1893, 374 for both Chinese and English). While a similar political meaning was available in the Latin term *pietas*, it does not seem to have survived when it crossed over into English initially, and it is only during the English Civil War that a political reading of filial duty and obedience (not piety) surfaces, and once it does, Hobbes and others have no problem subordinating filial duty to duty to the ruler, whereas in the Chinese tradition scholars were reluctant to say this explicitly, even if some of their works imply it. Moreover, the English understanding of the relationship between filial piety and loyalty is different from that in China, leading to restrictions in its scope in the second half of the seventeenth century. While filial and filial piety in English remain strictly related to one's immediate parents, in China, as we have noted, it extends back multiple generations; one's parents are only the closest generation to whom one owes filial feelings. To the extent that multiple lineage lines in a clan continued to give offerings to a common ancestor, often performing services together in an ancestral hall, filial piety tied those descendants together; if one treated an uncle or any member of a senior generation in the clan with disrespect, one could be labelled as unfilial.

Yet overall, there remains enough overlap in the two concepts that, after contact between Europe and China begins in earnest, 'filial piety' and 'filial duty' are established as English equivalents for xiao with little or no discussion of any of these important differences.

Filial piety and China in English: the early period

The history of Chinese-English interaction through translation is complicated by the fact that all early texts in English that contain translations from Chinese, or even much information about China, are translations from Spanish, Portuguese, Italian, Latin, or Dutch. Even after direct trade begins between England and China (the East India Company sends its first trade ships in 1635), the British rely heavily on either Catholic priests and Portuguese traders as interpreters, or Chinese who had learned pidgin Portuguese or pidgin English. Only a handful of British subjects learned Chinese before 1800 (St. André 2006). Since this study is about English-Chinese interactions, I will mainly limit my discussion to the English versions of all such materials.[6]

Up to 1638, none of the references to 'filial' in English texts make any mention of China. Conversely, early works on China, such as González de Mendoza (1588) and Linschoten (1598) never mention filial piety. The earliest example I have found that links China with the term filial is *Some Yeares Travels into Divers Parts of Asia and Afrique*, which says 'No people whatsoever, expresse more filiall respect unto their Parents than the Chyneses do'

(Herbert 1638). Like the examples discussed in more detail below, this text exalts the Chinese as being exemplary practitioners of a universal virtue.

Only in 1669 are China and filial piety linked in the English language. Then between 1669 and 1715, there are two examples of texts discussing China that use the term filial piety; one that uses both filial piety and filial respect; one that uses piety, filial respect, and filial duty; one that uses the term filial duty; and one that uses filial love. The first of these is Webb's *Historical Essay Endeavoring a Probability that the Language of the Empire of China Is the Primitive Language* (1669). On page 104, he says 'Thus, for fatherly affection and filial piety, *China may give example to all Nations of the World*' (my emphasis). Four years later, Nieuhof, in *An Embassy from the East-India Company of the United Provinces, to the Grand Tartar Cham, Emperor of China* (1673), at the opening of chapter four, when speaking of the mountains of China, notes that the Chinese are assiduous in their search of auspicious burial grounds: 'to advance a filial Piety to the deceased Parents'. Le Comte, *Memoires and Observations ... Made in a Late Journey through the Empire of China* (1697) mentions a series of loyal officials remonstrating with the emperor about a mistaken policy, and being killed, but they keep doing it, martyring themselves out of 'filial duty'. Bouvet in *The History of Cang-Hy, the Present Emperor of China* (1699) has three occurrences of the term filial, talking about the extraordinary piety and filial respect that the emperor exhibited towards his grandmother. Finally, in *The Portugues Asia* (Faria e Sousa 1695), the author describes how, as part of the funeral rites for a deceased emperor, taxes are reduced and prisoners set free 'all as an Oblation of filial Love'.

Worthy of particular attention is Wanley's *Wonders of the Little World, or, A General History of Man in Six Books* (1673). In a chapter entitled 'Of the Reverence and Piety of some Children to their Parents', Wanley collects examples from around the world, with a concentration of examples from Classical Greece and Rome, but also including Scotland, Poland, England, Sicily, Persia, and China. Here is the entry for China:

> The Emperour of China on certain days of the year, visiteth his Mother, who is seated on a Throne, and four times on his feet, and four times on his knees he maketh her a profound reverence, bowing his head even to the ground. The same custom is also observed through the greatest part of the Empire; and if it chance that any one is negligent or deficient in this duty to his Parents, he is complain'd of to the Magistrates, who punish such offenders very severely. But generally no people express more filial respect and duty than they.

Here we learn that not only does the emperor of China pay filial obeisance to his mother, but that this is a universal custom, and anyone who omits to do so is subject to severe punishment by government officials. Moreover,

Wanley takes care to emphasise that no people on earth are more respectful or dutiful towards their parents. This is also the first example of a text that is not specifically about China that discusses the Chinese propensity to filial piety.

In all of these quotations, filial piety is not unique to the Chinese. Rather, filial piety is a universal attribute and the Chinese are merely good examples of it. Therefore, these authors think that Europeans should learn to be better at filial piety through reading about China, just as reading stories from the Greco-Roman tradition can also inspire one to become a better person. It is also reciprocal; both the first and the fourth quotations stress that filial piety is linked to paternal affection, forming an inter-generational chain of affect.[7] Finally, in the fourth and fifth examples, filial piety is a trait that is implicitly linked to the ruler being fit to govern. In the last case, the emperor's display of filial love explicitly causes him to treat his subjects magnanimously, lightening their burden and forgiving those who had trespassed against the state by violating the law.

Filial piety in the eighteenth and nineteenth century

As we move into the eighteenth century, the number of occurrences of the terms 'filial', 'filial piety', and 'filial duty' in English increases dramatically. A search on ECCO (8 June 2019) yielded 19,837 texts that contain the term 'filial', of which 3616 texts contain 'filial piety', and 3622 'filial duty', for an average of sixty-five texts per year. In many of these texts the term occurs more than once. I have been able to identify a certain number of trends through recourse to three methods: examining those items with 'filial' in the title; sampling one in fifty items; and narrowing the search results by combining 'filial piety' and 'filial duty' with other search terms, such as 'China' or 'Chinese'.

First, the fame of the Chinese as practitioners of filial piety spreads. All but one of the six texts discussed above that link China and filial piety are essentially specialist works about China. In the eighteenth century more works not directly related to China also cite examples of Chinese filial piety. The most striking example of this trend is *A New Book for the Improvement of Young Gentlemen and Ladies. Filial Duty, Recommended and Enforc'd by a Variety of Instructive and Entertaining Stories* ... (1785). This work, which is a self-help/instructional work, discusses China in the introduction, and gives several examples of filial behaviour of Chinese children in the body of the work, the examples being drawn mainly from the Chinese work *Ershisi xiao* (二十四孝 *The Twenty-Four Paragons of Filial Piety*). In particular, there is the story of a child who lets insects bite him so that they will not bite his parents and they can sleep in peace, and the story of a man who dresses up as a child to make his parents think they are young.

All the examples that are drawn from China are positive ones; in other words, there are no unfilial children in China according to this book. This does not mean that the author believes there is no such thing as unfilial children; there is a whole section devoted to unfilial behaviour of *European* children, who are capable of all sorts of horrible acts towards their parents. This text thus shows that the image of the Chinese as being particularly good exemplars of a universal virtue, which emerges from the works on China discussed above, is now more generally reflected in British society.

At the same time, many important eighteenth-century texts continue to use the term 'filial piety', often along with 'filial', 'filial duty', 'filial obedience', and 'filial affection' with no reference to China and in a positive sense. Daniel Defoe, for example, uses 'filial' in a variety of combinations, including 'filial piety', although he prefers 'filial affection' and 'filial duty'. The first part of his *Complete Family Instructor: In Five Parts* (1715–18) is entitled 'Relating to fathers and children'. The term 'filial' also occurs in *Robinson Crusoe* (1719b), in *The Farther Adventures of Robinson Crusoe* (1719a), and in *The Political History of the Devil, as Well Ancient as Modern* (1726). Steele and Addison, in the *Spectator* of 1711 and 1712 use 'filial piety', once in a general discourse on pleasures at the sight of a parent after absence (Steele and Addison 1712), and once to describe a heroine: 'Leonilla too shall be still my Daughter; her filial Piety, though misplaced, has been so exemplary that it deserves the greatest Reward I can confer upon it' (Steele and Addison 1711a). Steele and Addison also cite Father Le Conte (sic) on China's abhorrence of patricide due to their extremely filial feelings (Steele and Addison 1711b).

Samuel Richardson uses the term 'filial piety' in *Clarissa* (1742a) and *Pamela* (1742b), and in *The History of Sir Charles Grandison* (1753) he frequently uses 'filial'. More interestingly, after having published these works, in 1755, Richardson compiled a *Collection of the Moral and Instructive Sentiments, Maxims, Cautions, and Reflexions, Contained in the Histories of Pamela, Clarissa, and Sir Charles Grandison ...* (1755) that has a separate entry for 'Filial Piety', with examples from his books. The phrase is also cross-listed under 'Parents and Children' and 'Education'. Clearly, Richardson felt that filial piety was an important concept in his writings, and that it was part of mainstream Christian morality.

In most of Richardson's works it is his heroines who exhibit filial piety; Henry Fielding, in *Tom Jones* (1749), gives us a hero who is still capable of this sentiment, as well as the woman he loves, who also (naturally) is filial towards her own father.

Despite the masculine example in Fielding, however, as we move into the second half of the eighteenth century, there is a more marked tendency for filial piety to be observed by women rather than men towards their parents. Moreover, in such works, especially plays and romances, there begins to be a tendency for filial piety to hold back the progression of the love interest. In other words, filial piety is still a good thing, and possessing filial piety is often a marker of what makes a woman worthy of being loved, but increasingly, a woman's filial behaviour leads to a delay in her finding true love. An early example is Haywood's novel *The Female Spectator* (1746), in which a woman, having lost her father, cannot bear the thought of marrying her sweetheart immediately.

Aaron Hill's play *The Insolvent: or, Filial Piety* (1758) is an interesting hybrid example. The title refers to the hero Chalons, who ransoms his father's corpse from his creditors with his own freedom. This act of filial piety results in him gaining the esteem of Valdore, who says 'The filial piety of young Chalons, demands reward/Beyond our admiration' (Hill 1758, 19).

Having first ordered his daughter Amelia to love a man he later considers unworthy, suddenly Valdore orders Amelia to love Chalons and marry him instead as the reward for Chalons's filial piety. Speaking with his daughter about her previous engagement, he says he was wrong to have urged her to love that man. Amelia, in her reply, raises the possibility that blind filial piety might not always be a good thing, because parents are human and therefore liable to err—as indeed her father had in initially asking her to love another man (27–28).

Another play, also featuring the phrase 'filial piety' in the title, *The Honest Criminal: Or, Filial Piety* (G. L. 1778), showcases two lovers, Cecilia and Andrew, who are forced to choose between filial piety and love. Cecilia first obeys her father and marries Mr Olban instead of Andrew 'offering myself a victim, to comfort the old age of an affectionate parent' (G. L. 1778, 25); then Andrew takes his father's place as a galley slave to save his mother, his father having been arrested for being a Huguenot (the action takes place in France). Only after Cecilia's parents are dead and Andrew's mother passes away are the lovers able to marry. Before that happens, the lovers meet by chance, and Andrew is offered the opportunity to marry her if he will explain why he is a convict. Andrew almost yields to temptation, but then cries out in agony: 'Ah! Wretch!—What am I going to do! Great God! what was I going to say!—Oh! my father! my father! ... Passion! Duty! Nature! combat my reason; and each take their turn to reign' (62). Thus filial piety is pictured as being at war with conjugal love; Andrew cannot reveal the reason for his imprisonment and clear his own name without calling for the arrest of his own father. That such a sacrifice on his part may be going beyond the call of reasonable duty according to eighteenth-century British norms is shown in a speech by his father late in the play, where he says to his son that 'thy tenderness has far exceeded the limits which Heaven itself has prescrib'd to filial love' (77).

Other works from this period also suggest a conflict between feelings and filial piety. In Ann Radcliffe's *Romance of the Forest* (1792), at the end of chapter twenty-six, the heroine Adeline, having discovered that her true father is the Marquis who was murdered more than fifteen years previously at the abbey, delays her marriage to Theodore until after a period of mourning. Only 'when she threw off the mourning habit which filial piety had required her to assume' (Radcliff 1847, 416) do they celebrate their nuptials. Tellingly here, the verb 'required' suggests that filial piety is not always something undertaken willingly, but is rather forced upon people, and she must 'throw off' the burden thus imposed before she can be happy with her lover.

The works of James Fenimore Cooper in the early nineteenth century are an important example of how far this process has gone. In *The Deerslayer* (1841), Judith exhibits filial love (Cooper 1963, 122), filial duties (193) and filial piety (343), while her sister Hetty displays filial affection (175); in both cases, these are towards an uncouth man who turns out not to be their father. More importantly, in *The Pathfinder* (1840) Mabel tells her father she wants to remain single to care for him (Cooper 1961, 285). At his deathbed, she is described as exhibiting 'sublime' filial piety (403), and it is only after that event that she is free to marry. In the first book then, both sisters' filial piety is misplaced, while in the second book Mabel's marriage is delayed until after her father's death, it not being possible for her to be both filial towards him and married to her lover. For Cooper, then, the opposition between filial duty and conjugal love is quite stark.

Indeed, Toll (1976, 148) tells us that the most common plot of nineteenth-century American melodrama is that of a woman torn between love for sweetheart and duty to family, usually consisting of marrying a rich villain to save parents from poverty. In the most famous example, *Hazel Kirke* (Mackaye 1880), which he discusses at length, the eponymous heroine rejects filial duty and instead marries her sweetheart, although this entails hardships for her parents.

We may contrast these later examples with two early texts from EEBO to see how far opinion changed. In *Gynaikeion* (Heywood 1624), one story also contains a conflict between filial piety and conjugal love, but in that case filial piety clearly wins out and the woman in question kills her husband to avenge her father, who had been killed by her husband previously. Even at the end of the seventeenth century, we find a daughter being chastised by the narrator for being 'all o'er Love, and Wanton with Desire' and therefore neglecting her filial duty to her parents (Phillips 1695).

The above discussion has centred around fiction and drama, focusing on famous authors or works with the term 'filial piety' in the title. To supplement this potentially biased selection, a sampling was taken of all texts in ECCO in which the term 'filial' occurred (19,837 items). After sorting by date of publication, one in every fifty texts was selected, for a total of 397 items, and then these 397 items were analysed in some detail. Many individual items contained multiple hits, so that the total number of occurrences of all forms, including 'filial' by itself, was almost 800 hits, or an average of two occurrences for each text.

First, in terms of relative frequency, filial fear, which had been the most common collocation in the seventeenth century, drops down to fourth place, with only fifty-five instances. This represents only 6.9 per cent of all hits, a precipitous drop from the 35.1 per cent it occupied in the previous century. Meanwhile, filial duty (111 hits, 13.9 per cent) and filial piety (104 hits, 13.0 per cent) are now the most common and essentially equal, followed rather closely by filial love (77 hits, 9.6 per cent). Since filial fear virtually always takes God or the Church as its object, while filial piety and filial duty are mostly used in secular, family situations, there is a marked shift away from religious associations for filial.

Second, there is a much greater variety of words that collocate with filial. I counted a total of ninety-five different binomes that began with filial. A large number of these can be grouped into a few major categories: emotions, abstract nouns (states of being, actions), body parts, and a small group of terms with negative connotations. Filial children experience a wide range of emotions, depending on the circumstances, from grief, sorrow, and agony at seeing a parent injured or dead, to rage and wrath at a parent wronged, through joy and rapture when their parents are saved. These emotions may also be expressed by filial sighs, shudders, or caresses, and filial body parts are also often connected with emotions (heart, eyes shedding tears, bosom heaving with emotion). Among the abstract nouns, many are also related to emotions, such as repentance, penitence, attachment, and disposition. Thus overall filial children are much more children of affect in the eighteenth century than they were in the seventeenth. The small number of negative terms (wickedness, contumacy, inhumanity, ingratitude, impatience, and unfilial) indicate that, although filial continues to enjoy very positive connotations, there are occasionally children who fail to practice this virtue.

Turning to the question of where the term filial occurs in the database as a whole, the fact that 'filial' features in the title of seventeen works is significant; no works in EEBO feature the term. These seventeen items are mainly novels and plays (nine), with a second significant grouping of books teaching good manners and letter-writing (four) and a book of moral education (one). There is also one religious text (filial fear), and there are two miscellaneous pieces; one a short, satiric poem about Grub Street that uses filial piety in an ironic sense, and one on the king.

The educational and religious material contain nothing surprising. Being inherently conservative genres, their use of filial duty, filial piety, filial obedience and filial fear are part of the social norms that must be maintained.

The dramas and novels, however, are a different matter altogether. As noted above in the discussion of texts that featured filial piety or filial in the title, other plays and novels also contain no references to filial fear. Instead, there is a concentration of filial piety, filial duty and, to a lesser extent, filial obedience. More importantly, there is a high incidence of conflict between filial piety or filial duty and other emotional bonds, chiefly romantic love, but also in some cases the bonds of friendship between two men of the same generation. In such instances, the son or daughter is usually a teenager or young adult, and the father is portrayed as tyrannical or arbitrary in the way he exercises paternal authority. As we have noted in the discussion of EEBO texts, a growing tendency to see filial piety as part of a reciprocal bond engendered by caring parents means that such an attitude on the part of the parents goes a long way to excusing the children's unfilial behaviour.

Meanwhile, as more texts begin to be translated from Chinese, the reputation of the Chinese concerning filial piety increases. Although the earliest partial translation/summary of the *Four Books* does not use the term 'filial piety', it does talk about obedience to parents being 'the first, and most important Virtue of Children to their Parents ... *Venvam*, [Wen Wang, an early sage-king] in the Relation of a Son, adher'd to this Obedience; and incessantly acquitted himself of this Duty with an extraordinary Piety' (Confucius 1724, 43). The term 'obedience' is used several times later in the text (77–79), but the term 'piety' also recurs when the text speaks of burying dead parents as the 'last Offices of Piety' (46). Then besides obedience, a man must 'above all Men ... love his Father and Mother' (80; used again p. 81). Other terms used include 'honour' (124), 'serve' and 'obey' (both 119). We can see, then, that at this time the equation between xiao and the term 'filial piety', although it has been established in the texts mentioned previously, is not yet fixed, but that stories about the Chinese as being dutiful children are being introduced, even when the term 'filial piety' is not always used.

One late example of this trend is the translation of a short story into English under the title of *Fan-Hy-Cheu: A Tale, In Chinese and English* (Weston 1814).[8] In the story, a man and woman meet during a rebellion and marry, only to be separated when the rebels are dispersed by imperial troops. Although they have no news of each other and do not even know if the other is alive, both refuse to re-marry. Instead, the woman tells her father that she will stay at home and serve him and her mother, and the man devotes himself to looking after his mother. Eventually they are re-united and live happily ever after. Although the term xiao is not used in the story and 'filial' does not occur in the translation, the tale is an interesting example of two people using the fulfilment of filial duties towards their parents as an excuse to avoid re-marriage and eventually give them the opportunity to be re-united. Far from there being a conflict between filial duty and conjugal love, there is an implicit assumption that a sense of filial duty and loyalty to one's spouse are mutually reinforcing virtues, and that the reward for filial piety may be conjugal love.

In the nineteenth century the link between filial piety in Chinese and English is strengthened by the direct translation of classical Confucian texts. Four important translations of the *Four Books* directly from Chinese between 1809 and 1900—Marshman (1809), Collie (1828), Legge (1861), and Wilson (1900)—use 'filial piety' for xiao as a noun, sometimes varying it with 'filial' when it is rendered as an adjective in English. The only exception to this rule, Ku Hung-ming's *Discourses and Sayings of Confucius* (1898), is instructive. Ku, who in his introduction says that he wants to translate the *Lunyu* into modern idiomatic English such as an English gentleman would use, avoids the use of the term 'filial piety'. Instead he uses the phrase 'to be a good son' or simply 'good son'. This indicates that Ku already feels that the term 'filial piety' is becoming outmoded in English.

Other translations in the nineteenth century, not necessarily directly concerned to expound Confucianism, also use 'filial piety' or some similar term for xiao. In the introduction to Davis's *Laou-Seng-Urh* (1817, xxxiv), he notes that his English readers 'have to remember that filial piety is paramount, and therefore taking inferior wives or concubines' is considered normal; later in his translation *The Fortunate Union*, he uses 'filial regard', 'filial disposition', and 'filial conduct' (Davis 1829, 93, 105, and 245). Tkin Shen's translation of *The Rambles of the Emperor Ching Tih in Keang nan: A Chinese Tale* (1843) uses it to describe one of the characters, who is reduced to tears upon losing the money he had saved for his mother's funeral (Shen 1843, 161).

Not just translations but also books that purport to describe the Chinese character use the term 'filial piety' extensively. Davis, in his two-volume work on China entitled *The Chinese*, which went through at least six editions between 1836 and 1857, uses the term 'filial duty', 'filial', and 'filial piety' interchangeably in a discussion of the relation between the family structure and the government (Davis 1836, 191–93).[9] Here we see the beginnings of a depiction of Chinese filial piety as not just extreme, but also as something negative. In particular, Davis argues that a paternal structure may be appropriate to small tribes, but for a large empire it becomes despotism, 'retaining little of the paternal character beyond its absolute authority' (190). He also quotes Sir George Staunton's view that this use of parental authority for government may be stable, but is not related to filial affection (192–93).

Later at the end of the century, perhaps the most (in)famous example is Arthur Smith's *Chinese Characteristics* (1894), whose chapter nineteen, entitled 'Filial Piety', contains an extensive discussion of this trait.[10] He begins by asserting the centrality of the concept for the Chinese: 'To discuss the characteristics of the Chinese without mentioning filial piety, is out of the question' (Smith 1894, 171), and then goes on to call it 'not merely a characteristic but a peculiarity' (172). Here we see a shift from the eighteenth-century emphasis on the Chinese as exemplars to one that emphasises oddity. This oddity includes the fact that Chinese children are expected not to feel resentment if, upon remonstrating with their parents about something the parents have done wrong, the parents should beat them, something that Smith finds it hard to believe any English person could stomach (174–75). He then gives three examples taken from the *Twenty-Four Paragons of Filial Piety* (which he renders as the *Four-and-twenty Ensamples of Filial Piety*) which he ridicules: why would the son of a rich official need to steal oranges for his mother? Who could believe the story of the carp that leapt out of water in response to a filial son lying on the ice? Who can imagine a boy lying perfectly still and letting mosquitos bite him instead of his parents? (176–77) Note that an example which *A New Book for the Improvement of Young Gentlemen and Ladies …* (1785) could cite as exemplary behaviour to be emulated, here a little over a century later is held up for ridicule. This is followed by a direct statement by Smith that the idea that it is better to murder one's child than let one's mother starve is abhorrent, and that cutting off one's own flesh to feed one's parents is barbaric (Smith 1894, 177–78). Smith goes on to argue that, taken to extremes in Chinese culture, filial piety is the driving force behind all sorts of decisions, such as child marriages, female infanticide, impoverishment of the family due to lavish funerals, and waste of manpower due to excessive mourning (178–83). Smith concedes that respect for elders, and perhaps the need to consult parents for important decisions even when one is an adult, are things Westerners might learn. 'Yet, on the other hand, it is idle to discuss the filial piety of the Chinese without making most emphatic its fatal defects in several particulars' (182). This is followed by a further catalogue of evils, including its being one-sided: there is nothing in the tenet of filial piety about how parents should treat children; it is sexist; it subordinates the young to the old; it encourages polygamy and concubinage; and it gives rise to ancestor worship and a generally conservative outlook that prevents the Chinese from changing and embracing Western Christian modernity (182–85). Smith effectively turns filial piety into a vice rather than a virtue, even while continuing to use the word 'piety' as part of the compound.

Despite the fact that some sinologists in the nineteenth century such as Davis suggested that 'filial piety' might not always be the best translation for xiao, by the early twentieth century, 'filial piety equals xiao' is more or less a fixed equation, with other terms such as filial duty or filial respect now less likely to be used when discussing the Chinese. The last time that another term is used in a translation of the *Classic of Filial Piety* was published in 1908, *The Book of Filial Duty*, as part of the Wisdom of the East series, translated by Ivan Chen (Chen 1908). Bertrand Russell's *The Problem of China* (1922) uses the term filial piety unabashedly. Following the lead of Davis and Smith, his argument is worth quoting at length:

> Filial piety, and the strength of the family generally, are perhaps the weakest point in Confucian ethics, the only point where the system departs seriously from common sense. Family feeling has militated against public spirit, and the authority of the old has increased the tyranny of ancient custom. In the present day, when China is confronted with problems requiring a radically new outlook, these features of the Confucian system have made it a barrier to necessary reconstruction, and accordingly we find all those foreigners who wish to exploit China praising the old tradition and deriding the efforts of Young China to construct something more suited to modern needs. The way in which Confucian emphasis on filial piety prevented the growth of public spirit is illustrated by the following story:
>
> > One of the feudal princes was boasting to Confucius of the high level of morality which prevailed in his own State. 'Among us here,' he said, 'you will find upright men. If a father has stolen a sheep, his son will give evidence against him.' 'In my part of the country,' replied Confucius, 'there is a different standard from this. A father will shield his son, a son will shield his father. It is thus that uprightness will be found.'
>
> It is interesting to contrast this story with that of the elder Brutus and his sons, upon which we in the West were all brought up. (Russell 1922, 40–41)

Here we see that filial piety is firmly associated with China, and especially with Confucius. Russell (1922, 41) goes on to say that filial piety is a universal 'at a certain stage of culture' for everyone, but that universality is qualified temporally: once those other cultures (he cites the Greeks and the Romans) attained 'a very high level of civilization', they left filial piety behind (41). So filial piety is closely linked to the past and 'the tyranny of ancient custom'. Therefore, attempts by a new generation of Chinese intellectuals to modernise the country have been frustrated by this custom, which Russell claims is consciously encouraged by foreigners who do not wish to see China modernise because then they would not be able to exploit it for their own gain. Russell juxtaposes a story in the Western tradition that is the exact opposite of the story of Confucius and his defense of family before state. Yet Russell also balances this discussion of filial piety out by saying that, although filial piety may lead to corruption and intrigue, what the West has substituted for it, patriotism, leads to killing and so is even worse (40–41).

Perhaps the strongest evidence for the fixed nature of the link between the two terms, however, is the fact that some people complain about it. Hamilton (1990) points out that by 1921, 'filial piety' was the obligatory translation of xiao, even by people who did not believe it was the best term for it, citing among others George Jamieson (1921, 4), who would prefer 'filial duty' or 'filial submission'. His position is essentially a stronger rephrasing of Staunton's remarks a century earlier that 'the pleasing appellation of filial piety' was too positive a term to use as a translation of xiao (cited in Davis 1836, 192).

From a high point in the early nineteenth century, the term 'filial piety', now firmly linked to Chinese Confucianism, gradually falls into disuse in the general language, but continues to be used in texts relating to China. Ku Hung-ming, who avoided the use of the term in his 'modern' translation of the *Lunyu*, uses it in *The Spirit of the Chinese People* (1915), where he argues that Chinese religion has two tenets: 'loyalty to the Emperor and filial piety to parents—in Chinese, *Chung Hsiao* (忠孝)' (Ku 1915, 44). Lin Yutang uses the term in virtually every one of his works, including his novels such as *Moment in Peking* (1939a), *Chinatown Family* (Lin 1948, 76 and 85), *The Vermillion Gate* (Lin 1954, 279), and *The Red Peony* (Lin 1975, 69); as well as his translations in *The Widow Chuan* (Lin 1952, 40).

In general then, there is a shift from male filial feeling (fear, duty, piety) towards God and parents, to women exhibiting filial piety towards parents but then having a conflict with love, thus giving negative connotations to filial piety as an excess, an extreme, a peculiar trait that holds back the natural life cycle. Gradually over a period of two centuries, filial piety becomes more of a backward-looking, secondary virtue at the same time that it is more firmly associated with China. There is thus a movement away from a general, or universal disposition, and a gradual emphasis of the particularity and the extremes to which the Chinese carry out filial piety, to the point that the peculiar custom of the Chinese becomes a vice, something associated with a more primitive stage of social evolution that prevents the arrival of modernity in China.

Filial piety in modern China

Many of the same people who are translating the Chinese classics into English in the early and mid-nineteenth century were also among the first to translate European texts into Chinese since the departure of the Jesuits.

Indeed, many of them learned Chinese precisely for this reason: they were Protestant missionaries intent upon converting the Chinese to Christianity. Although the term 'filial piety' is not used in the English version of the Bible, there are passages that have to do with children's obligations and feelings towards their parents; these passages were the basis for many of the sermons in EEBO and ECCO that use 'filial'. Most famously, the fifth commandment says 'Honour thy father and thy mother: that thy days may be long upon the land which the Lord thy God giveth thee' (Exodus 20:12) but there are also other passages such as 'Children, obey your parents in the Lord: for this is right' (Ephesians 6:1); 'Children, obey your parents in all things: for this is well pleasing unto the Lord' (Colossians 3:20;); and 'But if any widow have children or nephews, let them learn first to shew piety at home, and to requite their parents: for that is good and acceptable before God' (1 Timothy 5:4). There are also reverse cases where disobedience to parents is clearly bad, for example: 'For men shall be lovers of their own selves, covetous, boasters, proud, blasphemers, disobedient to parents, unthankful, unholy' (2 Timothy 3:2). In total, I identified thirteen passages from the Old and New Testaments, along with three additional passages in the Catholic version of the Bible, which includes sections excluded from the Protestant version.[11] We may look at how these passages are treated in some nineteenth-century translations by Protestant missionaries to get some idea of how the Christian concept of filial piety began to interact with the Chinese concept.

Two early translations of the Bible, one done in 1822 and one in 1823, provide some interesting data (Marshman and Lassar 1822; Morrison and Milne 1823). They both rely heavily on the Chinese character *jing* (敬 respect, honour, esteem) and compounds formed with it, as well as *shun* (順 obey, submit to, follow) and *zun* (尊 to respect) to translate these passages. Of twenty occurrences, only four in the 1822 version and two in the 1823 version use xiao, and in all cases it is in the compound *xiaojing* (孝敬 filial and respectful). Thus it seems that the early Protestant missionaries were reluctant to use the Chinese term xiao in their translation of the Bible, even in contexts where it might have seemed natural.

In the period between 1846 and 1854, a group of five missionaries compiled a new translation of the Bible based on drafts produced by earlier working committees (Cohen 1974, 20). This became known as the Delegates' Version, and was adopted by several different groups of Protestant missionaries, making it one of the most popular translations for the next six decades. In this version we see an even more marked preference for jing (respect) as a translation, occurring twelve times, while xiao is only used once, in the negative construction 'unfilial' (*bu xiao* 不孝) (Medhurst *et al* 1852; Medhurst *et al* 1854).

At the same time, some missionary translators of classical Chinese texts into English had a tendency to prefer filial duty as an equivalence of xiao rather than filial piety.

The picture changes somewhat with Chinese translations of the Bible published in the twentieth century, mostly because these new vernacular versions replace the single characters jing, zun, and shun, which are classical verbs that are not normally used in the modern vernacular, with binomes, often continuing to use the compound xiaojing, which becomes the single most commonly used term in all modern versions (between ten to twelve out of the twenty passages identified in the Protestant Bible), often coupled with the binome *fumu* (父母 father and mother) to form a four-character expression for 'honour thy father and mother'.[12] However, the other two most common expressions, *zunjing* (尊敬 respect) and *tingcong* (聽從 obey), do not contain the character xiao, and are of much more general use in situations of respecting or obeying someone. Still, twentieth-century Chinese Bibles contain between ten and fifteen uses of compounds featuring xiao for the translation of passages in the Bible where English versions still contain no uses of filial piety or even filial. Thus Christian texts in Chinese have their message pulled somewhat towards a Chinese orbit regarding child-parent relations. Significantly, the early translations were completed by European and American missionaries, while the twentieth-century ones were completed by Chinese Christians either working alone or with some non-Chinese scholars, but with the Chinese-speaking members leading the effort. This suggests that non-Chinese were more likely to equate firmly the English concept of 'filial piety' with xiao; since the term 'filial piety' did not occur in the English Bible, they were less likely to use the term xiao in their translations of the text. For the Chinese translators, however, xiao is a broader concept that can be adopted easily to situations that do not call for the exact term 'filial piety' or 'filial' in English.

We can cross-check this by consulting some of the bilingual dictionaries and teaching materials that were compiled in the nineteenth century by missionaries. In the early and for quite some time authoritative *Dictionary of the Chinese Language*, the main entry for xiao reads 'Duty and obedience to one's parents; filial piety, duty to superiors' (Morrison 1815–23, vol. 1, part 2:244). Where xiao appears in other entries, usage is split approximately half and half between filial piety and filial duty or dutiful. Similarly, his later *Vocabulary of the Canton Dialect* (Morrison 1828) gives either filial piety or duty for the vast majority of times that xiao occurs.

The later *Chinese and English Dictionary* defines xiao as 'filial piety, respect and reverence for parents' (Medhurst 1842–43, 1:173). In the sub-entries and in other entries where xiao occurs, Medhurst mainly uses either filial by itself or filial piety, or occasionally 'reverence' when xiao is a verb;

he seldom uses duty. Similarly, in his *Dictionary of the Hokëën Dialect of the Chinese Language* (Medhurst 1832), he overwhelmingly uses filial or filial piety.

A slight departure from Morrison and Medhurst is *A Chinese Chrestomathy in the Canton Dialect* (Bridgman 1841), which prefers filial, filial duty, or dutiful. Bridgman is also the only translator of the *Classic of Filial Piety* to use 'Filial Duty' in the title and for most of the occurrences within the text (Bridgman 1835).

Overall, then, nineteenth-century European and American translators firmly associated xiao with filial piety and/or filial duty; since those terms did not occur in the Bible, they were reluctant to use the term xiao in their translations of religious materials, and it was only in the twentieth century, when Chinese translators took the lead, that xiao emerges as a more common term in the Chinese Bible.

Thus few materials translated into Chinese in the early and mid-nineteenth century dealt with the concept of filial piety. It was not until almost the turn of the century, with the increase in translation of fiction, that we see many examples of filial piety in translated material. It is in this era, roughly 1895 onwards, that first sees a serious challenge to the traditional interpretation of that concept among the Chinese through translation.

The digitisation of material from this period is uneven and it is difficult to build up a reliable electronic corpus. Although there are large collections like Chinamaxx, the overwhelming majority of the texts are only available as PDF files, and OCR software does very poorly in converting late Qing and early Republican materials to text format, as Cao (2018) has detailed. This part of my study therefore relies more on close reading of a limited number of potentially rich texts, identified either because they have the character xiao in the title, are landmark translations that deal with parent-child conflict, or were identified in secondary material covering translation and social change in this period.

The texts that interest me can be divided roughly into two groups: those that apply the Chinese concept of filial piety to the situation found in a text being translated into Chinese, and those that contain material where the concept might have been used but was not. The majority of my examples are taken from works that were translated by Lin Shu (1852–1924) and his various associates.[13]

The very first novel that Lin Shu worked on was *La Dame aux Camélias*, by Alexandre Dumas *fils*. The translation, *The Legacy of the Parisian Lady of the Camellias* (巴黎茶花女遺事), was published in 1899 and was perhaps the most popular translated novel of its era. It established Lin Shu's reputation immediately, creating a demand that he continued to satisfy in an astonishing output (approximately 170 works over twenty-five years).

Everyone involved in attempts to reform or overthrow the Qing dynasty read it, as did the entire May Fourth generation of intellectuals.

The story details how a young man Armand Duval and a high-end prostitute Marguerite Gautier fall in love. After a brief idyllic period, Armand's father finds out and appears on the scene to alternately remonstrate, plead, and command his son to break it off, all in vain. The father then approaches Marguerite separately and tries to convince her that she is ruining Armand's life, again to no avail. Finally, the father explains to her that Armand's younger sister is engaged to a man of good standing, but that the fiancé's family now object to the marriage because of Armand's dalliance with a prostitute. To spare the daughter this humiliation, Marguerite agrees to break things off with Armand. She dies a year later of consumption, leaving a letter explaining all to the devastated Armand.

Early in the novel, before he meets Marguerite, Armand is described as a 'good son', something that could easily have been translated as xiao in Chinese, but is entirely missing from the translation. Likewise, later in the confrontation with his father, his behaviour could easily have been described as unfilial, a fairly common term of opprobrium in Chinese fiction. Yet in fact, in this translation of a novel where one of the main plot elements is the relation between father and son, nowhere does the term xiao appear. What is more, several key elements in the story challenge the patriarchal system that makes filial piety such a powerful force in Chinese society. First, Armand is financially independent from his father, receiving a quarterly sum from investments left to him by his deceased mother. This allows him to defy his father's will, even though the father threatens to cut off an additional stipend that he has been giving him. Second, the father is portrayed as being completely ineffectual in persuading his son and, as the story makes clear, the fact that Armand is an adult frees him from any necessity of obeying his father. In Lin's translation, Armand's own description of his father as 'extremely kind' (*en zhong* 恩重) only serves to make his disobedience more inexplicable and shocking to Chinese readers. Instead, the father is reduced to appealing to the better nature of Marguerite to 'save' Armand's sister and trick Armand into believing that she no longer loves him, and it is precisely because she is so in love with him that she is willing to sacrifice herself.

The Story of the Parisian Lady of the Camellias thus presents its Chinese readers with an alternate society where considerations of filial piety have been displaced by other concerns, namely romantic love and individuality. In this society, financially independent children interact with their parents on an equal footing, and even the best of parents cannot assume obedience, whereas in China, children are expected to be filial even when their parents are unloving, misguided, or cruel.

Lin Shu's translation of H. Rider Haggard's *Joan Haste* (1895) as *The Story of Joan* (迦茵小傳 1905b) is an even more glaring example of how some of his translations challenge the traditional virtue of filial piety. Yuan Jin (1998, 286) details how both the hero and the heroine defy their fathers in order to marry each other. The hero rejects his father's dying wish that he marry another woman, while Joan confronts her living father directly. Jin (286–87) also details how these flagrant violations of filial norms led to the novel being attacked by reformers for being too radical.

Lin Shu does use the term filial piety in some of his works, but even so, the stories are not necessarily an affirmation of that character trait. Hill (2012, 115–21) details how Lin Shu's translation of Charles Dickens' *The Old Curiosity Shop* (1841), which Lin entitled the *Biography of Nell, a Filial Daughter* (孝女耐兒傳 1907a), fails to live up to the promise of its title, because it is Nell's search for freedom from her grandfather's debts and harsh city life that dominate the action in Lin Shu's translation, not filial piety; filial piety is rarely mentioned in the novel until the closing chapters, where the dying Nell is praised for this characteristic that, in the bulk of the novel, is not in evidence, and which seems incompatible with her search for freedom.

> Filial Nell casts a darker shadow over Lin's project, because it begs the question of whether filial piety can serve as a universal principle in the same way that 'freedom' or international law might without being overwhelmed by cultural influences that bear the mark of industrial modernization and its tendency to 'liberate' individuals from the social bonds of extended family and community maintained by filial piety. (Hill 2012, 121)

Besides the *Biography of Nell, a Filial Daughter*, three other of Lin Shu's translations feature the term xiao in the title. These are: H. Rider Haggard's *Montezuma's Daughter* (1893), translated as *Record of a Filial English Son's Revenge at the Volcano* (英孝子火山報仇錄 1905a); David Christie Murray's *The Martyred Fool* (1895), translated as *Story of Two Filial Sons Returning Gratitude with Blood* (雙孝子噀血酬恩記 1907b); and Hendrik Conscience's *Arme Edelman*, translated as *Mirror of Filial Friendship* (孝友鏡 1918). In some of these translations, especially *Record of a Filial English Son's Revenge* and *Story of Two Filial Sons*, the acts and attitudes described as filial fit well into the Chinese concept of filial piety, and in the preface to the first of them, Lin Shu actually claims that filial piety is something that can be found in any country, echoing the seventeenth- and eighteenth-century English claims of universality (Hill 2012, 116). There are also other translations by Lin Shu and his collaborators that show an increase in filial piety. Huang (2009, 81–83) has shown how his version of *Hamlet* goes out of its way to foreground the concept.

Overall, then, Lin Shu is an interesting figure because his translations show us a range of material regarding how the Chinese concept of filial piety interacted with European and American literature. Although Lin himself was fairly conservative, opposing the overthrow of the Qing dynasty and the May Fourth Movement's call for the use of vernacular Chinese and adoption of many Western values, he cannot help but present his readers with many novels that challenge and subvert the role of filial piety in Chinese society, even though some of his translations still uphold it as a virtue and even propose it as a universal. Given the popularity of his translations and their sheer volume, this gives us some indication of how new ideas regarding filial piety were coming into China in the final twelve to fifteen years of the Qing, over a decade before the May Fourth Movement. Moreover, the fact that in many cases the reason that filial piety is portrayed as less than ideal is often due to its conflict with romantic love harks back to the gradual devaluation of filial piety in England and America, where exactly the same conflict is traced out in both theatrical performances and fictional texts.

Yuan Jin has traced the influence that such translated fiction had on the development of Chinese romantic fiction. Jin notes that by 1906, novels such as Fu Lin's (符霖 pseudonym; unknown author) *Qin hai shi* (禽海石 Rock in a savage sea, 1906), which criticises the idea of arranged marriage by parents, were being published. Also the later *Yu li hun* (玉梨魂 Jade pear spirit, 1912–13) by Xu Zhenya 徐枕亞 (1889–1937) is consciously modelled on Lin Shu's *The Legacy of the Parisian Lady of the Camellias*, and features a young man who falls in love with a widow and must choose between Confucian propriety (remaining a widow) and her lover. In the end, she is driven to suicide (Jin 1998, 288).[14] Jin also lists several other examples. By the time that the May Fourth Movement began, then, there had already been a large volume of material, both translations and original works, that challenged the concept of filial piety.

The flood of material coming into China through translation continues unabated after the 1911 revolution and the establishment of the Republic of China. Teruo (1998, 39) has done an exhaustive study of publications in this period and concludes that 44 per cent of all works of fiction published between 1896–1911 inclusive were translations.

It is, of course, famously during the May Fourth Movement (1917–21) that iconoclasts sought to overthrow much of Chinese tradition, including many tenets of Confucianism.[15] Although there had always been some resistance within China to certain social practices that the May Fourth Movement sought to abolish, such as footbinding, there were no significant voices calling for the overthrow of filial piety in this time period that were not influenced by foreign writers, either directly or through translation. Testimony from historians and literary critics alike regarding this point are numerous (see for example Chen 1989, 75; Chan 1998, 69). Tse-Tsung Chow, in his definitive study of the movement, shows how virtually all the important ideas of the movement came from foreign sources (Chow 1960, 15) and has an entire section detailing with what sorts of material were borrowed from which countries (28–41).

One early voice is Wu Yu, who in an important article in 1917 published in *New Youth*, argued that filial piety benefited the rich and powerful while harming the poor and weak (Wu 1917, 2). Moreover, to ensure their hold on power, the aristocracy elevated filial piety to the point where every virtuous deed could be explained by it, as every evil deed evinced a lack of it, and its principles were enshrined in laws that bound the people (2–3). According to Wu, this state of affairs is the opposite of Western countries, and in order to become a true republic, China must remove filial piety from the basis of society (3).

Turning to literature, we may consider the case of Lu Xun, perhaps the most emblematic of all Chinese writers from the modern era. Two works in particular by him help to shed light on the fate of filial piety in this time period. One is his story 'Kuangren riji' (狂人日記 Diary of a Madman); the other is a short essay, 'The *Picture-Book of Twenty-Four Acts of Filial Piety*'.

'The *Picture-Book of Twenty-Four Acts of Filial Piety*' (Lu Xun 1926) is at once a reflection on the state of children's literature in China (abysmal) and a personal meditation on how reading *The Picture-Book* affected him personally and, by extension, everyone who had received a classical education. An illustrated version of the *Twenty-Four Acts of Filial Piety*, which was one of the principal texts championing filial piety in late Imperial China, the book was widely available and, as discussed earlier, was translated by the Jesuits and then found its way into English-language works exemplifying filial piety in the eighteenth century and denigrating it in the nineteenth. Like the nineteenth-century English scoffers at this book, particularly Smith, Lu Xun points out the difficulty in a real boy carrying out many of the miraculous acts of filial piety, and expresses his disgust at others (Lu Xun 1976, 31–32). He also holds up the book as a mirror to the actions of his contemporaries in the civil or military service, pointing out that none of them can be seen performing similar acts (34). But the one story in the book that makes the deepest impression upon him is that of Guo Zhu, who dug a hole to bury his son because the family did not have enough food to keep both his son and his mother alive. In the story, Guo Zhu discovers buried treasure in the hole, a reward for his filial piety towards his mother that allows him to save both his mother and son (see cover for a Qing era illustration of this text). For Lu Xun, this story engenders a terror that his own father will bury him alive in order to be filial to Lu Xun's grandmother.

This feeling of anxiety persisted, Lu Xun tells us, until his grandmother died years later (33–35). Lu Xun's essay, then, sets up a stark equation: filial piety equals sacrificing a younger generation to save an older one.

If we look back at one of Lu Xun's first short stories, 'Diary of a Madman' (first published 1918), the focus in the second half of the story is on the narrator's five-year-old sister and his concern whether she has been eaten. In the final line of the story 'Save the children', we can see how Lu Xun's concerns regarding filial piety spill out into other of his works. It also firmly establishes filial piety as a backward-looking characteristic, just as filial piety in the eighteenth and nineteenth century gradually came to be viewed as a backward-looking trait in Anglo-American literature. But while Anglo-American literature often sets up filial piety as an obstacle to the forward movement of the plot, typically by delaying marriage of the next generation, in Lu Xun's imagination it is much worse: the younger generation may have to sacrifice their lives. Crucially, in the story of Guo Zhu, it is not the child who decides to sacrifice himself, but rather his father who decides to sacrifice the unwitting boy.[16]

By the 1930s, the idea that family centred values, including filial piety, were in opposition to modern society was firmly established both among left-wing writers and also among more conservative critics such as Feng Youlan (Lean 2007, 89). Moreover, as Lean demonstrates in her study of how Shi Jianqiao successfully used filial piety as a defense in her trial for the murder of the man responsible for killing her father, the concept of filial piety had undergone some modification by this time. Due to its identification with childish or womanish feelings, most legal reformers and many government officials were reluctant to admit filial piety as a justification at the trial (91–96). The large number of translations and fictional works that used the opposition between filial piety and romantic love seems to have moved the centre of gravity of filial piety from Confucian ritual to natural feelings, aligning it more with the English concept of filial piety as developed in the eighteenth and early nineteenth century and expressed in fiction of the time. The public debate over Shi Jianqiao's case reveals the extent to which most members of the elite had distanced themselves from filial piety, but it also shows that filial piety was by no means eradicated. This is seen both in public outpouring of sentiment and in the government's ultimate decision to pardon her, partly because of the government's own New Life movement, which re-embraced Confucian family values to the extent that they coincided with Christian values (Lean 2007, 120–22 and 150–54). Interestingly for this study, Lean notes that 'several telegrams demanded that Nanjing pay tribute to the filial devotion of the perpetrators *as something uniquely Chinese*' (154; my emphasis). In other words, the identification of filial piety as something specific to China had begun to re-assert itself in the Chinese discourse, influenced by the growing body of literature in English that identified it as peculiar to the Chinese. To the extent that it could be relabelled as part of the national essence, there continued to be some who took pride in how it marked China as different from other countries, even as the discourse about such traits holding China back from modernity also circulated.

The situation changes again after the establishment of the PRC in 1949, an avowed Marxist government. For the next thirty years, filial piety is barely acknowledged except in reports lambasting it as a feudal holdover, and there is no acknowledgement of it as part of a national essence. We can get a sense of how low the fortunes of filial piety had fallen when the government instituted the one-child policy in 1979. Although there were exceptions for ethnic minorities and for families in the countryside, tens of millions of couples whose first child was a girl were denied the possibility of having a son.

I conducted two surveys of material held in electronic format, both of which show the extent to which this time period was a nadir for filial piety in China. First, I searched through the *Selected Works of Mao Zedong* in five volumes (Mao 1977), and found no instances of the character xiao in his writings. While this does not mean that Mao Zedong never thought about filial piety, it certainly shows that the editors of his selected works felt that no work by Mao touching upon the subject was important enough to include in this extensive collection.

The second database I investigated was the Chinese Communist Party's flagship newspaper, the *People's Daily*, which is available in fully searchable format from its founding in 1946 through the present day. Of 4675 occurrences of the character xiao in various combinations, fully two-thirds (3105) occur in the thirteen years between 2007 and 2019 (inclusive).[17] In the 1940s through the mid-1960s, the term occurs an average of only eleven times per year; at the height of the Cultural Revolution, for seven years between 1967 and 1973, the term occurs only seventeen times in total. Moreover, in all instances before 1974, xiao is only invoked to be attacked or ridiculed. In 1974–75 there is a spike in use (141 occurrences over the two years) as part of the 'Criticise Lin Biao, Criticise Confucius Campaign' (批林批孔運動). All of these articles seek to link Lin Biao (林彪 1907–71) to Confucianism as a way of discrediting him and are unremittingly negative. After that campaign is over, usage again drops for the rest of the 1970s.

Usage begins to pick up in the 1980s (average of twenty-seven times per year) and the 1990s (average of forty-three times per year), but it is in late 2006 and then subsequent years that usage really takes off, with hundreds of hits each year. A quick sampling of articles reveals that since at least the early 1990s, the vast majority of references to filial piety are positive, a striking reversal from the situation when Mao Zedong was still alive. One good example is the article 'Giving Everything to the Fatherland' (把一切獻給祖國大地) from 1992, which among other stories of sacrifice tells the story of Qiang Xulin who had returned home to visit his dying father, but then was recalled to work:

> Since time immemorial, it has been difficult to completely fulfil the duties of both loyalty and filial piety. [Qiang Xulin] had quietly arranged everything for his father, fulfiling completely his filial duties. But then on 28 May, with tears in his eyes, he bid farewell to his father and left with many a backward glance, hurrying to the Xinjiang Survey Area.
>
> 自古忠孝難兩全.他默默地為父親料理着一切,盡最後一點孝心. 5月28日,他滿眶熱淚,一步一回頭,告別了即將理他而去的父親,急速趕往新疆測區.
> (Liu Yongnuo 1991)

Here we see filial piety again linked to the virtue of loyalty, not to a king or emperor, but to the modern nation state. Although there is a conflict in trying to maximise both filial piety and loyalty, the description of Qiang as filial is clearly meant in a positive sense. Indeed, *zhongxiao* (忠孝 loyal and filial) is one of the most common binomes in the *People's Daily* database.[18]

Other researchers have noted a slightly different way in which the Chinese government has exploited the link between loyalty and filial piety. Fong (2004) details how the government has used filial piety to promote nationalism among Chinese teenagers with an international outlook. Crucially, the idea that filial piety is unconditional is useful to the state because these teenagers often have a negative view of the government and of living conditions in China in comparison to life abroad; linking filial piety to loyalty to the government means that, despite their disapproval of various government policies and disappointment with the standard of living, these youths should remain loyal to the state. It also seems to indicate that the re-alignment of filial piety in Chinese to coincide more with affect than with ritual has persisted from the 1930s.

The surge since late 2006 is directly tied to a government initiative to promote filial piety. This initiative has included both carrots and sticks. On the one hand, contests to see who was the most filial and reward systems for filial behaviour were established both regionally and nationally. These include designating thousands of people as 'stars of filial piety' in local town and city drives (Fang Yunyu 2010) and national awards for youths presented on television (Li Wenrui 2019). Thus filial behaviour has been lauded and given rewards, both in terms of praise and monetary gain. At the same time, the government passed laws mandating that children were legally responsible for their elderly parents, and that this included not just financial support but also emotional support, usually in the form of periodic visits (Yu Hua 2013). There have been cases where children have been sentenced to jail time for neglecting their parents. One case in particular, the death of an elderly man in poor health resulted in his five children all being sentenced to time in jail for neglecting him, despite the fact that he was abusive towards them (Ni 2018). Finally, there were also educational initiatives. Probably first in importance among them is the *New Twenty-Four Paragons of Filial Piety*, a list of exemplary acts that any Chinese could perform towards their parents. This replaced the more mythological or magical ones in the original *Twenty-Four Paragons of Filial Piety*, and include such mundane items as teaching your parents how to use the internet, celebrating their birthday with them, and cooking for them on a regular basis. Crucially, all of the examples are for the care of elderly parents after their retirement. Former traditional facets of filial piety such as sacrifice to one's ancestors, the observation of proper mourning rituals and, perhaps most surprisingly, obedience to one's parents, are absent. There has even been a museum established exclusively to document and showcase filial piety (Hancock 2015).

If we wish to understand this resurgence of Confucianism in China in the first two decades of the twenty-first century, we must backtrack a bit. Despite the fact that filial piety, as part of Confucianism, was attacked both under the Republican government and the PRC, it did not completely vanish. We have already seen that during the Republican era the New Life Movement rehabilitated certain elements of Confucian values that could be reconciled to Christianity. More importantly, after 1949, filial piety continued as part of popular practices in many areas outside of the PRC. Among ethnic Chinese, it continued in Hong Kong and Taiwan, as well as among overseas Chinese communities around the world, particularly in Southeast Asia.[19] It also played an important role in Korea: 'Ancestral memorial rites and funeral ceremonies constitute the backbone of the Confucian heritage, and probably nowhere else are these ceremonies more intensively and extensively observed than in Korea' (Koh 1996, 195). In Japan filial piety was conscripted into the jingoist rhetoric of absolute loyalty to the emperor in the 1930s and 1940s as part of the war machine (Yamashita 1996, 152). Yet despite these negative associations in the post-war period, which meant that Confucianism as a whole was discredited, filial piety survived and even throve both with respect to living parents and deceased ancestors (Smith 1996, 157).

Moreover, in terms of intellectual movements and discussion about the relationship between Confucianism and modernity, a vigorous debate continued throughout the Republican period and, after the founding of the People's Republic in 1949, among overseas Chinese. The first generation of these new Confucians, as they are sometimes known, still wrote primarily in Chinese. Ch'ien Mu, who moved to Hong Kong after the founding of the PRC, where he co-founded New Asia College (now part of the Chinese

University of Hong Kong) and then in 1967 moved to Taiwan as a member of Academia Sinica, is typical of this generation (Dennerline 1988). The second generation, however, were mainly trained or worked overseas and increasingly wrote either in both English and Chinese or mainly in English. Typical of this second generation is Tu Wei-ming, who trained first in Taiwan, then in the United States, where he worked for many years while still keeping ties to institutions in Taiwan and Singapore. In 2010 he became the founder and director of the Institute for Advanced Humanistic Studies and Peking University chair professor (Tu n.d.).[20]

In fact, it has been argued that, from the 1950s through the 1980s, international discourse on cultural China in general and Confucianism specifically was shaped by academics writing in English and Japanese (Tu 1994a, 14). Moreover, not only was much of the work being published in English; there were also important contributions by scholars who did not read Chinese and therefore only accessed the basic texts of Confucianism through translation, including Herbert Fingarette, David L. Hall, and Robert Neville (Tu, 2000, 14).

In the 1980s, some of the new Confucians, as well as political pundits, argued that the economic success of Taiwan, Hong Kong, Singapore, and South Korea (the Four Asian Tigers) was linked to the fact that these countries had maintained 'Asian values', by which they meant Confucianism (Tu 1994a). Tu Wei-ming also sought to deflect the criticism of Confucianism going back to the May Fourth Movement that it had held China back from modernity by arguing that the problems in East Asian countries were due to the evils of colonialism and thus came from outside of China (Tu 1999, 67).

The Four Asian Tigers achieved their success under authoritarian one-party rule at least through the 1980s: Taiwan was controlled by the Kuomintang (KMT) under martial law until 1987 and, even after the lifting of martial law, the party remained in power until 2000; Singapore's government has been run by the People's Action Party since independence; Hong Kong, as a colony, had little self-government under the British and less after being handed over to the PRC; and South Korea was under the rule of two successive strongmen from 1961 through 1997. It should not be surprising, then, that Confucianism began to look attractive to the PRC in the 1980s as, in the post-Mao era, they moved away from communist orthodoxy but looked for models of governance that combined market reform with a continued centralised and authoritarian power structure.

What does this all mean for filial piety in the late twentieth century? First of all, as one of the basic tenets of Confucianism, filial piety receives plenty of attention. Leading figures of the new Confucians proclaim loudly and often that filial piety is either *the* root of all virtue, or at least one of the most important. In his early study of Wang Yangming, Tu notes that it was

Wang's filial feelings for his father and his grandmother that prevented him from becoming a Buddhist. Tu in an aside notes that 'he [Wang Yangming] came to the realization that the feeling for one's parents is so deeply rooted in man's nature that to expunge it is to deny the very foundations of humanity. This assumption is one of the most basic in Confucian teaching; indeed, it is the rationale underlying the practice of filial piety' (Tu 1976, 59–60). Elsewhere he quotes Fung Yulan on filial piety as the root of Confucianism (Tu 1984, 118–19).

There are, however, important debates concerning what Confucianism is all about, including what filial piety means exactly. This debate shifts the meaning of filial piety in various directions.

First, Tu Wei-ming has tried to argue that the five bonds, including that between father and son, are reciprocal, rather than hierarchical. This is perhaps because he is sensitive to the criticism levelled against Confucianism that it demands absolute obedience by inferiors towards superiors and thus easily legitimates authoritarian dictatorships. Thus he claims that 'The father must be loving to encourage filiality in the son.... If the father is not loving and the son fails to be filial, this is understandable' (Tu 1984, 23–24). This leads him into a rather tortured reading of the story of Shun, one of China's early sage kings, who was filial towards his father despite the fact that his father was a horrible person and treated Shun badly. For most scholars, this story is read as an example of how, despite the failure of the father to love his son, the son *still* has a duty of filial piety towards him. And in fact there are no passages in either the *Analects* or *Mencius* that state it is 'understandable' if the son of an unloving father is not filial; that is strictly Tu's modern interpretation. He further links this reciprocity to self-cultivation, claiming in a new reading of the need to provide grandchildren as the parents' wish that their children can become parents, because only when they become parents can they learn love in all its fullness, a good example of the heteronormative nature of the new Confucianism (Tu 1985, 14). Neville (2000, 99) points out that this new reading shifts emphasis away from having children as a means of economic security in old age to a religious and ethical motivation of parents wanting their children to become fully human.

Second, in the introduction to an important collection edited by Tu Wei-ming, he says 'being Chinese implies the practice of a code of ethics (e. g., loyalty and filial piety) toward one's homeland, the "mother country" (*zuguo*)' (Tu 1994b, v). This metaphorisation of filial piety as a feeling towards the nation state is a modern twist; in earlier times, filial piety might be *compared* to loyalty to the ruler, and the ruler might be *likened to* the father and mother of the people, but there was never any attempt to apply the notion of filial piety directly to the nation by anthropomorphising it as mother, which allows the complete conflation of loyalty and filial piety as one. It is also interesting that his English term, 'mother country', is feminine, whereas the Chinese in brackets '*zuguo*' is masculine; *zu* (祖) are one's paternal ancestors.

Elsewhere, Neville goes further to claim that Tu's modern interpretation of filial piety 'does not necessarily mean one's particular parents' (Neville 2000, 201). As the root of humaneness, filial piety becomes the basis for humane feelings that one has towards not just one's own parents and ancestors, or elders in the community, but also towards all humans. Thus the new Confucians extend the scope of filial piety in significant ways.

At the same time, however, filial piety is also modified due to the attack of feminists in the English sphere. Reporting from the first Confucian-Christian Dialogue Conference in Hong Kong in 1988, Neville notes that 'It was observed at the conference, for instance, that one major reshaping of Confucianism in the American context is that it places relatively more emphasis on the virtues of public life than on the virtues of filiality, although both are still important' (2000, xxiv). Neville also links the feminist challenge to Tu's emphasis on the reciprocity of the five bonds; indeed, Neville goes so far as to claim that Confucianism 'in its early and late basic texts emphasises reciprocity rather than oppressive subordination, and like Daoism Confucianism waged a critical and often losing war against primal patriarchalism' (Neville 2000, xxiii). Here the claim is that what has been rejected by the May Fourth Movement as the evils of Confucianism (patriarchy, hierarchy, blind filial obedience, and so on) are actually the evils of an earlier, primitive Chinese social system that Confucianism sought to combat.

This characterisation of Confucianism has not gone unchallenged, however. In the early 2000s, there was an important debate, first in Chinese and then in English, over the relationship between filial piety and nepotism. Briefly, one side took as point of departure passages relating to the sage king Shun, already alluded to, as indicating that Confucius and Mencius's philosophy, by putting one's father and brother above all else, led directly to nepotistic forms of government (Liu 2007). The other side dismissed this attack as based on a narrow interpretation of these stories out of context (Guo 2007). This debate, which began in Chinese (see Guo 2004 for a collection of the most important articles) then moved to the English-language forum of the journal *Dao*.

In sum, the concept of filial piety in the past thirty years in China owes much to developments in the English-speaking world since the 1960s, where a combination of overseas Chinese, Western sinologists, and philosophers have advanced a programme to make Confucianism relevant to modern-day China and, indeed, the modern world in general. This internationalisation of Confucian teachings has brought filial piety and xiao even closer together in both languages, partly by attempts to reinterpret it.

The convergence of filial piety and xiao

The close relationship between xiao in Chinese and 'filial piety' in English today can be seen by comparing information in several large databases.

First, Google Ngram Viewer (books.google.com/ngrams/) shows a fairly steady decline in the frequency of the term 'filial' from 1809–1985, from 0.0006560519 to 0.0001213455 per cent, just 18.5 per cent of the initial level. But filial piety is steadier, moving from 0.0000998298 to 0.0000292826, or about 29.3 per cent, and so occurrences of 'filial piety' as a percentage of all examples of filial rises significantly, from 15.2 to 24.1 per cent.

Ngram Viewer has the built-in problem that the material has all been automatically converted from image to text by OCR software. Yet if we turn to contemporary corpora constructed with proofread texts, we can get confirmation of these figures. The British National Corpus, compiled between 1985–93, has a total of 56 hits for filial, of which 14 collocate with piety, or 25 per cent, twice as common as the next term, affection (7 hits). Moving to the more contemporary Corpus of Contemporary American English, which covers 1990–2017, a search yielded 352 hits for the term filial. There were then 98 hits for piety as a collocation, or 27.8 per cent, by far the most common.

Turning now to two newspapers for some granularity in how these terms are used, in the *People's Daily* English edition website, a search between July 2007 and December 2019 for the word 'filial' yielded 200 hits. Out of these, an astonishing 138 hits, or 69.0 per cent, were for 'filial piety'. The next closest was 'filial' by itself (34 hits) and then duty (14 hits). The imbalance between filial piety and filial duty here (approximately ten to one) follows, but exaggerates the general trend in English in the modern period.[21] Naturally, these stories are almost exclusively concerned with China. Finally, in the *New York Times* in the same time period, there were 292 hits for 'filial', of which 60 were for 'filial piety', or 20.5 per cent. While this is slightly lower than the BNC (British National Corpus) and COCA (Corpus of Contemporary American English) percentages, it is instructive to look at who is being filial in these hits. Thirty-eight stories are concerned with the Chinese, while a further five are about Koreans, three are about Japanese, and one is about Vietnamese; moreover, in the case of Korea, Japan and Vietnam, the articles explicitly link filial piety to Confucianism. Therefore 47 of the 60 occurrences of filial piety, or 78.3 per cent, are concerned with

China and Confucianism, while only 13 are about non-Asians. Thus even in a US-based publication like the *New York Times*, the usage for 'filial piety' is overwhelmingly tied to China and other Asian countries that have been influenced by Confucianism.

This increasingly close connection between filial piety and China in English is also in evidence in *Webster's Third New International Dictionary*, which has a separate entry for 'filial piety' which it says is a translation of the Chinese term xiao, and then goes on to define as 'reverence for parents considered in Chinese ethics the prime virtue and the basis of all right human relations' (Gove 1993).

This is not to say that acts of filial piety completely vanish from Anglo-American culture, but rather that, increasingly, the term 'filial piety' is reserved for the Chinese. An example from the 1980s American police procedural series 'Cagney and Lacey', season five, episode eight, which first aired in the autumn of 1985, was entitled 'Filial Duty'. As with many episodes, this one paired up the crime plot with a sub-plot relating to one of the female detectives, in this case Cagney. The main story concerns a woman who had taken in her elderly mother, but then finds that this causes problems with both her husband and her twelve-year-old son, who loses his room to his grandmother and has to sleep on the couch. Her son winds up smothering the grandmother with a pillow and then he and his parents, who realise the truth, try to cover it up. The parallel story involves Cagney dealing with her ageing father, who is having health problems. Her brother in California wants to take their father out there, because the brother feels that she had been unfilial to their mother when she was still alive. The episode ends with the murder case unresolved; Cagney and Lacey have discovered the truth, but it looks like the son will not be prosecuted for it, and Cagney and her father have a difficult conversation about her (in)ability to care for him.

We may compare this television drama to the essay by Lu Xun in which he expresses fear of his parents killing him to save his grandmother in a struggle over resources. Only after her death does his fear that his parents might sacrifice him abate. In the Cagney and Lacey episode we have exactly the same initial situation: a struggle over limited resources, with the child initially losing out to the grandmother because his mother has chosen to allocate scarce resources to the grandmother. But when the child reacts by killing the grandmother, not only do the parents try their best to cover it up, but the detectives who discover the truth are also torn about how to react because, like Lu Xun, they want to 'save the children'. In other words, the future of the child, who at the age of twelve as a pre-adolescent is not legally responsible for his actions in the way that an eighteen-year-old would be, becomes the focus of the story. Will the detectives 'ruin' his entire life by exposing his crime, or will they decide that he was driven to an unthinking act and deserves to go free?[22] The fact that the case is left unresolved suggests the latter, a result that would be hard to imagine occurring in China.

Translations of Chinese fiction since 1995 have helped reinforce this trend, using 'filial piety' and associated terms, often with high frequency. Out of eleven contemporary novels and collections of short stories sampled, six contained the term.[23] In Wang Wenxing's *Family Catastrophe* (1995), translated by Susan Wan Dolling, 'filial piety' recurs no fewer than nine times (Wang 1995, 134, 197, 233 [three times], 234 [twice], 253 [twice]), along with filial (134), filial son (29 and 47), and filial feelings (159). Howard Goldblatt's translation of Gu Hua's *Virgin Widows* also has eleven instances of filial piety, filial devotion, filial obligations, and filial offspring (Gu 1996, 14, 28, 57 [twice], 60 [twice], 73, 78, 116, 133, and 163).

Julia Lovell, in the preface to her translation of Zhu Wen's *I Love Dollars* (2007), explicitly raises the issue of how Zhu Wen's work contains a 'merciless debunking of one of China's oldest social conventions: the bonds of Confucian filial piety' (Zhu 2007, xi–xii), and then uses 'filial duties', 'filial son', and 'filial respect' in her translation (12, 14, and 41).

Another example is Mai Jia's *Decoded*, translated by Olivia Milburn and Christopher Payne, wherein the protagonist is described as having 'an unusual sense of filial duty' (Mai 2014, 4); this results in his grandmother bequeathing him a large sum of cash 'as a reward for his filial piety' (7). Much later in the novel, in a discussion of care for the elderly, a man ruminates over the possibility that his son and daughter-in-law will not continue to care for him as he gets older:

> Of course, the possibility of this happening was not altogether remote—long-term sickness can weaken the resolve of even the most filial son. Nevertheless, I thought that there could be other possibilities; seeing him bedridden, perhaps we would have sympathised more, become even more filial. (239)

It also occurs in the writings of Asian-Americans, such as Wesley Yang, whose article 'Paper Tigers' begins a list of Asian values with filial piety (Yang 2018, 30).

In the twenty-first century, if we search for 'filial piety' in Google, the top twenty hits are all related to China.[24] These include several online reference works, all of which define 'filial piety' as a 'Confucian' virtue.[25] Other sites that come up include a video clip in Chinese exemplifying it (from Singapore); examples in Buddhist thought; the *Illustrated Twenty-Four Paragons of Filial Piety*;[26] and an article from *China Daily* October 2012: 'Filial piety cannot be overemphasised', surely a headline set to make Mao Zedong roll over in his grave.

Here we have filial piety for the twenty-first century: rather than being an issue of obedience, it is now an issue of support for the elderly in a country where the state apparatus increasingly withdraws from its role in the Mao era of cradle-to-grave care for its citizens.

Conclusion

It is perhaps impossible to weave a single coherent narrative out of so many disparate threads in the two languages over so much time. There are too many actors, both individual and group, with competing agendas and divergent views of filial piety.

On the one hand, we may fall back on the concept of 'contested concepts' and argue that filial piety remains a polysemous term precisely because it is so important. It will never be pinned down to a single definition or single genealogy. Its history is one of multiple roads not taken, dead ends and detours, but also of unexpected divergences and convergences. It will also continue to evolve in the future in ways we cannot predict or even imagine today.

On the other hand, there are certain tendencies that can be observed from the material and points that we can make, even if we must add the caveat that there are always exceptions and counter-currents.

First, because both cultures were patriarchal, filial piety began by being theorised mainly in relation to male descent, so that the son to father bond was the primary one upon which the edifice was built. In English, links to Christianity and the analogy of God as father and Jesus Christ as his son helped to strengthen this tendency, while in Chinese the emphasis on ancestor worship through the male line influenced the development, to the extent that in Chinese, when women began to be considered as filial actors, it was primarily to their in-laws, not their parents. Here we see a difference emerge: there is little significant literature in English wherein a woman is described as being filial to her in-laws.

Second, there is a strong assumption throughout the history of their interaction that the terms filial piety and xiao are equivalent or at least comparable. This is probably due to the common factor of patriarchal structures combined with the fact that the concepts in the two languages were based at least partly on affective bonding of child to parent. That bonding was sometimes thought to be a completely natural process, sometimes a result of nurture; but in either case, the assumption on both sides was that such child-parent bonding would be essentially the same regardless of culture.

Third, there are interesting things going on with how the nature-nurture debate proceeds, gender issues, the role of affect, and the way the two concepts converge and diverge at different points. In the early Chinese texts, filial piety seems to arise out of nature: it is in the nature of a son to be filial to his father. However, that 'nature' includes nurture within it, for many of these texts also stress that parental care for children, both the nine months spent in the womb and also the years of infancy and childhood, create a debt that must be repaid. While one might think that this would predispose filial piety towards the mother, as she is the one who carries the child in her womb and was often the primary care-giver in infancy, the exigencies of patriarchy, ancestor worship, and the tradition of women marrying into their husband's family ensure that this does not happen. In the English tradition, the introduction of the idea that filial piety is due to parents because of nurture quickly transforms it into a sort of contractual obligation which, if the parent should neglect their side of the bargain, frees the child of any responsibility towards them; furthermore, children are enjoined by their religion to ignore parental wishes when they are contrary to Church doctrine. As I have demonstrated, this is linked in turn to debates in the political sphere about the duties and rights of subjects to their sovereign.

This is not to say that no Chinese child ever hated their parents and neglected their filial duties, or that no English child ever loved their parents and fulfiled filial duties despite having been mistreated. We are dealing with how concepts are imagined and described, not how they were or were not realised in practice.

In terms of gender and affect, it would seem that when filial piety is associated with affect (filial love, filial affection, and so on), it is more firmly associated with women, and when it is associated with duty, it is more firmly associated with men. Early Chinese texts tended to emphasise the ritual nature of filial piety and play down affect; this is of course the period when filial piety is most closely tied to men. So on both sides the relationship between affect and duty is a tricky one. In the Qing, there are many stories of emperors being filial to their mothers, in particular Qianlong (Usui 2019, 14). In fact, if we go back to the earliest texts in English that discuss filial piety of the Chinese, Wanley (1673) speaks of the emperor's filial piety towards his mother, while Bouvet (1699) speaks of the Kangxi emperor's filial piety towards his grandmother. Likewise, while the *Twenty-Four Paragons of Filial Piety* mainly features the way in which male offspring treat their parents, in the majority of the stories from that text filial feelings are expressed towards both fathers and mothers or exclusively towards mothers. This would have made the concept of xiao appear less foreign to an English-speaking audience, where we have seen that some of the earliest texts refer to filial piety towards both parents.

Finally, there is clear and strong evidence that the meaning of the concept of filial piety in English and Chinese influenced each other. However, the direction of the influence was not always two-way, nor was it constant.

There are two waves of influence by foreign-language sources on the Chinese concept: from the late Qing through the early May Fourth Movement, and from the 1930s through the 1960s. In the first phase, many of the sources were English, either translated directly into Chinese or relayed through Japanese; in some cases, texts in various other European languages were relayed via English. In the second phase, from the 1930s through the 1960s, when Marxism exerted a powerful influence leading to the suppression of filial piety in China, the sources were more mixed, coming through English, German, Russian, and Japanese, and it is harder to demonstrate that the translation of specific English-language texts influenced the development. The May Fourth Movement tried to dethrone filial piety by negating its value completely, but this was never entirely successful in the Republican era, as the case of Shi Jianqiao demonstrates. On the other hand, the resolutely secular attitude of Marxist theorists seems to have had a more lasting influence, because filial piety in China today is less linked to ancestor worship or any religious sense. Instead, the government has relentlessly promoted it as a secular virtue that is aimed primarily at care for the elderly after retirement. This, in turn, returns us to a point made about filial piety in early Chinese texts, where it was primarily a virtue practiced by adults.

In the other direction, Chinese influence begins much earlier, in the eighteenth century, when the first details of how the Chinese were filial were translated into English, and they were upheld as exemplars. But the main influence comes in the nineteenth century and then, after a lull from the 1930s through the 1970s, accelerates towards the end of the twentieth century. At this stage, filial piety as a Christian virtue has completely disappeared in English, and the concept has been wholly colonised by the Chinese one, albeit not in its original form, as it has also been changed by earlier English, German, Russian, and Japanese sources.

Thus in the Chinese case we have a fairly clear relationship between the relative power of China vis à vis other nations and the receptiveness of filial piety to outside influence, while in the Anglo-American case we have a mixed bag, with filial piety being influenced both when Britain and America were strong vis à vis China (nineteenth and early twentieth century) and when they are weaker, in the late twentieth and early twenty-first.

One possible explanation for the anomalous case on the Anglo-American side is that, in the earlier period, the English and Americans were willing to take on board the Chinese concept of filial piety because it fit in with the larger ideological revolution of modernity. By associating China with filial piety, Anglo-American writers were able to associate what for them had become a backward-looking trait more firmly with a foreign country, and therefore distance themselves from it. By painting the Chinese as a culture that went to ridiculous extremes of filial piety, the British and Americans could, by contrast, define themselves as modern. Anglo-American culture essentially jettisons filial piety as a virtue in this time period and instead re-imagines it as a millstone wrapped around the neck of the Chinese, holding them back from modernity. Filial piety seems to be a good example of how unequal power relations between cultures may influence the flow of information and drive conceptual change.

Finally, in the late twentieth and early twenty-first century, the influence seems to be going in both directions. This is due to the internationalisation of Chinese Studies and the rise to prominence in more than one country of both bilingual and monolingual English scholars. On a broader scale, it is also linked to increasing connectivity, an effect of globalisation, suggesting that in the contemporary era that multi-directional crossflows of cultural information may increasingly become the norm.

Notes

1 Parts of this chapter are based on my article 'Consequences of the Conflation of *Xiao* and Filial Piety in English' published in *Translation and Interpreting Studies* (2018: 296–320). © John Benjamins. Reprinted with permission.

2 The character also functions as a surname, but this eighth meaning can be set aside here as irrelevant.

3 Search conducted July 2019; false positive hits excluded (OCR misrecognizing another word such as 'final' as 'filial', or returning texts that are not in English). Since EEBO does not include manuscripts, I could not search for other earlier examples but, as I am most interested here in tracing what happens after Chinese and English start to interact, I am not overly concerned with pinning down fine distinctions in the earliest meaning.

4 References to examples in texts taken from the databases do not contain page numbers because that information is not supplied when the data is captured.

5 See especially chapter twenty, 'Of Dominion Paternall, and Despoticall'.

6 I will essentially ignore any influence that the early translations into Chinese by the Jesuits may have had on the meaning of xiao in Chinese. Given their rather precarious foothold and limited success in proselytizing, I doubt that they would have had much impact on how such a core value would be interpreted. Their main intervention into discourse on the five bonds was concentrated on the concept of friendship (see Xu 2011).

7 Whereas in Chinese, filial piety is much more likely to be linked either to loyalty of a minister to the ruler or to ties between younger brother and elder brother. In other words, the Chinese discourse on filial piety tends to see it as one of several one-way, unequal duties towards one's superiors. This issue will re-surface in the twentieth century in the writing of Tu Wei-ming, discussed below, and of Fei Xiaotong, discussed in Chapter 4.

8 The original tale is number twelve in Feng Menglong's collection *Jingshi Tongyan* 警世通言, entitled 'Fan Qiuer Shuangjing chongyuan 范鰍兒雙鏡重圓'. A modern English translation, 'A Double Mirror Brings Fan the Loach and His Wife together Again' is available in Feng (2005).

9 All quotations are from the first edition (1836).

10 The work was first published serially in *The North-China Herald*, with a first book edition published in Shanghai in 1890, followed by a British edition in 1892, but I have used the enlarged and revised edition of 1894, which became the most widely available.

11 These are, in order of appearance, in the Old Testament: Exodus 20:12; Leviticus 19:3; Deuteronomy 5:16; 2 Samuel 10:3; Tobias 4:3, 10:12, 10:14, 14:13; 1 Maccabees 6:23; Proverbs 4:3; Sirach 3; Malachi 1:6; and in the New Testament: Matthew 15:4–6, 19:19; Mark 7:10, 10:19; Luke 15:29, 18:20; Ephesians 6:1–3; Colossians 3:20; 1 Timothy 5:4; and 2 Timothy 3:2.

12 I consulted six translations of the Bible, published between 1919 and 1992. They are: United Bible Association ([1919] 1988); Duns Scotus Bible Centre (1968); Lü Zhenzhong (1970); United Bible Association (1979); International Bible Society (1979); and World Bible Association (1976 [New Testament] and 1992 [Old Testament]).

13 Lin knew no foreign languages, but worked with a number of fellow countrymen who did read various foreign languages and orally interpreted the stories, which Lin then recorded in his justly famed elegant classical Chinese. He and his interpreters were responsible for some of the most popular translations to appear in the period from 1899–1924. See Hill (2012) for a detailed study in English.

14 Jin also notes that the description of inner psychological states of the characters, especially remorse, and the need for one of the lovers to sacrifice themselves for the other are both features that indicate such fiction is drawing upon translated models rather than the earlier scholar-beauty romances in the Chinese tradition.

15 I follow Chow (1960, 6) in this dating, although he notes that the founding of *New Youth* (*Xin qingnian* 新青年) in 1915 by Chen Duxiu (陳獨秀 1879–1942) can also be thought of as the beginning of the movement, and that other researchers extend the period further into the 1920s.

16 European literature of course has examples of adult children choosing to sacrifice themselves in order to save their parents; but perhaps only the story of Abraham and Isaac in the Bible, where Abraham prepares to sacrifice his son upon the order of God (the father), is comparable to the story of Guo Zhu.

17 The subscription database is available at http://www.oriprobe.com/peoplesdaily_tc.shtml.

18 It ranks fifth, with 510 instances or 10.9 per cent of all occurrences. The first four are *xiaoshun* (孝順 filial and obedient), 994 instances or 21.3 per cent; *xiaolao* (孝老 be filial to one's elders), 686 instances or 14.7 per cent; *jinxiao* (盡孝 make every effort to be filial), 641 instances or 13.7 per cent; and *xiaodao* (孝道 the way of filial piety), 532 instances or 11.4 per cent.

19 See King (1996, 268) for a 1982 survey in Hong Kong that identified filial piety as the single most important trait that differentiated Chinese from Westerners; see Kuo (1996) for a discussion of its importance in Singapore in the 1980s.

20 See Neville (2000, xxiv, xxvii, xxviii) for a detailed list of first and second generation new Confucians, as well as non-Chinese sinologists associated with the movement.

21 Based on Ngram Viewer. In the entire period 1809–1985, filial duty is less frequent than filial piety, and its usage drops even faster than filial piety, which means that it has a smaller percentage of total hits for 'filial' in 1985 than in 1809, dropping from 0.0000659737 to 0.0000050260 per cent.

22 Other police procedurals also have episodes where characters argue that crimes committed by minors should be excused, notably 'The Mentalist', where the lead character Patrick Jane, who is a consultant for the California Bureau of Investigation, persuades his detective partner Teresa Lisbon more than once to let a child go free. See 'Blood for Blood' (season three, episode fourteen), which aired 10 February 2011; a young girl shoots her father and Jane persuades Lisbon to let the girl go into the custody of her aunt, who promises to get her the psychological help she needs.

23 The sample was of works of contemporary Chinese literature translated and published between 1995–2014, where 'contemporary' is defined as post-Mao. These were: Wang (1995), Gu (1996), Yu (1996), Zhu (1998), Chen (1999), Zhu (2007), Lu (2006), Wang (2008), Xiao (2010), Yan (2011), and Mai (2014). In a random search of twenty works of fiction written originally in English from 1996–2005, only one work contained the word 'filial' (Cook-Lynn 1999), and none of them used 'filial piety'.

24 Search conducted 28 October 2012.

25 Wikipedia, Britannica Online, and Dictionary.com

26 女二十四孝圖說.

2

Fengshui

Fengshui, unlike filial piety, is a relatively minor tradition not directly linked to any key Confucian texts or, for that matter, Buddhist or Daoist texts. In the English tradition geomancy, the concept that is first posited as possibly equivalent, is a minor form of divination that was never widely practiced and is essentially extinct today. Yet as we will see, fengshui is intimately linked to filial piety through the intermediate practice of ancestor worship and, therefore, concern for the fate of parents, grandparents, and more remote ancestors after their death, and how the dead relate to the living. Also, in terms of the fate of the original English concept of geomancy, it too, like filial piety, suffers a decline as its association with China is strengthened in the second half of the nineteenth century, only to rise from the ashes at the end of the twentieth.

In terms of terminology, fengshui also offers interesting points of similarity and divergence with filial piety. Filial piety and xiao are independent terms that have both been remarkably stable over time. For fengshui, in Chinese we have at least three important terms over time: dili, *kanyu*, and fengshui. In the modern period the first two have fallen out of use, and we are left with essentially one term for the concept. In English, we start with one term, geomancy which, like filial piety, is independent of the Chinese terms and initially points to a practice that has nothing to do with China (it seems to have evolved in the Middle East or North Africa), but then a second term is introduced through borrowing of various transliterations of the Chinese term fengshui. These two terms then continue to co-exist in an uneasy balance, with the fulcrum of that balance being the question of whether fengshui is equivalent to geomancy or a subset of it. This relates back to the discussion of whether the Chinese practice of filial piety can act as an example for the rest of the world to follow, or a dangerous obsession that holds the Chinese back from modernity.

At the same time that we explore the interactions between dili, kanyu, fengshui, geomancy and 'fengshui' in English, and their relation to filial piety, we will also see how fengshui relates to two other important Chinese concepts: *yinyang* (陰陽 yin and yang; dark and light) and *wu xing* (五行 five phases). Finally, we will explore how fengshui relates to three broader categories in English: science, religion, and superstition, which returns us to the question of modernity.

Chinese terminology

There are at least three main terms for the practice of fengshui in Chinese sources. In rough order of age, they are, in a fairly literal translation, dili (地理 earth patterning), kanyu (堪輿 cover and support; thus, heaven and earth), and fengshui (風水 wind and water).[1] Between the eighteenth and the early twentieth century, dili and kanyu largely receded from use, leaving fengshui as the main modern term, with kanyu being used occasionally in more learned discussions, and dili now rarely used.[2] Practitioners of fengshui are generally referred to with the honorific *xiansheng* (先生 first born; hence senior, elder, master) attached to one of these terms, as in *dili xiansheng, kanyu xiansheng, fengshui xiansheng*, all of which translate as 'fengshui master'.

The history of fengshui has been recounted in great detail in a variety of sources (Eitel 1873; de Groot 1892–1910, vol. 3; Bruun 2003; Paton 2013). The short description below draws primarily on those four sources, along with Doré (1914–38, vol. 4), Smith (1991), and Feuchtwang (2002) on twentieth-century practice, limiting myself to pointing out elements that are important for the time period from the late Ming through the present, when interaction with Europeans and Americans led to it being introduced abroad.

The practice begins primarily with concern over the proper location and directional alignment of graves, which is associated with good or bad fortune for the descendants of the dead. In the early period this was primarily restricted to the ruler and the aristocracy, but over time it spread to encompass potentially everyone, and it became firmly associated with Chinese cosmological theories centring around the yinyang complementary pair, the five phases, the *Book of Changes*, and various heavenly phenomena. Indeed, so closely is it associated with yinyang theory that another name for a fengshui master is *yinyang xiansheng*. It also expanded its reach to encompass the houses of the living and all built structures including temples, public buildings, and bridges, as well as public works such as canals and roads. The emphasis remained on what effect these structures had on the fortunes of the living, who could be either the individual, the family, the village, the city, the province, or the entire nation. Fengshui practice as observed by Europeans and Americans from the seventeenth century onward seems to have evolved mainly based on the cosmological theories of Zhu Xi (1130–1200), including the fengshui compass, an instrument with a magnetic needle in the centre and then a number of concentric rings containing various cosmological indicators. There are two major schools of fengshui, the Fujian (or school of forms) and the Jiangxi (or compass school), each with their foundational figures, manuals, and key practices, although the difference between them seems to be more about loyalty than dogma.

One key element of fengshui is that all phenomena on earth are a reflection of phenomena in the heavens through a system of correspondences, which in turn are linked to the operations of yin and yang, the five phases, various constellations, the twenty-eight heavenly houses, and other heavenly phenomena as indicated by the concentric rings on the fengshui compass. When a location with excellent fengshui is chosen but the desired result is not obtained, or a family who buries their parents in a spot with bad fengshui becomes successful, this can be explained through *tianli* (天理 heavenly patterning; in this context, one's personal fate), which can overrule dili.

A second key element is that fengshui, concerned as it is with the future of the living, can be thought of as a means of divination. It is thus no coincidence that it is closely linked to the trigrams in the *Book of Changes*.

But beyond divination, which in many cases can be a relatively passive activity, a third key element is that fengshui is susceptible to human manipulation, both for better or for worse. So a fengshui master must not only try to locate the best available site for a grave or a building, but also recommend what alterations need to be done to correct any flaws. Conversely, damaging the fengshui of one's enemy is a tried and true tactic to harm them. According to many sources, the imperial government routinely would dig up the graves of the ancestors of rebel leaders in an effort to undermine their success. Thus even today, the verb *po* or *pohuai* (破/破壞 to break; to spoil) is often used for any action that might harm the fengshui of a locale.

I will leave discussion of what the deeper meaning of fengshui might be for later in the chapter, when discussing the modern period. For now, this short sketch of the practice will be sufficient.

English terminology

Geomancy is a term that occurs in English even earlier than filial piety, the word being taken over from Latin and possibly ultimately Arabic sources. The earliest example cited in the *Oxford English Dictionary* is from 1390, three years before their earliest citation for filial.

Geomancy at this point is defined as a type of divination made by casting stones or dirt upon the ground, or marking a series of random dots on a piece of paper. It is a fairly complicated process involving mathematical manipulation of sixteen rows of dots, reducing them to either odd or even, and forming them into groups of four rows each, which generates four figures.[3] These figures are then used to generate another four, after which an interpretation occurs that applies the general meaning of the result to the specific situation at hand. There is a complex relation between the figures and astral bodies, especially the planets, but also constellations, with each figure being given a name.

In its reliance of casting or choosing lots at random, its use of odd and even numbers to generate figures, and then the association of those figures with a set of general prognostic language that the expert interprets for the interlocutor's specific situation, geomancy has a superficial resemblance to divination based on the *Book of Changes*. It also somewhat resembles fengshui beliefs and practices, especially in its identification of these 'earth' figures with astral phenomena and with naming the figures; also of course, fengshui practices draw extensively on yinyang theory and the five phases, which link it to the *Book of Changes*. Coupled with the fact that the term dili means something like 'earth patterns', there is certainly justification for the use of the term geomancy as the closest equivalent term in English for these practices.

Unlike filial, however, geomancy never becomes a common term in English; EEBO yields only 246 hits in 122 different records stretching from 1473–1697. Moreover, most of these hits occur as part of a list of various types of magic, with no further explanation or discussion, for example: 'the several kinds of madness expressed in Geomancy, by Circles in the Earth; Pyromancy, by Fire; Hydromancy, by Water; Necromancy, by the Ghosts of the Dead' (*Strange and Terrible Nevves from Cambridge* 1659, 6). Also unlike filial piety, these references are almost always negative; geomancy is classified variously as witchcraft, warlockism, magic, or a black art, and few writers in this period have anything positive to say about it. Furthermore, as we move into the eighteenth century, hits in ECCO are actually fewer than in EEBO, just 179. Again, most of the results are the term cropping up in long lists of different types of magical practice, with only a small minority containing any detailed information (for example S. 1705; Curzon 1712).

Those writers who do engage in more detailed description of the term and how it is used write mostly in Latin for a European-wide audience. Texts in English are mainly translations of these Latin works (see for example Agrippa 1655). Many of the sources are vague as to what exactly geomancy is; even Roback (1854, 104), who gives a fairly detailed definition and multiple concrete examples with explanations of what the figures mean, finishes his exposition by saying that he has only given the simpler level of the practice and that interested readers who want more 'should apply to a competent astrologer and professor of magic'.

Geomancy is linked variously to the Middle East (Fraser 1742; Campbell 1753), specifically the Jews (Mackenzie 1713; Picart 1741) and the Persians, who are said by at least one source to have invented the practice (Chambers 1778–88); Africa (Rochon 1792); and the Greeks, especially Paracelsus (Barrow 1751). It is not linked to China in any way. Through the arrangement in book catalogues surviving from this time, we can see that geomancy and other magical practices were typically grouped together with medicine and the natural sciences (Wagstaff 1776; Lackington 1793), especially chemistry (Paterson 1773). In this respect at least, geomancy resembles Chinese fengshui, which was linked to Chinese medicine through its reliance on the concepts of yinyang and the five phases, and was therefore part of that knowledge system.

Early translations and descriptions

The earliest descriptions of fengshui practices in English seems to be *The History of that Great and Renowned Monarchy of China* (Semedo 1655), translated from the Italian. In a chapter entitled 'Of their Superstitions and Sacrifices in China', Semedo spends a paragraph describing the rudiments of fengshui practices:

> Others, whom they call *Tili*, pretend to *Divine* by meanes of the Scituation of the earth, and from the correspondence it hath with heaven, and with the parts thereof, pronouncing what places are *prosperous*, and what *unfortunate*, and where, if they build their houses, all will succeed prosperously, and with good fortune to the Family; or contrariwise, with sicknesse, misfortunes, disgraces and other evils: and in this facultie they have many skilfull professours, on whom they spend a great deale of money with out any profit at all. (Semedo 1655, 93–94)

Semedo's choice of transliteration of a Chinese term *Tili* signals that, for him, this practice has no equivalent in Italian and, by extension, probably in Europe.[4]

This initial text sets the tone for more than three hundred years of European understanding of fengshui practices. It classifies it as a superstition; notes that it is related to beliefs regarding good and ill fortune dependent on geographic location of buildings; mentions the large class of professional fengshui experts; and notes that the public spend large sums of money on it 'with out any profit at all', that is, Semedo believes it to be completely inefficacious. One other detail, its close relation to burial practices, is missing from this paragraph, but earlier in the work, in a chapter on funeral practices, he discusses the payment of large sums of money for purchasing plots of land for graves 'if their Astrologer do judge them lucky places, and fortunate for the Familie; for none do make choice of them, without his opinion' (74).

Another account of fengshui, this one based on Dutch sources that uses neither the term fengshui nor geomancy, occurs in *An Embassy from the East-India Company of the United Provincés, to the Grand Tartar Cham Emperor of China* (Nieuhof 1673). There are three passages. One, in the seventh chapter 'Of some Superstitious Customs, Fashions, and other Errors in use amongst the Chineses', claims that when burying their dead, the Chinese look for a place that looks like 'the Head, Tail and Feet of a Dragon' because the fortune of the family, and even that of 'Cities, Countries and of the whole Empire' depend upon it (184). The same passage also notes that there is a group of learned men who are consulted when choosing such burial plots or sites for public buildings. The second passage occurs in the thirteenth chapter, 'Of Hills and Mountains', again speaking of formations that look like parts of a dragon bringing good fortune (207). Finally, in the same chapter there is an anecdote of the emperor Xius employing five thousand men to alter the shape of a mountain, because 'deceitful Mountain-gazers' said that the mountain in question foretold that another man should become emperor, and Xius wanted to forestall this event (209). This last detail reveals a further important element of fengshui practices missing from Semedo's account: that human intervention can change the fortune associated with a particular natural feature, while the discussion of how the shape of the earth is linked to the mythical Chinese 'dragon' (*lung* 龍) gives us another enduring characteristic of fengshui practice.

Semedo's description is picked up by later writers, notably La Loubère (1693), who does not provide a name for this practice. In the case of the Dutch source, we find an interesting case of cultural substitution in a work that draws upon it in Bayle (1708), who says that 'the Chinese likewise pretend, that they who build Houses, shou'd beware of the fourth Degree of Scorpio, because a House built under such an Aspect is very subject to be infested with Dragons, Scorpions, and Vermin' (40). Here a Western zodiacal sign has been substituted for details concerning the choice of location, an example of what today we would call cultural substitution.

An extensive search of EEBO could find no instances of the transliteration of *fengshui*, despite having employed numerous possible alternate spellings and the use of fuzzy matching. It is only in the eighteenth century that we see the emergence of such transliterations in the literature on China. The key text is Du Halde (1736), which is translated into English twice in the space of a few years, once as *The General History of China*

(1736) and once as *A Description of the Empire of China and Chinese-Tartary* (1738–41). There are two passages where the term fengshui is mentioned, and in both cases it is accompanied by explanation. The first passage stretches over three substantial paragraphs, and gives a fairly detailed description of the concept similar to Semedo. In addition, Du Halde provides a literal translation of the term '*feng shwi*, that is, *Wind and Water*' (Du Halde, 1738–41, 1:664), and provides an example of how European missionaries came into conflict with local interests due to buildings they had erected.[5] In this case the offending building is a church with a tall steeple, and the affected Chinese is an official, who erects a gate to counter this attack on the fengshui of his own dwelling. Alas, the official falls ill, which illness is attributed to the gate being white, and it is re-painted in black, but he dies anyway. The story reveals that fengshui is not limited to the illiterate masses, and in the detailing of the official's death hoist on his own petard, as it were, takes an almost ghoulish delight. The myriad ways in which fengshui engenders conflict between Europeans and the Chinese, sometimes surprising twists in how fengshui influences may play out, and its lack of efficacy all become staples of later descriptions of the practice.

Curiously, the second passage in Du Halde's work that mentions fengshui somewhat contradicts this narrative. In the translation of excerpts from a Chinese writer, we are presented with a learned Chinese man who himself scoffs at the ridiculous practice of fengshui.[6] In a discussion of why a wise man should put his worldly affairs in order in good time, including securing a grave site, he says it is to ensure that the grieving widow and son do not have to worry about such details in their time of mourning. 'Not that I give any faith to Fables, or to the idle Stories about (*) *Fong shwi*; Wealth, Honour, and every thing that happens to Man, is regulated by the Orders of Heaven' (Du Halde 1738–41, 2:53). Du Halde here inserts a footnote to his translation, in which he explains that fengshui has to do with 'the laying out of a Burying-Place or a House'.

Du Halde's work was widely read, cited, and even reproduced wholesale in other works. In one case, after reproducing most of Du Halde's description of fengshui practices, a footnote added by the anonymous editor again shows a sort of cultural substitution: 'By this Word *Fong-shwi*, they understand not only a corrupt Air, which causes Diseases; but also a Kind of Curse, which extends even to Posterity' ([Green?] 1743–47, 4:225). Here, the very British preoccupation with salubrious or insalubrious air or vapours, much in vogue in British medical belief of the time, is introduced as the cultural equivalent of fengshui. Also, here the author assumes that fengshui is always negative or evil; there is no acknowledgement that a location can have good fengshui.[7]

The two English terms fengshui and geomancy seem first to occur together in 1815, with the publication of the first volume of Robert Morrison's *Dictionary of the Chinese Language* (1815–23), which also includes both Chinese terms fengshui and kanyu, but excludes dili.[8] Although Morrison uses transliteration more often than the term geomancy, on at least two occasions he uses both. When discussing the term *dadi* 大地, he gives one meaning as: 'in the language of Chinese geomancy, a lucky site for a grave. *Ta fung shwuy* 大風水, a spot of ground, and an adjoining landscape, which the geomancer pronounces indicative of prosperity' (Morrison 1815–23, vol. 1 part 1:573). The second one is under the character *feng* (風 wind), when defining the binome fengshui: 'wind and water; a kind of geomancy deduced from the climate; the aspect of buildings, doors, graves, and so on. *Fungshwuy koo hwo* 風水蠱惑 be fooled by the wind and water—superstition. *Fung shwuy seen sang* 風水先生 a professor of the Fung-shwuy Geomancy' (vol.1 part 2:189). By calling fengshui 'a kind of geomancy', Morrison suggests that geomancy is the broader, more inclusive term, of which fengshui is the local variant. This conforms with the fact that the term geomancy has over time become a broader, more inclusive term in English. Early definitions already noted that there was more than one magical practice labelled geomancy in the Middle East and North Africa; the OED gives an example of 'an other kinde of Geomancie, the which doth diuine by certaine coniectures taken of similitudes of the crakinge of the Earthe'. By the twentieth century this had broadened to include dowsing (also OED); numerous websites connect geomancy with earth energy, lines of power, earth acupuncture, and geopathic stress.[9]

As a Protestant missionary, it should also be obvious from Morrison's definition that he has a negative view of the concept, given his example of 'be fooled by the wind and water—superstition'. This negative view emerges in other, sometimes quite surprising, places in the dictionary. Under the character *ni* (泥 mud), we find the sample sentence '*ne yu fung shwuy* 泥於風水 bigotedly attached to the superstition of the Fung-shwuy' (vol. 1 part 2:612). Under the heading for kanyu, Morrison's definition could not be more withering:

A general term for the heavens and earth; it is also 神名 *Shin ming.* The name of a god, to whom a work on the sites of tombs is attributed. The phrase is also applied to the *super*stitious observances of the Chinese respecting tombs. (MS. Dictionary.) 堪輿看 *K'han yu k'han,* A person skilled in surveying the ground for graves; is otherwise called 風水先生 *Fung-shwuiy seen-sang,* Wind and water master. *This is one of the most idle and useless superstitions of the Chinese. They themselves say, that if ten Fung-shwuy Seen-ang be called in to give their opinions respecting the site of a grave, or a house, they have ten different tales to tell; no two of them agree.* (vol.1 part 1:521; my emphasis)

Here repeated judgemental terms on Morrison's part (superstitious; idle and useless superstition) are combined with what Morrison claims is a common saying among the Chinese themselves regarding the complete lack of agreement between the so-called experts regarding what is good or bad fengshui to paint a damning picture of this practice.

Other texts from this period do not always use both terms; indeed, there seems to be a preference for transliteration in various spellings over the term geomancy. In the notes of Sir John Francis Davis's translation of a play, *Laou-Seng-urh, or, 'An Heir in His Old Age'* (1817), there are two references to fengshui practices, although only in one case is it labelled as such. This occurs as an annotation of a line from the play 'Our tombs may be turned to the right aspect', for which the note supplies the additional information that: 'No Chinese will build a house, or a family tomb, until he has consulted some priest or other respecting the fung-swee (wind and water); that is to say, the precise line in which the several parts are to be placed' (Davis 1817, 73 and 114–15). Similarly, in Davis's later translation *The Fortunate Union* (1829), he uses transliteration only, but by the time he writes *The Chinese: A General Description of the Empire of China and Its Inhabitants* (1836), he is using both terms.

A database of 160 texts published between 1810–1900 that were either translations from Chinese or texts written in English about China was compiled, mainly by downloading texts from the Internet Archive. These works were then subjected to a search protocol designed to identify passages that discussed the concept of fengshui. Fifty-six of the texts contained some reference to fengshui; of these, twenty-eight (52 per cent) mentioned both terms, seventeen (31 per cent) mentioned fengshui only, seven (17 per cent) mentioned geomancy only, and four (5 per cent) managed to describe fengshui practices without using either term (Winterbotham 1795; 'Tombs of Ancestors' 1833; Quincy 1847; Allom 1858).[10] Moreover, most of the works that only mention one or the other term are from before 1850; over time, it becomes more common to use both.

There were three texts that used the term dili (using various spellings), although in all three cases this was in addition to either fengshui, geomancy, or both. Lay (1846, 122) speaks of 'this "te-le" and "fung shwuy", or soothsaying'; Fortune (1847, 323) quotes Lay verbatim; and de Groot (1892–1910, 3:1013–14) uses the term (transliterated as 'Ti li') in contrast with T'ien li ([tianli 'the natural influences' of the heavens in his translation). But these three instances are outliers, as we can see by de Groot's pervasive use of fengshui and geomancy but then only this one use of dili when contrasting it with heavenly influences. An interesting example of how different meanings of the same term come to be overlaid in translation is found in Henry (1885, 136), who talks about wind and water doctors, or 'as they style themselves, professors of geography, their geography, however, being only geomancy, or earth-divination, just as the astronomy of the Chinese is nothing more than astrology'. Here Henry has translated the Chinese term dili as 'geography', which is its modern sense, but not the sense to which the Chinese are referring, and then overlaying the (in his mind, debased) term 'geomancy' onto the modern 'geography' in English in order to establish a parallel between Chinese dili and Western astrology as debased forms of knowledge, a sort of degeneration of the scientific concepts of geography and astronomy.

Finally, a few texts use some sort of transliteration of fengshui, but then say that the best translation of the term is 'luck', such as Nevius (1868, 169). Morrison (1815–23, vol. 3, part 2:263), in the English to Chinese section of his dictionary, under the headword 'luck' gives as one of his definitions 'applied to a place, 風水好 fung shwuy haou [fengshui is good]', and then under the headword 'lucky' says 'when a place is supposed to be lucky it is said to have 好風水 haou fung shwuy [good fengshui]'. Moule (1871, 95), described a group of villagers almost mobbing a man for cutting holly at Christmas time, the villagers saying 'it's the luck of the place (the fung shuy)'. Even as late as 1910, Johnston (1910, 198) gives an example of a man whose house walls were attacked by a shrew from next door, claiming 'that they interfered with the good luck (fêng-shui) of her own habitation', and Murdock (1920, 306) defines fengshui as 'the Chinese science of luck'. The words luck and lucky occur frequently when describing the sites chosen by fengshui practitioners, much more often than more formal terms such as fortunate or auspicious. Brine (1862, 69) is a typical example: 'geomancers are the people whose business it is to select a lucky place for the interment of a deceased person'; Cockburn (1896, 32) uses the term 'professor of luck' for fengshui master.[11]

Given that there are no texts after 1847 that discuss fengshui practices without using either fengshui or geomancy, and that the term dili only occurs once in a text after 1847 in a very particular usage, it seems safe to say that between 1800 and 1850 the usage of fengshui and geomancy for the Chinese practice of *fengshui* was normalised.

Of note here is that the term geomancy is associated with fengshui in 65 per cent of the texts; furthermore, more than half the texts that do not contain the term geomancy occur before the end of the first Opium War (1839–42). Thus in the nineteenth century there is an increasing tendency to identify fengshui and geomancy so that, by the end of the first Opium War, two distinct meanings of geomancy had become firmly established. A small number of texts continued to refer to the Middle Eastern/North African practice. Towards the end of the century, most of these publications were associated with members of the Hermetic Order of the Golden Dawn; probably the best-known of these texts are Roback (1854), mentioned earlier; and Hartmann's *Principles of Astrological Geomancy* (1889), Hartmann being a member of the Golden Dawn. Regardie (1937–40, 4:112–36), also associated with the Order, contains perhaps the best modern explanation of this tradition.

On the other hand, an increasing number of publications use the term geomancy to refer to fengshui, as observed in the database, and there is only one text that mentions both meanings of the term. Gray (1878, 2:7) gives the Greek derivation of the term, and explains very briefly the method used citing classical sources, only to say that 'To the geomancers of China these two methods are altogether unknown'.

We can see the extent to which the two meanings of geomancy have diverged by the end of the century by looking at two texts from the late nineteenth and early twentieth centuries. De Groot's magisterial *Religious System of China*, in six volumes (1892–1910), contains an entire chapter devoted to fengshui practices, including its historical development, and frequently uses the term geomancy, but nowhere betrays any hint of the original meaning of that term in English. Likewise volume four of Doré's *Researches into Chinese Superstitions*, in thirteen volumes (1914–38), uses geomancy as the accepted translation for fengshui with no explanation of the Middle Eastern/North African tradition at all.

There are hints that the match between geomancy and the Chinese practice of *fengshui* is not perfect. De Groot says that 'Foreigners are in the habit of calling the Fung-shui experts geomancers, which is correct, *provided the earth be also considered as a depository of influences continuously poured down upon it by the celestial sphere*' (1892–1910, 3:940; my emphasis); in other words, he objects to a term that only points to the earth being used to describe a system that encompasses both earthly and heavenly principles. Couling (1917, 175) under the entry 'Feng-shui' goes so far as to say that it is 'often incorrectly called "geomancy" '.

We do, however, generally see from the way in which geomancy and fengshui are used together, that the English term geomancy is conceived of as a broader category, of which fengshui is a local Chinese branch. Starting from Morrison (1815–23) discussed earlier, several authors make this clear. Davis (1836, 2:137) says that fengshui is 'a species of geomancy' and Kidd (1841, 313) calls 'the wind and water profession' 'a sort of geomancy'; Langdon (1842, 59) uses the phrase 'Chinese geomancy', whereby we are to understand that the general category of geomancy has a specific subtype that is Chinese; Mayers, Dennys, and King (1867, 188) say that 'Fung-shuei' is a type of 'geomantic superstition'; and Brebner (1895, 65), speaking of Chinese objections to railways, says that 'One a semi-religious or geomantic one, which is founded on the prevention of offence to the Feng-shui, or crowd of spirits', which also clearly indicates that fengshui is only a part of a larger concept of geomancy.

At stake here is the relationship between universal categories and specific practice. To the extent that fengshui is identified by a transliteration, whether it is dili, Te-le, fung-shui, or even kanyu, it is exotic and local to China. Accounts that stress the unknowability of fengshui tend to favour such terms. To the extent that it is identified as a type of geomancy, it is brought within a larger system and therefore normalised and potentially knowable. But when the term geomancy starts to lose its original meaning and become uniquely identified with Chinese fengshui, it again becomes Other, just as we have seen with the term filial piety, which, once it loses its close ties to Christianity, then ceases to become a universal category and instead becomes identified as an extreme, cultural-specific trait of the Chinese.

The last example (Brebner 1895) also is an interesting case of how many writers in English struggled with the concept of fengshui, often interpreting it according to English concepts. Brebner thinks that fengshui designates various spirits that inhabit the earth. A generation earlier, a certain De '德', writing in *Notes and Queries on China and Japan*, refers to fengshui as 'the invisible, and intangible but all-pervading essence (or perhaps Genii)' (De 1867, 29), using the Middle Eastern term 'genii' to explain the Chinese concept.[12] Still earlier, Downing (1838, 258) says 'Priests and astrologers are consulted with reference to the locality, and the gods of the wind and water propitiated.' Another example is Hemyng (1904, 42), who says that 'their national weakness is a belief in Feng-shuy, who may be deemed as their god of luck, and has also some control over the wind'. In all these cases, fengshui is personified as a god.

Other writers tried to understand it in terms of a natural force, magnetism, possibly because of the common use of the magnetic compass in fengshui calculations. The first example of this that I found was Lo (1867, 7), who says that fengshui 'is simply terrestial [sic] magnetism'. Other examples include DuBose (1887, 433 and again 434) and Selby (1900, 266). Even Eitel (1873, 22 and 49), who writes an entire book on the concept and has a fairly thorough understanding, is forced back upon a magnetic explanation for the two 'currents, the one male, the other female' that run through the earth.

There are also cases where British conceptions of disease, specifically the Victorian preoccupation with drains, vapours, and miasma, intersect in interesting ways with fengshui. Davis, in his multivolume description of the Chinese published soon after his return to England, thinks that the Chinese preference for burying people in the hills is a sanitary device, designed to prevent disease by forbidding the burial of the dead within the city or town limits, and urges the British to consider adopting this practice (Davis 1836, 1:281–82). In his history of Hong Kong, Eitel (1895, 167) notes that the British had originally planned to locate the commercial centre of Hong Kong in Happy Valley; however, a combination of the Chinese merchants believing that the fengshui was bad and the 'malignant fever' experienced by the Europeans results in the commercial centre shifting westward. Another example, also from Hong Kong, is recorded in several texts; the account here is taken from Northrop (1894, 272):

> it is beyond question that the sites chosen by these professors are such as avoid many of the ill effects of the climate.

> Many years ago, when we first settled at Hong Kong, the mortality among the soldiers who occupied the Murray Barracks was terrible. By the advice of the colonial surgeon, a grove of bamboos was planted at the back of the buildings. The effect of this arrangement was largely to diminish the sickness among the troops, and it was so strictly in accordance with the rules of Feng Shui that the natives at once assumed that the surgeon was a past-master in the science.

He also tells how a plot of land chosen by the British for construction was declared by a fengshui master to have bad fengshui and, lo and behold, when the British built there the buildings were 'overrun as soon as built with white ants, boldly defying coal-tar, carbolic acid, and all other foreign appliances' (Northrop 1894, 272). In the one case, the British surgeon's advice agrees unconsciously with fengshui practice and succeeds; in another case, Western tactics for dealing with the natural environment fail when they encounter bad fengshui.

Yet the most enduring Western interpretation, or translation, of fengshui is an aesthetic one. Kidd (1841, 313) speaks of fengshui as being involved with the 'position and scenery' of the grave. Quincy (1847, 197) says: 'The great concern of a rich Chinese is to procure a pleasant spot for a tomb .... It must be airy, shaded by trees, watered by a running stream, and situated on an eminence commanding an extensive land and water prospect.' Robert Fortune, travelling in China in the 1840s in search of botanical specimens, detailed how he met a man who knew quite a bit about botany, and who also claimed to know about 'fung-shwuy (soothsaying)'. After giving Fortune a short lesson on how to select an auspicious site and showing Fortune his compass, Fortune interprets what the man tells him in terms of the aesthetics of the surrounding scenery. Thinking that he has understood fengshui, Fortune then identifies a different spot that he finds equally scenic, and points it out to his new acquaintance, only to be told that the site he had selected had terrible fengshui because of a furrow in a hill behind it (Fortune 1857, 184–85). Turning this around, Nevius (1868, 178) says that when a foreigner goes walking to enjoy the scenery, the Chinese assume that 'he is looking for *fung-shwuy*'. Finally Medhurst (1873, 126–27) recommends to the British tourist that, since good fengshui spots almost always have the most picturesque views, they should make graves of the rich their objective when hill walking.

The idea that a spot with good fengshui is necessarily a scenic one recurs in later texts as well (Macgowan 1907, 227–28). But the most surprising proponent of this translation of fengshui is made by Lin Yutang in his best-selling *My Country and My People*. It must be quoted at length to appreciate the intricacy of his argument:

> although geomancy is undeniably a superstition, it has a great spiritual and architectural value. Its superstition consists in the belief that by placing one's ancestors' tombs in a beautiful scenery, overlooking those dragon mountains and lion hills, one can bring good luck and prosperity to the dead man's descendants. If the location and the landscape scenery are truly unique, if, for instance, five dragons and five tigers unite in making homage to the tomb, it is almost inevitable that one descendant of the line should found an imperial dynasty, or at least become a premier.
>
> But the basis of the superstition is a pantheistic enjoyment of landscape, and geomancy sharpens our eyes to beauty. We then try to see in the lines of mountains and general topography the same rhythm we see in animal forms. Everywhere we turn, nature is alive. Its rhythmic lines sweep east and west and converge toward a certain point. Again in the beauties of the mountains and rivers and general topography, we see not a beauty of static proportions but a beauty of movement. A curve is appreciated less because it is a curve than because it is a sweeping gesture, and a hyperbola is more appreciated than a perfect circle.
>
> The aesthetics of Chinese geomancy has therefore a very close bearing on Chinese architecture in the broad sense of the word. It compels discrimination of the setting and the landscape. By the side of an ancestral grave of one of my friends there was a little pool. The pool was regarded as propitious because it was interpreted as a dragon's eye. And when the pool was dried up, the family lost its fortune. As a matter of fact, the pool, set at one side a distance below the grave, was aesthetically an important element in the general setting of the grave, balancing a line on the other side in a subtly beautiful manner. It was, indeed, like the last dot put on the picture of a dragon, representing its eye and making the whole picture alive. In spite of the superstition and occasional bitter family feuds or clan wars caused by it, as when someone builds a structure to obstruct the perfect sweep and rhythm of line enjoyed from the point of the grave or the ancestral hall, or someone digs a ditch somewhere and therefore breaks the neck of the dragon and dispels all hopes of the family's rise to power—in spite of all this, I wonder very much whether geomancy has not contributed more to the richness of our aesthetic life than it has hindered our knowledge of geology. (Lin 1939b, 301–2)

Several points are important here. First, fengshui is associated with aesthetics. That aesthetics springs from a 'pantheistic enjoyment of landscape' or the natural world, and makes us better able to appreciate beauty everywhere. This aesthetic appreciation is subtly tied in with one of the basic tenets of fengshui, which is that straight lines are bad, by reading curves as more natural and thus more beautiful. This rhetorical move takes the wind out of the sails of Western critics, who had often fastened on this point as being particularly ridiculous. He then offers an aesthetic reading of an anecdote about how the drying up of a pool by the side of his friend's ancestral grave led to misfortune for the family, by noting that the pool completed the aesthetic scene of the grave site.

In the paragraphs that follow, Lin moves on to tie fengshui with the field of architecture, claiming that the rules of fengshui had ensured that Chinese architecture was always concerned with blending all buildings harmoniously into their natural surroundings. He concludes this chapter, 'The Artistic Life', with the following:

> The terra-cotta walls of the Chinese temple merge harmoniously into the purple of the mountain sides, and its glazed roofs, laid in green, Prussian blue, purple or golden yellow, mingle with the red autumn leaves and the blue sky to give us a harmonious whole. And we stand and look at it from a distance and call it beautiful. (Lin 1939b, 303)

In and around the description of fengshui as aesthetics, he acknowledges the less appealing (to Western readers) aspects of fengshui. But by situating the topic, not in a chapter about religion, custom, or superstition, as most English and American writers before him had done, but rather in one on the artistic life, he radically alters the terms by which we understand the phenomenon, even as he harks back to earlier descriptions of the practice.

This line of thought is picked up by Joseph Needham, the great historian of Chinese science. Despite calling fengshui 'a grossly superstitious system', he also says 'all through, it embodied, I believe, a marked aesthetic component, which accounts for the great beauty of the siting of so many farms, houses and villages throughout China' (Needham and Wang 1956, 361; see also Sivin 1980, 23–24 and Feuchtwang 2002, 32 and 190–95).

Fengshui and filial piety

It is time now, however, to turn to how the Anglo-American understanding of fengshui tried to make sense of it by relating it to other concepts that related to China.

First, it should be noted that many foreigners simply labelled fengshui as superstition and felt that this term itself provided an explanation—that the

Chinese held an irrational belief, and there was no point in trying to understand such belief or understand it as a system, because something that was irrational was inherently unsystematic and therefore unknowable. Yet there were some Europeans and Americans who sought to make sense of fengshui by investigating the cosmological concepts that underlay it. There are many mentions of yinyang, the five phases, and other concepts that are used in fengshui in late seventeenth and early eighteenth-century descriptions of China, sometimes quite detailed, and there are mentions of fengshui in this time period as we have seen, but the two are not brought together until the nineteenth century. One of the earliest that I could find was Kidd (1841, 313), who says 'From the supposed relation of the elements to the five points, east, west, north, south, and centre, a distinct superstition, designated "the wind and water profession", has been derived—a sort of geomancy'.

Less obvious, but nonetheless important, is the link between fengshui and filial piety, which is basically twofold.

First, several accounts latch onto the fact that the government condemned delaying the burial of one's parents for reasons of fengshui to posit that fengshui was inimical to filial piety. As early as 1810, Sir George Staunton, in his translation of the Qing Penal Code, notes that a statute promising punishment by bambooing for anyone who fails to bury their parents within twelve months 'vainly seeking an auspicious time and place' was put in place 'to check the absurd consequences of a superstitious notion universally prevalent among the Chinese, of an intimate connexion always subsisting between the advantageous or disadvantageous mode and place of interment of persons deceased, and the future good or bad fortune of their surviving relations' (Staunton 1810, 190). Davis (1836, 1:282–83) also notes this conflict between filial piety and fengshui, giving the details of a story about a man who delayed the burial of his father for reasons of fengshui and was successfully sued in court by his younger brother. Another writer cited the *Sacred Edict* (Sheng yu 聖諭) of the Kangxi Emperor which similarly condemns the practice of waiting for long periods of time before burying the deceased (Moule 1871, 95–96); this point is picked up by later writers as well (Morris 1892, 230).[13]

The idea of a conflict between fengshui and filial piety finds its most poignant expression in the translation of a short story by Pu Songling into English by Herbert Giles (Pu 1880, 2:322–24). 'Feng-shui' details how two brothers fall to quarrelling about the proper time and place for the burial of their father. The first sign of trouble in the story is that the brothers have set up separate households, signalling a want of fraternal regard for each other, as the relation between brothers was seen as a corollary to filial piety, and was one of the five bonds. Each man engages a retinue of fengshui masters separately, and of course they determine on different spots that would yield the best fengshui to one brother or the other. The brothers engage in a pitched battle over the coffin, which lies neglected on the roadside and, in the end, only the death of the two brothers ends the feud. After their death, the two widows inspect the two grave sites and pronounce both unsuitable, whereupon they jointly engage some geomancers to select a spot which satisfies both women, with the younger pronouncing that the fengshui of the grave would certainly mean that someone in the family would achieve high military honours. This in fact comes true three years later when one of the grandsons passes the military examination. Giles also translates a note by Pu Songling saying that 'to indulge a morbid belief' in fengshui is folly, and that the actions of the two brothers go against propriety, filial piety, and fraternal love (Pu 1880, 2:324).

While the story certainly demonstrates that fengshui can be divisive, and the two brothers come to a bad end, at no point are we told that the fengshui masters are incorrect in their prognostications. More importantly, the story clearly indicates the efficacy of fengshui in the ending, when the prediction of the younger widow is borne out by later events. Thus the story reminds us that the criticism of fengshui practices within the Chinese context, including the legal strictures, are against excess, not the system itself. Returning to Staunton's translation of the relevant statute, we can note that the penalty only applies if someone remains unburied for *more than a year*. In other words, taking several months to decide on an auspicious location and select an auspicious date according to the dictates to fengshui is perfectly acceptable.

Running almost completely contrary to this idea of a conflict between fengshui and filial piety, a second and more common link is one of mutual support. Since early descriptions of fengshui practice are almost exclusively concerned with burial practices (for example Winterbotham 1795, 357), and burial practices are linked to ancestral worship, it is not long before fengshui is conceived of by Europeans and Americans as a form of filial piety. One early description, although hazy on the details of how fengshui works, is clear on this point. Care of ancestral tombs is a filial duty; part of that care is the selection of the location according to 'the gods of the wind and water', as well as upkeep and regular sacrifices afterwards (Downing 1838, 3:257–58).[14]

This connection is made over and over again in the English-language literature, especially in the second half of the century (see Fortune 1847, 322 and Williams 1848, 2:262–65 for examples before 1850). Yates, in an important article in the first volume of the *Chinese Recorder and Missionary Journal* (1868–1912), states at the outset that linking ancestor worship and fengshui is one of the main points he wishes to make. He likens ancestors to the branches of a tree, and the root to the living family; the branches capture and collect good fengshui (wind and water), which they transmit down to the root, or the living family (Yates 1868, 38–39). More importantly, Yates then attacks, not fengshui, but ancestor worship, because rather than being prompted by a spirit of true filial piety, it is prompted by a 'servile fear' of the dead and a selfish desire to better one's own prospects. The phrase 'servile fear' harks back to numerous sermons from the seventeenth and eighteenth century on man's filial duty to God, which should be motivated by true piety rather than servile fear. By activating a Christian discourse that equates Chinese filial piety with servile fear, Yates undercuts Chinese filial piety and contributes to the devaluation of this by now peculiar Chinese trait, as argued in the previous chapter. That undercutting is achieved through the link to fengshui, which the British and Americans had long classed as superstition, and is reinforced by his contention that current filial piety, because it has been reduced to 'mainly ... devotion to deceased ancestors', is degenerate (Yates 1868, 23). Worse still, '[t]he living are the slaves of the dead. Yea, the generation of to-day is chained to the generations of the past. Their thoughts do not trend forward, but backwards' (38). This means that innovators cannot achieve distinction, and that fengshui and filial piety are holding the Chinese back from (Western) modernity.

> The great question is, how are we to correct their views of their relations and obligations to the dead? How are we to liberate them from their present cruel bondage? Commerce will not do it. Science and civilization will not accomplish the end effectually, neither will formal Christianity do it .... The gospel, then, is the only antidote for the woes of China. (43)

Not surprisingly, Yates the preacher ends with this exhortation to spread the gospel as China's only hope, not only to save their souls from going to hell, but also to bring them into the present.

Yates's essay is one of the first attempts by a foreigner to consider fengshui in any detail, but he was by no means the last. From this point onward, there are more than a dozen extensive treatments of the subject, with many books on China in the next fifty years devoting an entire section to the topic (Nevius 1868; Moule 1871; Eitel 1873; Moule 1878; Dukes 1880; Henry 1885 [whose chapter title, 'Ancestral Worship and Geomancy' explicitly links the two]; DuBose 1887; Moule 1891; Morris 1892; Cockburn 1896; Douglas 1901; Ball 1904; Macgowan 1907; Macgowan 1909; Johnston 1910; Ball 1911; Macgowan 1912; Couling 1917). There were also two important multivolume works on Chinese religion and superstitions (de Groot 1892–1910 and Doré 1914–38) that contain extensive treatment of the topic. In most of these, the link between filial piety and fengshui as proposed by Yates is repeated in some variation or another.

Pride of place goes again to Eitel, who states that:

> The deepest root of the Feng-shui system grew out of that excessive and super-stitious veneration of the spirits of ancestors, which, though philosophical minds like that of Confucius might construe it on an exclusively moral basis as simply an expression of filial piety, was with the mass of the Chinese people the fruitful soil from which the poisonous weed of rank superstition sprang up in profusion. Ancestral worship naturally implied the idea that the spirits of deceased ancestors could and would somehow influence the fortunes of their descendants. (Eitel 1873, 61–62)

Here we see clearly laid out the steps from filial piety to ancestor worship to fengshui, due to the 'excessive and superstitious' nature of ancestral wor-ship in the days after Confucius, which provided the fertile soil from which the 'rank superstition' of fengshui soon emerged. This is because ancestral worship ipso facto implies that they must have an influence on the fortunes of their descendants. Later Eitel goes further to argue that, because fengshui is entwined with ancestral worship and all major events in domestic life, it is an ineradicable part of Chinese culture (78).

Moule (1878, 104) repeats Eitel's link between filial piety and fengshui, again echoing Yates's attack on filial piety as containing 'a vast admixture of selfishness' because of its links to fengshui. He also sets up a parallel: feng-shui is to 'railways and other modern improvements' as ancestral worship is to Christianity. In other words, the former blocks technological modernity while the latter blocks spiritual modernity. He also calls fengshui a 'mighty foe' (Moule 1878, 106). At least three sources go further to identify that foe by explicitly linking fengshui to Satan (Turner 1874, 347; Henry 1885, 151; Woodbridge 1919, 42). DuBose (1887, 431) calls it a 'black art'.

Most of these accounts are concerned with the present state of affairs in China, or posit a degeneration from an earlier high civilisation to today's state of affairs. However, De Groot (1892–1910, 3:979) provides an inter-esting early example of the link between filial piety and fengshui from the Jin Dynasty (266–420 CE), wherein filial piety is first a motivating factor in a young man choosing a good location and proper time for the burial of his father, and then that filial action being rewarded by later success.

De Groot is fairly neutral in describing such ancient practices, but when it comes to the contemporary practice of fengshui, he makes no secret of his disapproval both of filial piety and fengshui. saying that it is:

> the product of egotism under the guise of filial piety; a sure criterion that this highest among the national virtues of the Chinese, so often extolled to the skies by European authors, is much less sincere than generally supposed; that it is not spontaneous, but calculating; not generous, but thoroughly selfish. Fung-shui is fetishism applied to the dead and their corporeal remains. It is a

hybrid monster, *born of the union of filial devotion in its vilest form with blind gropings after natural science*. At the outset a benumbed viper, it has, carefully fostered by the nation, developed into a horrid hydra suffocating the whole Empire in its coils and deluging it with its venom throughout its length and breadth. (de Groot 1892–1910, 3:1048 my emphasis)

We may pause to wonder over the vituperative nature of this description, as well as the extended metaphor de Groot employs here. Eitel (1873, 61) already used a rather colourful metaphor of fengshui as a 'poisonous weed' striking deep roots in the 'fruitful soil' of excessive ancestral worship. De Groot replaces the botanical image with a much more disturbing one of dead bodies, unnatural copulation, and a viper that becomes a hydra, that acts both like a boa constrictor 'suffocating the whole Empire in its coils' and a venomous snake, 'deluging it with its venom throughout its length and breadth'. All this from a man who supposedly was setting out to give an academic survey of China's religious system.

Yet if we go back to one of the early works we have cited, Morrison's dictionary, we can now note that this almost hysterical fear and loathing of fengshui runs throughout the writings of the nineteenth century. To understand why, it will be necessary to shift our focus away from the question of how fengshui was related to Chinese concepts and look instead at how it interacted with Anglo-American concepts of science, religion, superstition, and magic.

Among these terms, we can broadly conceive of a series of oppositions and affinities. Religion is true, superstition is false; science is true, magic is false. Yet while at times science and religion are both considered true, at other times they are also in opposition, with either science or religion claiming to be true as opposed to the other, which is then labelled false. In general, to the extent that an author believed strongly in science, religion tended to move towards superstition and, conversely, to the extent that an author believed strongly in religion, science would move towards superstition or magic; this thinking harks back to the story of the Garden of Eden and the eating of the forbidden fruit, which was knowledge. The majority of the authors of works about China that deal with fengshui in depth were missionaries who mostly avoided a confrontation between science and religion, choosing instead to emphasise that they were on the same side, with religion playing a dominant role as concerned with the transcendent revealed Truth of God, whereas science was concerned with truth in the world. Other correlates include the belief that science and religion are rational and systematic, while superstition is irrational and lacks any system; it is often associated with luck.

Early texts, in which fengshui is discussed, mostly briefly and in little detail, tend to simply label it as superstition. Winterbotham (1795,

357) puts his discussion of fengshui in a paragraph that begins 'There are other superstitious practices to which the Chinese are also much addicted', while Staunton's note in his translation of the Qing penal code calls it 'a superstitious notion' (Staunton 1810, 190), and we have already seen that Morrison's dictionary uses 'superstition' (1815–23, vol. 1 part 1:521 and 530). Davis (1836, 2:137) also calls it 'the strangest and most unaccountable of the Chinese superstitions'. For these and most other writers up until the 1860s, fengshui was not worth serious consideration, and was considered to be irrational, unsystematic, and false, all classic hallmarks of superstition.

Even writers who might be more systematic in their treatment of the concept often classified it under superstition by including it in chapters that were explicitly labelled 'superstition' or some similar term. Examples include 'Superstitious Notions Respecting Spirits, and the Science of Fung-shwuy, or Geomancy' (Nevius 1868, chapter twelve); 'The Superstitions of the Chinese' (Moule 1871, chapter three); 'Superstitions as to Various Objects' (Dennys 1876, chapter six); 'Primitive Survivals' (Cockburn 1896, chapter one); 'A Chapter on Some of the More Shady Professions in Chinese Life', which begins with a discussion of geomancers (MacGowan 1907, chapter eleven); and in one case an entire work, whose title is *Researches into Chinese Superstitions* (Doré 1914–38).

However, by the 1860s, with the publication first of Yates (1868) and Nevius (1868), and then Eitel (1873), a sense emerges that fengshui is based upon a system, and that it has an internal logic of its own. This shift comes about as it is associated with yinyang and five phases theory. Although most foreign writers still refuse to credit it with truth and may classify it as superstition, they begin to use the words science, pseudo-science, or proto-science to describe it. This leads to a seeming paradox of scientific superstition or superstitious science, but we should keep in mind that the definition of superstition in the *Oxford English Dictionary*, with plenty of examples from the nineteenth century, is 'religious belief or practice considered to be irrational, unfounded, or based on fear or ignorance; excessively credulous belief in and reverence for the supernatural'. The second clause is the crucial one: 'excessively credulous belief' or, in other words, in the realm of science, scientism or magic. As early as 1836, Davis (1836, 1:282) says that fengshui is 'a sort of science'. Ball (1911, 33) encapsulates this neatly, calling it a 'farrago of nonsense' that 'has been worked up into what the Chinese consider an exact science'. Leong and Tao (1915, 144) refer to 'the bogus science of geomancy [that tends] to show the persistence—nay, domination—of the primitive beliefs that had their root deeply planted in the remote ages of the past'. Here and elsewhere we can consider the term science to refer to a *systematic* and *internally consistent* understanding of how the world works. Internal consistency is often important because they sometimes attack fengshui for a lack of it (Dukes 1880, 235). Giles, in a footnote to the story 'Feng-shui' discussed earlier, explains that it is 'a *system* of geomancy, by the *science* of which it is possible to determine the desirability of sites ... and to foretell fortunes of the family based on such selection' (Pu 1880, 2:322). Here the two key ideas that it is systematic, and therefore not irrational, and that it is a science, and therefore concerns the collection of information about the natural world, are reinforced by the ending of the story in which fengshui is proven to be efficacious. In other words, it is based at least partly on empirical observation.

There are also texts that claim to dig beneath current-day practice to a bedrock of observation of the natural world. Dukes (1885) goes into some detail to explain that on the Chinese continent, the north wind is the wind of autumn, cold and death, while the south wind is associated with the spring, warmth, and life, and argues that this insight into where warm and cold weather come from was the basis upon which the rest of fengshui was built. He does not make it explicit, but this view obviously accords well with yinyang theory. A similar passage occurs in DuBose (1887, 432). Northrop (1894, 272) says that fengshui contains faint ideas of the natural sciences 'overlaid and infinitely disfigured by superstition'. He goes on later to add that 'through the mist and folly of this superstition there appears a small particle of reason, and *it is beyond question that the sites chosen by these professors are such as avoid many of the ill effects of the climate*' (Northrop 1894, 272; my emphasis). Thus there are even cases where foreign writers grudgingly admit that there might be something to this 'science'. We should also remember those texts that try to translate fengshui in terms of magnetic currents mentioned earlier (Eitel 1873; Lo 1867; DuBose 1887; Selby 1900, 266), as well as stories of how British decisions, ostensibly made based on concerns for health, coincide with principles of fengshui. Other examples include Smith (1901, 57), who refers to 'the highly rudimentary "science" of Fengshui, or geomancy'; MacGowan (1909, 88), who says that 'the Chinese have reduced fêngshui to a science';[15] and Dukes (1912, 835), who calls fengshui 'this blind groping of the Chinese mind after a system of natural science'.

More typical, however, is the idea advanced in many publications that fengshui is opposed to science. De Groot (1892–1910, 3:937–38) again furnishes us with one of the more extreme statements concerning this opposition:

> Nature having *never been studied in China in a scientific manner*, Fung-shui is not based on any sound ideas acquired by an experimental and critical survey of the heavens and the earth. Starting with the *hazy notion* that Nature is a living organism, the breath of which pervades everything and produces the varied conditions of heaven and earth, and with some *dogmatic formulae* to

be found in the ancient works and confided in as verdicts of the most profound human wisdom, Fung-shui is a mere *chaos of childish absurdities* and refined mysticism, cemented together, by *sophistic* reasonings, into a system, which is in reality a *ridiculous caricature of science*. (my emphasis)

Later (3:1055) he adds: 'The only power capable of overthrowing it, or weakening its all-pervading influence, is sound natural science'.[16] Moule (1891, 298) makes a similar argument, while Dukes (1885, 157–58) says: 'There is no idea in the cranium of a Chinaman more difficult to uproot than this *absolute faith* of his in the *almightiness* of Feng-Shui. Argument apparently fails to loosen his hold in the least. He cannot grasp the elementary principles of a sound theory of natural science, for his prejudices are infinitely stronger than his reason' (my emphasis). He goes on to say 'From the above it will be seen how much what we might call the *gospel* of natural science is needed in China, to assist in clearing away the tangled undergrowth that hinders the feet of the *messengers of the Truth*' (my emphasis). Here Dukes uses an interesting but ultimately contradictory blend of science and religion. First, fengshui is described using terms that could be used to describe a Christian's faith in 'Almighty God', and that faith is seen as preventing the Chinese from understanding natural science. Thus in the first quotation, he seems to array science on one side and religion and fengshui on the other. Yet in the second quotation, he uses religious imagery to describe how the 'gospel' of science will be spread by its messengers (disciples) of 'Truth' with a capital T, suggesting that (Christian) religion is on the side of science.

Dukes's work thus signals that another opposition is just as likely to emerge in writings from the second half of the nineteenth century and the beginning of the twentieth, namely, the opposition between fengshui and religion. Yates (1868, 43), while arraying science together with religion in opposition to fengshui, believes that science alone is insufficient to overcome it. Rather, it is only the true Christian religion that can do so. This requires 'knowledge of the true God, and faith in our Lord Jesus Christ' and the power of the Holy Spirit. 'The gospel, then, is the only antidote for the woes of China.' Henry (1885, 151) says: 'the great antidote for this system of grossest error is the spread of Christian science'. But while the first step involves introducing Western astronomy and physical geography to 'break down this mass of superstition', this must be followed by the Gospel, because fengshui 'shows much of the genius of the "prince of the powers of the air", against whose devices only the "Sword of the Spirit" will prevail'. In other words, fengshui is the work of Satan, and only Christianity can overcome this foe, against whom science is powerless. Woodbridge (1919, 42) echoes this idea that, being the work of the devil, science alone cannot conquer it.

These theoretical pronouncements on the status of fengshui as an oppositional force to science, Christianity, or both, are echoed by complaints about the practical force of fengshui in preventing the spread of Western technology and the conversion of Chinese to Christianity. Virtually all of the authors who discuss fengshui for more than a paragraph or two give details, often repeated from one publication to another, of specific instances where a railroad, telegraph line, mining interest, or canal was opposed on the grounds of fengshui. I found twenty-six instances in the database (Moule 1871, 95–96; Eitel 1873, 1; Moule 1878, 106; Dukes 1880, 225; Dukes 1885, 153–54; Henry 1885, 136 and 150; DuBose 1887, 431; Moule 1891, 229; Morris 1892, 232; de Groot 1892–1910, 3:1040; Northrop 1894, 271; Brebner 1895, 65; Cockburn 1896, 29–30; Douglas 1899, 417; Selby 1900, 267; Selby 1901, 216; Smith 1901, 1:96; Douglas 1901, 340; Smith 1901, 96; Northrop 1903, 375; Ball, 1904, 314; MacGowan 1909, 94–96; Ball 1911, 32; Dukes 1912, 834; Moule 1914, 56–57; Murdock 1920, 136–37) Moreover, there are numerous stories of Christian mission buildings being opposed (Kidd, 1841, 313; Nevius 1868, 175; Yates 1868, 42; Moule 1871, 97; Dukes 1880, 229–30; Moule 1891, 73 and 228; Morris 1892, 234; de Groot 1892–1910, 3:1042 and 1046; Cockburn 1896, 29; Selby 1901, 142; Smith 1901, 1:57; Northrop 1903, 376; Beach 1903, 172–73; MacGowan 1907, 70–71; Ball 1911, 37 and 39; Dukes 1912, 834; Couling 1917, 22; and Woodbridge, 1919, 42). The most 'absurd' story recounted is by Dukes (1885, 152), who says that a *proposal* by the Episcopal Church Mission in Foochow to build something was blamed for catastrophes in the city in 1876.

Moule (1878, 106) brings this discussion back to filial piety, for he argues that, just as fengshui is an obstacle to 'railways and other modern improvements', so too ancestral worship is the great obstacle to Christianity. This syllogism can be mapped back onto the four Anglo-American concepts of science (modern improvements) and (Christian) religion on one side, with superstition (ancestor worship) and magic (fengshui) on the other.

This refusal of the Chinese to embrace enthusiastically Western science and religion infuriates the writers. To understand this infuriated tone, the work of historians of science, religion and anthropology may help us in pulling together certain threads of discourse from the seventeenth through the early twentieth century.

In *Magic, Science, Religion and the Scope of Rationality*, Stanley Tambiah (1990) draws upon a wide array of sources to give an insightful history of how these three concepts have developed in an interrelated fashion from the Renaissance through the twentieth century. Importantly, Tambiah notes the acceptance of these concepts as distinct yet somehow interrelated for virtually the entire period he covers, and the fact that the nature of their relationship has been the subject of wide and enduring debate in anthropology, religious studies, and sociology. Tambiah is ultimately interested in exploring 'the issue of "rationality" itself, and the limits of western "scientism" as a paradigm' (1990, 3), which is somewhat beyond the scope of this study. But he is a useful guide to the development of these concepts as the social sciences emerge in the nineteenth century.

While the authors who discuss fengshui seldom use the term 'magic', it seems clear from their use of the related term superstition, and from their descriptions of it, that they see it as a sort of magic, especially when practiced by fengshui masters. Following Tambiah rather loosely, magic may simply be defined as a (usually) systematic attempt to manipulate the universe for personal gain through invoking correspondences between the real and symbolic orders. In the nineteenth century, magic tended to be seen as a type of proto-science or pseudo-science, as indeed we have noted above in reference to fengshui, one that was not based on empirical evidence, but rather through attempts at pure theorising and the construction of abstract systems often based on the analogical mode. It was also distinguished from religion by the fact that magic, in attempting to manipulate the universe, displays mankind's hubris in challenging the supremacy of God; religious prayer, rather than trying to directly change reality, supplicates the Deity to intervene *if it so chooses*. Tambiah traces this distinction back to the Jewish faith, with developments in the Protestant Reformation, thus linking it to the outbreak of witchcraft trials during the Enlightenment (Tambiah 1990, 4–14). Finally, with the conception of God as designer of a universe with regular laws, science becomes in a sense the handmaiden of religion, investigating and mastering truth in the physical world while yielding to religion regarding transcendent Truth about God and the afterlife. This harmony between religion and science is not broken until Darwin's theory of evolution, which introduces the idea of ongoing and open-ended change that is neither maximally functional nor necessarily progressive (Tambiah 1990, 16–18). The break between science and religion is not accomplished overnight, however, with many branches of the sciences still firmly continuing under the older paradigm into the twentieth century.

Having established the rough relationship between these concepts, Tambiah goes on to consider how they then play out in the work of Edward Tylor, thought by many to be the father of social anthropology, in his landmark *Primitive Culture* (1871), which went through several editions and remained in print well into the twentieth century.[17]

Tylor certainly embraces the Reformation idea that magic is false. But if magic is false, why has it persisted in so many cultures down to the present day? Tylor gives a long list of reasons, including 'the cunning [magician's] shrewd guesses at the past and future'; covering over the fact that magic fails in the great majority of cases (he assumes) by 'rhetorical shift and brazen impudence', the use of ambiguous phrases, faulting others for improper performance of rituals, interference from other magicians or higher powers; and finally, the tendency of people everywhere to cling to beliefs once they are established (Tylor 1871, 1:121–23).[18] However, the magician is not wholly to blame; he is described as both 'fraud' and 'dupe' of his own practice, and Tylor theorises that magic is, in its origins, not consciously fraudulent; rather, it is a sincere but misguided attempt to understand and control the universe (1:120).

Be that as it may, magic is not just false, but evil. The rhetoric that Tylor employs at points parallels some of the more extreme rhetoric employed to describe fengshui. This can be seen in several passages, where he describes it as 'one of the most pernicious delusions that ever vexed mankind' and linked to the 'lowest known stages of civilization, and the lower races' (1:101). He also calls it 'a contemptible superstition' (1:102) and a 'monstrous farrago' that has 'no truth or value whatever' but yet has somehow enthralled the world for ages (1:120). Luckily, the rise of experimental testing by 'progressive races' has led to magic eventually breaking down; thus 'the modern educated world, rejecting occult science as a contemptible superstition, has practically committed itself to the opinion that magic belongs to a lower level of civilization' (1:101).

That last quotation brings up the next important point, which is that Tylor firmly believes in the evolution of culture from primitive to advanced. He explicitly traces the development of certain facets of belief systems, such as the evolution of sacrifice to the gods, which implies reciprocity (I give you a sacrifice and you do me a favour), through homage, and finally abnegation, by which point the sacrifice of the worshipper is voluntarily made for ethical or moral reasons rather than for personal gain (2:340–41; also 356–62 for examples). It also comes up in his discussion of the belief in the continued existence of the soul after death, wherein he establishes Christianity as the most advanced religion (2:2).

Furthermore, Tylor is a universalist; he believes that all humans have equal potential to develop their intelligence and thus will pass through the same stages of development. Therefore, it is the duty of more advanced cultures to help others to evolve to the same level as themselves—what was sometimes called the 'white man's burden'—and this will be accomplished through science and the spread of Christianity. Thus he states in the conclusion his firm belief that science will do away with animism and other superstitions (2:407–9). The closing sentence of the work is 'Thus, active at once in aiding progress and in removing hindrance, the science of culture is essentially a reformer's science' (2:410). In other words, the anthropologist should help to educate more primitive people both in terms of science and religion so that they can reform their society and become modern.

Tylor was an armchair anthropologist; rather than collecting data himself in the field, he combed through existing written records of travellers, missionaries, merchants, and foreign service officers from all over the world, including China. In his earlier work, *Researches into the Early History of Mankind and the Development of Civilization* (1865), he had drawn mainly on works by the Jesuits concerning China, but in *Primitive Culture* he draws on a wider range of contemporary sources. Far and away his favourite source is Doolittle's *The Social Life of the Chinese* (1865) with twenty-four citations, followed by a German work on Chinese religion and cults by Plath (1862), with eight citations, Davis's *The Chinese* (1836; Tylor uses the later edition of 1851) and the first volume of James Legge's *Chinese Classics* (1861) with six citations each, and then a variety of other sources including recent articles from various journals such as the *Transactions of the Ethnological Society*, published by the Royal Anthropological Institute of Great Britain and Ireland in the 1860s.

Since neither Doolittle nor Davis dwell at length on fengshui, it is not surprising that Tylor never mentions it in his work, but he does discuss ancestor worship.

> Nowhere is the connexion (sic) between parental authority and conservatism more graphically shown. The worship of ancestors, begun during their life, is not interrupted but intensified when death makes them deities. The Chinese, prostrate bodily and mentally before the memorial tablets that contain the souls of his ancestors, little thinks that he is all the while proving to mankind how vast a power unlimited filial obedience, prohibiting change from ancestral institutions, may exert in stopping the advance of civilization. (Tylor 1871, 2:108)

Moreover, this ancestral worship is, like the most primitive type of worship described by Tylor, strictly reciprocal: 'Among the Chinese, manes-worship is no rite of mere affection. The living want the help of the ancestral spirits' (2:108). Here, then, we see laid out explicitly the equation that will be repeated over and over by writers from the 1860s through the 1920s regarding ancestral worship: it is a primitive system that, because it holds China back from modernity, must be eliminated. While Tylor may not tie ancestral worship to fengshui, we have already seen that the authors of all sorts of books on China that come after Tylor strengthen the claims that filial piety is based on reciprocity, which is often glossed as greed or cupidity, and that *this cupidity expresses itself through fengshui practices*. Thus fengshui practices become part of the argument, following Tylor, that the Chinese must be saved from themselves because they are in a primitive state of development.

Tylor's work was widely known in the late nineteenth century; as mentioned earlier, he drew upon, and corresponded with, many missionaries in the field. We can see his direct influence on the work of Cockburn (1896). Cockburn's first chapter, entitled 'Primitive Survivals' is taken directly from Tylor's *Primitive Cultures*, volume two of which was devoted almost entirely to the 'survival' of primitive beliefs in the modern age. Cockburn also uses terms such as 'fetishism' and 'totemism' to categorise Chinese beliefs, which categories derive from Tylor.

This Anglo-American discourse of evolution and universality of the human experience, then, enmeshes the Chinese concepts of fengshui and filial piety firmly in the debate about magic, religion, and science in the nineteenth century, with *both* fengshui and filial piety (through its avatar ancestral worship) being treated as magical practices. This is in part accomplished by denying any truth claims to either fengshui or to the cosmological beliefs that lay behind it. Thus even though Eitel and several other writers connect fengshui to yinyang and five phases theory, they are always careful to label those systems as false and, more tellingly, lacking any basis in empirical evidence. Eitel (1873, 5), for example, says that the Chinese 'evolved a whole system of natural science from their own inner consciousness and expounded it according to the dogmatic formulae of ancient tradition' in the complete absence of experimental observation. This prevents it from being classified as science.

We can now begin to understand the extremity of the Protestant writers' revulsion against these superstitions: 'thou shalt not suffer a witch to live' (Exodus 22:18). The witchcraft trials of the sixteenth and seventeenth centuries might have died down in Europe, but the depth of feeling was still there, and we see it here transferred abroad to Chinese practices that seemed bent on undermining the narrative of the British as bringers of modern civilisation to the Chinese.

This revulsion is also linked to a strong suspicion that fengshui is being used cynically as an excuse to block foreign incursions (or helpful development, depending on the point of view). Northrop (1894, 271) claims that local government officials are selective in when they listen to local complaints about fengshui: if it is opposed to foreign activity then it is supported, but if it is opposed to the needs of the Chinese state then 'the terrors of Feng Shui disappear like the morning mists before the sun'. Moule (1914, 59) draws his readers' attention to the fact that steam traffic along the coast, which had no competition from native junks, also met with no opposition based on fengshui, whereas steam-powered ships on inland waterways, where it competed with local barges, was vehemently opposed on fengshui grounds. Up until foreigners began to gain access to wide areas of China in the wake of the Second Opium War and consider investment in technological development, foreigners did not consider fengshui to be important enough to write about in English. Bruun notes that the *North China Herald*, founded in 1850, contains no mention of fengshui up until an article he cites from 1868; yet in the same time period, Chinese-language periodicals edited by missionaries contain many articles decrying fengshui practices in strong terms.

Ole Bruun has argued precisely that in the late nineteenth century, fengshui was used consciously as a tool of resistance against colonial incursions by foreign powers. In particular, Bruun (2003, 45–46) cites cases reported in the *North China Herald* in June of 1868 where the government had vetoed petitions for the construction of roads to open coal mines by foreigners based partly on fengshui concerns of local residents. Importantly, the British government's response, expressed by Sir Rutherford, was that references to the local people's faith were 'unanswerable'; in other words, the British accepted such claims as legitimate, even though the British themselves did not believe in fengshui. This gave the Qing government ammunition to use in other disputes with foreigners, including a reason to deny foreigners the right to build missions, which right had been granted to them by the Treaty of Tientsin negotiated during the Second Opium War (1856–60). In the wake of the massacre of Christians in Tianjin in June of 1870, the Chinese memorandum on foreign missions (1871) included language that explicitly enjoined foreigners wishing to establish a mission station to consult with local authorities on whether such a station was in accord with local fengshui, and further to consult with local residents, before proceeding. Although this memorandum was never ratified by the foreign powers, it gives an indication that the Qing already recognised that fengshui was one of several possible tools to resist foreign incursions (54). For Bruun, the discussion in English in this period and the decades immediately following demonstrate that fengshui was increasingly seen by foreigners as a belief system and cosmology and that, *as a result*, it became more prominent in Chinese discourse as an anti-foreign tool and anti-foreign discourse (57–60). As evidence that this was a conscious plan by the government is the fact, widely reported, that while foreign efforts to open mines, build railways, and string telegraph lines were resisted in the name of fengshui, Qing government projects were not subject to similar problems (62–64).[19]

It is possible to search for instances of fengshui in a wide range of newspapers from North America, the United Kingdom, and Ireland in the same time period to get a sense to what extent the specialist knowledge from books about China, and the experience of foreigners reporting in English-language papers in East Asia, penetrated into popular discourse. A search through ProQuest Historical Newspapers of sixteen possible spellings for fengshui plus the term geomancy shows virtually no instances of the concept before 1863; furthermore, several of the early instances of the concept occur in advertisements for books about China or about the occult. The first instance of a news article that mentions the concept is from the *New York Times* on 29 August 1866, which discusses the role of 'Fongshwe, which we may render by geomancy, [which] is the most formidable obstacle in the way of every kind of internal improvement' ('Affairs in China' 1866, 2). A similar article two years later in the *Cincinnati Daily Enquirer*, 23 October 1868, says

> They believe the erection of poles and the stretching of wires would disturb the currents of 'Fung Shuey' (good luck), just as some of the residents of Tennessee and Alabama, ten or twelve years ago, believed the telegraph wires caused a lack of rain. Hence their opposition to the construction of the telegraph; and it remains for the prejudice to be overcome, before electric communications in China will be a success. ('Commercial Progress in China' 1868, 3)

The comparison to superstitions in the United States, which presumably were overcome, is typical of the attitude that, over time, the forces of modernity would impose themselves on China. Similar results multiply into the early twentieth century. A 1908 headline in the *Washington Post* announces 'PROBLEM FOR CHINESE: Far-Reaching Superstition is Great Bar to Progress' (Freedman 1908, E12), while another from 1919 shouts 'SUPERSTITION FOE TO PROGRESS IN CHINA' (The Statesman 1919, A12).

In terms of absolute numbers, however, references to fengshui never exceed five per year until 1898, after which there is a sharp rise in 1900 and 1901 (totally thirty-nine references) due to the Boxer Rebellion, only to drop down to zero in 1902. After that, numbers are again mostly below five per year except when there is some widely reported event concerning China, such as the funeral of the emperor Guangxu in 1909, which results in fourteen hits for that year. Finally, there are a handful of articles in 1912 and 1924 that refer to fengshui among overseas Chinese in San Francisco, when turf wars between rival tongs made national news. While these stories take place in America, there is no mention of fengshui as something that might be practiced by non-Asians.

Up through the 1920s then, fengshui remains largely in the realm of specialist knowledge in English, widely referenced in literature on China from 1860 onwards but otherwise largely ignored by the general populace. That specialist literature contains much information, some of it quite detailed, but situated firmly within an Anglo-American discourse of science, religion, superstition and magic. To the extent that it is reported more widely, it is a strange superstition that holds the Chinese back from joining the Western nations in their march to modernity.

Fengshui in Late Imperial China

Chinese authors, especially of a more Confucian bent, had certainly criticised both fengshui and the underlying correlative cosmological thinking of yinyang and five phases before the advent of European and American writings on the subject. In terms of the cosmology, Henderson (1984, 97–99 and 103–5) notes that as early as the Later Han dynasty, certain aspects of correlative thinking had been attacked by Wang Chong (27–100 CE), and that in the eleventh century a 'cluster' of sceptics emerged, only to be overwhelmed by the neo-Confucians, who returned to correlative thinking with a vengeance. This later led to a rise in popularity of fengshui practices in the Ming dynasty (Liu 1971, 72–75 and 82). But it was scholars starting in the early Qing who, bent upon uncovering the authentic core of Confucianism by peeling away later layers of commentary and interpretation, mounted the most concerted attack upon yinyang and five phases theory as late and therefore inauthentic material (Henderson 1984, 155–59). This desire to return to the roots of Confucianism, coupled with advances in astronomy partly fuelled by Jesuit mathematicians, led to the gradual decline in respect for such systems among the educated in the late Qing. As we have noted earlier, *The Sacred Edict* (1724) condemned it for interfering with filial piety; thus there was some governmental censure of excesses of the practice, although the Qing government continued to employ fengshui experts in the planning of government buildings (Yang 1961, 264).

What Henderson does *not* document is a corresponding decline of such thinking among the general population. In fact, he explicitly avoids popular material such as divination manuals, which continued to be published in good numbers throughout the Qing, because they drew mainly on Han or post-Han texts, all of which were imbued with correlative thinking. Despite the attacks on correlative cosmology by some members of the literati class, 'most, if not all, Chinese scholars shared with commoners a belief in some popular religious ideas, such as geomancy, the notion of a predetermined fate (*ming*), fortunetelling ("knowing fate"), and moral retribution particularly in the civil service examinations' (Ropp, 1981, 152). The exceptions were few and far between; Ropp details four of them in his chapter discussing the supernatural, but stresses that these men were a small minority among the literati, who in turn were a small minority of the entire population (Ropp 1981, 153).

If we turn to literary representations of fengshui in the Qing, there is however some evidence of scepticism. Pu Songling 蒲松齡 (1640–1715), the collector, editor, and author of the compendious *Strange Stories from the Leisure Studio* (Liaozhai zhiyi 聊齋誌異; first published 1740) tells one story entitled 'Kan yu' (Geomancy) which, as noted earlier, was translated by Giles (Pu 1880) as 'Feng Shui' in his selection of stories from that collection. Nowhere in the story is the efficacy of fengshui questioned; rather, it is the unfilial behaviour of the sons—dividing the family property and then going to war with each other, rather than thinking of themselves as a unit—that causes the problem, and it is the wisdom of the widows to reunite the two branches of the family that then resolves the problem. This accords well with Feuchtwang's (2002, 246 and 262–67) observation that ancestral worship brings families together, while fengshui practices tend to pull them apart—or rather, fengshui may give *expression* to such centripetal forces (Feuchtwang 2002, 271). By entitling the story 'Geomancy' rather than something like 'Two Unfilial Sons', Pu Songling directs the reader's attention away from the more controversial aspects of the story, yet still delivers that message.

By contrast, the slightly later vernacular novel *Rulin waishi* (儒林外史 *The Scholars*) by Wu Jingzi (吳敬梓 1701–54) contains a quite hard-hitting critique of fengshui practice. Ropp (1981, 173) details how 'Wu gave his most extensive and passionate critique of any popular religious practice'. In chapter forty-four, readers are presented with a reasoned critique of fengshui that attacks it for subverting ancient Confucian burial practices, anachronistic claims relating to fengshui's supposed founder, and cases of people who succeed despite ignoring fengshui of their ancestors, or of people failing in life despite having procured excellent fengshui grave plots (175–76). This is followed in chapter forty-five by a satirical portrait of two self-styled fengshui experts, who calmly munch on clods of earth to test the fengshui of different plots and then give hyperbolic claims relating to the sites (177–79).

Yet even as Ropp details these critiques of fengshui in the novel, he notes that fengshui had a particular relevance for the literati, who were more likely to have the disposable income necessary to expend on a fengshui master, and who were heavily invested in success at the imperial examination, which was the pinnacle of worldly success. Thus

it was not uncommon for examination halls to be remodeled in accord with the dictates of geomancers, in an effort to improve the candidates's chances in subsequent examinations. While some intellectuals expressed doubts regarding the reliability of geomancers, few were willing to discount their effectiveness entirely, and it was not uncommon to find amateur geomancers among the upper classes. (160)

In the late Qing we can also find some condemnation of fengshui practice in literature. Li Ruzhen's (李汝珍 1763–1830) *Jing hua yuan* (鏡花緣 *Flowers in the Mirror*) in chapter twelve rehearses the complaints against fengshui for delaying burial services and the illogic of poor fengshui masters claiming to know the secret to graves that will make the owner rich and successful

(Li Ruzhen 1991, 47–53). Again, the first critique does not deny the existence of fengshui, while the second could be interpreted either as a critique of the system or, more likely, as anticlericalism—exposing frauds among practitioners *because* the author holds these beliefs and is upset at tricksters misusing them.

Finally, there is a pair of courtcase novels, both based on a real-life feud between two families in Guangdong Province, that features fengshui beliefs. *Jing fu xin shu* (警富新書 New warning about wealth) was published anonymously in 1809, while the second, *Jiu ming qi yuan* (九命奇冤 A strange case of nine murders) which is based on the first but with significant differences, was authored by Wu Jianren (吳趼人, aka Wu Woyao 吳沃堯, 1866–1910) and published in serial form in the magazine *Xin xiaoshuo* (新小說 New Fiction) between 1904 and 1906, and then published in book form in 1907.[20] The story revolves around two men whose parents were business partners but who fall out with each other. A deadly feud develops when the richer and more well-connected of them, Ling Guixing, upset that he has not passed the imperial examination, hires a geomancer who pronounces that a stone house owned by the other man, Liang Tianlai, has damaged the fengshui of his father's grave and is thus preventing him from succeeding at the exams. The stone house has been the Liang's home for generations, and Tianlai refuses to sell it. Ling Guixing eventually orders the storming of the stone house, which is set on fire, killing everyone inside; Tianlai only escapes because he is away from home at the time. The rest of the novel follows his attempt to obtain justice through the courts, which he eventually does after a long series of narrow escapes from the clutches of his enemy.

This case, which revolves around the relationship between fengshui of a grave and success at the imperial examinations, supports Ropp's claim that those aspiring to hold official posts through the examination system were among those most likely to engage fengshui masters, as they had the necessary funds, and were competing for a vanishingly small number of places.

There are some salient differences between the first and second version. First, the quarrel between the two men in Wu's version begins *before* the question of fengshui arises, when the two men meet to divide up the business. Although they are not kin, this situation echoes that of the short story by Pu Songling, where I have interpreted the division of the property by the brothers as the 'true' underlying cause for the quarrel over the grave of their father. During the division, the richer Guixing proposes a sort of closed bidding process to determine who will get the last few items that they cannot agree upon, but unexpectedly Liang outbids him and gets the objects. Guixing is unhappy and tries to renege, but neighbours intervene and say that he must abide by the rules that he himself set. When the issue of fengshui of his ancestral grave is raised, then, he is already predisposed to blame Tianlai for his own failure in the examination.

Second, in Wu's version, Ling Guixing tries to cheat at the examination through a large bribe passed on through connections, and is so sure of having passed that he makes preparations for a feast on the day that the results are to be announced. Having paid a large sum of money for nothing, his disappointment is therefore double.

In a sense, these two changes make the issue of fengshui less important in the overall plot. Instead, the focus is on the greed, rapacity, and dishonesty of Ling Guixing, who is portrayed significantly worse in Wu's version of the story.

There are other changes in the second version that show how a Western sensibility has begun to influence the discourse in Chinese about fengshui. Although Wu did not know any foreign languages, it is well established that he was influenced by translations of foreign literature, including Sherlock Holmes stories (Martin 1986, 905–7); his decision to write for *New Fiction*, a reformist magazine run by Liang Qichao (1873–1929), who himself was heavily influenced by foreign ideas, is therefore not coincidental. This is evident in the very first chapter, which begins *in medias res* with the destruction of the stone house and the murder of all its inhabitants, and then backtracks in chapter two to the beginning of the story as told in the 1809 version. This structure is quite out of keeping with traditional Chinese fiction, especially the courtcase genre.[21] In terms of the discourse on fengshui, the most telling difference is revealed in the penultimate paragraph of the novel: 'Poor Ling Guixing! that with all his riches he should come to such an end as this was all the fruit of one single seed: "superstition" ' (可憐凌貴興財雄一方, 卻受了這般結果, 都是 '迷信' 兩個字種的禍根) (Liu and Zhu 2003, 322). Here Wu uses the modern term '*mixin*' (迷信), which was a loanword through Japanese, coined as a translation for the English word 'superstition'.

The term mixin erupts into the Chinese discourse on fengshui in the period 1904–06, precisely the time that Wu was writing *Jiu ming qi yuan*. We can see this through an examination of collocations with fengshui in *Zhongguo jin-xiandai sixiangshi quanwen jiansuo shujuku* (中國近現代思想史全文檢索數據庫 Indexed Corpus of Materials Relating to the History of Chinese Late Imperial and Modern Thought).[22] A search for the keywords fengshui and kanyu in a list of 37 periodicals stretching from 1834–1948 generated 173 articles containing mixin, all of which were collocated with fengshui, not kanyu.[23] The first article to use mixin dates from October 1904. From that point to the end of the database, there are 96 articles that contain fengshui, of which 24 (exactly 25 per cent) use mixin either as a verb, noun, or adjective.

If we compare these results to the Qing fiction discussed above and to the European perception of fengshui, one point of interest is that all of the Qing literature cited focuses exclusively on the fengshui of graves; there is no mention of houses, temples, or government buildings, and there is certainly no mention of it standing in the way of progress. Also, these few critics must be balanced against a healthy number of neutral or positive references to fengshui in other works from this time period. A cursory search through a selection of Ming-Qing works turned up twelve neutral or positive references to fengshui from *Xi you ji* (西遊記 *Journey to the West*, circa 1592) through *San xia wu yi* (三俠五義 Three heroes and five gallants, 1879). Yet in the Indexed Corpus of Materials Relating to the History of Chinese Late Imperial and Modern Thought, the vast majority of references to fengshui are negative, regardless of whether the journal is run by foreigners or Chinese, and regardless of the time period: 154 articles attacked fengshui actively, fifty contained neutral descriptions of fengshui practice (fengshui is mentioned but no judgement is made), and only three articles have positive things to say about it. This seems to indicate that the Chinese periodicals established at the end of the nineteenth century and the first few decades of the twentieth inherited certain dispositions from the foreign-run periodicals of the earlier period, which advocated a number of reforms in Chinese society, among which was the abandonment of fengshui, and were all founded and run by missionaries. Indeed, many of the late Qing journals were explicitly reformist in tone and were run by the likes of late Qing reformers Kang Youwei (1858–1927) and Liang Qichao.

The attacks on fengshui in late Qing and early Republican Era periodicals in China begin earlier than the attacks on filial piety, yet there is a large degree of overlap in the types of attacks, the journals in which such attacks were published, and the link to holding China back from modernity. Also, if we take the 1904 introduction of mixin as the point at which foreign discourse on fengshui clearly enters into the equation, then there is a closer match. Bruun (2003, 72–73) has detailed how fengshui was attacked by Sun Yat-sen after his conversion to Christianity, and how 'modern-educated elite intellectuals' mirrored the viewpoint of foreign visitors that uneducated superstition was holding China back.

These attacks continued throughout the Republican era. Of special note for us is the belief that Western science was the answer to overcoming Chinese superstition (Yang 1961, 364–65), and the 1929 promulgation of the 'Procedure for the Abolition of the Occupations of Divination, Astrology, Physiognomy and Palmistry, Magic and Geomancy', all of which led to the precipitous decline in fengshui practices in urban areas of the Republic, thus establishing a split between urban and rural views of fengshui (Bruun 2003, 76–77). That urban-rural split endures down to the present, although not necessarily in the same form.

The PRC also consistently held an anti-fengshui view. Unlike the Republican era, however, they also had strong anti-religious views, partly because orthodox Marxism viewed religion as the opium of the masses, but also because they viewed with suspicion the motives of foreign Christian churches vis à vis state power (Bruun 2003, 81). This meant that they grouped fengshui and religion together as superstitions, as opposed to Marxist-Leninist thought and science, whereas in the Republican era many high-ranking members of the KMT were Christian, and Christianity was seen as part of the modernising forces in China. Bruun (82–102) goes into great detail regarding the pressure on all forms of religious observance from the 1950s through the mid-1970s. While the intensity rose and fell according to different movements, the basic understanding of fengshui as backward superstition remained consistent. A search through the *People's Daily* archive mentioned in Chapter 1, note 17 easily verifies this consistency of official tone throughout the period. I found 137 occurrences of fengshui between 1947 and 1976, inclusive. Of those, not a single one has anything good to say about it. Forty attack fengshui as superstition (mixin) and twenty-three attack it as feudal (*fengjian* 封建, a term widely used to mean anything from China's imperial past). Other labels include 'outmoded thought' (*sixiang luohou* 思想落後), 'conservative thought' (*baoshou sixiang* 保守思想), 'nonsense' (*huyan luanyu* 胡言亂語), 'unenlightened thought' (*sixiang wei juewu* 思想未覺悟), 'trickery' (*pian ren baxi* 騙人把戲), the workings of 'class enemies' (*jieji diren* 階級敵人) and, in logical contradiction with 'feudal' but in keeping with the general tone of enemy of the people, 'capitalist restoration' (*zibenzhuyi fubi* 資本主義復辟).

At the same time that official rhetoric remains constant, however, Bruun argues that the nature of fengshui for practitioners gradually changed in this time period in response to governmental pressure. He notes in particular that, as a decentralised practice, fengshui masters were less susceptible to mass campaigns and therefore better adapted to surviving in such an atmosphere than clerics of organised religions (Bruun 2003, 82 and 96). This meant that, as other types of religious figures were rounded up and eliminated or forced to return to secular livelihoods, fengshui masters were increasingly consulted for a wider variety of 'life-cycle rituals', leading to the boundary between fengshui and popular religion becoming more blurred (96). Second, he sees the link between fengshui and traditional burial practices as key to fengshui's survival during this period, and to the resurgence of fengshui after 1976. In other words, the link between filial piety and fengshui I have already discussed, and the continued central status of ancestral worship, assured the survival of fengshui in the countryside. Since the reforms begun under Deng Xiaoping in the late 1970s, fengshui has made a comeback there, thanks in part, Bruun says, to widespread poverty and growing income inequality, the retreat of medical practitioners from the countryside, and the restriction of much scientific knowledge as state secrets (for example pollution levels, which affect both agriculture and individual health) (105–6). This has occurred despite continued negative press in *People's Daily*.

In urban areas, however, where many people still had their family home in the countryside, fengshui was both less prevalent and of a different nature, because it was not primarily associated with graves, but rather with dwellings, and those dwellings were increasingly flats rather than houses. But before discussing urban fengshui in China, it will be instructive to return to what was happening in the Anglo-American sphere in the mid-twentieth century.

Fengshui for the New Age

I had earlier noted that up to the 1920s, the English discourse on fengshui was fairly developed but mainly specialised. This continues to be true right through the mid-1970s; annual hits in the ProQuest Historical Newspapers database continue to be in the low single digits up to that point, only beginning to rise consistently from 1980.

There are a few important trends in the articles that do appear up to this point. First, the refusal of many countries to recognise the PRC, especially the United States, which holds out until the mid-1970s, means that access to news coming out of China is limited. What does come out is often from the *People's Daily*, and so a significant portion of the articles in the Anglo-American press in this period concern the various anti-superstition campaigns launched by the government against, among other things, fengshui. Second, there is a shift in focus to territories outside the control of the PRC, especially Hong Kong; twenty-two percent of the articles that mention fengshui from 1956 through 1989 are directly related to the British colony.

These reports about Hong Kong show a shift in the discourse surrounding fengshui in English. Although we still find articles noting that it is a hindrance for government development projects (see note nineteen above for some examples), more and more frequently the articles begin to tell of the influence of fengshui on real estate prices and development, of the efficacy of fengshui and certain 'cursed' buildings, and finally of foreigners doing business in Hong Kong who consult fengshui masters either in relation to their office or to their home.

These articles are followed in the mid-1970s by articles concerning the effect of fengshui on the real estate market in North America: first Los Angeles and San Francisco, followed by New York, then Vancouver and Toronto, all cities with large immigrant Chinese populations. This includes an increasing number of immigrants from Hong Kong, where uncertainty about the fate of the British colony sets off a wave of outward migration beginning in the mid-1970s.

In conjunction with this growing interest in fengshui in newspapers, we find from the late 1960s an increasing number of academic books, articles, and dissertations devoted to the topic, often taking a markedly positive attitude as opposed to the earlier writings by China experts from the late nineteenth and early twentieth century. Finally, two books are published by non-academic presses for popular consumption: one by a Singaporean in 1979 and one by a New Yorker in 1983. Both received favourable reviews in the press and seem to initiate a fengshui craze in the English-speaking world. Evelyn Lip's *Chinese Geomancy: A Layman's Guide to Feng Shui* is published simultaneously in Singapore, Malaysia, London and the United States (under the title *Feng Shui: A Layman's Guide to Geomancy*), but the American press is a small independent one and it garners little attention there. Most of the attention is in Southeast Asia and the United Kingdom, where it is reviewed in the *Guardian* (15 February 1980), which claims that it is the first English-language book to popularise the practice of feng-shui to a non-Chinese audience. Four years later, Rachel Rossbach, who had lived in Hong Kong for an extended period of time, publishes *Feng Shui: The Chinese Art of Placement* (1983) through E. P. Dutton, a major New York publisher, and is reviewed in the *New York Times*. The review is followed by articles about Rossbach herself as a fengshui practitioner in New York and her later publications, including a second book, *Feng Shui: Ancient Wisdom for the Most Beneficial Way to Place and Arrange Furniture, Rooms and Buildings* (1984). Lip's and Rossbach's works are quickly followed by what becomes an avalanche of books in English on fengshui, this time describing it, not as a Chinese superstition, but as a contemporary practice to improve anyone's life. In 1999 there were over one hundred separate titles published.

The single most important shift in this period is the almost complete suppression of any link between fengshui and filial piety or ancestral worship. Rossbach does discuss briefly the fact that, traditionally, fengshui included this as a component, but this occupies a mere four pages out of 189, the bulk of which is devoted to three topics: proving that fengshui works in the modern world, detailing her own fengshui lineage, and giving instructions on how anyone can use fengshui principles themselves based on a mixture of rules and ad hoc advice, all while stressing the mystic element of fengshui.

I have compiled a database of all the records between 1968 and 2009 in WorldCat that come up when the keywords 'feng shui' are inputted, controlling for language (English) and type (book), and then checking manually for false hits, leaving a raw total of 2096 items. After deleting all duplicates, the resulting database contained 1436 records. The titles of all these works were then converted into a plain text file and fed into the concordancer program Wordsmith (version 8), and a word frequency list was generated. Lemmas and, in a few cases, closely related terms such as house and home were combined, resulting in 1807 items, of which almost 1000 were hapax legomena.

The list reveals that, despite some continuity from the late nineteenth-century material, the topic of fengshui in the English-language material of the period is significantly different, bearing out the changes already clearly visible in Rossbach's 1983 work.

Not surprisingly, 'fengshui' is the most frequent word in the entire list; at 1020 occurrences, it is far more common than even the definite article 'the' (773 hits). It is used alone as the title of 33 books, and begins the title of a further 368 books. All lemmas of geomancy/geomancer only total 36, so clearly the transliteration is winning out over the proposed native equivalent, although a quick look inside some of the books reveals that the term 'geomancy' is often at least mentioned occasionally.

The use of the transliterated term strengthens the foreign origins of the concept, and so when we turn to geographic names (Table 2.1), it should be no surprise that fengshui remains closely tied to China. There are 27 occurrences of either the country name or cities within it, plus 136 occurrences of the adjective 'Chinese'. The next most frequent is Hong Kong, with 16 occurrences, which bears out the findings from newspapers which, as discussed above, carried frequent news stories of fengshui in that territory. If we group these with the results for other East and Southeast Asian countries, we get 220 occurrences, versus 55 occurrences for all other geographic terms, exactly 80 per cent versus 20 per cent.

In terms of the basic cosmology underlying fengshui practice, 'qi' ('breath' or 'vitality'; 14 hits), and yin and yang (10 hits) are not overly common in the titles of English-language books, but when we begin reading them, it emerges that almost all books on fengshui in English make at least some mention of these cosmological concepts and, in many cases, enter into fairly detailed discussion of their role, along with the five phases.

In terms of the purpose of fengshui, we also find quite a bit of continuity. Table 2.2 lists words associated with goals: health and wealth

Table 2.1 Distribution of geographic names in English fengshui book titles, 1968–2009

Geographic location	Noun	Adj	Sub-unit[1]	Subtotals
China	24	136	3	
Hong Kong	16	0	0	
Macao	1	0	0	
Japan	0	2	0	
Singapore	6	0	0	
Korea	4	0	0	
Himalayas	1	1	0	
Indonesia	1	0	0	
Malaysia	0	0	4	
Pacific	1	0	0	
Asia	0	11	0	
East	6	0	0	
Orient	0	5	0	
East/Southeast Asia	60	155	7	220
				80.00%
Australia	3	4	2	
America	0	7	8	
Canada	0	0	6	
New Zealand	1	0	0	
Africa	1	0	0	
Babylon	1	0	0	
Germany	0	0	1	
United Kingdom	0	0	6	
India	1	12	2	
Rest of world	7	23	25	55
				20.00%

Note:
[1] Any sub-division of the larger unit, such as a city, county, or region.

Table 2.2 Distribution of goals in English fengshui book titles, 1968–2009

Goals	Hits	Subtotal	Percentage
Heal/health	104	104	20.27%
Wealth	37	172	33.53%
success	32		
prosper	28		
money	8		
rich	3		
career	10		
fortune	54		
Harmony	100	212	41.33%
love	48		
romance	8		
passion	2		
happy	43		
joy	7		
serenity	4		
Destiny	9	9	1.75%
Family	4	4	0.78%
Fertility	2	12	2.34%
daughter	2		
offspring	0		
child	7		
infertility	1		
son	2		
Total	513	513	100.00%

Note: 'Power' (24 hits) is not an aim, but what helps you to achieve that aim, and therefore is excluded from this table.

(grouped with success, prosperity, money, rich, career, and fortune) remain as two main items. These findings largely mirror the traditional goals of fengshui practice, which many observers have noted are firmly rooted in the here and now. The surprise is that harmony (grouped with love, romance, passion, happiness, joy, and serenity) constitutes the largest single block, which seems to represent a departure, or development; it was noted by more than one observer that fengshui often seemed a channel for competition and strife within a community, with numerous fights arising from fengshui disputes. Hits for 'power' turned out to be not a goal, but a means to achieving other goals and are not included here. The other difference is an almost total absence of interest in family matters (four hits). Moreover, there are no occurrences of 'son' in the database and only two occurrences of 'daughter', neither of which is about offspring as a goal. There are a very few titles that talk about fengshui for children, but they are not about *having* children, but bringing them up properly. Only two titles, *Natural Fertility* and *Fertility Wisdom: How Traditional Chinese Medicine Can Help Overcome Infertility*, are connected with the topic of having children.

Fengshui involves a highly developed sense of spatial orientation and the relation between individuals and different types of environments. Turning to terminology related to human geography, it should be no surprise that home, house, and cognate terms occur frequently. Table 2.3 lists a total of 186 occurrences; when combined with related terms such as bedroom, kitchen, and so forth, plus the large number of hits for garden (50), there are 292 hits. The next most important space is the workplace, with business, office and work totalling 96 hits. By contrast, there are just 14 hits for terms associated with schools (including universities), five for market, five for temple and two for museum. We can see that fengshui in these sources is concerned with little other than home and office; other spaces, in particular public spaces, are of little concern. Thus the idea of communal fengshui seems entirely absent; cases of villages or neighbourhoods complaining about damage to their collective fengshui, so prevalent from 1860–1960 in English-language materials, have vanished. The number of references to gardens indicates the continued importance of aesthetic concerns, as do the large number of hits (175) for architecture and building design. Interior spaces are much preferred over exterior ones, as urban spaces are preferred over suburban or rural. Most importantly, however, is that there are only three hits for cemetery and zero hits for grave; even when combined with the related but non-spatial terms burial, death, and ancestor, there are only a total of ten hits. Contemporary English fengshui, then, almost totally ignores what was and has been for hundreds of years arguably the most important human geographic term, at the same time cutting virtually all ties to filial piety (0 hits for 'filial') and ancestor worship.

In the raw list of results, the most common word after 'fengshui' and some articles, prepositions, and conjunctions, is 'you' and its lemmas (300

Table 2.3 Distribution of locale in English fengshui book titles, 1968–2009

Built environment	Hits	Subtotals	Percentage[2]
Home[1]	186	292	60.33%
room	18		
bedroom	6		
kitchen	5		
cook	2		
food	4		
recipe	2		
living room	1		
garden	50		
dorm room	1		
residential	8		
domestic	5		
apartment	3		
flat	1		
Work	45	96	19.98%
office	29		
business	22		
School	4	13	2.69%
classroom	4		
university	3		
academy	2		
Other locations		12	2.48%
market	5		
temple	5		
museum	2		
Interior	26	30	6.20%
inside	4		
Exterior	4	7	1.45%
outside	3		

(continued)

Table 2.3 (Cont.)

Built environment	Hits	Subtotals	Percentage[2]
Urban	11	20	4.13%
city	5		
town	3		
suburb	1		
Rural	0	4	0.82%
country	2		
village	2		
Burial	4	10	2.07%
cemetery	3		
ancestor	2		
death	1		
grave	0		
Total	484	484	100.15%

Notes:
[1] Includes: Homes, homebuyers, homeowner(s), homier, house(s), household, and housing.
[2] Does not total 100% due to rounding.

hits). Looking at all pronouns (Table 2.4), we can see that other pronouns are almost completely absent; all first-person pronouns occur only twenty-four times, and third-person pronouns occur only six times. This feature seems related to the high number of occurrences of 'guide' (133 hits) and cognate terms; Table 2.5 lists over a dozen such terms, totalling 300 hits.

These two features firmly establish the genre of most of these works as being self-help books. We can see this more clearly in the high number of hits for 'easy' (forty-two) and cognate terms in Table 2.6, where sixteen items have a total of 207 hits. This is in contradistinction with the antonyms 'hard', 'difficult', and other synonyms, totalling just nine hits; it is also in line with the preference for practical and practice (seventy-four hits total) versus theory (nine hits), also in Table 2.6, as well as the number of hits for 'complete' and its cognates (fifty-five total). Finally, we can link this emphasis on ease with the use of terms such as 'dummy' (as in the Dummy's guide to series), 'layman', 'idiot', 'beginner', 'everybody', 'learn', and 'manage' (thirty-six hits).

Table 2.4 Distribution of pronouns in English fengshui book titles, 1968–2009

Pronouns	Hits	Subtotal	Percentage
you	47	300	90.91%
your	246		
yours	0		
yourself	7		
she	1	6	1.82%
her	0		
herself	0		
his	0		
himself	0		
he	1		
they	2		
them	2		
theirs	0		
their	0		
I	3	24	7.27%
my	6		
mine	1		
me	2		
myself	0		
we	1		
our	8		
us	2		
ourselves	1		
Total	330	330	100%

One of the things that both English-language and Chinese-language sources stress over and over again in earlier periods is how difficult fengshui is to comprehend and to practice. All manuals of fengshui in Chinese are written for specialists, and are rarely if ever owned by non-professionals. Feuchtwang (2002, 255) makes the interesting observation that anyone in

Table 2.5 Distribution of terms relating to guidance in English fengshui book titles, 1968–2009

Guidance	Hits
guide	137
guidebook	2
book[1]	53
handbook	16
encyclopedia	13
workbook	11
manual	9
element(s)	8
companion	7
resource	6
almanac	5
bible	5
key	5
anthology	4
calendar	4
compendium	3
abc	2
checklist	2
dictionary	2
directory	2
map	2
planner	2
Total	**300**

Note: [1] As in 'the little book of'.

China might claim to be able to diagnose that a given (usually bad) situation is due to fengshui, but that prognosis, or what to do about it, was strictly left to the professionals. Here in our database, we see the opposite happening; fengshui is easy for you to comprehend and correct in your own home, without the need to employ a specialist.

Table 2.6 Distribution of terms relating to ease/difficulty in English fengshui book titles, 1968–2009

Ease/difficulty	hits	subtotal	Percentage
Easy	42	207	54.05%
simple	31		
step	25		
tips	19		
day[1]	16		
natural	14		
clear	12		
fast	10		
introduction	9		
quick	6		
basic	6		
key	5		
instant	4		
demystify	3		
explain	2		
just	3		
Difficult	1	2	0.52%
effort	1		
hard	0	2	
Practical	54	74	19.32%
practice	20		
Theory	9	9	2.35%
Everybody	1	36	9.40%
dummy	5		
layman	2		
idiot	4		
beginner	8		
learn	8		

(continued)

Table 2.6 (Cont.)

Ease/difficulty	hits	subtotal	Percentage
manage	8		
Complete	27	55	14.36%
comprehensive	3		
everything	13		
every	4		
all	8		
Total	383	383	100%

Note: [1] Includes daily, everyday.

Another group of words worth noting for their departure from previous meanings is the association with Western astrology and various other New Age practices, which occur a total of 103 times (Table 2.7). Although none of the terms except astrology and magic are very common, together they point to a firm linkage being established between fengshui and various other 'alternative' understandings of the way the world works, and thus to feng-shui being interpreted in contemporary English usage as neither mainstream science nor superstition, but rather something that is validated through personal experience. Indeed, 'superstition', so firmly attached to fengshui in earlier English and twentieth-century Chinese discourse, is almost absent (three hits). 'Science' fares better at twenty-nine hits, but much more common is the term 'art' (sixty-six hits).

Finally, the term environment, which with its lemmas environments, environmental, and environmentalist, gives fifty-three hits, points to a further cluster of terms which tie fengshui to environmental concerns with 176 hits (Table 2.8). This is yet another departure from earlier understandings of fengshui in both languages, and again shows the concept being interpreted in the context of emerging environmental concerns in the English-speaking world starting in the 1960s, which included a re-evaluation of 'alternative' or 'traditional' views of non-European peoples.[24]

In sum, while there is much continuity with certain core elements of the concept, such as concern with the improvement of one's situation through manipulation of one's environment, there are also significant changes, including a shift from professional to amateur agency as fengshui is fitted into the self-help-guide model, and association of fengshui with late twenti-eth- and early twenty-first-century concerns in the English-speaking world, including New Age beliefs and environmental concerns. At the same time,

Table 2.7 Distribution of New Age terms in English fengshui book titles, 1968–2009

New Age	Hits
astrology	34
magic	20
crystal	8
gem	8
holistic	7
tarot	6
New Age	4
aromatherapy	2
herbal	2
reiki	2
witch	2
conjure	1
complementary	1
fairy's	1
fragrance	1
pagan	1
palmistry	1
wiccan	1
meditation	1
pulse	2
detoxify	2
dowse	2
alternative	8
holistic	7
chakra	3
meditation	1
Total	**128**

Table 2.8 Distribution of environmental terms in English fengshui book titles, 1968–2009

The environment	Hits
planet	0
global	2
world	0
Cosmos	2
Earth	28
Environment	53
Mountains	7
Nature	9
Nature's	2
Water	27
Wind	9
ecology	7
sustainable	7
Total	153

the link between fengshui, ancestor worship, and filial piety is severed, as it becomes almost exclusively an urban, home-office-centred model for the individual, not the community.

Some, though not all, of these shifts can also be perceived in Chinese discourse on fengshui. Bruun (2003, 234–41) has documented the adoption of an environmental discourse relating to fengshui in China, first proposed by foreigners in the 1960s. Specifically, he documents the citation of English-language sources by Chinese writers, especially Joseph Needham, crediting the shift to their work, which is linked to a continued orientalist discourse regarding China as the mystical and harmonious East versus the soul-destroying, instrumentalist view of nature in the West (Brum 2003, 235–38).[25]

Bruun also documents a continued split in urban versus rural uses of fengshui, a trend that we saw emerged during the Republican era. Rural fengshui has tended to maintain more of the tradition, with a continued emphasis on burial sites and communal fengshui concerns (often in opposition to state intervention in local affairs). Urban fengshui, on the other hand, shares more characteristics with contemporary English practice, with the emphasis on home, on the individual rather than the community, on amateur versus professional agency, and with the (relative) downplaying of ancestor worship and filial piety.

We may take one Chinese manual from the 1990s as representative of these trends. Hong Pimo's *Zhongguo fengshui yanjiu* (中國風水研究 Research on Chinese fengshui, 1993) features eight chapters on fengshui for the home, followed by only a single chapter on fengshui for the grave, and then one chapter on critics of fengshui.[26] All of the discussions of basic cosmological theory occur in the second chapter, and are explicitly linked to the home as opposed to the grave. Chapter three then discusses basic concepts, with an emphasis on the need for the owner's time of birth to align with the positioning of the house. Chapter four gives explicit instructions for both location and orientation for all major items in the house which anyone could follow without recourse to an expert. Likewise, chapter five details how to arrange things like the colour scheme and lighting. Chapter six then gives several concrete examples of how these instructions may be carried out. It is only in chapter seven that we get to issues relating to the construction of houses and, in chapter eight, the house's relation to its environment.

The work thus mirrors English-language materials in important ways. It privileges interior home space as the central locus of fengshui practice; it devalues graves and burial practices, as well as community fengshui; and it empowers individuals to make decisions without recourse to a professional. Hong even feels the need to devote an entire chapter to explaining the theoretical underpinnings of fengshui, indicating he does not believe that his Chinese readers will be familiar with them. There are certainly also differences, including the fact that grave siting is still given an entire chapter, and the fact that the office as a space for fengshui practice is totally absent, but all in all, the work, if translated into English, would not be out of place in the American or British market.

Conclusion

In tracing the long and complicated journey of the concept(s) of fengshui between Chinese and English, we can see that fengshui practices, which have been around since at least the Han dynasty, continue today despite repeated attacks both from within China and without. Yet fengshui is a system of practice and, like all such systems, must constantly be maintained and renewed by succeeding generations, who adapt it to fit their evolving needs. It has undergone important changes between the nineteenth and twenty-first centuries, in a process involving intercultural dialogue between Chinese and English.

Moreover, fengshui has been bound up in discussions of the nature of Chineseness and the definition of Chinese culture. This is due to at least two reasons.

First, fengshui is intimately interconnected with other concepts that are important to the Chinese. Most importantly, it is linked to ancestor worship and filial piety which, as noted in the previous chapter, have long been central to the Confucian worldview and the organisation of Chinese society. It is also based upon certain cosmological concepts that were normalised in the Han dynasty. This correlative system of yinyang and five phases ties fengshui to the *Book of Changes*, one of the enduring classics of Chinese thought. It also links fengshui to Chinese medicine. Although I have chosen not to investigate that connection in any depth here due to considerations of space, it is indicative of the struggle to define what is considered true (bound up with discussions of what is efficacious), what is considered scientific, and therefore what is modern. The tension in English-language book titles about fengshui since the 1980s, where claims that fengshui is both ancient/traditional and modern, is beautifully mirrored in the designation 'traditional Chinese medicine' to denote what claims to be a modern, scientific, and efficacious practice handed down unchanged from antiquity. It is precisely that tension that allows fengshui to be both particular to the Chinese and yet claim to universal application.

Second, there is the Anglo-American desire to use the concept of fengshui as a short-cut to understand China and explain why it was so intractable to 'civilizing' and modernising influences. This was used as a justification for colonial and imperial attitudes towards the Chinese. That message was in turn taken up by the May Fourth generation of intellectuals in China, who rejected much of Chinese tradition in an attempt to become modern.

Yet despite claiming that fengshui is one of the keys to understanding Chinese culture, Anglo-Americans have consistently attempted to understand it in terms of their own frames of reference. We have seen this in some of the earliest writings in English on fengshui, which equated it variously with Western astrology, Middle Eastern genii, local gods, vapours and miasma, magnetism, aesthetics and, in the twentieth century, ley lines, ecology, environmentalism, and a wide range of New Age beliefs.

Throughout this period, we have also seen that the concept of fengshui has been enmeshed within the larger discourse on truth, which plays out in the intersection of science, religion, magic, and superstition. Since the 1980s, the linking of fengshui to New Age beliefs has complicated this equation. New Age beliefs have challenged the hegemonic claims of science to define truth, and the tendency to associate fengshui with this wide spectrum of beliefs and practices thus in a sense once again asserts the primacy of

Western categories in understanding fengshui even when it is used to challenge Western orthodoxy. We will see in our discussion of face that this is also an important factor in the history of that concept.

This Anglo-American understanding has had a significant impact on the way that fengshui is conceived in Chinese. In the nineteenth century, it prompted some Chinese to make instrumental use of it in quarrels with foreigners. During the May Fourth Movement it led to the wholesale denunciation of fengshui along with other traditional values such as filial piety, and after 1949 in the PRC, the government has been vociferous in branding fengshui as superstition, in opposition to science and orthodox Marxism. Even the partial tolerance of fengshui can be seen as at least partly justified by the more positive evaluation of fengshui in English-language publications since the 1980s.

Finally, we have seen that today there are at least three overlapping spheres of fengshui practice, which exhibit significant differences: the Chinese countryside, Chinese urban areas, and Western urban areas. Although they share a common cosmological theory and a basic understanding of fengshui as the manipulation of one's environment in order to improve one's health and success, they differ markedly in how those goals are to be achieved.

Notes

1 Based on a survey of 150 texts in the online electronic corpus of the Chinese Text Project (http://ctext.org/), the earliest use of fengshui in its modern meaning occurs in the *Collected Conversations with Master Zhu* (朱子語類 Zhuzi yu lei), dating to 1270 CE, while the other two can be traced back to the Han dynasty (202 BCE–220 CE). Bennett (1978, 1) notes that their order of popularity in use before the twentieth century also followed this order.

2 See Smith (1991, 131) for a list of other terms that have sometimes been used, and Shi Zhen (1995) for a more detailed discussion of the origin and meaning of each term.

3 In fact, at least one source classifies geomancy under 'arithmetic' (Curzon 1712, 2:124 and 328).

4 The term that he transcribes, 地理 (*dili* according to modern hanyu pinyin transliteration), at some point in the nineteenth century became the translation for the concept of geography, and it remains the standard term for that concept today in China. This initially led me to believe that geomancy must have been coined as an equivalent for this earlier Chinese term, due to the link between it and the earth (geomancy means literally 'earth magic'). However, the earliest text that I have been able to find that uses 'geomancy' to describe any of these practices dates to 1815 (Morrison 1815–23), so this remains to be proven.

5 Since the 1736 edition omits some material, including the second passage relating to fengshui, I use the 1738–41 translation in my discussion.

6 I have been unable to identify the Chinese writer, who is nowhere named in the text. In terms of its substance, the text upon which the translation is based seems to be very much in the neo-Confucian tradition of Zhu Xi, but if it is a translation of his work, then it is a very loose paraphrase. The introduction to the translation calls the Chinese author 'modern', so it might be by a later neo-Confucian.

7 Another example of a text that reproduces Du Halde almost word for word, but without the attempt at cultural substitution, is the anonymous *Chinese Traveller* (1772). Winterbotham (1795, 357) also reproduces in a more digested form the same material on fengshui but omits the term, saying only that there are 'quacks' who offer advice about choosing burial sites.

8 Although we have seen that dili is still in use in China in the nineteenth century to refer to fengshui practices, Morrison already equates it with 'geography'.

9 See for example Mid-Atlantic Geomancy https://www.geomancy.org/index. php/dowsing, Geomantica https://www.geomantica.com/, and Geomancy Australia https://www.geomancyaustralia.com/

10 Of these, Allom (1858, 2:103) uses the phrase 'influence of the atmosphere' as his translation of fengshui, while the other three use no term at all.

11 Although not exhaustive, a partial list of examples where luck or lucky is used to describe the function of fengshui include Semedo (1655, 74); Mayers (1867, 188); Gray (1878, 1:315–17 and 2:7–8); Henry (1885, 136–38); Moule (1891, 64); Smith (1899, 20–21 and 314); Selby (1901, 142); Ball (1904, 500); Hemyng (1904, 42); Johnston (1910, 118 and 267–68); Wilson (1913, 1:15); Moule (1911, 309); Moule (1914, 56); Couling (1917, 417); Buck (1931, 252); Hobart (1936, 130); and Lin (1939b, 301).

12 A good example of how knowledge regarding different parts of the 'East' were often conflated. See St. André (2018c, 36–54 and 114–19) for more on this tendency.

13 The passage that Moule alludes to is not actually part of the original *Sacred Edict* composed by the Kangxi Emperor, but rather belongs to one of the commentaries appended to it. The relevant passage can be found in Milne's translation (1817, 165–66).

14 These two views about the relationship between fengshui and filial piety can be found in Chinese sources as well. See Smith (1991, 152–55) for other examples besides the *Sacred Edict* and Pu Songling's story.

15 Elsewhere, MacGowan (1907, 65) says 'The Chinese are an exceedingly superstitious people, but they are capable of being intelligently religious when they become acquainted with the truths of the Gospel'. This nicely encapsulates both the difference between superstition and religion—superstition is something that others (erroneously) believe in, while religion is an intelligent and rational belief system—and also points to the fact that they are closely allied, as both are belief systems, which is why the Chinese can transition from one to the other.

16 He goes on to make the classic colonial argument that, since the Chinese have not shown themselves capable of discovering natural science, it falls on foreigners to save them from themselves.

17 Tambiah's discussion of Tylor occurs on pages 42–51 of his book; below I have gone directly to Tylor and quoted from his work, because some of the points I want to make about Tylor are not made by Tambiah.

18 After listing these characteristics from Tylor's work, Tambiah (1990, 46) notes that most if not all of these strategies are also a very good summary of what Thomas Kuhn refers to as 'normal science'.

19 Bruun does not go so far as to embrace a purely instrumentalist view of fengshui and, interestingly, neither do later British colonial officers who had to negotiate with local villagers in the New Territories over fengshui matters every time they wanted to implement any sort of public works project. More than one report by acting officials bring up the charge of crafty villagers cynically using fengshui concerns either to block development or to squeeze as much compensation as possible out of the government, only to reject the hypothesis and emphasise the sincerity of the people's belief in fengshui (Hayes 1963, 143–44; Hayes 1967, 22). Hayes (1967, 28–30) in particular also cites similar earlier cases from the 1920s, while Coates (1968, 171–74) gives a fine example of the persistence of Tylor's view of the magician as both fraud and dupe, arguing that the villagers both believe in fengshui sincerely (they are duped) and use it instrumentally to extract maximum advantage from their conflict with the government (they are frauds). Boxer (1968, 230–33) gives confirmation of these reports and adds others examples, while Hayes (1980, 155–56) provides an example from 1978.

20 Carlitz (2007) provides a detailed analysis of these two plus a third version. The two versions are available together in a modern reprint, which I have used for my analysis. See the afterword for details regarding earlier records of the historical case and details of the publication of both accounts (Liu and Zhu 2003, 323–25).

21 See St. André (1998) for a detailed discussion of the differences in plot structure between Chinese courtcase fiction and Anglo-American detective fiction.

22 https://www.cuhk.edu.hk/ics/rccc/database_main.html

23 Dili was excluded from the search because by the late nineteenth century this term was increasingly used as a translation for 'geography'. There was some overlap in the two results lists, which I ignore here because I am interested in when and how often 'mixin' collocated with either term. Coverage between 1834–90 is relatively sparse, because periodicals were basically unknown in China until they were introduced by Westerners; the six journals in the database that began publication before 1890 were all managed by foreigners, mainly missionaries.

24 See Bruun (2003, 233–35) for a conclusive refutation of the idea that fengshui before 1950 was in any way concerned with environmental thought.

25 After spending most of his book offering a sympathetic view of fengshui as empowerment of the individual and locus of local resistance to state power,

Bruun (2003, 248–52) concludes his discussion of the relation between feng-shui and the environment in China on a much bleaker note, arguing that the supposedly environmentally friendly system has not prevented peasants from extracting the maximum yield of a limited range of crops and farm animals from the land, to the detriment of all other species. For an example of the opposite view, see Anderson (1980, 15–27).

26 The latter is rather short (twenty-six pages) and probably included to forestall problems with the censors, as fengshui was and remains classified as superstition by the Chinese government.

3

Face

Face, like fengshui, is not a 'mainstream' concept in Chinese thought. While even fengshui practitioners can trace their roots back to the *Book of Changes* and the development of Han cosmology so that they can at least claim a lineage that links them to classical learning, face has no such genealogy. In fact, it could be argued that, until face is taken up in Anglo-American discourse of the nineteenth century, it may not even have existed as a distinct concept separate from a variety of related terms in Chinese such as honour, reputation, or standing.

Like filial piety and fengshui, however, face undergoes a similar fate of rapid devaluation in the nineteenth and early twentieth centuries, first in English and then in Chinese. We will also see that there are strong links with the term guanxi, to be discussed in Chapter 4, both in terms of content and in terms of its modern fate. This relationship with guanxi, in turn, links face to filial piety.

In the modern period, however, face sees a radical departure from either filial piety or fengshui. The latter terms mean essentially the same thing in populist and specialist discourse, and there is even a tendency as we have seen for fengshui to become more popular and less specialised, the proliferation of how-to manuals attesting to the loss of the fengshui expert's monopoly on diagnosis. Face, however, moves from being a strictly popular term to being adopted as a 'scientific' one, first in sociology and then in linguistics, in a much more rigorous fashion than fengshui ever was. This leads to a vigorous but possibly ever-more-abstruse debate about the relation of face both to politeness theory and to other concepts related to reputation and, ultimately, to the thorny question of whether it is possible to develop a universal definition for face or if each culture has its own variety.[1]

Face in Chinese culture up to 1800

As Hu noted decades ago (1944, 45), mian, usually in the compound *mianmu* (literally, face and eyes), is the older of the two terms in the metaphorical sense of reputation. The earliest texts that I found date approximately to the end of the third century BCE for mian, whereas I did not find an occurrence of lian in this sense until the late Ming, approximately 1600CE.[2]

Face in the metaphorical sense does not appear in any of the ancient classics, and is by no means conceived as important. The earliest example I could find was the *Shuo yuan* (說苑 Garden of stories), compiled probably in the Qin or early years of the Han dynasty (circa 200BCE), where in four passages mianmu is being used in this way (*Shuo yuan* 4, 10; 4, 14; 5, 24; and 9, 20).[3] All instances are in direct speech, and three of the four are quite similar in structure: 'what face do I have (to do X)' or, in one case, 'I cannot face people'. There is also one example where face is linked with another term *yu* (譽 'reputation' or 'repute'): '[his] face is disreputable' (面子不譽) (*Shuo yuan*, 2, 16). Thus in all cases it is the *lack* of face that receives comment and, in one case, as a result the person commits suicide by slitting his own throat (*Shuo yuan*, 9, 20).

This pattern of being limited to reported speech, dearth rather than plentitude, and sometimes extreme reaction (suicide) continues in other Han dynasty texts. Yet the term remains relatively scarce; many more of the texts I examined in this period, some quite lengthy, did not have the term. From 209 BCE, the putative date of the first two texts that include the term, through the end of the Later Han dynasty (220CE), the term occurred in fourteen texts, while there were forty-seven texts in the database with no occurrences; thus only 23 per cent of the texts contained the term, always as part of reported speech. This suggests that the term mianmu to mean metaphorical face or reputation was considered colloquial. It does not occur in poetry, in formal essays, or in any classical compositions.

In later dynasties, the term becomes somewhat more common, occurring in twenty-two out of forty-five texts examined up through the end of the Ming Dynasty, but this may partly be due to the fact that the texts in the database from later periods rapidly become more vernacular in nature. In these texts it is still restricted to dialogue, still mostly in the sense of lack, and instances of suicide as a result of not having face continue to occur.

In the later period there are some uses of mian in the literal sense of 'face' that are cognate and do not involve dialogue. An example from the tenth-century compendium of stories *Tai ping guang ji* may illustrate this. After having wasted all of the money that an old man had given him, Du Zichun sees the same old man again and 'Zichun, overcome with shame, covered his face and walked on [so as not to be recognised]' (子春不勝其愧, 掩面而走) (*Tai ping guang ji*, Shen xian 16, Du Zichun, 6). Here we see that Zichun literally cannot 'face' the old man, Zichun having wasted the opportunity given to him. The phrase 'to cover one's face' (*yan mian* 掩面) is associated with a sense of shame (kui 愧).

Gradually, we begin to see other sentence patterns in which metaphorical face occurs, notably '*kan* X *zhi/de mian*' (看X之/的面), which means literally 'seeing X's face, [I will or will not do something]'. This is often translated more loosely as 'out of respect/consideration for X', 'seeing we are friends', 'for X's sake', or 'as a favour to you'. The earliest example I found comes from the novel *The Water Margin* (*Shui hu zhuan* 1334), where this formula occurs eight times in the first five chapters alone. The formula often involves A not punishing B out of consideration for the face of X (where X can sometimes be A or B, or sometimes be a third party C). An interesting example occurs in the slightly later novel *Romance of the Three Kingdoms* (*San guo yanyi* 1360), the opening paragraph of chapter four, where Dong Zhuo wants to kill Yuan Shao for having challenged his authority at the end of chapter three, but is restrained from doing so. After Yuan Shao leaves, Dong Zhuo says to Yuan Kui: 'Your nephew has no sense of propriety, but "seeing your face", I will pardon him' (汝姪無禮, 吾看汝面, 姑恕之) (*San guo yanyi*, 4, 1). In this case, face seems to be linked not just to reputation, but also to power and, more importantly, looking ahead to the discussion of my fourth key concept guanxi, to connections. A discussion follows in which Dong Zhuo's advisors worry that the Yuan clan is strong enough to cause serious problems, and so Yuan Shao is not only pardoned, but also given an official post. In this formulation, face is consistently something that is possessed in abundance, rather than the usual lack that we have seen in other expressions. Person X has so much face that the normal course of events (often a punishment of some sort) is averted; here 'face' is far removed from any possibility of shame, being rather honour, reputation, or status, a quality that translates into (political) power.

Lian in the metaphorical sense of 'face' finally makes an appearance in the late Ming, in *The Plum in the Golden Vase* (*Jin ping mei*). This novel, which is rich in colloquial expressions, contains a wide variety of usages both for lian and for mian. Based on a count of occurrences in the first twenty-five chapters (one-quarter of the work), the most common expression is the one just discussed, 'seeing X's face', but there are at least nine others:

- *Mei mian* (沒面; lacking face)
- *Mei lian jian* X (沒臉見X; lacking the face to see X)
- *Shuo mianzi hua'r* (說面子話兒; speak the language of face, i.e. 'put a good face on things'
- *Bo mianpi* (博面皮; to thin the skin on one's face, i.e., 'lose face')
- *ti mian* (體面; appearances)
- *po lian* (破臉; to break one's face, i.e. put oneself forward without regard for face)
- *tian xiulian* (添羞臉; add shameful face, endure opprobrium)
- *na shenme lian jian* X (拿什麼臉見X; what face do you have to meet X)

- *zai X lian shang wu guang* (在X 臉上無光; on the face of X there is no light, i.e. lose face)
- *[you] lian zuo zhu* ([有]臉做主; have the face to make decisions)

Doubtless these expressions, and more, were circulating in speech prior to the publication of this novel. Of note is that the usage continues to be in reported speech only and, although no one commits suicide because of a loss of face, it is seen as a motivating factor in many minor decisions throughout the novel.

In the Qing dynasty (1644–1911), the number of different expressions continues to multiply, while the early compound mianmu largely drops out of use, replaced by *mianpi* (面皮 face skin) *mianzi* (面子 where zi is a nominalising suffix), *lian zui* (臉嘴 face and mouth), *lian kong* (臉孔 face hole), *she lian* (舍臉 house face), and *lian mian* (臉面 the two terms combined). The most common verbs used with it are *you* (有 to have) or *wu* (無 to lack; also its synonyms *mei* 沒 or *meiyou* 沒有); other verbs include *gei* (給 to give; also its synonym *shang* 賞), *shang* (傷 to injure or destroy), and *zhang* (仗 to rely on). Intriguingly, the verb *diu* (丟 to lose), which is borrowed into English in the early nineteenth century as part of the phrase 'to lose face', is a relative latecomer. The first occurrence I found was in the mid-Qing novel *Dream of the Red Chamber* (circa 1791; see *Hong lou meng*, 101, 13).

In none of the works consulted in Chinese up through the early nineteenth century is face a problematic category. Indeed, as hinted in the introduction to this chapter, face flies so far below the radar that no one discusses it, let alone criticises it. Unlike filial piety and fengshui, there are no books, or even essays, devoted to the topic of face as far as I have been able to determine right up through the nineteenth century. There are not even cautionary tales regarding people who are overly concerned with face; although large collections of tales by Feng Menglong and Ling Mengchu contain fairly frequent references to face, it is always incidental to the plot. Face is simply not considered to be an important concept in China up through the nineteenth century.

Since it does not appear in classical texts and was not a mainstream concept, it should be no surprise that the early Catholic missionaries paid no attention to it.[4] It is rather the British who bring 'face' to the attention of Europeans, first through dictionaries and glosses of translations from Chinese, and then through the gradual adoption of these phrases into English.

The earliest occurrence I have found is in Morrison's dictionary, where this metaphoric meaning of face occurs twice in the first volume (Chinese to English) and several times in the third part (English to Chinese), but always as a literal gloss on a Chinese expression (Morrison 1815–23, vol. 1 part 1:324; vol. 1 part 2:537; vol. 3, part 2:159; vol. 3, part 2:198; vol. 3, part 2:363; and vol. 3, part 2:234). Morrison captures several of the current usages, but in no case does he represent any of these phrases as being part of the English language.

Similarly, there are two uses in English texts from 1818 and 1829, where it appears as a literal translation of something spoken by a Chinese. Abel (1818, 391), in an appendix to his account of the Lord Amherst mission to China, presents the translation of a document supposedly written by the Chinese emperor to explain why the British ambassador's audience with the emperor did not proceed: 'I, the Emperor, have really not the face (am ashamed) to appear before the ministers beneath me, who are labourers for the state.' A decade later, Sir John Francis Davis, in his translation of a Chinese novel, includes the sentence 'I truly have not the face to go back to her just now', accompanied by a footnote that explains that this is a literal translation of a Chinese expression (Davis 1829, 1:225).

We have to wait until 1834 for the first intimation that face is being used in its metaphoric sense by people speaking some variety of English. This comes through the word-for-word translation of the phrase 'diu lian' as 'to lose face', which John Morrison lists in his *Chinese Commercial Guide* (1834). Although the expression does not contain any loanwords, Morrison places this phrase in a 'Glossary of words and phrases peculiar to the jargon spoken at Canton', where 'jargon' refers to the pidgin English that had emerged in the eighteenth century in Canton and Macau, partly modelled on pidgin Portuguese. Thus at this time he obviously considered this phrase, and the other terms he listed, as not a phrase in general circulation. The *Oxford English Dictionary* also attributes the meaning of face as 'reputation, credit; honour, good name' to the English community trading in China, linked to the expression 'to lose face'.[5]

Although the term is attested in pidgin English in 1834, it does not seem to have been in widespread use in publications on China until after 1890. It occurs occasionally in translations, most notably the translation of a short novel by one of James Legge's Chinese converts, which has the rather awkward 'with what face can you stand before any man?' (Shen 1843, 223). Yet the vast majority of texts about China ignore its usage. John Francis Davis's *The Chinese* has a chapter on 'Character and Manners' and two chapters on 'Manners and Customs', in which he describes how the Chinese consider it rude to refuse a request directly and therefore often lie (Davis 1836, 243–44), as well as the niceties of gift-giving (287) and the courtesies involved in visiting (295–97), but no mention of the term face, even though we have seen that he was familiar with it from his translation in 1829 and elsewhere in *The Chinese* he gives a derivation of another pidgin term, 'chin-chin' (1836, 296). Neither does Gutzlaff's *China Opened*, which describes 'excessive' politeness at banquets (1838, 486–87) and the use of 'ridiculous' politeness at formal occasions, which he links to a tendency to lying and deceit (504–5). Gutzlaff also had extensive knowledge of Chinese and worked in Canton on and off, so must have been familiar with pidgin.[6] Henry Sirr's *China and the Chinese* has a section on national character but no mention of face, although he talks about the upper class's sense of honour and preference for death over capture (1849, 2:416–23); Scarth's *Twelve Years in China* (1860), which discusses the 'Chinese character' at length and describes the sort of polite behaviour associated with face, makes no mention of this term either. Likewise W. H. Medhurst jr, in *The Foreigner in Far Cathay* (1873), devotes an entire chapter to 'The Character of the Chinese', discusses how the Chinese have a sense of dignity which is different from Western honour, but does not use the term. The latter two men spoke at least one Chinese dialect, so it is unlikely that they had never come across it.

Of 132 texts related to China examined between 1804–93, there were a total of only twelve occurrences of 'face' in the metaphorical sense, or 9.1 per cent, inclusive of the ones already discussed. Two examples from these works, Huc's *Chinese Empire* (1855) and Cooke's *China* (1859), will demonstrate its usage between 1834, when it is listed as a phrase in pidgin English, and the point when it emerges into more general use. In Huc, face is presented as part of the translation of a speech given by a Chinese man: ' "How shall I dare to show myself?" he kept repeating. "I have *lost my face* (that is, been dishonoured)" ' (Huc 1855, 1:382). Note that Huc used italics to mark the phrase off as unusual, and felt that an explanation needed to be added after it in parentheses, indicating that this usage of the word 'face' was not deemed current.[7] This conclusion is reinforced by the way in which the two occurrences of 'face' in Cooke are framed in quotation marks, as part of the indirect reported speech of a Chinese mandarin taken prisoner by the British and interrogated at various times (Cooke 1859, 404 and 406). In sum, face is evoked in these works solely as an explanation of Chinese behaviour, not in a general sense, but rather to explain the actions of specific people in one-off usage. It is still, as with the case in Chinese, largely confined to reported speech or enclosed in quotation marks to mark it off as a foreign expression that is a literal translation from Chinese.

The association of 'oddity' with the English spoken in the trading port, remarked upon as early as George Anson's *A Voyage Round the World* (Anson 1748), in which he refers to it as 'the ridiculous jargon of broken English', grew as pidgin English came into wider use in the nineteenth century (Bolton 2003, 159). This 'strangeness' of pidgin English was, by extension, taken to be a mark of inferiority of the Chinese. An 1858 anonymous

jingoistic jingle in Punch serves as a good indication of the negative connotations associated with it:

'A Chanson for Canton'
John Chinaman a rogue is born,
The laws of truth he holds in scorn;
About as great a brute as can
Encumber the Earth is *John Chinaman*,
 Sing Yeh, my cruel *John Chinaman*
 Sing Yeo, my stubborn *John Chinaman*;
 Not Cobden himself can take off the ban
 By humanity laid on *John Chinaman*.
With their little pig-eyes and their large pig-tails
And their diet of rats, dogs, slugs, and snails,
All seems to be game in the frying-pan
Of that nasty feeder, *John Chinaman*.
 Sing lie-tea, my sly *John Chinaman*
 No fightee, my coward *John Chinaman*
 John Bull has a chance—let him, if he can
 Somewhat open the eyes of *John Chinaman*

        (London *Punch*, 10 April 1858)

Pidgin constructions (or at least, what the editors of Punch considered to
be Pidgin) employed here ('Sing lie-tea', 'No fightee') are directly associated
with negative characteristics (sly, cowardly behaviour) and also indirectly
with other undesirable characteristics, such as a disregard for truth (line
two), a characteristic widely imputed to the Chinese (see Davis 1836 and
Gutzlaff 1838) that becomes directly associated with the concept of face in
Smith (1894). Two decades later, Charles Leland could compose an entire
book mocking such language. His *Pidgin-English Sing-song, or, Songs and
Stories in the China-English Dialect* (1876), which made the Chinese out to
be ridiculous through the employment of pidgin as a comic language, contains three examples of face (Leland 1876, 44, 54, and 79). Although Leland
provided an introduction that outlined the rules of pidgin and a vocabulary
list of pidgin expressions, he still felt that he had to provide a footnote for
it: '*To take one's face away*, the common Chinese expression for causing
shame or defeat' (54). In all three cases, face is a negative attribute, part of
the overall problematic nature of the Chinese. No wonder, then, that as having, losing, or preserving face became associated with the Chinese national
character, it was taken as a negative attribute.[8]

 Thus we should not be surprised that Cooke's use of the phrase 'to lose
face' is an early example of negative connotations that coalesce around the
term. In his book where he uses the phrase, Cooke is describing a Chinese

official who was in charge of putting down a rebellion in South China and had supposedly ordered the killing of over 100,000 rebels. Cooke notes that the official Yeh

> goes to bed about eight o'clock, and while we are reading or writing, or playing chess, he sleeps the sleep of infancy—an unbroken slumber, apparently undisturbed by visions of widowed women or wailing orphans. This man-killer, after slaying his hundred thousand human beings, enjoys sweeter sleep than an innocent London alderman after a turtle dinner. So false are traditions; so false are the remorseful scenes of Greek and English tragedies.

> But, although our great mandarin is at peace with his own Chinese conscience, he has an evident horror of his living countrymen. He has 'lost face' with them, and the greatest fear he has is the being made an exhibition to a Chinese rabble. We were malicious enough to ask whether he would like to go to the Hongkong races. (Cooke 1859, 404)

Here Cooke is making a sharp contrast between Europeans, who have consciences, and the Chinese, who are motivated only by a fear of other people's bad opinion. For Cooke, there can be no question that there is something wrong with a man who can execute 100,000 people, many unjustly (this is the subject of subsequent conversations with Yeh regarding how the rebels were tried), and not feel any pangs of guilt, only to be horrified by the possibility that the 'rabble' might jeer at him.

These findings regarding the use of 'face' in books about China are confirmed by ProQuest's Historical Newspapers database. An extensive search was carried out across forty newspapers using a variety of keywords in tandem (since the word 'face' can be used in many different ways, most unrelated to the concept under consideration here). Of the 171 instances of metaphorical face found between 1824 (first hit) and the end of 1894, all but a handful limited the application of the term to Chinese people. The first non-Chinese example refers to Koreans (1877), the second to the British colonial government of Hong Kong (1882), and then there is one reference to an American in 1890 and two referring to foreigners in China in 1893. The vast majority of examples are still reported speech and, as with the Chinese usage, there is sometimes a tie with suicide. The application of the formula to a few non-Chinese, however, and the occasional use of it in discursive prose rather than in reported speech signals a gradual adoption of the phrase in English.

The situation changes drastically in the 1890s, due to the work of Arthur Smith, who seems to have done more than any single author to fix the association between face, national character, and inferiority. The first chapter of his *Chinese Characteristics* (1894) is in fact entitled simply 'Face', which he argues is 'a key to the combination lock of many of the most important characteristics of the Chinese' (1894, 17). Smith argues that face is based on a love of theatricality among the Chinese; in other words, 'face' is a mask that the Chinese wear, and as such it is contrasted with 'reality' and 'fact', which are associated with Westerners (16–17). He draws an explicit comparison with the concept of taboo from the South Sea Islands, and claims that they both are 'deserving only to be abolished and replaced by common sense' (17). His two main examples of how face operates are especially telling. The first is of a coolie who steals a tennis ball and then, when accused, 'finds' it in a corner of the court; the second is of a servant who steals a penknife and, again, 'finds' it somewhere when accused. In both cases, we can see that, first of all, the Chinese are being portrayed as thieves, and second, that 'face' consists of the desire to avoid owning up to some bad deed; they 'save face' by 'finding' the objects when it becomes clear that their master suspects them of the theft. These tales of how inferior domestics, when confronted, refuse to admit their mistakes, stand in stark contrast to the many stories for children in British and American fiction where owning up to one's fault is key to becoming a better person.[9] Although the chapter is only three pages long, its pride of place establishes it as the 'key' to understanding the Chinese.

Smith also seems to introduce, or at least popularise, several new expressions relating to face, principally through the use of new verbs; before him, face is almost exclusively associated with the verbs 'to lose' and 'to have'. Besides these two expressions, Smith tells us that one can 'keep face' or 'give face' (17). There must be a 'balance of face' among parties in a quarrel in order to resolve it successfully, and face is something that must be preserved 'intact' (17).

More importantly for later developments, Smith seems to have coined 'to save face', which is not a direct translation from Chinese, but rather a neologism formed as the opposite of 'lose face'. This phrase is also bound up with negative Anglo-American stereotypes of the Chinese, being often used to describe the great lengths to which someone will go to *avoid* losing face, and is associated with that lack of respect for the truth that the *Punch* doggerel attributed to the Chinese.[10] Thus 'to save face' is instrumental, while the original 'lose face' refers to a post-factum situation. This phrase does not seem to pre-date Smith's text; the earliest example for it given under the entry on 'face' in the *Oxford English Dictionary* is from 1899. This 'native' neologism in English is now firmly established in the lexicon, and has become much more common than the original 'to lose face': a search on Google (27 January 2021) for the phrase 'to save face' generates roughly five times as many results as 'to lose face'.[11]

In Smith's later work, *Village Life in China*, he insistently brings up 'face' in his discussions of goings-on in the village, continuing the idea that face is the single most important characteristic of the Chinese. In particular, he repeats his argument that the Chinese are theatrical and that saving face is a form of putting on a show for others (1899, 69). This theatricality means that 'the Chinese frequently appear as if psychologically incapable of discriminating between practical realities which are known to be such, and theoretical "realities" which, if matters are pushed to extremities, are admitted to be fictitious' (68). Other examples revolve around important social rituals such as funerals (181, 187, 190, 191, and 194); divorce (289); the explanation for high suicide rates (322–23); the mechanism by which bullying works (214); and how discord both within the family and between in-laws often arises or is worsened (325–26 and 335). Of particular note is that, in the discussion of face at funerals, Smith links face concerns to economics: poor people cannot afford to save face (187). Concomitantly, rich people are sometimes forced by face concerns to disregard monetary issues. When a rich man has lost his father, he would lose face if he did not act the part of a grief-stricken son, too distraught to care about money. This allows his relatives and friends to fleece him mercilessly during the funeral, and he has no recourse, because to admit knowledge of the theft would cause him to appear unfilial (186–87).

In Smith's work then, face ceases to be simply an expression that the Chinese use, as reported in direct quotations, and starts to become an independent concept in English to explain what makes the Chinese different from Europeans and Americans. It is endowed with an economy, both in the sense that it is something that can be gained, lost, and saved, and also in the sense that its workings are linked to the economic standing of the individual in question. It is also linked to filial piety on the one hand and to international diplomacy on the other, the idea of balance of face being explicitly compared to the balance of power in Europe.

Face, national character and Chinese modernity, 1895–1939

After the great success of Smith's book (Hayford 1985, 153), the term 'face' as an explanation for what is peculiar to the Chinese becomes more common. Among fifty-nine texts relating to China in the two decades following the publication of Smith's book, twenty-two (37.3 per cent) used the phrase, up from the 9.1 per cent we saw in texts published up to 1894. The fact that sinologists such as E. H. Parker feel they can use the term to explain actions of the Chinese government with no need to gloss it attest to it becoming more commonly known (Parker 1903, 75). Many of these works follow Smith's lead in devoting extensive sections to the concept. MacGowan, like Smith, devotes the entirety of a chapter to the term in two books (MacGowan 1909, 283–94; 1912, 301–12), and uses both the expressions 'save face' and 'lose face' in several other parts of both books (1909, 148, 171, 172 [3 times], 243, 275, and 278; 1912, 165, 189–90, 261, and 297). Gilbert (1932, 27–29) repeats many of the points made by Smith, and his examples also include those of a servant stealing and then needing to 'save face' over the theft.

A particularly interesting example can be found in the translation of a famous essay of the reformer Zhang Zhidong by Samuel Woodbridge. In the original, at the beginning of part two, chapter five, when discussing what is wrong with the use of foreign teachers paired with interpreters as a means of educational reform in China, Zhang notes that such teachers may know English but not be learned in the particular subject matter on which the foreign teacher is lecturing, leading them either to omit or distort some of the meaning (Zhang Zhidong 1990, 111). Woodbridge's translation amplifies this point, saying that a teacher would do so 'in order to save his face' (Chang 1900, 110). Here Woodbridge draws a clear connection between face as an undesirable characteristic and China being held back from modernising, a lesson that is completely missing from Zhang's original text.

Since MacGowan is one of the three sources cited by Goffman, an important mid-century theorist of face, it is worth noting three facets of his discussion of the concept. First, like Smith, MacGowan emphasises the theatrical nature of face (1912, 301, 305–6). Second, he is perhaps the first person to divide face into two different aspects. One he identifies as 'honour, reputation', bestowed by others on the self; this is realised literally in his example, where a departing magistrate is presented with an 'umbrella of the myriad people', a physical object he will bring home to hang in the ancestral hall as a token of the face he has been given by the populace (302–4). The other aspect of face is 'self-respect, or dignity', which is more an inner feeling, but which in turn leads to an outward show (hence the theatricality of face); his examples here are very similar to Smith, involving coolies and servants (304–7). Finally, MacGowan ends his discussion by noting one positive aspect of face: because the Chinese are conscious of their own face needs, they can be extraordinarily sensitive to the face needs of others, going to great lengths to help everyone preserve their face. As we will see later in the chapter, this aspect is crucial for Goffman in making face into the glue that binds individuals together in social interaction.

Despite the occasional positive note regarding how face functions in Chinese society, these works by and large continue to emphasise that a preoccupation with face is one of the things that is wrong with China. Douglas (1899, 382) uses it when describing the cowardly actions of the Tongzhi emperor, and in another work to describe the machinations of the Empress Dowager during the Boxer Rebellion, when she is portrayed as willing to let the country go to wrack and ruin 'to save our "face" in the eyes of the world' (Douglas 1901, 443). Johnston (1910, 210) gives it as a rather sordid motive for the parents of a woman who, after completely ignoring her during her lifetime, suddenly take an interest in her after her death by insisting upon a lavish funeral for her as a way of gaining face, while Woodbridge (1919, 89) notes how an act of face-saving ruined an expensive gift from the British to the Chinese emperor.

Gilbert, whose book title *What's Wrong with China* already indicates that the characteristics he discusses are negative, contains a good example of how Smith's emphasis on international relations is taken up by later writers. After theorising that the basis cf face in China is the inability of the Chinese to laugh at themselves or to be laughed at by others because of 'the ingrained self-esteem' that gives them 'a sense of dignity commensurate with their imagined importance' (1932, 26–27), he predictably gives an example involving a servant who had cheated his mistress. Because his mistress was Chinese, rather than expose him, she let him know indirectly that she knew he had embezzled funds entrusted to him and he found a way to repay her, in the process inventing a 'little fiction' about 'mythical' repairs.

> She accepted the money without demur and the servant went about his usual duties as though nothing had happened. The old lady had recovered her money and the servant had saved his face.

> *In the same way* both the Imperial and the Republican Governments of China have, in their relations with foreign Powers, published thousands of the most transparent lies in official and very solemn proclamations, to save the nation's face without deceiving anyone, and have felt satisfied in each case, because their pretensions were not challenged, that the nation's face was fully and adequately saved. (28–29; my emphasis)

The bridge between the private individual and the state here, 'in the same way', reaffirms a homology between states and individuals. Gilbert goes on in the following pages to detail how considerations of face are behind all of the moves that China has made, and to explain that face considerations mean that China cannot be expected to accept foreign countries as equals; China can only conceive them as inferiors or, at gunpoint, temporarily as superiors. Thus the Chinese concept of face forestalls any possibility of 'normality' in international relations as Europeans and Americans conceive it (30–33).

Besides the non-fiction works about China published by Anglo-American publishers, there was also a certain amount of 'missionary fiction', stories written either by missionaries or their children and set in China. Alice Tisdale Hobart's *Yang and Yin: A Novel of an American Doctor in China* (1936) provides an excellent example of how ingrained the idea of face

as an explanatory concept for everything that was backward about China
had become by the 1930s. In the novel Peter Fraser, a medical missionary,
causes his cook to resign because working for a foreigner who washed his
own floors was too great a loss of face, in a continuation of the long line
of stories involving servants being concerned about how their master's status reflects upon themselves (Hobart 1936, 88).[12] After this setback, Fraser
becomes more aware of face and how it works among the Chinese, leading
him later in the novel to use it as an argument to help stop the theft of opium
from the medical stores of the mission, noting that the subsequent misuse of
the stolen opium represented a 'loss of face to the Christian church' (124).
He also persuades the local prison warden to improve hygiene, saying that
it will give him 'great face' if the prisoners do not fall sick (329). Loss of
face is given as the reason that the matriarch of Scholar Sen's family drives
everyone in the family to commit suicide: 'The family was disgraced. Face
was gone. The wild scene of frantic women and frightened men, as the lao
tai tai drove them to the killing of themselves' (208). Face is also given as a
reason for the decision of someone to leave on a pilgrimage (276).

But the crowning moment in the discussion of face comes when Fraser's
former apprentice, now in charge of the mission hospital and working with
Fraser on a study of snails as the possible intermediate carrier of flukes that are
plaguing the locals, is offered a job elsewhere. At first, he is tempted to take it,
as he feels that his position as head of the mission hospital is a 'face-losing' one
(360), but it would mean giving up the study of the snails, and so he decides
to discuss it with Fraser, who advises him that the people who are offering him
the job are only doing so because they want to use him for something:

> 'That price you know. I am speaking frankly, John, disregarding that great
> matter of face.' It was the first time that Peter had ever spoken openly to any
> Chinese of the matter of face. 'I have never alluded to the wiping out of your
> family or its causes, or to your position since. But I know there is some special
> price they ask of you in going to the capital.'

> And for the first time in his life, Lo Shih looked at himself with the mask of
> face removed. It gave him a curious feeling of intellectual vigor, which cut
> through the subterfuges of his present life. Influence in far-away Szechuan was
> what they wished to buy from him. He did not hide the fact now behind the
> high-sounding word 'service'. Through him they wished to gain control of the
> revenues of that center of opium, the province of Szechuan. (362)

Here we see clearly presented Smith's idea that face is theatrical, a mask
that, once removed, allows the Chinese man to see his 'true' self for the first
time in his life. The 'intellectual vigor' that he feels is that of clear Western
logic, which enables him to understand that his life has been a web of sub-
terfuges, glossed over with high-sounding but ultimately empty words like

'service'. As a result of this revelation, made possible by Fraser, Lo Shih decides to turn down the offer, remain in his 'face-losing' position and complete the medical study they have begun. In sum, he learns to disregard face and becomes a modern, Western doctor.

Usage in newspapers supports the idea that Smith's understanding of face as a negative characteristic of the Chinese was widely accepted. An article from the *Chicago Daily Tribune* in 1898, more than four years after Smith had published his revised edition, draws extensively on his work to argue that 'face' allows foreigners to understand recent political events in China, specifically why the Chinese leased land to Germany indefinitely for a nominal fee rather than cede it outright; it was to 'save face'. The article ends by wondering if 'the belated and luckless Oriental personage [China]' will be able to 'catch on to the inevitable modern world movement' or if he will be 'compelled to swallow his "face" and get off the stage as best he can' ('Chinese "Face"' 1898, 30). The use of the verb 'swallow' here, which is unusual, suggests that for the author of the piece 'face' is linked to pride and anger. It also makes clear, as already noted, that face has negative connotations in English; this is not the 'pride in a job well done' but rather the 'pride that comes before a fall'. At the same time, we see the now familiar link between a characteristic peculiar to the Chinese and a resistance to the forces of modernity. Other articles from this time period also make this link, for example an article from 1893 in the *North China Herald*, which compares the internal revenue collectors along the canals, which are run by the Chinese, with the Maritimes Customs office, which is run by foreigners. In the former, graft and corruption are rampant and, when foreigners resist paying bribes to expedite delivery of goods, the Chinese revenue collectors claim that this would make them lose face ('Chinese Internal Customs' 1893, 536).[13] Face is thus linked to bribery, corruption, inefficiency, and backwardness, versus the modern workings of the Maritime Customs, where such customs have been banished.

Finally, an example from a slightly later date both illustrates this link between face and a refusal of modernity and also connects it to filial piety:

> Hit a Chinese suddenly with a new idea and he will rebel. It is not by any means a matter of stupidity. Down in his heart he may from the very first realise that the new idea is an improvement, but he is not going to 'lose face' as it were, and play false to the ancestors whom he worships, by showing any precipitancy in admitting this intruder upon his regular routine of thought and action. (Missemer 1925, 18)

Here losing face is associated with change, which change is, of course, necessary for the arrival of modernity in China. It is also linked to ancestral worship, because if a Chinese loses face, then it also reflects badly upon his ancestors, first because his own loss of status reduces the status of his family, and second because by adopting a new way of doing things, he is obliquely criticising his ancestors for not having done the same.

At the same time, the borrowed phrase 'to lose face' and the coined phrase 'to save face' begin to be used more frequently to describe the actions of people other than the Chinese, along with the less frequently used expressions 'to have face', 'to give face', and 'to gain face'.[14] In these cases, the negative connotations already established are retained; in other words, since concern with 'face' is a bad thing, whenever you want to criticise someone for their concern with appearances, honour, or reputation, using 'face' to describe those motivations in English automatically stigmatises the person. Returning to the ProQuest Historical Newspapers database, for the period from first record to 1894, 'face' is limited to China, Korea and the United States; between 1895 and 1914, that list expands to twenty-four countries and then in the next two decades to forty-two, with a similar number of different nationalities or ethnic groups.[15] It also becomes increasingly common for face to be attributed to abstract entities, such as towns, cities, states, nations, and corporations. Moreover, as seen in Table 3.1, although China and the Chinese continue to represent the lion's share of cases, there is a steady growth in the number of cases that occur in other countries, especially outside of Asia. Here we can clearly see 'face' becoming a naturalised concept in English by the beginning of World War One, and growing more common as time goes on.

Entrenched as the concept of face had become in English discourse about China that circulated in China's treaty ports and among missionary writers, Chinese intellectuals in the late Qing and early Republican Era (1895–1925) debated this concept as well, linked to the notion of national character (Huters 1998, 575–76).

Table 3.1 Distribution of face according to country and ethnicity in newspapers, 1824–1932

	1824–94	1895–1914	1915–32
China	92.2	65.9	52.7
Other Asian countries	4.7	7.7	10.8
Non-Asian countries	3.1	26.4	36.5
Chinese	88.3	60.6	47.7
Other Asian people	5.0	8.0	11.7
Non-Asian peoples	6.7	31.4	40.6

Wu Jianren, the hard-hitting reformist satirist of the late Qing, whose work *A Strange Case of Nine Murders* was discussed in the previous chapter on fengshui, also attacked face, albeit obliquely. In his *Ershi nian mutu zhi guai xianzhuang* (二十年目睹之怪現狀 *Bizarre Happenings Eyewitnessed over Two Decades*), which was serialised in Liang Qichao's reformist magazine *New Fiction* and then published in book form in 1909, eighteen different expressions use either lian, mian, or a combination of the two. In several cases these are satirical scenes, and so by association face has negative connotations in the text. More interestingly, however, are two passages where he links economics and face. The first one is rather straightforward: while discussing what the narrator should do about a certain Master Li (李公) who has been trying to force him to sell his land, a friend You Yunxiu (尤雲岫) says 'nowadays, if you have money you have face' (此刻世界上, 有了銀子, 就有面子) (*Ershi nian mutu zhi guai xianzhuang*, 19, 9). Yunxiu then goes on to discuss how this rich person's son is 'spreading bribes around Beijing to buy connections' (到京裡去買關節), and therefore his friend should forebear from getting involved in a dispute with the family; the narrator takes his advice and, in the type of comic reversal typical of the novel, decides to give his land to the bully for free. Here face as social reputation is reduced to a simple economic equation, whereby the more money you have, the greater your face, a rather cynical view of the increasing role of money in modern society, while at the same time linking it to connections and corruption, which will be taken up in the next chapter on guanxi. The second passage, which reinforces this message about the almighty dollar, features Shu Danhu (舒淡湖), who seeks out a reporter friend Hou Aochu (侯翺初) to ask a favour. Aochu first upbraids him for only seeking out his friend when in need and then, when Danhu promises to 'thank' him for his help (i.e., offers money), tells a tale of being cheated by another acquaintance who promised to 'thank' him for a favour. Danhu then takes out one hundred dollars and gives it to Aochu up front, at which point Aochu completely changes his attitude and starts to call Danhu his 'old friend' (老朋友); Danhu explains what he wants Aochu to do, and Aochu 'seeing the "face" of the hundred dollars, nodded his head in agreement' (看在一百元的面子上, 也就點頭答應了) (*Ershi nian mudu zhi guai xianzhuang*, 66, 1). Here what seems to be a straightforward bribe is transformed into a matter of face by anthropomorphising the money so that it can be said to have 'face' which Aochu respects by acceding to its wishes that he help Danhu.

There is also some evidence in early Chinese-language Hong Kong newspapers that face had begun to have more negative connotations in this period. A search through the titles of news reports from this period in the database 'Old HK Newspapers' with a restricted set of keywords turned up some interesting results from the first decade of the twentieth century.[16]

In an article '*Shuo qingmian*' (說情面 'Speaking of Face') from June 1904 in *The Chinese Mail* (香港華字日報), the anonymous author bemoans the fact that China only pays attention to face, not the welfare of its citizens, and that 'thus all the weakness and chaos [described earlier in the article] stem solely from face' (是種種弱昧亂亡之因無不由情面二字) ('Speaking of Face', 1904). In September of the same year another article is published whose title makes a similar point: '*Banshi zhi gu mianzi*' (辦事只顧面子 'Prioritizing face when working').

But the concept of face as the basis of the Chinese national character is most famously taken up in Chinese by Lu Xun (魯迅 1881–1936) in the 1920s. Lydia Liu has a perceptive discussion of the way in which Lu Xun took over such arguments about national character. Besides noting the importance that virtually all modern critics place on face as part of national character, especially in the character of Ah Q from 'The Story of Ah Q' (Liu 1995, 65–69), she also picks up on the way in which Smith's understanding of Chinese character is based on his relations with his servants (57). Just as another May Fourth intellectual, Hu Shih, had criticised his fellow for being anti-scientific underachievers with his Mr Approximation (差不多先生), Lu Xun effectively internalises the European and American critique of Chinese culture under the Qing dynasty. Face for Lu Xun becomes one of several markers of traditional China, which must be rejected in order for modern China to emerge; in this sense he agrees with Smith's pronouncement that face, like taboo, must be abolished if China is to become a modern nation. Liu notes that this is accomplished by the creation of a modern, Enlightenment-like literate narrator who can be both Chinese and yet transcend this national character (75–76).

Besides the figure of Ah Q, Lu Xun also takes up the concept of face elsewhere in his voluminous writings, in particular two of his short prose works. In a 1926 piece, which is an entry in his 'Mashang zhi riji' (馬上支日記, Instant branch diary), Lu Xun for the first time discusses Arthur Smith's work directly. He records buying a Japanese work by Hideo Yasuoka on the character of the Chinese people that was heavily influenced by Smith. Yasuoka devotes the first chapter, like the 1894 edition of Smith's work, to face (which Lu Xun here translates consistently as timian), while other chapters are devoted to topics such as fatalism, lack of sympathy and cruelty, stinginess, and being extremely superstitious.[17] Lu Xun then moves to a direct discussion of Smith's work, where he notes Smith's emphasis on the link between theatricality of the Chinese and their concern with face (Lu Xun 1998, 3:326). Because this is a diary, the entry is not very systematic and moves on to other topics, but it is important in documenting the fact that discussion of face as a national characteristic was already in the air; Lu Xun notes that a translation of Smith in

Japanese had appeared twenty years previously (326). More importantly, Lu Xun seems to accept the criticism of the Chinese as being overly concerned with face 'if we examine the matter from inside and out, we can see that this [discussion of face] is not overly harsh' (我們試來博觀和內省，便可以知道這話並不過於刻毒) (326).

Eight years later, Lu Xun penned what may be the first essay in Chinese devoted exclusively to the topic, 'Speaking of Face' (說面子) (1934), where he develops his ideas more systematically. He begins by noting the fact that, unlike the Chinese, who take face for granted, foreigners pay great attention to the topic, seeing it as the key to understanding the Chinese (Lu Xun 2006, 4:514). He then goes on to tell an anecdote of foreigners bullying a minister in his office into acceding to their demands, only to be shown out by the side door rather than the main entrance. This slight allowed the Chinese official to feel that the foreigners had no 'face' while the Chinese had plenty of 'face', and therefore that China had gained an advantage over them (514). This example of the illogic of face concerns then prompts Lu Xun to reflect on broader questions of what face means for the Chinese.

In his discussion, he uses a variety of expressions with both lian and mian, and posits that there is a line, above which actions cause people to gain face and below which actions cause people to lose face. Yet the line is not fixed; sitting by the side of the road with your shirt off to pick lice out of your clothes is not a loss of face for a rickshaw puller, while the same action would be a terrible loss of face for a young woman of good family. Thus he argues that people of higher status are more likely to be concerned about losing face, although there are some actions that a rich person can do without losing face that would cause a poor person to lose it (514–15). He goes on to give three examples of the types of problems caused by wanting face, but then notes that it is one thing to say that 'wanting face' can be bad, and another thing to say that 'not wanting face' is good. Here he explicitly ties his criticisms of face to existing criticisms of filial piety: 'if we support the idea "don't practice filial piety", there will be people who accuse us of encouraging people to beat their parents; if we support the idea that men and women are equal, there will be people who accuse us of promoting indiscriminate sex' (如果主張"非孝"，就有人會說你在煽動打父母，主張男女平等，就有人會說你在提倡亂交) (515). He then gives an example of a beggar who thinks he has gained face because a rich man has deigned to speak with him, although what he said was only 'get out of here!' (滾開去) (516), and notes that in Shanghai, getting kicked by a foreigner is not considered a loss of face. These two anecdotes illustrate the ridiculous lengths that people will go to in order to claim some sort of connection with the rich and powerful, and again point to the close connection between the concepts of face and guanxi.

Lu Xun's works reveal the extent to which the Chinese concept of face had changed by the 1930s. First and foremost is the fact that face has emerged as a concept that needed to be discussed, driven by foreign discourse about its importance in explaining the Chinese character. Not only had the Chinese taken over foreign belief that face was important, they also accepted that face was a negative characteristic that made the Chinese look ridiculous, and that face was a theatrical mask that allowed the Chinese to divorce themselves from 'reality' as perceived by Europeans. Important for later developments is the idea that face is relative, not absolute, with the rich and powerful being more concerned about saving or losing face than the poor. We also see that face is linked with other 'national characteristics' holding China back from modernity; for the current study, it is especially noteworthy that both filial piety and guanxi are linked to face. Finally, we see the continued indiscriminate mixing of expressions using both lian and mian for what seems to be the same concept.

Another iconic writer of the period who addressed the issue of face was Lao She (老舍 1899–1966). In the novel *Er Ma* (二馬 *Mr Ma and Son*), set in London, a Mr Ma and his son try to run an antique shop that his deceased brother had started. About halfway through the novel their shopkeeper Li Zirong has a conversation with the elderly Mr Ma about how poorly the shop is doing and offers to resign in order to save them the expense of his salary. Mr Ma, however, cannot believe that Li is being straightforward with him and interprets this as a way to ask for a raise, and in the ensuing cross-purpose dialogue, when Mr Ma says to Li 'let's not damage anyone's face now' (自要別傷了面子), the narrator interrupts the story with a three-paragraph disquisition on face, giving various examples of how face interferes with modern life, including one about its pernicious influence on business practices (Lao She 1999, 1:509). The narrator goes on to rant about how 'Everything that the Chinese people care about crouches underneath "face"; as long as everyone's face is kept up, well then, who cares about reality!' (中國人的事情全在 '面子' 底下蹲著呢, 面子過得去, 好啦, 誰管事實呢!) (1:509). Here and later in the section, the idea that we have seen in Smith's work that the Chinese are not concerned with 'reality' but only appearances is brought out forcefully.

Lao She also later wrote an entire play entitled '*Mianzi wenti*' (面子問題 The problem of face). Written at the end of 1940 and published in 1941, it details the trials and tribulations of Mr Tong Jingming. According to the cast of characters at the beginning of the play, Tong is an upper-class official whose 'life's work has been a fight for face' (畢生事業在爭取面子) (Lao She 1999, 9:297). He is surrounded by a cast of like-minded sycophants who first aid and abet him in acquiring face so that they, too, can gain face, only to abandon him after he loses his job due to incompetence. Tong's obsession with face leads him to make a series of bad decisions, for example playing mahjong with his 'friends' even though it is bad for his health, being forced to accept people sponging off him and his daughter, and even to consorting with collaborators, which costs him his job and drives him to suicide (9:298, 320–21, 360, 370–71).

By contrast, two groups are represented as not being concerned with face: the workers, represented by the character Zhao Qin, who suddenly finds himself rich and is pulled into Tong's orbit because of it; and the modern man and woman, represented by the doctor Qin Jianchao and his nurse Ouyang Xue. Interestingly, there seems to be some danger that the worker will become enamoured of face, as he is cultivated by various people in Tong's orbit in order to try and cheat him out of his money, while the modern professionals seem completely immune to the attraction of face and indeed make the strongest statements condemning face in the play, seeing it as lies, a waste of time, nonsense, trivial matters, et cetera (9:306, 340–41, 313, 325–26, and 341). Since it is wartime, face is also opposed to patriotism, with the doctor and nurse volunteering to go to the front while the others sit around talking about face; the nurse even says to Tong at one point 'you people talk of face, we doctors and nurses talk of the spirit of service!' (你們講面子, 我們當醫生和護士的講服務的精神!) (9:313).

By associating face concerns with the aristocratic Tong and his bourgeois hangers-on, Lao She clearly implies that face concerns are part of the old order, and that the workers and modern professionals do not share them. By extension, face is something that does not concern the Communist Party.

Both Lu Xun and Lao She were members of the League of Left-wing Writers and associated with the Chinese Communist Party, but antagonism towards face was not limited to the left. Lin Yutang, writing in English for an American audience in the 1930s, echoes the sentiment of his countrymen that face is holding China back from modernity. After calling face 'that hollow thing which men in China live by' (Lin 1935, 200) and giving a long list of examples of how consideration of face leads to absurdities, he closes his discussion of the matter by saying: 'When face is lost at the law courts, then we will have justice. And when face is lost in the ministries, and the government by face gives way to a government by law, then we will have a true republic' (203). In other words, face is a negative characteristic that must be eliminated from China in order for it to become part of the modern world. He reiterates this point in the epilogue, when he claims that the triad of 'Face, Fate and Favour .... have made the rule of Justice and the weeding out of official corruption impossible' (363). Although the work I am quoting from here was published in English, its content was largely assembled from a series of articles written in Shanghai, published for an English-speaking Chinese audience in his journal *The Little Critic*.

May-ling Soong Chiang, the wife of Generalissimo Chiang Kai-shek, also wrote an article condemning the Chinese propensity to be concerned with face, along with six other 'deadly sins'. First published in Chinese in the *Central Daily News* (中央日報) in Chongqing, she later self-translated the essay into English as part of her book *China Shall Rise Again* (Soong Chiang 1941). Of the seven characteristics, face receives by far the most attention (four out of fifteen pages in the English translation). She calls it a 'curse' and claims that 'more incompetency and ruin have been engendered by "face" in social, official, political, and national phases of our life than one could conceive or care to admit' (39). She gives an example of how face interferes with the efficient running of government, and then goes on to note that it has 'direful reactions in other directions' including discouraging patriotism, frustrating idealism, lowering morale, and making people 'spiritless automatons', suppressing creativity and leading to disaffection that could foster rebellion (40). Most especially, she notes that it has interfered with

> the full and intelligent utilization of the knowledge and experience of foreign technical and other experts who have, from time to time, been engaged at great expense from many countries, and been employed in many spheres, by our government. In this respect the old regime permitted the initiation of a system of fanatical face-saving which even now, if not suppressed, will impede the aims of our government, discourage and render idle the experts, rob the country of wealth and power, and irreparably retard industrial expansion. (41)

Here again we see the insistence that concerns over face are holding China back from modernity, being antithetical to experts and industrial expansion.[18]

The negative associations of face in Chinese continue after the establishment of the PRC in 1949. A search for all permutations of terms relating to face in the *People's Daily* database proved too unwieldy because of the large number of hits, but a search for the binome 'mianzi' limited to titles of articles shows a clear trend. There were 143 hits stretching from 1958 through 2020, and in all of them face is portrayed in a negative light. The first article in 1958 contains an unequivocal condemnation of face: 'Face and arrogance can kill' (面子、架子，是害死人的東西; Wei Yiqing 1958). Other articles emphasise that certain actions, judged to be a loss of face under the old order, were no longer so, for example 'Admitting One's Mistakes to the Masses Is Not a Loss of Face' (向群眾承認錯誤並不丟面子) (Qu Yaoxin 1965), whose title is in direct contradiction to the earlier understanding we have seen in Cooke about the Chinese official having no conscience yet fearing to lose face in front of the masses. In others we see the contrast between face and reality, first popularised by Arthur Smith, repeated, as in 'Face and Truth' (面子與真理; Wen Hua 1980), an article that calls face a 'feudal class concept' (封建等級觀念); or the more explicit 'Speak Truth, Not Face' (要講真理，不要講面子; Chen Yun 1981), which is a speech first given in 1945 but reproduced in 1981 as a call to reform after the excesses of the Gang of Four. The most recent example continues in this vein; 'Wasting Food and Drink Does Not Mean You Have Face, It Means You Have Lost Face' (餐飲浪費，不是有面子而是丟面子; Zhang He 2020). In official discourse, face remains thoroughly discredited right up to the present.

Gain in translation?

By the late 1930s, then, one might expect that 'face', having acquired negative connotations both in China and abroad, would be on its way out as an analytic category. Far from disappearing, however, depending on one's reading of face, it either rises from the ashes like a phoenix or, like the hydra, grows back heads as fast as they can be chopped off.

First, despite the fact that the concept of face in English was originally restricted to the Chinese, its gradual movement into the general lexicon has meant that it continues to be available for a wide variety of usages, most often with negative connotations but sometimes in a more neutral sense. The online *Oxford English Dictionary* gives a quotation from Evelyn Waugh's *Brideshead Revisited* (1945) that illustrates the former and a quotation from G. Jones, *History of the Vikings* (1968) as an example of the latter. It occurs in a wide variety of genres, from science fiction (Herbert 1965, 185 and 429; Laumer 1973, 39; Foster 1979, 10) to fantasy (Pratchett 2011, 162), detective fiction (Packard 1930, 283), biography (Malan 1990, 59, 72, 158 and 357), and such classics as *From Here to Eternity* (Jones, 1951, 163, 339, and 597). Many native English speakers are unaware of its origins as a calque from Chinese, as it has entered the general lexicon.

It does still, however, have a tendency to be associated with China, often as a marker of 'Chinese' thought, with a large number of works that are either translated from Chinese or set in China employing the concept. Justin Hill's *The Drink and Dream Teahouse*, set in Shaoyang, contains dialogue such as ' "Have you no face?" he demanded, "shaming the family"?' (2002, 29). The series of thirteen crime novels written in English between 2000 and 2023 by Qiu Xiaolong, a Chinese immigrant to the United States, and set in Shanghai featuring Inspector Chen, all employ the concept of face on average three to five times per novel. In the first novel, *Death of a Red Heroine*, a potential loss of face is one of the reasons that spurs Inspector Chen on in his investigation when he comes under pressure to abandon a case for political reasons (Qiu 2000, 517). In *A Loyal Character Dancer*, face comes up in several different places, including concerns over China losing face in front

of foreigners (Qiu 2002, 22, 207–9 [four times], and 318), government officials or departments losing face (151 [three times] and 277), and even as a
motivation of one of the criminals (334). In *Red Mandarin Dress*, besides
several casual uses of the term, Inspector Chen reflects on the concept of
face and wonders if Western psychology has an equivalent term (Qiu 2007,
74). In all these works the dialogue is meant to represent speech or thought
processes in Chinese, and there is a clear implication that face concerns are
somehow unique to the Chinese.

The Garden of Forking Paths: fissures in the meaning of 'face'

In English, whether one is perceived as having lost or saved face, the underlying message is that one is overly preoccupied by keeping up appearances.
In Chinese we have seen that there exists a wider variety of expressions
relating to the concept of 'face' and, indeed, there are two different nouns,
lian and mian that can be used.

In the 1940s, an article appeared in an anthropological journal that
attempted to differentiate between these two terms in Chinese and establish
them as having slightly overlapping but largely complementary meanings.
Hu (1944) locates the meaning of both terms within the umbrella English
term 'prestige', a native English category which she claims is universal in
human societies everywhere. By contrast, different cultures have a variety
of local terms to express ways in which one may attain prestige; lian and
mianzi are two of these. She then makes the claim that mianzi is associated
with 'the kind of prestige that is emphasised in this country [the United
States]: a reputation achieved through getting on in life, through success and
ostentation. This is prestige that is accumulated by means of personal effort
or clever maneuvering' (1944, 45). Such prestige is mainly dependent upon
the external environment. Lian, however, is more of an 'internalised sanc-
tion' and something that, although perhaps present in American society, is
not 'formally recognised' (45).

Hu is anxious to establish that the word mianzi, which is a kind of prestige
that Americans know and love, is present from earliest times in China. Toward
that end, she quotes two texts from the fourth century BCE that use the term
mian (1944, 53), and argues that lian is a recent North China upstart that has
slowly encroached upon the older, Central-Southern term (46). In doing so she
perpetuates the myth of Southern Chinese as being the 'true Chinese'.[19] Most
of the rest of the article is taken up by a detailed list of phrases using these
two terms but, interestingly, she discusses lian first, even though she has just
argued that mianzi is much older and, by association with American 'success
and ostentation', seemingly more central to the universal category of prestige

into which she places both (45). She begins with 'diu lian', precisely the phrase that was translated from Chinese into English in the nineteenth century as 'lose face', and dwells at length upon this expression for almost five pages, as the most common one. She then lists four additional uses of lian before going on to detail sixteen uses of mianzi in the sense of 'prestige'.

In retrospect, it seems clear that Hu was operating within a 'scientific' linguistic discourse that believed that different terms necessarily denoted different concepts. There had to be a reason for why there are two different terms in Chinese, and it was up to the linguistic anthropologist to try and find a rationale for it, based on different collocations. Moreover, the labelling of these two contrasting types of prestige as external and internal clearly indicated the influence of the contemporary dichotomy between externally imposed shame and internally felt guilt, a distinction that was then used to label cultures as either 'shame cultures' or 'guilt cultures' (see inter alia Benedict 1946). Oddly, although Hu presents China as inventing, or at least valuing the internal lian, most writings on the subject put China and Japan under the 'shame' category, that is, a society where the *external* pressure exerted by society was the main check on the individual's selfishness. This disjunction between internal lian and external shame may be the reason why, although the relationship between preserving or losing face and shame should be obvious, she never draws the readers' attention to it.[20]

Hu's argument can be read in two ways. On the one hand, we can interpret her splitting of lian and mianzi, and the association of mianzi with a known type of prestige in America, to a desire to argue for the peculiarly 'Chineseness' of lian, specifically diu lian, to lose face. In this reading, 'to lose face' is again strongly associated with a particular region of China and a particular time period (roughly the Mongol invasion, so by implication nomadic, foreign, and barbaric), a local aberration of prestige that, by spreading across China, has warped the Chinese concept of prestige and led to the deplorable situation described by Arthur Smith, Lu Xun, Lao She and Lin Yutang.[21] Or, if we wish to emphasise what she says about lian as not being formally recognised by Americans, but by implication present in American society, then we can see her article as an attempt to say that lian describes a second universal facet of prestige, one which has hitherto not received proper scholarly attention merely because English lacks a term to distinguish it. It is this indeterminacy that makes her work so interesting.

In either case, there is a definite revaluation of the concept of face, although at the price of it becoming subservient to the concept of prestige. There is also an overlap between the two concepts of mianzi and lian with contemporary anthropological debates over the difference between shame and guilt cultures and other dichotomies in social science research.[22]

Hu's distinction between lian and mianzi has been widely reproduced in subsequent literature in Chinese writings (see for example Ho 1976), even though we have seen that there is a richer, more complex range of vocabulary to describe overlapping phenomena in Chinese. To my mind the division is, like that between shame and guilt, hard to maintain, but we will see that Hu's distinction was used in the 1980s and 1990s to argue against Brown and Levinson's model.

That the split in meaning between lian and mianzi is not necessarily obvious to native speakers of Chinese, even acting as trained ethnographers, can be seen in the work of Martin C. Yang, who three years after Hu's article wrote an ethnographic monograph describing his home village of Taitou, located in the northeast of China. Here is his definition of face:

> 'Face' is a literal translation of the Chinese character *lien* or *mien*. Although *lien* or *mien* means just what the English word face does, the Chinese expression *tiou lien* (losing face) or *yao mien-tze* (wishing a face) has nothing to do with face in our usual understanding of the term .... When we say in Chinese that one loses face, we mean that he loses prestige, he has been insulted or has been made to feel embarrassment before a group. When we say that a man wants a face, we mean that he wants to be given honor, prestige, praise, flattery, or concession, whether or not these are merited. Face is really a personal psychological satisfaction, a social esteem accorded by others. (Yang 1947, 167)

Yang does not make Hu's crucial distinction between the two terms, yet, like Hu, he sees face as a local Chinese term used to describe social facts that are basically a subset of prestige, insult, honour, or embarrassment. Since face is only a subset of prestige, there are many places elsewhere in the monograph where shameful or embarrassing situations are discussed without mention of the term face (29, 71, 104, 109, 117, 119, 133, 149, and 152). Yang also puts great stress on the social nature of face, but for him the social means, crucially, onlookers, not the interlocutor. If only the two participants are present, 'then bitterness may be roused but not the sense of losing face', which seems to tie it to shame rather than guilt (168). Since loss of face is a social event, restitution must also be social; in his village, the most common way of doing this is a public banquet, ostensibly to thank the mediator(s), with one or both parties admitting responsibility by paying for it and, in good theatrical tradition, involving speeches (166, 168).

Given later developments, it is of particular interest that the discussion of face occurs in Yang's thirteenth chapter, entitled 'Village Conflicts', and that the sentence immediately preceding the above definition reads 'Since a number of village conflicts are caused by hurting somebody's "face", it is necessary to discuss the losing or gaining of "face"' (167). Elsewhere he notes that social conflicts may be resolved through the intervention of someone with greater face than the participants (165) or through the desire of one or both participants to give face to the mediator (171). Thus face is identified primarily as an issue that both causes and, at times, helps to resolve conflict. Outside of this chapter on conflicts, face is only mentioned five times, mainly in relation to the difficulties of acting as a local official (which involves many conflict situations; 178 [twice] and 185) and as part of a saying Yang translates 'When you are going to beat a dog, you had better consider the "face" of the animal's master. If one does not punish a neighbour's child, one should not punish a neighbour's dog' (49), which again situates face in conflict situations. Nowhere does he tie concerns with face to politeness. The saying just quoted, for example, merely encourages people to refrain from aggressive acts in order to avoid hurting someone's face, rather than to act politely, and the description of what happens at a restitution banquet implies that, far from behaving politely, the parties may be barely civil to each other (166).

Again of interest because of the later model developed by Brown and Levinson, Yang develops a list of factors that influence the degree of face involved, including power relations and social distance. Yang comes up with a total of seven factors.

More interestingly, unlike Brown and Levinson, for at least three of the seven factors Yang sees the relation between varying the intensity of the factor and face as being parabolic rather than linear. For social distance, Yang states categorically that there can be no issue of face between close relatives, for example husband and wife, but that with more distant kin, with neighbours, et cetera, as distance increases face concerns also increase within the social circle (168–69). Therefore, an arbitrator brought in from a neighbouring village may be able to resolve a conflict between men of high standing in the village, because he has more face (165). A man visiting a distant city where no one knows him, however, may do all sorts of face-losing actions with impunity (169). So face concerns for Yang are centred around the circle of people with whom one has regular contact, or who may know one's family and neighbours. Only if the deeds of the man in the distant city become known in his village will he lose face (169). For Yang, then, face is clearly linked with shame, a social pressure on the individual to conform, where the social is circumscribed by local boundaries.

In terms of social status, again, face concerns increase if the action or insult is committed by someone of inferior status towards a superior (whereas an insult by a superior will involve less or no loss of face; here we may recall Lu Xun's dictum that being kicked by a foreigner in 1930s Shanghai represents no loss of face); but when the distance is extreme, say a member of the gentry and a beggar, then face concerns again diminish and the gentry will take no notice of the beggar as someone so far removed as not worthy of attention (167–68). Indeed, the gentry may *gain* face among onlookers by ignoring a beggar's insult and preserving his equanimity (168). Equally, Yang notes that the lower one's class, the less face one has to lose, and so interactions and insults between poor peasants do not result in loss of face, whereas the same action between two members of the gentry might result in great loss of face and a major feud (167 and 170). This finding to an extent matches with Lu Xun's and Lao She's association of face concerns more with the upper classes.

Finally, age is likewise a parabolic factor. The very young are relatively immune to face concerns, whereas increasing age involves increasing concern with face, until a maximum is reached by those in middle-age, because they have acquired more social prestige and therefore have the most to lose. In old age, however, face concerns diminish (169).

To sum up, for Yang face is a unified concept but influenced by a wide variety of factors, mainly in a parabolic fashion that mirrors the limits of various social groups. While it arises in social interaction, it seems to be a type of prestige closely related to the inverse phenomenon of shame, and can be stored up and maintained by the individual. Yang's understanding of face is therefore not radically social, as some people have argued Goffman's to be. This can be seen clearly at the beginning of Yang's discussion, quoted above, where he says he needs to discuss 'the *losing* or *gaining* of "face"'; in other words, face is a *thing* that individuals can accumulate or lose. The final sentence of his definition, 'Face is really a personal psychological satisfaction, a social esteem accorded by others' (167), seems to embody the paradox of something that is at once socially bestowed but becomes personal property. Finally, going against the grain of the gradual extension of face beyond China that we have seen in general English writing, it is firmly situated within Chinese culture; while Yang describes a wide variety of situations in his village to demonstrate how it works in practice (170–72), he never suggests that the term is applicable outside of China.

De-racinating 'face'

In 1955, Erving Goffman published a paper entitled 'On Face-work: An Analysis of Ritual Elements in Social Interaction' which was later republished in a collection of his essays on social interaction (hereafter cited as Goffman 1967). Goffman acknowledges in a footnote that he has read Smith (1894), Hu (1944), Yang (1947), and one other work on Chinese society that discusses the Chinese concept of face. Yet his own development of the concept departs fairly radically from those discussions in several ways.

First, Goffman attempts to divorce the term from its Chinese origins. His text opens with the universal claim that 'Every person lives in a world of social encounters', and goes on to define face in terms of the 'line', that is, 'a pattern of verbal and nonverbal acts by which [someone] expresses his view of the situation and through this his evaluation of the participants', that in turn leads to a 'stand', that in turn constitutes one's 'face' (1967, 5). The essay ends with a return to this notion of 'a universal human nature' comprised of various parameters which each society may emphasise more or less, but are constrained to take into account (44–45).

Whereas for both Yang (1947) and Hu (1944) face was firmly rooted in Chinese culture, for Goffman, 'to lose face' can already be described as a colloquial expression 'in our Anglo-American Society' (1967, 9). When he wants to use another collocation that is not usual in English, 'to give face', he does however characterise this as Chinese, and there are several footnotes that refer to Chinese conceptions of face. Thus there persists a trace of the Chinese origin of the concept. Certainly Goffman draws on the writings about Chinese face for some of his categories, not just 'to give face', which he acknowledges, but also for example on page forty his discussion of people who are either too thin-skinned or too imperceptive seems drawn from Hu's discussion of thin and thick-skinned behaviour (Hu 1944, 54). He may have drawn on Yang's discussion of the social nature of face, although his understanding of what this means is somewhat different, because Goffman does not seem to need a third person present in order for face concerns to arise. He also seems to have been influenced by Smith's discussion of face as being essentially a mask when he refers to a line as something that everyone 'tends to act out' (Goffman 1967, 5), to face as 'the role he appears to have chosen for himself' (11), and face-saving actions as 'traditional plays in a game or traditional steps in a dance' (13).

Second, Goffman rejects the phrases 'to lose face' and 'to save face' as analytical categories, preferring to coin a whole range of new collocations for the term face, and assigns them meaning based on their relation to a person's 'line'. A person can 'have face', 'maintain face', 'be in face', 'be out of face', or 'be in wrong face' (6–8). This relation between 'line' and face further divorces his understanding of the term from its origins. Only after detailing the meaning of these new expressions does Goffman note that 'in our Anglo-American society', the colloquial 'to lose face' 'seems to mean to be in wrong face, to be out of face' while 'to save face' is tortuously defined as 'the process by which the person sustains an impression for others that he has not lost face' (9). Goffman thus divorces the term face from its Chinese and pidgin English roots.

Goffman may have chosen it because his interest in micro-sociology, or 'the study of face-to-face interaction in natural settings' (1), meant that a certain amount of serendipitous linguistic play was thereby made possible. There is first his dwelling on 'face-to-face' social interaction as the arena of face-saving; on page nine he uses the term 'shamefaced' as an extreme form of being out of face, and on page thirty there is a pun: 'Hinted communication, then, is deniable communication; it need not be faced up to'. This playfulness belies the otherwise scientific tone of the article.

Although Goffman departs fairly radically from earlier conceptions of face, divorcing it from the Chinese context, a tradition of studying face as a concept with Chinese roots continues at least up until the 1990s, mainly following Hu (1944). Thus after face had acquired two rather specialised meanings for internal and external sense of prestige, a second split develops between the work of those who have followed Goffman, of divorcing the concept of face from the original Chinese context, stressing its universal features, and coming up with new collocations and further subdivisions; and those who continue on from Hu (1944) to treat face as mainly associated with Chinese culture. To a certain extent, this mirrors the split in popular usage between face as a general lexical item that can be used to describe anyone and the persistence of a strong association with the Chinese.

In contrast to Goffman, who deracinates the term face, Ho (1976) begins by drawing attention to the Chinese origin of the concept, citing etymological dictionaries of English that identify it as a loanword. He then goes on to adopt Hu's distinction between mianzi and lian, although, rather confusingly, he says that the terms mianzi and lian are often interchangeable in Chinese, even if there is a distinction in the way in which face is judged, either on character (lian) or on 'amoral aspects of social performance' (mianzi) (Ho 1976, 867). In other words, he believes that Hu was mistaken in inventing a distinction between lian and mianzi, but then accepts the distinction as creating two valid categories, even if it is inaccurate to use lian and mianzi as labels for those categories. He then observes that despite the work of Goffman and others, face is not a commonly used category in the social sciences. The rest of his paper is spent demonstrating first that face is a distinct and therefore useful category, and second that it has application outside of Chinese society, even if the term originates there (868–69).

For the purposes of this study, the most interesting part of Ho's discussion comes on pages 878–80, where he advances an extremely detailed argument to distinguish face from prestige. This is vital to his two main conclusions, that face is a distinct and therefore useful category for social scientists and that face is a universal. Earlier both Hu (1944) and Yang (1947) had argued that face was a subcategory of the larger, universal category of prestige mainly applicable to China. Ho turns this argument on its head, claiming that while prestige is almost identical to face and the two are easily conflated, face is a broader and more basic category than prestige. This paves the way for the concluding section, which argues that face is in fact universally applicable. In the end for Ho, face is useful in highlighting the problems of Western cultures, which over-value the individual, and therefore tend to deny the importance of face in the maintenance of social structures.

Given this gesture towards the universal and the lure of an 'outside', corrective view of Western culture, it is not difficult to see why Brown and Levinson's politeness model of face became so popular in pragmatics and sociolinguistics. *Politeness: Some Universals in Language Usage* proclaims in its very title their universal aspirations, and one of their self-declared goals is 'to rebut the once-fashionable doctrine of cultural relativity in the field of interaction' (1987, 56). Tellingly, when discussing face, we see for the first time a definition that completely fails to mention the Chinese origin of the term: 'Our notion of 'face' is derived from that of Goffman (1967) and from *the English folk term*, which ties face up with notions of being embarrassed or humiliated, or "losing face"' (1987, 61; my emphasis).

Like Hu, Brown and Levinson also split the term, with negative face being defined as the individual's desire to be free from imposition, and positive face as the individual's desire to be accorded prestige and goodwill from the group (1987, 62–63). Although Brown and Levinson thus split the term into two sub-categories, these are not linked to the perceived etymological differences between lian and mianzi.

Brown and Levinson's work established face as a mainstream sociolinguistic concept. This is easily demonstrated by a keyword search for 'face-work' and 'face AND politeness' in the Social Science Index, which resulted in hits for articles in a wide range of journals,[23] or looking through the table of contents of one journal, the *Journal of Pragmatics*, which between 1987 and 2010 had no fewer than five special issues devoted to the topic of politeness and face (April 1990; May 1994; October–November 2003; April 2007; August 2010), as well as dozens of articles scattered through the other issues (I counted twenty-seven, judging from the titles alone). Several edited volumes, from Ting-Toomey's *The Challenge of Facework* (1994) to Bargiela-Chiappini and Haugh (2010) also attest to the popularity of the topic. While quite a bit of the theoretical literature suggested refinements or amendments to Brown and Levinson's model (see Haugh 2010 for an overview), most seemed to accept the underlying validity of using the concept of face to explain politeness behaviour. In the foreword to the re-issued text as a stand-alone volume ten years after its first appearance, Gumperz already can claim that it is the 'classic treatment on politeness in communication' (Brown and Levinson 1987, xiii).

Challenges to Brown and Levinson in the 1980s and 1990s: the campaign to rectify names

The move to deracinate face and elevate it to an abstract universal was welcomed by some Chinese scholars, who either introduced Goffman's and/or Brown and Levinson's definition of face or applied them to Chinese case studies (Chen Rong 1986; Zhang Ren 1994; Ma Dengge 1995). It was also featured in Chinese textbooks of sociolinguistics (Zhu Wanjin 1992, 158–66). It is, after all, more or less a vindication of the Chinese after 150 years of slurs, to claim that a category of social behaviour despised by the Victorians was in fact an essential element of all societies, including their own. In this reading, one might see the extremely negative view of face as an example of how one often hates another, not because they are different, but because they share traits which one does not like to acknowledge are part of oneself.[24]

However, the rise of nativist studies, postcolonial studies and subsequent calls in many disciplines in the humanities and social sciences to become less Anglo-centric or Eurocentric resulted in an embrace of cultural difference. This, in turn, led to a re-valuing of local knowledge and local concepts, among which in the Chinese context face figures prominently. In Taiwan and Hong Kong, Yang Kuo-Shu (楊國樞) and colleagues were responsible for several publications, notably two collections of essays, *Essays on Modernization and Sinicization* (現代化與中國化論集 1985) and *The Psychology of the Chinese* (中國人的心理 1989). In the first of these, the article by Hwang Kwang-kuo about face begins by tracing the uniqueness of Chinese culture back to Confucianism, which he argues emphasises 'harmonious bonds between people' (人際關係的和諧). As an outgrowth of that valuing of interpersonal relations, he identifies five concepts (renqing, face, guanxi, *yuan* [緣 fate], and *bao* [報 repayment]) particular to Chinese culture, of which 'renqing and mianzi are the two core concepts central to understanding social behaviour of the Chinese' ('人情' 與 '面子' 是了解中國人社會行為的兩個核心概念) (Hwang 1985, 126). Hwang's article is in some sense a hybrid one because, even when arguing for the uniqueness of Chinese concepts at the beginning, he speaks of using 'global concepts' (整體性概念) in order to understand Chinese culture, his definition of face later in the paper comes straight from Goffman, and he uses Chinese translations of some of Goffman's terms throughout the essay (125 and 141–42).[25]

The second book is a collection of essays that deal with several concepts that Yang and his colleagues claimed were unique to Chinese culture. Four essays were devoted to face (including a reprint of Hwang's article), the largest group in the collection, while filial piety and guanxi featured in two articles each and fengshui was discussed in one article (Yang Kuo-Shu 1989).[26]

These and other scholars have continued to publish, with much of their work revolving around these few concepts as 'unique' to Chinese culture. Yang was the editor of a book series entitled 'Works about the Chinese People' (zhongguo ren 中國人叢書), which published twenty-five titles between 1988 and 1999.[27] This included *The Chinese People's Outlook on Face* (中國人的臉面觀), a four-hundred-page monograph by a scholar from the PRC (Zhai 1995). Zhai explicitly acknowledges that foreigners were the first to apply the concept of national character to Chinese society, and that Arthur Smith played a key role in putting the concept of face at the centre of that discussion (Zhai 1995, 4). His survey of works in Chinese relating to national character shows that, although some attention was paid to face in the 1920s, it was not really until the 1930s and 1940s that face received much attention (9–11). Even then, face was generally considered as only one of several concepts. The work of Zhuang Zexuan, for example, abstracted fifteen characteristics from Smith's book, among which he listed face thirteenth (Zhuang Zexuan 1938, 304–7). Face comes up several times later in the book, mainly as one of the negative characteristics that should be changed (346, 354, 453, 539), but it is classified as merely a subcategory under 'tolerance and humility' (*rongren qiangong* 容忍謙恭) (397), a move that downplays its significance overall.

Thus the identification of these concepts as part of the 'Chinese national character' must be laid at the door of Arthur Smith and other English-language China observers of the late nineteenth and early twentieth century. Further, the link between face and Confucianism is something of which no nineteenth-century Chinese scholar ever dreamed. Despite the writings of Lu Xun, Lao She and Lin Yutang, face does not seem to have been considered a key concept in the overall Chinese national character by academic researchers in Chinese until after it was adopted by Goffman and raised to universal status.

The discussion of Chinese or Asian exceptionalism, which first occurred in Chinese-language academic publications in the late 1970s and early 1980s, led subsequently to some of the sharpest criticisms of Brown and Levinson's model in English-language scholarship coming from Japanese and Chinese scholars, who have argued that this sociolinguistic model of face and politeness was not applicable to their cultures.

Matsumoto led the way in English-language scholarship with a rather devastating critique of the universal applicability of Brown and Levinson's division of face into negative and positive. She claimed that there was no such thing as negative face in Japanese culture, and that therefore Brown and Levinson's model was not universal (1988, 405). This claim was backed up by a survey of social science research showing that Japanese culture completely lacked this desire of the individual to be unimpeded (406–8) and then a consideration of some sentences in Japanese that seemed to contradict Brown and Levinson's predictions based on assumptions concerning negative politeness.

In the course of this critique, Matsumoto claims that Brown and Levinson's model of both negative and positive face revolved around 'an individual who desires to defend his/her own territory from the encroachments of others' (1987, 405). For Matsumoto, this 'notion of individuals and their rights ... cannot be considered as basic to human relations in Japanese culture and society' (405). The crux of the matter, then, is that Westerners are individualists and Japanese are collectivists. In this respect Matsumoto's argument relates back to Ho (1976) and to Yang (1947).

The collectivist/individualist issue has been picked up and echoed by subsequent scholars who also question Brown and Levinson's model. Gu (1990), for example, declares that Brown and Levinson have focused too exclusively on a model of politeness involving two rational model persons, neglecting the wider social context, which for Gu is vital in the Chinese context and makes politeness not just instrumental but also normative (1990, 242–43). Scollon and Scollon (1994, 151–52) claim that the boundary of the self in Chinese culture is wider than that in Western ones, including close relatives and intimate friends, a restatement of Yang's argument that there can be no face concerns between close relatives. This is a modified version of Matsumoto's critique; rather than deny that there are individuals in Chinese culture, they argue that the boundary of that self includes one's in-group. They conclude that if the boundary of the self is different, and if Chinese culture is collectivist rather than individualist, it may not be possible to come up with a theory of face which is at once simple enough to apply and also encompasses such radically different notions of self and society (152–53). Finally, critiques of Brown and Levinson were not limited to scholars of East Asia, with articles on politeness and face in Greek, Polish, and Igbo all either explicitly or implicitly foregrounding similar problems (O'Driscoll 1996, 3).

Based on the work of these scholars, we might argue that the adoption by European and American linguists of the term 'face' has resulted in a transformation through translation of the concept. In this process the original 'Chineseness' of face was first broken off and isolated as lian (versus mianzi, which Americans also acknowledged). Emptying the word 'face' in English of its cultural specificity then allowed its elevation to a universal category, but at a price. Their critique rests upon the supposition that the emptying of face of its Chinese cultural specificity allowed it to be covertly filled up with another, 'western' bias based on individualism. This *new* term was then applied willy-nilly to other cultures, seemingly with no awareness that the concept of face as defined by Brown and Levinson is culturally specific to the West and therefore invalid as a universal category. Adopting a postcolonial perspective, we might see this as an example of orientalist discourse being used as an analytical tool to control the Other with its 'own' terms through a highly selective and biased translation.[28]

From forking paths to labyrinth: is face universal or culturally specific behaviour?

Since the beginning of the 1990s, research on face has increased exponentially and been applied in a wide variety of studies. This has not meant, however, that final consensus has been reached regarding any of its important features; indeed, part of the reason for the volume of publication is precisely the continued controversy over all aspects of this concept. It would be impossible in even a monograph devoted solely to face to do full justice to the range of debate; the following brief sketch of this 'afterlife' of the term will therefore focus mainly on how these debates relate to the historical roots of the term, and to what extent the (lack of) connection with that history continues to inform the debate.

First, the 1990s saw the emergence of a further split in the definition of face, with the emergence of a sense that non-scientific usage of the terms 'politeness' and 'face', both in English and their equivalents in other languages, should be kept distinct from the sociolinguistic use of the terms. Watts ([1992] 2005) is one of the earliest examples of a discussion of this problem, but only in relation to politeness; he distinguishes 'first-order' and 'second-order' conceptions of the term, and points out the danger of confusing them. This bifurcation is given at least four different sets of names in the literature: first- versus second-order, politeness1 versus politeness2, academic versus folk, and emic versus etic.

Sometimes these discussions are accompanied by reflection upon the advisability of using terminology that could so easily lead to confusion. Indeed, most of Eelen (2001) is taken up with a long catalogue of how and why the two levels had often been confused in earlier research. At least one researcher (Watts 2003) proposes replacing a large portion of the phenomena previously labelled as polite with the term 'politic', and moots the possibility of discarding 'politeness' altogether for second-order discussions.

On one level, it might be argued that, confronted with evidence that Brown and Levinson's model did not satisfactorily explain politeness in all cultures, researchers sought to try and take into account what research subjects had to say about the category or categories of face to explain variations from predicted behaviour, and to distinguish how research subjects understood what was happening in social interaction, as opposed to the researcher's analysis of it. After Watts ([1992] 2005) and Eelen (2001), the distinction can be said to have become common in the literature (Haugh 2007; Ruhi and Isik-Güler 2007).

In terms of the relation to Chinese culture, the emic/etic distinction weakens the tie between Chinese culture and conceptions of face, because Chinese becomes just one of many emic 'notions' or 'folk understandings' of the term, and therefore has no special status vis à vis how the etic notion is deployed. Thus the relationship between lian and mianzi becomes a local-ised issue, completely unrelated to how face is deployed in sociolinguistics, whereas for Hu (1944) there could be no understanding of 'face' without an understanding of the two Chinese terms.

In one sense, it could be said that the emic/etic split allows researchers to have their cake and eat it: politeness (or face) can be at once culturally specific (emic) and universal (etic), thereby resolving the apparent conflict between the two. Thus Culpeper and Kádár (2010, 23), in their introduc-tion to a volume on (im)politeness, argue that the term 'politeness' is of recent coinage and not all cultures have an easy translation of it; therefore, it should either be abandoned as a term or used only to designate the research-er's definition (etic use) rather than pretend to be a label for anything in the culture being studied (emic use); for the latter, only terms that the particular culture has coined should be used.

While the emic/etic discourse structure allows for this compromise, such compromise has been attacked vigorously, as in Eelen (2001) and Watts (2003). However, their critique of the possibility of constructing a universal etic category has been limited to politeness.

Face, on the other hand, has by many researchers been allowed to retain a universal function even as politeness is carefully divided into emic and etic variants. O'Driscoll (2011, 18), in summarising Goffman, says: 'face, it is argued, is an ideal concept for engaging with the crosscultural and intercultural precisely because it does *not* implicate specific cultures (see Section 4) or construals of politeness which are inevitably culture-specific (see Section 3)'. Similarly, while Watts ([1992] 2005) contains a powerful critique of politeness research as often confusing emic and etic notions of politeness, nowhere does he suggest that the same might be true about face. Here it is useful to recall that Hwang, writing in Chinese and arguing for the uniqueness of Chinese culture, could still adopt Goffman's 'global concept' of face.

This discourse on emic versus etic notions of politeness and (more rarely) face largely ignores the growing criticisms of the initial emic/etic distinction in anthropology, of which Mayfair Yang (1994, 26–27) is a good example. In a discussion of guanxi, Yang critiques the notion that an observer from another culture has a privileged vantage point from which to view 'local' or 'native' behaviour; rather, she sees this as a masked form of imperialistic power, the 'Westerner' setting himself (the masculine pronoun being used advisedly) up over the natives. Yang's critique, which draws on the work of James Clifford (1992), is advanced perhaps more strongly in Binsbergen (2003, 500–4), where the etic is postulated as no more than a 'North Atlantic' emic interpretation that has been raised to an underserved status of universality and cultural neutrality. The early critique of 'face' as being biased towards Western individuality by Matsumoto (1988) is perhaps one of the few papers in sociolinguistics that advances such a critique of core concepts in sociolinguistics, but her work comes before the emic/etic debate, and later researchers do not seem to have made this connection.

Instead, it almost seems that the term 'politeness' is being sacrificed as emic in order to preserve 'face' as an etic concept. Major attempts to construct a new universal model of face, such as Locher (2008, 14), seem to locate all cultural specificity at the level of politeness, while facework remains a cross-cultural constant tied to basic psychosocial processes of identity formation.

It should come as no surprise, then, that the second major development in research on face has been the problematising of Brown and Levinson's linkage of face and politeness. Watts (2003) contains probably the strongest argument against this linkage, with subsequent scholars often citing him as justification for not seeing politeness as always linked to face (see Chang and Haugh 2011; Hambling-Jones and Merrison 2012; Haugh 2010). Other scholars, such as Arundale (2010 and 2103), may continue to see face as a possible explanation for (im)politeness, but do not posit a necessary link. Conversely, Culpeper and Kádár (2010, 9) manage to avoid the use of the term 'face' when giving a general definition of politeness, even though the example they give of politeness, rephrasing something to avoid hurting the listener's feelings, could be seen as a classic example of attending to others' face needs.

The increasing disconnect between face and politeness means that research on politeness in China has to a certain extent been freed from involvement with discussions of any definition of face, Chinese or otherwise. Kádár (2010) indeed succeeds in writing a very perceptive article on 'Historical Chinese Polite Denigration/Elevation Phenomenon' without ever mentioning the term face, while at the same time insisting on the historical rootedness of Chinese notions of politeness. Similarly, Okamoto (2011) and Hudson (2011) both write papers on politeness in Japan without mentioning the term 'face', something probably unthinkable in the period between 1990–2005.

At the same time, the reason Watts (2003) and others seem to want to disconnect politeness and face is that they feel an etic or universal notion of politeness (second-order politeness) is impossible to achieve, but at the same time seem more disposed to retain face as a universal. This is perhaps due to the manifest shifts in emic notions of politeness over time in English, whereas there does not seem to be a corresponding historic shift in the meaning of 'face' in that language. It would seem that this lack of change over time in the term 'face' is due to its relative recent appearance in English, and that this lack of shifts in meaning in English predisposes scholars working in that language to treat it as a universal.

Thus both of these issues, the emic/etic distinction and the (dis)connect between face and politeness, are bound up with the continuing debate about the universal applicability of facework models, which is the third major strand in ongoing discussions of face.

Regarding the role of China in this debate over the universal or particular applicability of face, there seem to be three possible stances in the literature. First, some researchers attempt to undo the deracination and subsequent individualistic bias of the term in Brown and Levinson's model by reinserting the notion of face into Chinese culture. Second, other researchers accept the critique of scholars who say that Brown and Levinson's conception of face and politeness is flawed, and add to or modify Brown and Levinson's model in order to come up with a universal model. Third, still other researchers attack the notion of exceptionalism and re-affirm the validity of face as a universal. Like the second group of researchers, this stance believes in a universal concept of face, but they do not accept the initial criticisms of it as being ethno-centric.

The three possible stances can be seen to derive from two choices: first, whether or not one believes that the term 'face' as used in socio-pragmatics has a specific origin which may have had a (continuing) influence on the meaning. The first two groups believe this to be true, while the third group does not. The second choice is whether 'face' can be considered a universal. The first group says no, due to their answer to the first question; the second group says yes, if and only if the question of origins is given careful consideration and ethno-centrism is avoided in the construction of a definition; the third group says yes of course, because the answer to the first question was no, there is nothing wrong with the term 'face' in the first place. If the three stances are broken down according to those two questions, we should note that there appears to be a null set: no researchers who answer the first question with 'no' go on to answer the second question with 'no'. In other words, all of the critiques of a universal concept of face are tied to the historical specificity of the term, not to other issues such as flaws in the rationale of the model or doubt of its robustness qua model.

A good example of the first stance is Chang and Holt (1994, 102), who consistently use the term mianzi instead of 'face', and relate it to two other 'Chinese characteristics: guanxi and renqing', in an interesting echo of some of the late nineteenth- and early twentieth-century English writers and the

Taiwanese scholars writing in Chinese in the 1970s and 1980s.[29] Chang and Holt gloss these terms as 'Chinese relations' and 'human emotions' respectively, an interesting split between local (Chinese) and universal (human). This refusal to translate, adopting transliteration instead, is linked to the insistence of the cultural specificity of the terms, and the debates in translation studies about the impossibility of perfect translation (Whorf 1956; Nida 1959; Quine 1959; Steiner 1975). This stance is also widely represented in early twenty-first-century literature in Chinese, being perhaps the most commonly held view in China today (Wang Wenbin 2012; Li Fuqiang 2019; Lu Peijin 2019).

The work of Chang and Holt, which focuses on contemporary usage, is complemented by the work of Gu (1990, 238–40), who traces the concept of Chinese politeness back to Confucius and the *Book of Rites*, maintaining that *li* (rites, ritual) is the origin of politeness in Chinese, with the modern compound *limao* being the closest equivalent to the English word politeness. This leads to some mental acrobatics, where he claims that the great proletarian revolution has swept away the remnants of feudalism, but somehow the torch of li continues to be passed down from generation to generation; thus Chinese civilisation can be at once modern and traditional. This argument implicitly loops back to Lu Xun and Lin Yutang, who associate face with the past of Chinese civilisation, only for Gu there are positive aspects of the term, and so his work represents a rehabilitation of the past in the wake of the political rehabilitation of Confucius in China.

Mao (1994) tries to argue that mianzi and lian are distinct categories, as Hu (1944) and Ho (1976) had claimed, at the same time arguing that Brown and Levinson's negative face does not really apply to China. To achieve this, he analyses two segments of dialogue using the terms mianzi and lian, rather than Brown and Levinson's positive and negative face. Unfortunately, since both segments he chooses are 'positive [felicitous] outcomes', with the invitation among friends being accepted, it is not clear that his examples have proved that negative face is never important in Chinese, as in such cases Brown and Levinson would not expect negative face to be relevant. A more recent example is He and Zhang (2011), who are concerned exclusively with mianzi as a Chinese concept of face.

In none of these cases do the authors claim that Chinese mianzi or lian is a universal category. Indeed, even when they continue to argue that there is a distinction between these two terms, they maintain that the distinction is a purely emic one, and has nothing to do with general models of face or politeness. Rather than challenge the existing paradigm by coming up with a new one (based on Hu and Ho's work, for example), they may be seen as either totally uninterested in the attempt to construct a universal paradigm applicable to all cultures, or challenging the very notion that such a paradigm could exist.

Allied with these voices within sociolinguistics are studies in anthropology and Chinese studies that use face as a marker of Chinese difference. Brownell (1995, 291–95) argues that the notion of fair play, which emerged in Britain in the nineteenth century, has now been enshrined as a universal value by the International Olympic Committee. By contrast, the Chinese concept of face, where winning gives face to one's coach, leader, town, and country, has remained a 'local' (or emic) Chinese value, and worse still, become associated with being a 'bad sport', since the perception is that one will do anything in order to win, including cheating. In the twenty-first century, the work of Nathan and Scobell (2012, 25–26), published by a prestigious North American university press, could still claim that face can be used to explain the uniqueness of Chinese diplomacy; moreover, this use of face was praised by a reviewer as 'one of the truly brilliant contributions' of the monograph (Mirsky 2013, 53).

Finally, a certain number of business and management studies engage in explaining to a Western audience how face works in Chinese culture and, therefore, how they should modify their business and management practices in that country (Cardon 2005; Langenberg 2007, 90–96; see Chapter 4 for more on this genre in relation to guanxi).

Moving to the second stance, early attempts to come up with additional or complementary notions that allow for a universal theory of politeness include Hill *et al* (1986), who advance a modified version of Brown and Levinson by introducing the notions of discernment and volition; and, Ide (1989) who follows along from Hill *et al.*

Since the publication of Watt (2003), this trend has become more prominent, with a multiplication of either modified versions of Brown and Levinson, or radically new frameworks being proposed. In some cases these works seem to ignore the objections raised to the possibility, *pace* Eelen, of a universal notion of politeness and face. Most interestingly, many of these works propose a return to Goffman's model of face (Fracchiolla 2011, Gerholm 2011, Hambling-Jones and Merrison 2012); in such cases Brown and Levinson are accused more or less explicitly of deviating from Goffman's definition, to which these more recent researchers wish to revert. Spencer-Oatey (2007, 649) even calls Goffman's definition of face 'classic', whereas we have seen that in 1987 that term was being applied to Brown and Levinson. Yet a return to Goffman, who does note the origins of the concept face in descriptions of Chinese culture, albeit rather furtively, has not resulted in an attempt to ground a new universal paradigm of face in Chinese emic notions of the term; in this sense, this group of researchers are in agreement with the first group.

An important element of this new urge to universalism is the attempt to draw on other disciplines, especially the biological sciences and psychology. Terkourafi (2007, 321–24), for example, states baldly that the etic notion of face is universal because it is biologically grounded in the dualism of approach and withdrawal, as well as phenomenological conceptions of intention. Arundale (2010, 2078) draws upon 'the study of human communication, as well as on research in conversation analysis' to construct a 'Face Constituting Theory'. As perhaps the most resolutely theoretical approach to the problem of constructing a newly grounded conception of face that can be universal, Arundale (2010, 2088) raises the issue of whether the word 'face', which he recognises as a metaphor, may still be profitably used to describe what he calls a conjointly pro-duced social phenomenon. Interestingly though, he fails to come up with a better one and so continues to use 'face'. Coming at the problem from a very different angle, both Spencer-Oatey (2007) and Locher (2008) make a connection between identity theory and face. For Spencer-Oatey, iden-tity theory, and more specifically social psychology, provides 'a universal framework of value constructs that has been empirically validated in over 63 different cultural groups' (2007, 649) as a replacement of Brown and Levinson's positive/negative dichotomy. Locher, using a different (post-modern) model of identity, posits homologies between identity construc-tion and facework, so that face effectively becomes the bridge between identity construction and politeness.

Third, rather than skirt around or ignore Chinese conceptions of face, some researchers have chosen to attack the notion of China and Japan as 'special' cases that do not operate according to the rules of face in order to re-affirm the validity of face as a universal category. Fukada and Asato (2004) take issue with both Matsumoto's (1988) argument that face is not applicable to the use of honorifics in Japanese and later attempts to intro-duce a new category, *wakimae* or discernment, as an alternative (Hill *et al* 1986; Ide 1989). These scholars clearly recognise the nature of the attack mounted on universal models by the first group.

One indirect strategy of rebutting the argument that face is culturally bound (to China) that is sometimes used consists of citing examples of Chinese behaviour within a study of face; this implicitly disarms criticisms that the model does not explain Chinese behaviour. Spencer-Oatey (2007), in developing her work on face and identity as intertwined, repeatedly uses the example of a Chinese business delegation that visited Cambridge in the UK. Using both remarks made in English and translations of transcripts from Chinese remarks that were then rendered into English by an inter-preter, Spencer-Oatey builds up a rich understanding of the links between the identity of the Chinese as first members of a firm and members of the Chinese nation to explain the facework involved, and their reaction to cer-tain events during their visit to the UK.

However, the slippage between lian, face, mianzi, timian, prestige, honour and other terms as these concepts circulate back and forth between English and Chinese highlight the need to use concepts and debates within translation studies to understand what is happening here.

First, it should be pointed out that there is an interesting homology between attitudes towards translatability and universality. Researchers who lean towards cultural specificity tend to eschew translation from Chinese, transliterating the terms lian and mianzi rather than translating them. This equates with the commonly accepted thesis in translation studies that an absolute or perfect translation is impossible. On the other extreme, if we return to the universalist paper of Spencer-Oatey (2007), we can see that in a bilingual exchange facilitated through an interpreter, Spencer-Oatey assumes absolute transparency in the translation process. It is as if the Chinese speakers are actually using English in their interaction with their British counterparts and with each other, and the question of whether differences in the way in which language is used in Chinese and English is affecting the exchange never arises. For example, the transcript of example four includes, after a line of Jack speaking in English, the line: 'Int: [interprets into Chinese]' (648). No back translation into English of the interpreter's rendering of Jack's English speech in Chinese is provided because of the underlying assumption that there would be no difference between what Jack said in English and what the interpreter said in Chinese, just as later when one of the Chinese speaks, it is followed by 'Int: [interprets into English]'. Instead, in places where, in the original exchange, someone is speaking Chinese, Spencer-Oatey provides a post facto written English translation of a now erased Chinese speech, which practice glosses over the real-time lag between segments of speech in the exchange and possible differences between the original speech and the interpretation. The only point where the interpreter comes into view is when, after one of the exchanges, the British learn that the interpreter had intervened in an exchange and cut off the Chinese speaker (648). This, significantly, means that the only time interpreting is problematic is when the interpreter does not do her or his job properly, that is, when the interpreter is not acting simply as a conduit for the original speaker. This conduit understanding of the act of interpreting or translating has been thoroughly discredited in translation studies (Martín de León 2010).

In fact, none of the examples in Spencer-Oatey's paper involve two native speakers of English interacting with one another; rather, in each case one or more British are shown interacting with foreigners. The other major example Spencer-Oatey discusses is a personal encounter with a Hungarian student whose 'mixed' compliment caused Spencer-Oatey some anguish (2007, 645; recurs 649). In none of these cases does Spencer-Oatey make any attempt to investigate how differences in culture might have been affecting the exchange, and how those differences might then affect the way in which the different speakers might have understood or constructed face concerns.

What Spencer-Oatey has done, in effect, is a three-step process. First, she has chosen examples where people of different nationalities, specifically British and Chinese, interact. These interactions, which in some cases are bilingual, therefore appear to support a universalist model of face. However, this bilingual exchange is theorised as totally transparent through being presented in a monolingual format, a format that essentially argues there is no difference between the Chinese and the English language. Therefore, exchanges involving Chinese can be represented in English and then analysed according to rules that have also been formulated in English.

In a slightly different manner, we see the return of the repressed (Chinese) in Arundale (2010, 2085), not by introducing Chinese examples to prove that his model is universal, but rather by integrating a different Chinese binary, yin and yang, into his definition of face. He conceptualises the relation between the individual and the social as face in an 'Yin/Yang dialectic that is neither a dualism nor a bipolar continuum in that it involves two phenomena "that function in incompatible ways such that each negates the other".' By explicitly rejecting a Hegelian dialectic and embracing a Chinese yinyang one, Arundale argues that he can transcend the Chinese/English, East/West dichotomy and achieve a new abstract universalism. Yet this rejection of Hegel for yinyang essentially acknowledges that Matsumoto's critique of Brown and Levinson is correct, and that their model of face was based on an individualistic notion of the self involved in an essentially oppositional relation with the Other, instead of a mutually reinforcing yinyang one.

Conclusion

Unlike the other two concepts filial piety and fengshui, face only emerges as a key concept in the nineteenth century as a direct result of the interaction between British and Chinese in the treaty ports. Face became an important concept, first to explain the uniqueness of Chinese culture, and then later in sociolinguistics as either a universal or a culturally specific concept. This was accomplished through a continued back and forth between the two languages. Starting at least from Lin Yutang, many of the participants in the Chinese-language debates have also published in English, and the work of these bilingual scholars, along with the early translators of Smith and other English writers into Chinese, has been crucial at every stage in the process.

In terms of popular usage, the concept has been relatively stable in English. Originally restricted to China and the Chinese and with heavily negative connotations, there has been a gradual broadening of its usage, although the association with China is still strong, as are its negative connotations. The judgement by foreigners that face was holding China back from modernity was internalised by Chinese thinkers, and therefore the connotations of the terms lian and mianzi in everyday Chinese today still have negative connotations that derive ultimately from the English term. The fact that Lu Xun used the term timian, and that Gu goes back to the Confucian notion of li in search of alternative words with more positive connotations, supports this conclusion.

It seems possible that the negative connotations of the word face in the English language both prior to and continuing after Goffman and Brown and Levinson's use of the term are partially responsible for the rejection of this notion as a universal by Chinese and Japanese scholars, who may perceive this as a type of orientalist discourse. This conclusion is reinforced by the fact that, in translating face from a popular to a scientific concept, Brown and Levinson abandon the distinction made by Chinese scholars and substitute one that can be read as based on a Western bias towards individualism. Among other things, this may be linked to ongoing discussions in anthropology and areas studies regarding on the one hand other Chinese concepts such as guanxi, and on the other hand to debates over the 'imposition' of Western values under the guise of universal human rights. Although some Chinese researchers seem to have accepted Goffman's and/or Brown and Levinson's model, Chinese-language research is more likely to follow Hu and Ho, treating face as a doubled Chinese concept consisting of lian and mian.

Further attempts to refine the category, first Goffman and then more notably Brown and Levinson, have continued this multiplication of meanings of the term. We can thus theorise the debates over universal applicability in terms of debates over conceptual terminology. To adopt a line from the Confucian *Analects*, 'If names be not correct, language is not in accordance with the truth of things. If language be not in accordance with the truth of things, affairs cannot be carried on to success' (Legge 1861, XIII.3). These scholars are engaged in a campaign to rectify names. Kuhn's (1962) notion of paradigms can be a useful way of characterising these debates over terminology, with the different groups conceptualised as either 'normal', 'radical', 'conservative', or 'alternative paradigm' scientists, all having different relations to the existing paradigm(s).

Regardless of where researchers stand in relation to these various issues, running through the vast majority of the literature from MacGowan right down to the present day has been the persistence of a dichotomous view of face. What exactly that dichotomy is varies greatly (inner versus outer, guilt versus shame, positive versus negative, emic versus etic, lian versus mianzi, volition versus discernment, avoidance versus attraction, the individual versus the social), but the idea that face must somehow have an obverse and a reverse side seems perhaps to be its most universal feature. The last scholar to analyse face as a single concept was Yang (1947).

At the same time, attempts to argue that face has more than two facets all seem to run into the problem of Occam's razor. Spencer-Oatey (2007, 649–51), who proposes using Schwartz's wheel of ten values, notes that once the number of categories surpasses two, researchers are often confronted with the question of why this particular set or list of categories, no more and no less. Terkourafi (2007, 315) also notes this bind, where the multiplication of principles opens up the question of irreducibility and universality. Yet if researchers can argue that face is a universal because it is grounded in a neurobiological dichotomy, we might also argue that the persistent need to see face as a dichotomy, which first emerged due to the historical accident that Chinese has two interrelated terms, may be grounded in another biological fact, that our bodies are symmetrical. This insight should allow us to reflect critically on the way in which, in this instance, proponents of universalism are in effect arguing that the biological determines the social.

Here I am mainly dealing with sociology and sociolinguistics; but face also persists in Chinese studies, business studies and, to a lesser extent, anthropology. In these disciplines, which do not seem to cross over to sociolinguistics, face remains firmly attached to China. This divide is not a linguistic one, but rather a disciplinary one; scholarship both in Chinese and English in these fields tend to treat face as unique to Chinese culture and ignore the work of Goffman and his successors (Jiang Caifen 2009). In the popular literature, a linguistic divide does seem to exist: there are popular works in Chinese devoted to the concept of face, and these see it as unique to Chinese culture (Zhang Tao 2006; Wuyue Sanren 2013). In English there are no popular works devoted to the concept of face. In terms of casual references to face in non-academic works, the situation is less clear-cut, but perhaps the tendency in Chinese is to see face as unique to Chinese culture, while in English, as we have seen, while the link to China persists, it can and is applied widely to people and situations everywhere.

It should be clear by this point that I adopt an essentially postmodern and relativistic view of the history of the term 'face' and its cognates in Chinese, English, and sociolinguistics. It is, finally, impossible to decide whether any of the positions described is 'correct'. Just as there is no perfect translation, so too there is no perfect model that will explain all social interaction. The existence of universals is not a question of finding them 'out there' and convincing everyone of their truth value, but rather of constructing a paradigm that is acceptable to all scholars. Such an attitude at once frees researchers from an all-or-nothing critique, whereby one exception invalidates the entire model, while at the same time reminding researchers of the particular situatedness of all knowledge and therefore the need to acknowledge and learn from exceptions. In this case, I would argue that Brown and Levinson have not completely succeeded in constructing a universal model due to their failure, whether through ignorance or wilful decision, to take into account certain cultural factors relating, not to the structure of Chinese and Japanese societies, but rather to the history of the terms face, lian, and mianzi. In the resulting free-for-all following on the wake of initial critiques, no one paradigm has succeeded in establishing itself decisively. This brings me back to what I saw as the indeterminacy of Hu's argument. One wonders what might have happened if Goffman had not been beguiled by the puns available through the use of the term 'face', and had instead chosen another term, whether the absence of those historical connotations might have led to the development of a different, and perhaps more readily acceptable form of universal face theory. Yet certain key aspects of Goffman's work, such as the theatricality of facework, probably derives from its Chinese roots and Smith's description. So although the choice of the term has led to the continued controversy over models of both face and politeness today, it might not have been possible for Goffman to come up with his theory without the rich history of face in both Chinese and English.

Notes

1 Parts of this chapter were originally published in *The Journal of Pragmatics*, volume 55, James St. André, 'How the Chinese Lost "Face"', 68–85. Copyright Elsevier (2013).

2 Hu dates lian to the Yuan dynasty (1277–1367), but this is based on citations in the *Kangxi Dictionary*, which does not give the metaphoric sense of the word, only its literal meaning.

3 All premodern texts cited in this chapter are from the open-source Chinese Text Project https://ctext.org/. Since that website is organised chronologically by book title, then (sometimes) sections, chapters and finally paragraphs, citations will be in the format TITLE (SECTION,) CHAPTER, PARAGRAPH. Thus here (*Shuo yuan*, 4, 10) means *Shuo yuan*, chapter 4, paragraph 10.

4 Recently Keevak (2022, 23–35) has tried to argue that there is a sort of pre-'face' discourse in Catholic missionary writings about China regarding polite behaviour among the Chinese, but he was unable to point to any texts that explicitly reference face and, as we will see in the twentieth-century debates on face, there is no necessary link between it and politeness.

5 There are early references to someone not being able to face someone from a feeling of shame; these are usually couched as 'could not face X'. The more general meaning of 'outward show; artificial or assumed expression or appearance; pretence' for face has some quite early references, but this is not necessarily related to one's reputation or social standing; likewise, the phrase 'put on a good face' (meaning to act boldly or confidently) pre-dates the Chinese loan, so face as an outward appearance was not a new usage, but as reputation it was.

6 See St. André (2007) for a discussion of Davis and his role as translator and as an employee in the East India Company; see Gutzlaff's own *Journal* (1834a) for details of his activities.

7 Huc's work was originally published in French, where the phrase 'I have lost my face' is 'j'ai perdu ma face' with a footnote explaining that it meant 'je suis déshonoré' (I am dishonoured) (Huc 1854, 1:414). While the history of the phrase 'to lose face' in other European languages is beyond the scope of this study, here I will just mention that the website 'Expressio.fr: Les expressions françaises décortiquées' gives another publication by Huc in 1850 as the locus classicus for this expression in French, and gives two contemporary examples, one from 2002 and one from 2011. The website also lists equivalent expressions in German, Dutch, Polish, Spanish, Portuguese, Italian, Swedish, Russian, and Hebrew, demonstrating that this particular expression has become widely disseminated across a range of languages. https://www.expressio.fr/expressions/perdre-la-face

8 The use of literal translation of Chinese expressions to mock the Chinese was a strategy that emerged in the 1820s and 1830s among translators mainly associated with the East India Company (including Davis and Gutzlaff). See St. André (2007) for a more detailed discussion of this phenomenon.

9 In the United States, the story of George Washington chopping down the cherry tree and then admitting it when asked by his father is only the most famous of these. In the United Kingdom, *Tom Brown's School Days* is perhaps the most iconic nineteenth-century example of a genre that sought to inculcate a sense of sportsmanship, fair play, and being a good loser. See Brownell (1995, 290–304) for a discussion of how these ideas became enshrined in the modern Olympics, and an extended argument that there is a cultural clash between Chinese face and British 'fair play'.

10 My thanks to an anonymous reviewer for this point.

11 The search was conducted twice, once enclosing the phrase in quotation marks and therefore searching for an exact match of the phrase, and once without, with a similar proportion. For the exact match, 'to lose face' generated 595,000 hits while there were 2,490,000 results for 'to save face'; for the inexact match, the results were 808,000,000 and 4,140,000,000 respectively.

12 Another excellent example of this from a slightly earlier non-fiction work is *Houseboat Days in China*, wherein the servant of one of the foreign hunters who is a poor shot contrives to buy birds in local markets and hang them up as if they had been shot by his master (Bland 1919, 61), and on the return trip *all* of the servants on various boats contrive ways of maximizing the bulk of the game bag in order to gain face (253–54).

13 Although this article was published before the revised version of Smith's book, it should be noted that his work was first published serially in that very newspaper in 1890.

14 The first two of these, which we have seen are employed by Arthur Smith as early as 1890, are probably also borrowed from Chinese through translation; 'have face' being a literal translation of 'you lian/mianzi' and 'give face' from either 'shang lian' or 'gei mianzi'. 'Gain face' seems to be a spontaneous coinage in English. In the earliest example of it that I found, it was used in opposition to 'lose face' and presented as being spoken by an American who did not know Chinese (Carpenter 1896).

15 Statistics were collected on the country in which an act of saving or losing face occurred, as well as the nationality or ethnicity of the actors involved. All cases where this was unclear were excluded. In some cases, more than one country or nationality was involved, and so the total number of the two factors is not identical.

16 The database does not support full text search and also does not support single character search, so five binomes were used to search through titles from the 1880s through 1929: 面子, 情面, 顏面, 丟臉, and 有臉. There were 35 results in total from two newspapers: *The Chinese Mail* (香港華字日報) and *Universal Circulating Herald* (循環日報), all involving the binomes containing mian. There were an additional 50 results from 1930 to 1949 with occurrences of all five terms and in five additional newspapers: the *Kung Sheung Daily News* (香港工商日報), *Kung Sheung Evening News* (工商晚報), *Tien Kwong Morning News* (天光報), *Ta Kung Pao* (大公報), and *Wah Kiu Yat Po* (華僑日報).

17 Lu Xun gives a Chinese translation of the title (從小說看來的支那民族性); the original Japanese is 小說から見た支那の民族性 (The ethnic character of the Chinese, as seen from their fiction).

18 See Soong Chiang (1935a and 1935b) for the Chinese originals.

19 See Friedman (1994) for a detailed discussion of the North-South divide in China, along with its social and political implications.

20 See Dodds (1951) for the application of the shame/guilt divide to Greek culture. There are also links to the work of Claude Levi-Strauss and the emergence of structural anthropology, for example *Le cru et le cuit* (1964).

21 For a more detailed discussion of the convenience of attributing anything bad in China to the influence of northern barbarians, see St. André (2018c, 64–67).

22 Morisaki and Gudykunst (1994) explore the relation between face and the shame/guilt divide.

23 *Communication Quarterly*; *Communication Research*; *Journal of Experimental Psychology*; *Memory and Cognition*; *Psychological Science*; *Human Communication Research*; *Applied Social Psychology*; *Journal of Communication*; *Social Science and Medicine*; *Journal of Social History*; *Social Psychology Quarterly*; *The Social Science Journal*; and *Journal of Personality and Social Psychology*.

24 See St. André (2018c, 3) for a discussion of this tendency in relation to translation practices described as blackface.

25 See Hwang (1987) for a slightly revised version of this article in English that retains all of these points.

26 The other concepts were *yuan* (緣 fate), *baoen/fuchou* (報恩/復仇 repayment and revenge), and *jice xingwei* 計策行為 tactical behaviour), each covered in one or two chapters. This volume was reprinted, first in Taiwan at least once (1990), and then in Mainland China at least twice (2006 and 2012).

27 See the website of the Chinese Native Psychology Research Foundation (華人本土心理研究基金會): http://www.indigpsych.org/publications/69?scope=chinese

28 See Edward Said's argument about the translation and appropriation of Hindu law into English as then being used to control Indians, under the guise of merely putting into effect their own laws (Said 1978).

29 Chang and Holt use a different romanization system, so the terms are spelt mien-tzu and lien in their paper.

4

Guanxi

Introduction

Proponents of the importance of fengshui for understanding Chinese society today can point to a hoary tradition of Chinese cosmology, a long series of written texts, and widespread popular practice at least as far back as the Ming dynasty. Proponents of guanxi as the key to understanding Chinese culture, however, have a tougher job cut out for them, because the term is a modern loan word from Japanese (Liu 1995, 334).

Many researchers have sought to get around this problem by discussing other terms in Chinese, notably *qing* (情 emotion, affection, sentiment) and various compounds formed with it (especially *ganqing* [感情 emotion] and *renqing* [人情 'affective ties', 'the human touch' or simply 'humanity' (as in the phrase 'show some humanity').], *li* [禮 rite, propriety] and its various compounds [notably *liwu* (禮物 gift, present)], and *lun* [倫 order, logic, relation]). Notably, however, there is no etymological link between any of these terms and guanxi.

I will trace quite a different path of development. Following up on the fact that this is the only loanword in Chinese for one of my four key concepts, I will argue that the concept of guanxi, and the discourse surrounding it, far from being a 'native' Chinese concept, has its roots in the birth of the modern civil service in Great Britain and the United States. From the early nineteenth century there were extensive debates, first in the United Kingdom and then later in the United States, regarding the role of interpersonal relations in determining hiring, promotion, and firing in government service and related areas such as the clergy, the armed forces, and universities. On the one hand was patronage, seen as a legitimate use of personal influence, position, and power to determine these matters, and a cluster of terms to denote illegitimate, excessive or flagrant use of personal influence: nepotism, cronyism, corruption, et cetera. In contrast to this existing system, the concept of merit emerged as an alternative, determined by examination. The idea of using some sort of an examination system, in turn, ultimately derived from reports regarding the Chinese Imperial Examination system. Similar to filial piety, then, China was initially held up as an example for others to emulate; yet by the early twentieth century, emphasis had shifted one-hundred-and-eighty degrees and European powers were seen as having modern professional civil servants appointed and promoted strictly on merit, while China remained mired in nepotism, corruption, and cronyism. Out of this discourse emerges the twentieth-century concept of guanxi as somehow central to Chinese culture, either as an evil to be eradicated in the writings of foreigners and early twentieth-century Chinese reformists, or as a unique and precious cultural heritage that has enabled Chinese society to be more just, humane, and successful in business than 'Western' models.

Patronage, gift, living, preferment

The earliest meaning of patronage in the *Oxford English Dictionary* is the right to confer ecclesiastical benefice. The term gradually came to be extended to other realms, especially in universities, which were initially linked to the Church, but also eventually anywhere involving the conferment of some benefit by a member of the royal family or aristocracy. Most literary works written before 1750 were dedicated to a patron, who supported the author in some fashion, for example.

Victorian fiction is full of references to local squires having the power to appoint the local parson; this was called variously a gift, living, preferment, or presentation (Badeau 1886, 216). In Jane Austen's *Sense and Sensibility*, Colonel Brandon offers the living of a curacy at Delaford worth two hundred pounds per annum to Edward Ferrars, who has been disowned by his mother after he refuses to marry the woman of her choice (a rich heiress) and instead insists on marrying the penniless Lucy Steele for love (Austen 1811, 3:63–65). Ferrars is no relation of the Colonel, but rather the friend of a woman whom the Colonel esteems. He offers the living to Ferrars because of her connection between the two of them, despite the fact that Ferrars has never studied divinity and has not yet been ordained. It is manifestly *not* because he is qualified for, or even particularly interested in, the job. Rather, he is broke and searching around for a living; in the nineteenth century, penniless sons of good families went into the Church, and they did so through their connections. Similarly, in Austen's *Pride and Prejudice*, there are two men whose preferment are mainsprings of the plot: the obsequious Mr Collins and the villainous Mr Wickham.

As seen from these examples, patronage was a normal part of nineteenth-century British society. These two examples also illustrate the advantages and disadvantages of such a system. In the first case, Ferrars is an earnest young man who embraces his role as a member of the clergy and does a fine job. In his case, the patronage system has succeeded in identifying a man who, although lacking technical qualifications, proves his worth on the job and therefore vindicates the process by which he was selected.[1] This is not true, however, for either Mr Collins or Mr Wickham. Collins is shown to be an obsequious toady who hovers around aristocrats in the hopes of preferment, and who proposes to Elizabeth's best friend Charlotte days after he had proposed to, and been refused by, Elizabeth herself. Austen is scathing in her condemnation of his actions through the reaction of her main characters. Worse still, Wickham defames the character of Mr Darcy after that man denies him the preferment promised by Darcy's late father, based on his reading of Wickham's character. This defamation is one of the main obstacles to the resolution of the love interest between Mr Darcy and Elizabeth, and Wickham's marriage to Elizabeth's sister is the crisis of the entire novel. That people like Collins could obtain preferment through such obsequious actions, and that the wicked Wickham almost succeeds to a preferment, prevented only by the timely death of his erstwhile benefactor, exposes the fragility of such a system.

Reports of the Chinese civil service in Europe

Meanwhile, reports had been arriving since the sixteenth century about the Chinese civil service examination system. The earliest reports were from the Jesuits and other Catholic missionaries in the field, who wrote glowingly of how the Chinese had an impartial examination system that identified the best-educated, and therefore best qualified, candidates for public office. González de Mendoza (1588, 1:80–84 and 95–99), Semedo (1655, 36–47) and Du Halde (1738–41, 1:251–52 and 374–77) among others all contain descriptions. The main point they make is that appointment to office is determined on merit through a uniform examination system based on a set curriculum open to all, rather than being hereditary or by direct appointment. The examinations had different levels, from lower local ones to higher ones in the capital and were rigorously policed to prevent cheating. A small number of appointments were also based on meritorious actions (for example, being exemplar of filial piety), and degrees could also be purchased, but such purchased degrees could only be at a low level with limited privileges. Once appointed to office, civil servants could not serve in their natal region to discourage partiality and make sure that connections through family ties or friends did not lead to perversions of justice; to discourage the taking of bribes, all hearings had to be public and they were paid a good salary (Mendoza 1588, 1:80–82).

These ideas were picked up by many French Enlightenment thinkers, including Voltaire, Montesquieu, Diderot, and Rousseau. François Quesnay especially is the first one to explicitly recommend that France adopt a similar system in his essay 'Le despotisme de la Chine' ([1767] 1888) (Teng 1943, 281–83). They also began to impinge on the British consciousness as early as the 1730s, when the London journals used the example of the Chinese civil examination system to attack then prime minister Walpole, who was accused of, among other things, using his political power to shield friends and connections from prosecution over the South Sea Bubble and controlling patronage so that Members of Parliament and peers became dependent on him (Taylor 1998, 4 and 7); later Adam Smith in his *Wealth of Nations* (1776, 2:270) advocated for examinations in order to combat corruption in the civil service (Teng 1943, 285 and 296).

At the close of the eighteenth century, the Macartney embassy and other early reports also noted the Chinese civil service examinations. These are the first direct reports in English, and are important because, as I have argued elsewhere, the British by this point in time were mistrustful of secondhand reports and translations of Chinese texts regarding reality in China (St. André 2006). Teng (1943, 308–12) lists over seventy sources from the 1790s through the 1860s that cite the Chinese civil service examinations. Among the more notable is Robert Morrison's dictionary, which contains a thirteen-page entry on them under the headword *xue* (學 to study); this entry is essentially a digest of the 1813 edition of the *Kechang tiaoli* (科場條例 Examination regulations), followed by a digest of a short work on how to write compositions for the examinations (Morrison 1815–23, 1:759–85). This entry was considered so valuable that it was later reprinted in somewhat altered and condensed form in the *Asiatic Journal* for 1826 (Teng 1943, 288). Other early British descriptions include passages in Gutzlaff's *Sketch of Chinese History* (1834b, 1:46) and *China Opened* (1838, 2:346), and Medhurst's *China, Its State and Prospects* (1838, 151) (Teng 1943, 288).

Pride of place, however, goes to Thomas Taylor Meadows, who in two separate works advocated strenuously and at length, not just that the Chinese system worked in China, but that it should be adopted by Great Britain for its civil service. In chapter eleven of his *Desultory Notes on the Government and People of China* (1847), entitled 'On the Cause of the Long Duration of the Chinese Empire', Meadows stresses that everyone who knows anything about China is aware of the examination system, but that most sinologists perversely insist upon attributing the longevity and stability of successive Chinese empires to filial piety, when in fact it is due to the examination system (1847, 124). He then goes on to discuss the great merits of the system, including the fact that its absolute fairness means that 'the untalented submit cheerfully to whatever is founded on it; and as a certain path is open

to every man of real talent, able demagogues are rare' (138); that 'by securing for the government the services of the wise and talented, public business
must, generally speaking, be efficiently performed' (145); that 'the certainty
of attaining wealth and rank in the state, merely through personal qualifications, stimulates the whole nation to healthful exertions, thus diffusing
prosperity throughout it, and multiplying its powers to a great extent' (148);
and concludes by saying in all capital letters 'FOR THE RULERS OF ALL
OTHER NATIONS, THE CHINESE EMPIRE CONSTITUTES A GREAT
PRACTICAL LESSON OF FOUR THOUSAND YEARS' STANDING'
(154). Crucially, the final chapter of the book is a call for the application of
a Chinese-style civil service examination in Britain where, because Britain
has juries, a parliament, and the free press, the examinations will be even
more impartial than they could ever be in China. Here Meadows carefully
separates the *idea* of a fair examination system as a basis for civil service
from the various problems he sees existing in the Chinese *implementation*
of it. Such a system would ensure impartiality, standardisation, and 'a con-
sequent unity of feeling throughout the empire' (248–49).

Nine years later Meadows published a second work, *The Chinese and
Their Rebellions* (1856), which includes a preface entitled 'Plan for the
Union of the British Empire and the Improvement of the British Executive',
which is essentially a twenty-seven-page argument for the adoption of a
competitive civil service both in Britain and in its colonies. More importantly, he details how he himself instituted such a system in the British factory at Canton, where he wound up hiring 'perfect strangers' who turned
out to be the ablest men in the factory (1856, xxii–xxiii). Meadows outlines his idea of how to implement such a system on a much wider scale in
Britain, and then goes on to reiterate the advantages he sees in such a system
(xxv–xlviii). Furthermore, in the main body of the book, he argues that, just
as there is 'an intimate connection between "ignorance and vice", so on the
other hand high intellectual faculties are, as a general rule (which the exceptions but prove) associated with moral elevation' and therefore the use of
examinations will identify not only the talented, but also the virtuous (21).
This may be seen as an attempt to answer charges, as we will see below, that
examinations are precisely incapable of that function.

Teng traces the development of various types of examinations in Great
Britain and its colonies. As Foucault has argued, colonial possessions were
often the site of experiments in modernisations that were then later imported
into the home country (Foucault 2003, 103; see also Lloyd 2011). This
was also true of the civil service examinations. The East India Company's
training college Haileybury, designed to train men up for service in overseas posts, had examinations as early as 1806, and in 1833 there was a
regularised system of civil service examinations for the Indian civil service

extending beyond that college. By 1850 the Indian Civil Service had a full-blown competitive examination system; fifteen years later Britain followed suit at home.

Debates in Parliament, as recorded in *Hansard's Parliamentary Debates*, were long and protracted, with advocates of patronage fighting a rearguard movement to preserve the privilege of patronage for as long as possible in whatever form possible. The process of adopting a civil service examination in Britain thus proceeded by stages, with various combinations of patronage and examinations being used together. One worked by allowing patrons to nominate a limited number of candidates for a post (say, three), and then having an examination to decide which of the three got the job; another had a dozen or more candidates nominated by patronage, followed by an examination to determine the top five or six candidates, who would then be proposed for heads of departments to select from for posts in their offices; another had an open examination, after which the head of department was allowed to choose which of the highest scoring candidates would get the job.

Throughout the debate, proponents of an examination system sought to portray the existing system of patronage in the worst possible light. Terms such as 'favouritism', 'nepotism', 'bribery', 'irresponsible family patronage', [abuse of] 'power', 'corruption', and 'jobbing' occur frequently (see for example *Hansard's Parliamentary Debates*, series 3 [1829–92], 127:1317–18; 129:573; 146:1467–68; 148:1676–77; 163:1033). This marks a shift in collocation for the term patronage, which, as we have seen, was often used in a neutral or positive sense in the early nineteenth century.

Several of the key speeches in Parliament referenced the Chinese system. The Earl of Granville cited the Chinese example as early as 1853, during preliminary debates, saying:

> I have heard it stated that one of the principal reasons why a small Tartar dynasty has governed the immense empire of China for upwards of 200 years, has been that they have got the talent of the whole Chinese population by opening every official situation to competition. (128:38)

Later in the year, due to others questioning the veracity of such reports, Granville spoke again at greater length about the Chinese example, going out of his way to say that he had sought out the opinion of a British Sinologist, Dr John Bowring. Bowring not only backed up the Earl's earlier statement but also added that, so ingrained was the sense of fairness of the civil service examinations in the popular opinion, one of the rallying cries of the Taiping rebels was that the Qing government had tampered with the degrees which had been obtained by recent examinees; the Taipings promised 'if victorious, to restore the ancient system in its pristine purity' (129:1340–41).

Even critics of the civil service reform brought up the Chinese case, although of course for these critics, the Chinese case was hardly exemplary. In 1860, Mr Laing, a Member of Parliament, noted that 'The only practical instance which they yet had of the complete working of competitive examinations in the Civil Service was in China, and that was hardly a test by which the merits of the system could be fully judged' (156:1194). In other words, Laing does not believe that China should serve as an example for Britain, but he is aware that they have a working competitive examination system. Other Members of Parliament went further than this. Mr Baillie Cochrane first echoes Mr Laing's proposal that a Chinese example is no example at all (158:2062–3)[2] and then goes on to say that the same John Bowring, whom the Earl of Granville had cited, *also* said that:

> The war in 1841 was called the Opium War, and he believed it would never have taken place, if the Emperor had not sent down a *very learned Chinese—* Commissioner Lin—*but a man of incontestable ignorance as to countries and nations*, and who, above any one, was likely to involve China in a quarrel. He had risen from the ranks; for among the Chinese it was a rule that the humblest may rise to the highest station in the empire. It was all the result of competition. (158:2062–3, my italics)

This attack is a restatement of a criticism often levelled against the idea of a general examination, that the knowledge tested is not necessarily applicable to the job for which the candidates are being selected. Cochrane concludes his attack by saying 'the qualities most desirable in public men—zeal, diligence, public honour, and private integrity—were precisely those in which candidates could not be examined' (158:2066). In a move that finds an echo in early twenty-first concerns in the United States about teaching for examinations, Members of Parliament avowed that a civil service examination would lead to 'cramming' and rote learning of useless knowledge at the expense of developing students' judgement and powers of reflection (128:13–15; 150:1698; 166:339–41; 167:93). Some even claimed that because cram schools were expensive, the examinations would preclude the poor and middle classes from succeeding (172:966).

Another attack that was aimed at the British civil service examination was that it would ruin the lives of thousands of young men because they would set their sights on a job in the civil service, spend years preparing for it, and then be disappointed when they were not successful. Again, China was held up as a (bad) example of this: Mr Monckton Milnes, Member of Parliament, quotes a Chinese gentleman who 'mentioned with pride that in his native country he came out of an examination where there were no less than 8,000 candidates'; Milnes then goes on to say that such a system is not worth it (163:1437).

There is thus quite a mass of evidence gathered both by Teng (1943) from various sources and myself from the Parliamentary record that the example of the Chinese civil service examination system informed the debates around the adoption of a civil service examination in Britain and its colonies. The United States followed suit slightly later, with first a failed effort in the 1860s and then eventually the passage of the Pendleton Civil Service Reform Act of 1883. Advocates for civil service reform such as Thomas Jenckes, a congressman from Rhode Island, and leading intellectuals such as Ralph Waldo Emerson cited the Chinese example, while W. A. P. Martin, president of the Tung-wen College in Beijing, read a paper on the Chinese examination system before the American Oriental Society in 1868 that was later printed in the *North American Review* (Hoogenboom 1961, 647; Teng 1943, 306). Teng (1943, 306–7) provides additional examples from books and magazines from the period.

From example to villain

Yet even as Britain and the United States were emulating the Chinese civil examination service to combat abuses of the earlier patronage system (often called the 'spoils system' in the United States), China's government was at the same time being identified as a classic case of rampant patronage, corruption, nepotism, and bribery, despite the fact that it had both a civil service examination system for appointments and various other measures in place to combat such abuses.

Meadows, whom we have seen was perhaps the most ardent proponent of importing the Chinese civil service examination to Britain and its colonies, was far from having a starry-eyed view of China. In both works he has plenty of negative things to say about the Chinese and the way that the government is run, especially at the local level, citing widespread corruption, routine bribery, flaunting of laws and regulations, and the widespread use of torture to extract confessions (1847, 106–9 and 113–15); he also has an entire chapter entitled 'On the Principal Defects of the Chinese Government' and another entitled 'On the Extortions and Oppressions of the Mandarins', in which he elaborates at length on these and other problems (1847, 155–70 and 175–86). Chapter nine, 'On the Yamun and Their Various Inhabitants', discusses at length the way that key members of an official's staff rely on a variety of personal connections in their business, which is notoriously corrupt (109–16). The *chaiyi* (差役 runners, a sort of low-level police or bounty hunter), for example, have 'connections' with local gangs, and the *yemen* (爺們 trusted personal retainers of the official) normally obtain their posts either through family ties to the mandarin or through recommendation from the mandarin's superior. Meadows sees these ills as mainly due to the low or non-existent pay for officials and their underlings (contradicting earlier reports that pay was ample; see Mendoza 1588, 1:80–82) as well as a system that rewards low reports of crime, which leads to widespread bribery and the routinisation of corruption. This argument about institutional causes of corruption is repeated by later writers (Giles 1877, 58; Pu 1880, 1:219 footnote; Dukes 1885, 93; Moule 1891, 26; Smith 1894, 236; Cockburn 1896, 104; Ball 1904, 321). At the end Meadows is careful to point out that such problems could be avoided in the British case due to differences in institutional structures.

Likewise, in the Parliamentary debates, we see that even proponents of the civil service reform bill who cited the Chinese example sometimes indicated that it might not be proper for Britain to emulate Chinese *practice*. Earl Granville, one of the strongest supporters of the bill who cited the Chinese example twice and even confirmed his opinion with a China expert, Dr Bowring, notes that sometimes the Chinese may carry things too far: 'It is probable we may not be required to carry out our examinations in the same strict manner as in some instances is adopted in China—Dr. Bowring having informed me of a case in which the examiner was sent down to one of the provinces locked up in a box' (*Hansard's Parliamentary Debates*, series 3 [1829–92], 129:1341). The tone of gentle jest arises from the speaker's disbelief that anyone should carry measures to such extremes. This extremism of the Chinese is, as we have seen in the evolution of foreign perceptions of Chinese filial piety, a step towards identifying the Chinese not as a people to emulate, but rather a people who go beyond the bounds of reason.

We must keep in mind that at the time these debates were proceeding, British subjects were witnessing the depredations of the Taiping Rebellion and also entering into the Second Opium War (1856–60) with China, both of which led to a serious readjustment of British opinions of the Chinese. There are debates in Parliament about the reprehensible behaviour of both the rebels and the government troops, using especially the terms 'perfidy' and 'cruelty' several times by different speakers (see for example *Hansard's Parliamentary Debates* series 3 [1829–92], 173:215–16 and 1463–71). Summing up the situation, Colonel Sykes says 'there are two faults which must be matter of reproach to the Chinese—one is cruelty, and the other is perfidy' (173:1473). There were also the reports, as noted earlier, that one of the reasons for the rebellion was that the Qing government had watered down key provisions of the civil service examination, both by favouring Manchu candidates in order to ensure that a good number of Manchus were members of the bureaucracy, and then later in widespread sale of degrees, and of such degree holders being able to attain higher offices than previously was possible. Reports relating to these two events thus helped to worsen British opinion of the Chinese government.

Meadows and Lord Granville were able to separate out the potential of the civil service examination from the reality of its flawed implementation. They also did not connect it to Chinese values or social structure, tending more to note institutional problems, such as low pay for officials, as the underlying cause of abuses to the system. However, as the century wore on, more and more foreign writers complain about the breadth and depth of corruption, bribery, and miscarriages of justice in China (Nevius 1868, 285 and 429; Cockburn 1896, 139; Douglas 1899, 257). Although some positive discussions about the attempts of the Chinese to control nepotistic tendencies still occur in the 1870s (for example Gray 1878, 1:186), already in 1877 Giles makes damning remarks about how the Chinese are 'behind the rest of the civilised world in theory and practice alike' (1877, 60). By the end of the century, Douglas (1899, 448) thought that corruption was so extensive that it impeded all attempts at modernisation (harking back to the link between Chinese characteristics and a refusal of Western modernity discussed earlier), while Selby (1900, 28) claimed that China had 'a Government which is perhaps the most colossal piece of corrupt incompetence the world has ever known', and that China, once the model for Europe in terms of civil service, was decried as a hopeless case, and was being urged to copy British institutions (284). Ball (1904, 161–62) said that 'rapacity and corruptions pervade every department of the State'. Similarly, Johnston claims that 'so long as bribery and "squeeze" system are practically recognised as necessary features of civil administration', reform is impossible (1910, 442); earlier in the same work he also claimed that

> until the existing departments of Government have been thoroughly reorganised, corruption stamped out, and a spirit of loyalty and patriotism infused into all ranks of the Civil Service, the creation of a great spending department, such as an Admiralty or Naval Board, will merely add enormously to the financial burdens of the country without providing it with any reliable safeguard or protection in the event of war. (437)

Thus by the early twentieth century, China and corruption are almost synonymous.[3]

In the same time period, there is a certain number of descriptions of various types of social ties, both those of kinship and those of influence, in the literature, which today would probably be labelled as guanxi. Cockburn noted the importance of connections as a social safety network in a land where insurance, pensions, and social welfare programmes were almost unknown (1896, 151). In some cases missionaries even advocated using the importance of connections in Chinese villages to obtain converts to

Christianity, hypothesising that converting 'key' people in the village would lead to mass conversions through their ties to other villagers (Selby 1900, 3 and 226).

More importantly for my argument, connections were also linked to corruption in the Chinese civil service and the law courts. Cockburn emphasised how jobs in the local customs offices multiplied endlessly so that an official 'can always find employment for his poor relations' (1896, 139). MacGowan furnishes an excellent example of how deeply entrenched the misuse of connections had become:

> This official happened to be one of those upright men that are found occasionally in office, who was impervious to a bribe, and who was desirous that justice should be done without respect to the position or character of the parties. He foresaw, however, that there would be difficulties in the case, as the rich man had not only wealth to back him but also influential family connexions that would enable him to resist any judgment that might be given against him. (1909, 122)

In other words, the system is so corrupted by the misuse of social networking that even an upright official stands little chance of successfully prosecuting a rich and well-connected man who can give bribes and pull strings. Clearly, by the early twentieth century, there is ample discourse in the English literature that China's bureaucracy is hopelessly corrupt and backward, and that it is linked to the improper use of personal connections.

Tellingly, some of the most detailed descriptions of corruption and cheating are related to the Chinese civil service examination system. Doolittle has an entire section entitled 'Examiners often influenced by bribes' (1865, 1:427–44, 2:381, and 2:422), and many others discuss the topic (Nevius 1868, 60; Smith 1899, 132; Selby 1900, 39).[4] Again, this allowed the British to claim that the Chinese needed to learn about fighting corruption in government from the British, after having just borrowed the idea of civil service examinations to solve the same problem of corruption in Britain.

This required an active form of forgetting, one which continues to this day. Eighty years after the various works by Reichwein ([1925] 1968), Teng (1943) and Maverick (1946) conclusively demonstrated the importance of the Chinese civil service as a model for Europeans, and especially for the British, histories of the British civil service continue to ignore their role. Chapman's book-length study in 2004 only mentions the Chinese example twice. The first time, it is not as an example from which the British drew, but as a point of contrast when discussing standards. After noting that the Commissioners for the civil service in India expected a high standard of integrity to be maintained, Chapman quotes an example from Meadows regarding the draconian measures taken by the Chinese government when corruption was detected: twelve officials were executed due to 'conniving of the substitution of a set of essays for the Ken-jin (the second counting from below)' (Chapman 2004, 118–19). Chapman here reproduces the Victorian logic of citing the extremities to which the Chinese went as a counterfoil to the British, who 'of course ... were not as extreme as in Imperial China' (119). On page 233, buried in a discussion of civil service systems in other cultures, Chapman is willing to admit that the Chinese system may have influenced 'the development of the examination systems in Britain and India', but only in regard to the emphasis placed on classical studies.

Having conveniently forgotten China's role as a model, the British and then the Americans, as I have demonstrated, were quick to condemn the Chinese as hopelessly corrupt, mired in nepotism, cronyism, and other forms of favouritism. Although they do not go so far as to claim that guanxi is a national characteristic, they do note the importance of family ties (and therefore the propensity to nepotism), as well as the ties of mutual responsibility at even the level of neighbourhood or village (Smith 1894, 208). Smith, whose work we have seen was so important in the 1890s and early twentieth century, has a few telling passages:

> The individual who has done you a favour may refuse your subsequent offer of money, either because he thinks it is too little, or because he is hoping that in the future you will be able to do him a service in return; (67)

> The same greater or less disregard of orders appears to prevail through all the various ranks of Chinese officials in their relations to one another, up to the very topmost round. There are several motives any one of which may lead to the contravening of instructions, such as personal indolence, a wish to oblige friends, or, most potent of all, the magnetic influence of cash; (78)

> The influence of an elder brother over a younger, or indeed of any older member over a younger member of the same family, is of the most direct and positive sort, and is entirely irreconcilable with what we mean by personal liberty; (227)

> For a local magistrate to be guilty of all kinds of misdemeanours for which he gets into no trouble whatever, or getting into it, escapes scot-free by means of influential friends or by a judicious expenditure of silver; (232)

> Some Chinese officials cannot be tempted by any bribe, and refuse to commit a wrong that will never be found out, because 'Heaven knows, earth knows, you know, and I know'. But how many Chinese could be found who would resist the pressure brought upon them to recommend for employment a relative who was known to be incompetent? Imagine for a moment the domestic consequences of such resistance, and is it strange that any Chinese should dread to face them? But what Chinese would ever think of carrying theoretical morals into such a region as that? When it is seen what a part parasitism and nepotism

play in the administration of China, civil, military, and commercial, is it any wonder that Chinese gate-keepers and constables are not to be depended upon for the honest performance of their duties? (317)

In these passages we note the idea of reciprocity and storing up of favours for future use; obligations of connections leading to disregarding the law, the (excessively) strong ties in families, the calling in of favours in time of need, and the overwhelming pressure that family members can exert on other members. The topic also occurs in his later *Village Life in China* in several places (Smith 1899, 164, 185, 191, 223, 302, and 305). Pages 181–82 in particular contain a description of the careful recording of the value of cash presents at weddings and funerals to maintain reciprocity, one of the key features of guanxi dwelt upon by guanxi researchers in the 1990s.

As we have seen with filial piety, this Western discourse penetrated into the Chinese public sphere during the early twentieth century. I have dwelt upon the example of Arthur Smith precisely because, as we learned in earlier chapters, his book was translated first into Japanese and then Chinese, and was available to members of the May Fourth generation.

In twentieth-century Chinese literature there is plenty of evidence that corruption is a popular theme, as indeed it was in some major fiction of the Ming and Qing dynasties, but beyond nepotism, connections do not play a major role.[5] I had to search long and hard to find a few passages that link connections and corruption. An extensive keyword search of related terms turned up one late Qing novel and a work by Su Qing (蘇青 1914–82) in the 1940s as the only significant examples where terminology relating to connections was related more than once to some form of corruption.[6]

Likewise, writings in English by Chinese academics may discuss corruption but seldom dwell on the importance of connections. Lin Yutang, who certainly pulls no punches in his critique of various facets of Chinese society, writes that

> Face, favour, privilege, gratitude, courtesy, official corruption, public institutions, the school, the guild, philanthropy, hospitality, justice, and finally the whole government of China—all spring from the family and village system, all borrow from it their peculiar tenor and complexion, and all find in it enlightening explanations for their peculiar characteristics. (Lin 1939b, 167)

Favour, privilege, and official corruption are all aspects of corruption; yet although he links these to 'the family and village system', he does not explicitly point to guanxi as being involved. Likewise Yang, whose work I discussed earlier regarding the importance of face in social life of his natal Chinese village, contains no special mention of connections as a defining characteristic, even though the stated purpose of his study as a sociologist was to describe the connections that bind Chinese society together, 'start[ing] with the interactions between the individual in the primary groups, go on to those between primary groups in the secondary group, and finally those between the secondary groups in a large area' (Yang 1947, x). Although he does talk about face and filial piety at length, and mentions fengshui in at least a couple of places, as discussed in earlier chapters, nowhere in his book does he raise the possibility that Chinese social relations are unique, despite the fact that in several places he records practices of what is today considered central to guanxi, such as the careful recording of gifts at births, weddings, funerals, and other important social events so that equivalent gifts can later be given in return (152).

In Chinese, the situation is slightly more complicated. In 1947, Fei Xiaotong (費孝通 1910–2005), one of the founders of sociology in China who trained at the London School of Economics, published 鄉土中國 (*From the Soil: The Foundations of Chinese Society*). In this work he employs the term 'guanxi' and also the compound *shehui guanxi* (social relationships) and he identifies certain characteristics of such relationships. The three most important characteristics are that social networks are centred around each person (in other words, each person has their own unique network); each network link is a dyad, is unique, and is an example of guanxi; and networks have no explicit boundaries, extending outward, like ripples in a pond (Fei 1992, 20–24). Therefore, the moral content of an individual's behaviour in the network is situation specific; or, as Andrew Kipnis rephrases it in 1997, 'the art of guanxi invokes a moral emphasis on the relational ethics of gan-qing exchange at the expense of universalistic ethics of state normalization' (Kipnis 1997, 150).

Fei's argument, which contained most of the core ideas relating to guanxi as defined in today's sociological and anthropological literature, did not receive much attention at the time, probably because shortly after the establishment of the PRC in 1949, sociology was banned as an academic subject and he was branded as a Rightist. One early exception was the Chinese-American academic Francis K. L. Hsu, who knew Fei Xiaotong's work and began researching and publishing in the field of psychological anthropology.[7] As early as 1948, Hsu noted the importance of official connections vis à vis the local standing of different clans in the village where he conducted his fieldwork, and specifically linked widespread nepotism among officials to the unique characteristics of Chinese society, where generosity to one's own in-group leads to praise and prestige locally, which is all that one cares about (Hsu 1948, 124–25, 225–27, and 263; also see Hsu 1963, 167 for a recurrence of this argument). He did not use the term guanxi, or any other term to denote this particular nexus of connections and favours, but his is the first discussion in English of Chinese characteristics described in a neutral or positive manner, for the emphasis in his work is on the security and groundedness that the Chinese individual finds in their web of interpersonal connections. This comes across particularly strongly in his *Americans and Chinese*, where discussions of problems in Chinese society are carefully balanced against discussion of problems in American society. A discussion of why Chinese are partial to opium addiction is followed by one on Americans being prone to marijuana use (at a time when this was considered a serious social ill) and suicide (1955, 52–65); a discussion of the problems inherent in Chinese marriage is balanced by a consideration of problems in American marriage (125–34), and so forth. In the final section, an entire chapter is devoted to drawbacks of American society, followed by one devoted to the problems of Chinese society (327–80).

Back in the Chinese world, Fei's ideas lay fallow until in the 1960s and 1970s they were picked up by a group of sociologists and psychologists in Taiwan and Hong Kong, including Hwang Kwang-kuo 黃光國, Li Yih-Yuan 李亦園, Yang Kuo-shu 楊國樞, Wen Chung-i 文崇一, and Ambrose Yeo-chi King 金耀基, all trained in Western universities, who were interested in establishing Chinese psychology, Chinese sociology, and Chinese anthropology. Their basic premise was that the various academic disciplines that had developed in European and North American universities claimed to be universally valid but were in fact built upon a narrow base of data collected from European and North American societies; these theories and models of how society worked were thereby incomplete and inherently biased. They then took Hsu's argument one step further from a neutral description of Chinese characteristics to a positive one, celebrating the characteristics that distinguished Chinese society from Western ones as advantages rather than disadvantages. It is these scholars who for the first time elevate guanxi to the status of key concept in Chinese culture, building upon Fei Xiaotong's work.

Two of the earliest studies of guanxi produced by this group were by Ambrose King and Chiao Chien 喬建, both from the Chinese University of Hong Kong. King is a sociologist who clearly shows the influence of Fei Xiaotong on this group of scholars, quoting extensively from Fei's work (King [1980] 1989, 76, 86–87, and 99). King also begins his essay by stressing the importance of researching Chinese cultural concepts both to test those supposedly universal concepts on new data from different societies and also to introduce some of these new, Chinese-based concepts to the wider field, one of the major goals of their work (76–77).

King equates the modern term guanxi to the Confucian term *lun* (倫) in Classical Chinese. He takes the five relationships (*wu lun* 五倫 father–son, ruler–subject, elder brother–younger brother, husband–wife, and friend–friend) as the classic statement on the centrality of guanxi as an integral part of the Confucian social order. He then links it to both renqing and *bao* (報 reciprocity) to conclude, like Fei Xiaotong, that ethical standards in Chinese society are based on valuing relations between private individuals while at the same time understanding the difference between close and distant relations and superiors and inferiors, leading to relativistic standards of behaviour based on an ego-centric view of society (86–87). He then posits two types of exchange in society, which he labels social and economic, the former being based on renqing and bao, the latter being based on impartiality and contract (89–91). Most of the rest of the essay is taken up with the tension between these two types of exchange in the individual bureaucrat and businessman, who must constantly choose, not between right and wrong, but between two different sets of moral values (97). Yet despite the fact that King begins by calling for introducing Chinese concepts into sociology, in the end King says that as Chinese societies in Hong Kong and Taiwan modernise, social relations are slowly being replaced by economic ones. Thus there is an implicit narrative of progress towards modernity through the rejection of Chinese tradition, much as was also the case in the May Fourth Movement.

Chiao Chien's article is one of the foundational texts for the study of guanxi practices as they developed in Mainland China, identifying some of the key features that would distinguish guanxi practiced there as opposed to Taiwan, Hong Kong, and overseas Chinese populations. He is the first to notice the emergence of a group of terms related to guanxi, including: *guanxixue* (關係學 guanxi-ology), which he links to the conscious establishment of a wide network of connections mainly for instrumental purposes; the term *guanxi hu* (關係戶 guanxi household, that is, a regular/stable guanxi connection); and the term *guanxi wang* (關係網 guanxi web, the sum total of your guanxi hu) (Chiao [1980]1989, 107 and 114–15). He also pays special attention to collocates, especially verbs used with the term, and what those different verb-object combinations mean (108–10). He also documents the extent to which guanxixue is vital for all facets of life under the Chinese Communist Party (CCP).

Chiao concludes by arguing that guanxi should become a new universal concept in the social sciences, because he believes that the type of social structure seen in China is more common around the world than those seen in Western nations. Unlike King, he does not conclude that guanxi will slowly diminish as China modernises, and he argues for using kuan-hsi, a romanised form of the Chinese term, rather than any of the terms proposed by other researchers in English, such as 'personal network' or 'particularistic ties', because he feels that the multifaceted meaning of guanxi is not completely covered by any term in English. This is one of the strongest arguments for the establishment of guanxi as a universal academic concept, similar to the way in which face was adopted by sociolinguistics at about the same time.

Two other examples occur in a later edited collection (Yang and Hwang 1991). Ho *et al*, in their paper on guanxi, first identify it as the single most important characteristic that distinguishes Chinese psychology from Western psychology, because it means that the self is largely defined by its connection to others, and therefore the boundary of the individual is not as clear-cut as in the West (Ho, Chen, and Chiu 1991, 58–62), and then explicitly link it to face, a characteristic that Ho had written an important paper on in 1976 (see Chapter 3 for discussion of his work). The other article on guanxi in this collection links guanxi to renqing (human connections or obligations). Here we get one of the more important statements on guanxi as divisible into good and bad. Good guanxi based on affective ties leads people to value emotional rewards, which can aid the company for which one works, while bad guanxi based purely on instrumental motives leads to people putting their private gain over the good of the company, which results in all of the evil practices decried by earlier critics (Yu and Hwang 1991, 220–21). This article is also of interest because of the way it explores how one or more of these characteristics then played out in various facets of contemporary Taiwan, Hong Kong, Singapore, Korea, Japan, and (occasionally) China. Yu and Huang (1991) investigated the influence of renqing and guanxi on the development of Taiwan's national industries, showing how guanxi often *helped* these industries to develop. This was in the time of the 'Asian miracle' and the Four Asian Tigers (Taiwan, South Korea, Hong Kong, and Singapore), with Tu Wei-ming at Harvard trumpeting Confucian values as the underlying basis of their success.

Finally, the book 中國文化的深層結構 (The deep structure of Chinese culture), by Sun Lung-Kee 孫隆基, brings us back full circle to the arguments of Smith and his colleagues of the previous century. Andrew Kipnis puts it well in his work:

> As the title of his book implies, Sun uses an essentialized, psychologised notion of Chinese culture, of which guanxi subject construction is the central component, to paint a negative picture of Chinese the globe over. Sun describes a series of 'Chinese characteristics'—including an underdeveloped sexuality, an inability to control bodily fluids and functions in public, a sycophantic personality, a rejection of rationality, and political despotism—as entailments of a desire to construct and be constructed by guanxi subjects. Sun's analysis was originally written as a cultural self-critique for a Chinese-language audience, and I fear a total appropriation of his work into English would border on racism. (Kipnis 1997, 187–88)

The main argument about guanxi subject construction occurs quite early. Sun first characterises the Western notion of the self as existing outside of all social constraints, using Existentialism as his example of the extreme of this viewpoint. By contrast, for the Chinese ' "the individual" only manifests within social guanxi—the individual is the synthesis of all social roles, and if these social guanxi are emptied out, "the individual" evaporates' ("人"是只有在社會關係裏才能體現的—他是所有社會角色的綜合，如果將這些社會關係都抽空了，"人"就被蒸發掉了; Sun 1988, 11). Guanxi thus becomes *the* most basic Chinese characteristic; he then links guanxi variously to the Confucian concept of *ren* (仁; usually translated as 'benevolence' but here better understood as humanity, or how we interact with others), renqing and face (11–195). Interestingly, Sun decentres filial piety, placing the emphasis squarely on the ramifications of subject construction based on guanxi and therefore an extended, group definition of the self; when he talks about the family, he emphasises more the power of the father over the son rather than the son's filial duty towards the parents (177–81 and 201–3). The rest of the book is devoted to the ramifications summarised by Kipnis.

These works were published in Chinese, although the same authors also occasionally published in English. They also often cited English works, and their influence was widely felt among academics overseas, especially those who were originally from Taiwan. Chief among these was Mayfair Mei-hui Yang, who in 1994 published the first book-length study of guanxi in English: *Gifts, Favors, and Banquets: The Art of Social Relationships in China*. The cover features the Chinese characters guanxixue (which she renders as 'the art of guanxi' or 'the art of social relationships'), and in the course of the book she develops the distinction between guanxi and guanxixue first noted by Chiao. Crucially, she also links it to the distinction between good and bad guanxi established by Ho and Hwang, a distinction taken over by many later researchers in English-language studies; she then explicitly blames the CCP for causing the emergence of guanxixue due to its disastrous policies in the Great Leap Forward and the Cultural Revolution (154–59). Yang follows King in linking guanxi to Confucian values, and, while she compares guanxixue to the concept of *blat* in the Soviet Union, she claims that because guanxi is linked with ganqing, renqing, and *yiqi* (義氣 which Yang glosses as ' "loyalty" or "ethic of righteousness" ' [119]), it is unique to China; in a later article in 2002 she refutes the idea that guanxi is going to wither away as rule of law becomes established in China, because she believes that it is an integral part of Chinese culture (Yang 2002). In effect, these arguments combine to suggest that guanxi is an age-old (good) practice that has been corrupted into (bad) guanxixue by the evil excesses of the CCP, similar to the argument by Hu (1944) that face in Chinese is split into an older mianzi and a newer lian, with lian being associated with the more negative aspects of face.

Another important study of guanxi in the same year was the English article by Ambrose King in Tu Wei-ming's edited volume *The Living Tree: The Changing Meaning of Being Chinese Today*. In this updated English-language study, King ties guanxi to face and renqing, and notes its persistence in the modern period despite the CCP's attempts to root out all feudal elements of culture, specifically attempts to substitute a universal comradeship over personal connections (King 1994, 109 and 117–18). King again stresses the Confucian roots of guanxi. Finally, although he still claims that as the rule of law becomes established, guanxi declines in importance in places like Taiwan and Hong Kong, he brings in the argument first developed by Chiao that in the PRC, the gap between socialist universal values and market rationality provides a space within which guanxi can flourish (125–26).

Mayfair Yang's work was mainly based on research collected in cities; a few years later Andrew Kipnis's book *Producing Guanxi* looked at the role of guanxi in a rural setting in Mainland China. His thesis is that *ganqing* (感情 emotions) rather than renqing is the real basis of guanxi; he says that ganqing and guanxi are two sides of one coin (Kipnis 1997, 23). More interestingly, he argues that the split King posits in all societies between social and economic relationships (with the social involving renqing and therefore being guanxi) is actually only a split in modern Western societies; in Chinese society, guanxi is more of a total relationship that encompasses both (Kipnis 1997, 24). Like Mayfair Yang, regarding the question of whether guanxi is rooted in Confucian values or is a response to communist rule and scarcity of goods, he argues for both. He posits that it initially evolved in a society where legal protection was minimal, but continues to be important today both in the diaspora and in the emerging private firms in China of the 1990s (Kipnis 1997, 6–7 and 153). Kipnis also notes that, although the CCP has long perceived guanxi as a threat and tried to root out old forms, in fact various new forms of guanxi have also been important for the CCP (158–64).

Kipnis also shows the continued influence of Fei Xiaotong's work, expanding upon Fei's idea that the self in China is relational. One good example is Kipnis's discussion of the large number of different names for a single person, including relational appellations such as 'mother of X', which would be used by different people depending on their relation to the person; for Kipnis, this can only suggest that the self is radically relational rather than fixed.[8]

It should be clear by this point that since some time in the late 1970s, the discussion in academia of the meaning of guanxi has been essentially bilingual, carried out both in English and Chinese, with some scholars writing in both languages and all scholars reading and citing works in both languages. This is possible mainly because guanxi, unlike face, has remained firmly attached to China and the Chinese, and so therefore all studies of guanxi revolve around Chinese communities, whereas many studies of face are conducted by sociolinguists with no knowledge of China or Chinese. Despite Chiao's claims that guanxi is more common than Western-style relations worldwide, to date there have not been studies showing how the concept of guanxi can be used to understand other cultures. Instead, when comparative studies are conducted, each country has its own special term. Horak and Taube (2016), for example, use guanxi for China and *yongo* for Korea, while Karhunen *et al* (2018) compare Chinese guanxi to Russian blat, and García (2014) uses clientelism for Europe and guanxi for China.

The extent to which guanxi remains linked to China can also be seen by a survey of its use in English-language newspapers. A search for the term in the *New York Times* and the *Wall Street Journal* from 1980–2020 generated 140 hits. All of these hits were related either to China, to foreigners trying to understand how guanxi affects their lives in China, or to how guanxi continues to be used among overseas Chinese populations. Each time that the term was used, it was invariably defined for the reader, usually in a short parenthetical phrase, sometimes in a longer and more detailed separate sentence or paragraph. This is in sharp contrast to both face and to fengshui, which as we have seen have put down roots in American culture and are used by a large number of people who know little or nothing about China and apply them to non-Chinese situations.

In the English-language press, guanxi is still generally portrayed in a negative light. This is also true in Chinese-language newspapers and periodicals, especially state-owned media in China. The *People's Daily* first ran an article devoted to guanxi in early 1980 (Xi 1980); this article was quickly followed by several others in the same year, and then in 1981 there was an explosion of interest, with thirty-three articles. The number tapered off sharply in the following year to nine and then settled in to an average of four to eight per year through 1988, after which the *People's Daily* largely lost interest in the topic. Between 1990 and 1994 and again between 2001 and 2006 there were no articles at all; in other years typically there were one to two articles right up until the present, with a slight increase in 2015 and 2017.[9]

In all of these articles, the attitude is uniformly critical of guanxi. The tone is set from the very start, associating guanxi and guanxixue variously with feudalism, capitalism, colonialism, Lin Biao, and the evil Gang of Four (Xi 1980; Zheng 1980). In the only article in which a party member admits to practicing guanxixue, the author bemoans the fact that he is driven to these desperate measures in order to help the local population under his care, and he calls upon the leaders of the party to root out such corrupt practices from the party and the state (Wan 1989).

People's Daily makes an interesting attempt, again, to distinguish 'good' social relations from 'bad' social relations, but they do so, not by contrasting guanxi and guanxixue, but rather by contrasting comradely relations (*tongzhi guanxi* 同志關係) with individual relations (*geren guanxi* 個人關係). This first happens in an article in February of 1980, a month before the first broadside against guanxixue, The article argues that comradely relations, if taken as the basis of work relations, establishes an equality that allows people to work together to overcome all obstacles and realise the ideals of socialism. Yet the article warns that recently, individual relations have been replacing comradely relations and threatening socialism, splitting people into cliques and putting profit before all else (Yin 1980). In 1982 this is followed up by an important article which stresses first that CCP members of course are full of all kinds of sentiment (*qing* 情; the common denominator in renqing and ganqing), but that their sentiments for all sorts of people do not interfere with their ability to treat everyone equally and avoid any whiff of 'special relations' (*teshu guanxi* 特殊關係). 'Sentimental' comradely relations are then sharply contrasted with guanxixue, which is the essence of individualism, combining the worst parts of feudalism and capitalism and resulting in the plundering of public goods for private gain (He 1982).

Despite this uniform official condemnation in the *People's Daily*, by the 1990s it was possible to find self-help books in Chinese that promised to 'teach you how to grasp China's most complex yet most practical body of knowledge' (教你掌握中國最複雜但卻是最實用的學問; Dong 1998, dust cover; translation provided in Gold *et al* 2002, xvi).[10]

It is also true that, among the general population, if someone says that so-and-so managed to accomplish something through guanxi, the implication is that it was done improperly. However, it is also true that people may sometimes brag about the quality or reach of their own guanxi. Thus we have a sort of schizophrenic popular view, wherein if one uses guanxi oneself to attain a desired end it is a good thing, whereas if one describes how someone else attained a desired end through guanxi it is reprehensible.

Guanxi and business studies

Returning to the academic sphere, from the social sciences, guanxi studies are quickly picked up by business studies.[11] Such studies aim to apply the belief that guanxi is a unique characteristic of Chinese culture to the world of business, commerce, and human resource management. Most of the earlier debates in the social sciences are carried over into the new domain, notably over whether guanxi is declining, steady, or growing in importance in the world of business; whether its origins lie in hoary tradition or recent political events; and whether it is a unique advantage that allows China to prosper, or is a millstone hung around the neck of the economy. But on one thing they all agree: guanxi is crucial to understanding how business works in China today. Thus any foreigner wanting to do business there must understand guanxi in order to be competitive.

Perhaps due to this 'deal with it' attitude, business studies overall have seen some of the most positive statements about guanxi. In particular, guanxi was celebrated as one of the unique and central features of the Chinese economy (Buderi and Huang 2006, 269; Bian 2019, 81 and 102–67). It was even proposed as one of the main reasons for the success of Asian economies in the 1980s and 1990s (Meuer and Krug 2011, 156; Rühle 2011, 188–93). Guanxi is also celebrated as one of the few concepts in business studies that comes from studies of Chinese data (Tsui 2012, 30), which argument aligns with the critique of Eurocentric bias of social science models, both for guanxi and also as we have seen earlier for face. Meuer and Krug (2011, 151), in their overview of research on guanxi in business studies up to 2010, note that much research emphasised its role in improving performance through access to resources.

The argument that guanxi is a positive characteristic is aided by the continued tendency to split guanxi into good and bad facets. Meuer and Krug (2011, 158) note that of the two, 'there is a strong tendency towards explaining the beneficial factors of guanxi, while the "dark side" remains underrepresented'. Buderi and Huang (2006, 6) begin their work by stressing that good guanxi fosters deep and lasting relationships, while bad guanxi leads to favouritism and cronyism. The trick, of course, is somehow to have the former without the latter. Luo (2020), whose work has gone through three editions over twenty years, is another good example of this tendency. After introducing the topic in the first chapter, he devotes the entirety of chapter seven (eighty-five pages) to the topic 'Guanxi, Corruption and Governance'. He spends quite a bit of time and effort arguing that guanxi is distinct from bribery and corruption (206–10). He argues that, because guanxi is intimately bound up with feelings and obligations (ganqing and renqing), although it may be instrumental, it does not cross over the line to become bribery or corruption (Luo 2020, 15–18). In a rather circular argument, he goes on to define bribery and corruption as gifts that are given without first developing feelings or sentiment, and also posits that the same gift given to the same person under differing circumstances may be an innocent gift given out of affection, an instrumental gift between friends, or an outright bribe (11 and 209). Since his book is written primarily with foreign businessmen in mind, he gives explicit advice on how to avoid crossing this line (avoid giving cash gifts and consult local contacts about appropriate gift-giving 27–28). Finally, he posits that 'face' serves as a regulatory brake on the possibility of people exploiting guanxi for nefarious ends, a possibility that he acknowledges exists (vii, 26). In his understanding, actions such as outright bribery or exploiting guanxi to rob state enterprises of wealth for private gain lead to a loss of face and therefore the collapse of one's guanxi network, meaning a loss of opportunity to engage in exchanges with many people (14–15).

Luo is also a good example of how business studies draw heavily on the work of social scientists; he frequently cites Mayfair Yang (4, 8, 22, 27–28, 97, and 291) and, although he does not name Fei Xiaotong, he uses Fei's metaphor of concentric rings and hierarchical relations (9, 13, and 70).

In this sense, business studies provided an opportunity for the now rehabilitated guanxi to be sometimes endorsed by government officials. One example of this is the government of Singapore, which in the 1990s welcomed Tu Wei-ming and the other neo-Confucianists as justification for their policies and as celebrating the achievements of the Singaporean economy and the other Asian Tigers. The dichotomy posited by academics between 'good' and 'bad' guanxi was vital for this move. In the wake of the Asian economic crisis, however, less is now heard of this argument.

It is also true that a second, persistent trend in business studies continues to see guanxi as a distortion or departure from the rule of law and norms of good business practice. Luo (2020) certainly falls into such rhetoric occasionally in his otherwise largely sympathetic portrayal. More clearly, we can see from the titles of such articles as 'Extra-Legal Protection in China: How Guanxi Distorts China's Legal System and Facilitates the Rise of Unlawful Protectors' (Wang 2014) and 'Guanxi Deviant Behaviour in the Chinese Context' (Guo *et al* 2017) that terms such as 'distort' and 'deviant' betray a clear negative attitude towards guanxi, and that many researchers in business studies view guanxi as an alternative to business practices as preached in European and North American business schools.

Conclusion

Guanxi remains a contested key concept much like face, both in Chinese and English.

Moreover, the contestation often relates to prior political or cultural views. Questions relating to its origin, for example, often indicate political bias. Critics of the Chinese Communist Party may be more likely to attribute the origin and rise of guanxi to failures of the Chinese state since 1949, especially the Great Leap Forward and the Cultural Revolution; while those with strong Chinese nationalist sentiments may seek to connect it to ancient texts and hoary tradition. Likewise, championing the uniqueness of guanxi by some social scientists is likely linked to postcolonial and anti-imperialist views, whereas in business studies there is a tendency to decry the 'persistence of cultural essentialism' and call for empirical studies that will 'put the record straight' by showing that guanxi networks are rooted in recent historical developments since the founding of the PRC (Meuer and Krug 2011, 157).

Attempts to connect Chinese classical texts and the discussion of five relationships to the modern concept and practice of guanxi typically omits intermediate steps; in other words, there is no discussion of how the five relations leads to the modern practice of guanxi, and no intermediary texts are cited as proof. There is thus little evidence that guanxi was conceived of as being central to Chinese culture before the modern period.

By contrast, I have shown that in English there is a long and detailed history of associating China with the concept of universal civil service examinations as a way to ensure fairness and impartiality, and then the flipping of this association and the repeated assertions that various sorts of corrupt practices based on connections are rife among the Chinese. The first discussions of connections as being central to the Chinese occur in English-language sources, as an outgrowth of discussions of the high prevalence of corrupt practices based on such connections.

Therefore I contend that the modern concept of guanxi emerges in an interlingual dialogue and that, without that dialogue, guanxi would not today be conceived of as important for, and unique to, Chinese culture, by anyone. Also because of that historical dialogue, the link between guanxi and various forms of corruption remains strong; attempts to rehabilitate it have been only partially successful in restricted fields (anthropology, business studies).

Despite the fact that as early as 1980, Ambrose King raised the question of whether a society based on guanxi and renqing is the norm and modern Western societies that are based on contract rule of law are the exception, guanxi remains firmly tied to China. We can contrast this both with the concept of face, which has entered normal vocabulary and become a mainstream concept in sociolinguistics; as well as with feng-shui, which now circulates widely in popular literature and New Age beliefs. One searches in vain for references to guanxi in discussions of British or American corruption scandals. One might speculate that it was the fact that face first went through a long process of indigenisation (over 150 years from being introduced into pidgin English) that allowed it to be adopted as an academic concept. In the case of guanxi, native English terms such as relationship and network are used as universal terms instead, while guanxi is firmly established as a subspecies of this category limited to China.

It is thus too early to tell whether guanxi will establish itself in English as a concept independent of China. It took 'lose face' approximately a century to move from being part of the 'peculiar jargon' spoken in treaty ports to being accepted as a common phrase in English and applicable in circumstances not involving China, whereas guanxi has only been around for about thirty years.

Notes

1 That system, in turn, is based on the idea of class and breeding; we will see later that opponents of an examination system in the United Kingdom often argue precisely that examinations cannot test for good breeding or gentlemanly traits.

2 He repeats this argument even more forcefully a few years later, when he says 'The only other country where such a mode of examination was introduced was China, and he did not know that it was necessary for them to take lessons from the Celestial Empire. The public service had not improved under that system' (172: 953).

3 Other indications of the link between China and corruption include the rise of 'yellow peril' discourse in the 1890s and the portrayal of Chinese characters in fiction, notably Fu Manchu in a series of novels written by Arthur Henry Ward under the pen name of Sax Rohmer beginning in 1913.

4 There is also an interesting case of an author linking influence to fengshui; Nevius (1868, 178) complains that the influence of a wealthy family may inconvenience many people, when, for example, they insist on low bridges so as not to disturb the fengshui.

5 Notably *The Water Margin*, *The Plum in the Golden Vase*, and *The Scholars*. Yet even that last novel, which features extensive discussions of official corruption, contains only a few instances where terminology relating to connections occur.

6 The two works are 官場現形記 (*Officialdom Unmasked*; published serially 1903–05; modern reprint 1956) by Li Baojia (李寶嘉 1867–1906) and Su Qing's 歧途佳人 (Beauty gone astray; 1948).

   The keywords were: 關係, 交情, 鑽營, 私相授受, 仰攀, 攀高, 攀扯, 攀親, 門路, 人情, 關節, 趨附, 干謁/幹謁, 攀附, 攀龍, 攀鱗附翼, 借譽, 請託, 私近, 私謁, and 請謁. Additionally, several keywords were searched that yielded no results at all: (走)後門, 用人唯親, 借勢, and 打招呼. 86 books published between 1902 and 1948 were surveyed, mostly from the Chinese Text Project (described earlier) and Apabi Reader, an electronic text subscription service.

7 Hsu collaborated with Fei on a translation of a work by a Chinese economist (Shih, 1944), so they actually knew each other personally.

8 Another possible explanation for some of his data is deep-rooted sexist attitudes in what remains a very patriarchal social structure. His most extreme example is of married women, whom he notes may be entirely deprived of any

given name and only referred to relationally, whereas he never suggests that a man would not have a proper adult name that everyone would know even if they did not always use it when addressing him.

9 As with the concept of face, it is difficult to search for the concept of guanxi in a Chinese database because the word has many common meanings that far outnumber its use in the sense meant here. Using collocates such as la (拉 pull) and gao (搞 engage in) as filters might prejudice the results, as such collocates tend to be used by people when describing negative effects of guanxi. Therefore a search was conducted wherein the results were limited to articles in which the characters guanxi appeared in the title, with each hit then being examined to see first whether the article was talking about guanxi in the specialist sense, and then if so, what attitude was being expressed relating to it. The search ran from January 1975 through December 2021.

It is possible that the reason stories denouncing guanxi drop off after 1990 is that guanxi networks have indeed, as Kipnis argues, become important to members of the CCP and therefore rhetoric denouncing them has been reined in.

10 I found a total of fifteen such titles published between 1998 and 2010 using the search term 'guanxixue' in Hong Kong Academic Library Link (HKALL).

11 This is foreshadowed by a pair of articles in the *People's Daily*, where guan*xi*xue is contrasted with guan*li*xue (管理學 management science); see Ye Ban (1983) and ' "Management science" beats "guanxi science" ' (1983).

Conclusion

Despite various surface differences, the four case studies examined in the previous chapters—filial piety, face, fengshui, and guanxi—are all examples of a bi-directional, interlingual practice. On the theoretical level, then, the project demonstrates the multifarious ways in which such interlingual practice may evolve, and the diverse pathways that it may follow. Filial piety exists in both cultures prior to contact; after equivalence is established, changes in its valence first in English leads to a concomitant shift in valence in Chinese, followed later by a resurrection of the concept in post-Mao China that now is having implications for the meaning of the term in English again. Face starts as a loan from Chinese, becomes naturalised in English, spawns new expressions, and then goes on to become a universal in sociolinguistics, only to be challenged by Chinese social scientists as inappropriate to describe the situation in China, where alternate taxonomies of face are developed and promulgated; to this day there is no consensus regarding this concept. Fengshui also travels from Chinese to English, first through phonetic transcription of two different terms, but then also by equation with a pre-existing concept, geomancy. This results in the emptying out of geomancy's original meaning for most English speakers, with the two terms coexisting in English now both pointing to the Chinese concept. As with the other terms, fengshui's valence in Chinese shifts under the weight of English usage, only later to see that practice being borrowed and appropriated in the English-speaking world as one of several New Age practices, taking on new, positive meaning. Guanxi, also a borrowed term from Chinese into English, itself is borrowed from Japanese, and its meaning has shifted rapidly over the past century, again due first to pressures in the English-speaking world, then later due to the growing economic success of China and other Asian economies. Unlike fengshui, however, it remains firmly 'local' to China.

The case studies also reveal that, in relation to Chinese culture specifically, such practices have been part of the development of a restricted number of concepts used to create a stereotypical image of China, both in

Anglo-American culture and also in China itself. What are we to make of this enduring practice?

First, we may note that different key concepts interact, merge, emerge or become prominent at different points in time, and undergo change at different points in time. Filial piety, for example, emerges at least two thousand years ago in Chinese, and six or seven hundred years ago in English. In both cases it was certainly an important concept in Confucianism and Christianity respectively. Fengshui, or its earlier incarnation dili, is also quite old in Chinese, but in English is a fairly recent loan, with only scattered references before the nineteenth century. Moreover, it was not considered an important concept before the second half of the nineteenth century either in Chinese or English. Meanwhile, as I have shown, guanxi only really emerges in the early twentieth century both in Chinese and English, in response to developments in English; even though its roots may be traced back to earlier concepts, the lack of discussion in Chinese texts points to this as being very much an ex post facto derivation.

However, there do seem to be a few key periods in time that are important for any term relating to China and Chineseness. The first of these is the nineteenth century when, in English, we see changes in the meaning of filial piety, and an increasingly negative interpretation of all characteristics ascribed to the Chinese. Yet it is not until the May Fourth period in the early twentieth century that we see a major rupture for some of these terms in China, at which point in time they are not necessarily undergoing major change in English. Then after the Cultural Revolution, we see a period in which terms seem more liable to change in English under pressure from developments in Chinese, with certain keywords such as fengshui and guanxi coming to have more positive connotations, while another term, filial piety, continues to languish. Meanwhile filial piety is rehabilitated in Chinese across the board, face and guanxi are rehabilitated and even elevated to new heights in academic discourse, and fengshui is rehabilitated in academic and popular usage, but not in official government publications.

Noteworthy is the key role that academic discourse has played in several of these shifts. Face is given a whole new lease of life when Goffman takes up the term in the 1950s, and it is largely in academic circles that we see changes in its meaning, and discussions about its universality or particularity debated. On a more general level, the pioneering work of Fei Xiaotong launched the revisionist discussion of Chinese characteristics, rejecting the extremely negative views put forth in many English-language publications up to that point, and further positing that they could be described in a neutral or even positive fashion. His work led, by fits and starts, to an extended discussion both in English and Chinese. In English, the main early proponent of this view was the American-based Francis Hsu. In Chinese, the work coming out of the social sciences in Taiwan and Hong Kong in the 1970s and early 1980s played a crucial role. Here in particular the concept of guanxi was developed, along with a cluster of other terms including face and fengshui. It was this work that led to the major readjustment in the valence of these terms in subsequent decades. All of these works were predicated on tracing the uniqueness of Chinese culture back to Confucianism. Since at least the 1980s, this conversation has also been a bilingual one, with researchers in both languages reading and citing each other.

These shifts in academic meaning, especially as these terms travel between popular and academic, or from one academic discipline to another, as with guanxi, hark back to Bal's work (2002) on the changing meaning of concepts as they travel between disciplines, and point to the range and complexity of such processes.

The concentration of shifts in meaning at certain periods also provides some corollary evidence for begriffsgeschichte, or history of concepts, which noted that there are certain periods of time in German history when key concepts underwent rapid change (Richter 1986). In particular, the period from about 1900–30 and then again the period from about 1980 through the present seem to be two periods of rapid and intensive change in Chinese, while the nineteenth century and the late twentieth century seem to be the key times for shifts in English.

It is also clear that what are considered to be the key concepts change over time. One of the terms I have investigated here, filial piety, has arguably been considered a key concept in China for over two thousand years. Yet the others have not been considered so until more recently; fengshui perhaps in the mid-nineteenth century in English and slightly later in Chinese; face in the late nineteenth century in English and, again, slightly later in Chinese; and finally guanxi only well into the twentieth century.

This list of four concepts is also by no means exhaustive; we have briefly come across other concepts (renqing, ganqing, bao, yinyang, the five phases, et cetera). I must again stress that these four were chosen because of the extent to which their development over time can be documented as the result of interlingual exchange between Chinese and English, which was my primary interest, not because I think that they are the four key concepts that explain Chinese culture.

Despite all the changes in the list of key concepts and changes in their meaning, throughout this period, from at least the publication of the work of Arthur Smith in the 1890s, everyone seems to agree that a small number of key concepts are able to define Chinese culture and identify what makes China unique. This is true regardless of which characteristics are considered to be defining, and whether they are good or bad. So for example when first Fei Xiaotong, Francis Hsu, and then Yang, Hwang and several others take over the idea of Chinese characteristics from Western writers, these researchers interpret these characteristics in a neutral or positive light, and link them to the idea that Chinese society is collective while American is individualistic. Others such as Sun (1988) interpret these characteristics in a quite negative light but still believe that understanding a restricted number of concepts will explain all differences between Chinese and Western culture. Right up until the present, the view that a handful of concepts can explain everything is commonly found in research papers (Ng 2008; Wang *et al* 2021), webinars ('China, Ready or Not? Chinese Concepts' 2013), and written materials for Westerners moving to China (Canada China Business Council 2021; 'What Sort of Cultural Awareness Training Do You Need To Work in China?'). Most make quite explicit lists; for example 'Chinese Culture Core Concepts' (2022) enumerates 'modesty, filial piety, guanxi, interdependence, stoicism, "face", [and] unity' as the core concepts to be discussed, after which, presumably, readers will understand everything they need to know about China and Chinese culture. Thus like Smith and the other English writers over a century ago, these Chinese researchers see guanxi and other characteristics as together making up a distinct pattern that differentiates Chinese society from Western (increasingly focusing on American) ones.

To the extent that these concepts are thought to explain Chinese culture, they relate to ongoing debates about the uniqueness of Chinese culture. This comes out perhaps most clearly in the academic debates about face, beginning in the 1970s and continuing today, wherein claims for universality on the part of Western academics beginning with Goffman have later been contested by Chinese academics, who insist on the cultural specificity of mianzi. We have also seen this with filial piety, where that term in English loses its original meaning as a Christian virtue and instead becomes firmly attached to China over the course of the nineteenth and early twentieth century.

These arguments, in turn, are part of enduring ideas about an East-West, European-Asian split. Such discourse in Europe goes back at least to the records kept by Venetian ambassadors regarding their contacts with Constantinople, and the emergence of the Asian despotism model (Koebner 1951; Valensi 1990). This split has over time taken on many forms and included many concepts. For our purposes here, the most important ones are individualistic versus collectivist social organisation, egalitarian versus hierarchical social structures, and individual independence versus collective interdependence. Since at least the time of Arthur Smith, these oppositions have been applied to the West versus China. But they have also been taken up by Fei Xiaotong, by Francis Hsu, and by the Hong Kong and Taiwan academics discussed earlier.

In all of these academic works, not only are these individual oppositions of characteristics discussed, but also various combinations of two or more characteristics are discussed together. It is therefore difficult to discuss any single term in isolation from the others, as the terms are interconnected. The four concepts I have analysed—filial piety, fengshui, face, and guanxi—are interconnected to a certain extent, especially through the Confucian concept of li (rites). Filial piety, as a bond between child and parent, is at once an example of a particular type of guanxi and, through ancestor worship, also what gives rise to fengshui. To the extent that filial piety is conceived of as unique to China, it also is seen as part of the underlying structure that gives rise to the particular type of interpersonal connections labelled as guanxi. But filial piety can also be linked to face; at least one researcher has argued that filial piety drives children to want to maximise the prestige, or face, of their parents (Teon 2017). Guanxi, in turn, is motivated either by renqing or ganqing, as is face; in turn, face is also linked to corruption and, therefore, guanxi. Fengshui, to the extent that it relies on the correspondence between heaven, earth, and people, also draws on early Chinese cosmology, underpinned by Confucianism through the *Book of Changes* but also supported by yinyang and five phases theory. Since these concepts are theorised as being the key to the whole of Chinese culture, it should not be surprising to us that they are also perceived as interconnected among themselves and also to other concepts.

Although these concepts are interconnected in both academic and popular literature in various ways, this does not mean I think that these four concepts taken together actually explain the difference between China and Anglo-American culture, or that any other combination of a limited number of concepts would be able to do this. Rather, I am trying to show how these concepts have been and continue to be used to reify difference. While I do not dispute that some knowledge of these and other topics might help someone to make sense of cultural differences, I do not believe that a limited set can stand in for the whole. To me, this synecdochical view of cultural difference is too reductive.

Let us look briefly at astrology as a counter-example from American culture. Many people in America believe in astrology to a greater or lesser extent. Almost everyone, whether they believe in astrology or not, is familiar with the signs of the zodiac and knows that, according to astrology, the time of your birth is supposed to influence your fate, as twelve different constellations are dominant at different times of the year. Fewer Americans will know how the movement of the planets are supposed to interact with the different signs, or that the period of six days between signs is known as the 'cusp' and means that the individual is influenced by both signs.

Some people's belief in astrology is limited to reading their daily horoscope in the local newspaper or online, or perhaps asking about a potential lover's star sign to see if they are compatible—or more likely, if things go wrong with a relationship, incompatibility in star signs will be used as an ex post facto explanation as to why things went wrong.

For some people, however, it seems that no major decision can be made without reference to one's horoscope. At this level, believers in astrology would probably consult a specialist. For example, when Ronald Reagan was president, it was reported that his wife and, to a lesser extent, he himself were both firm believers in astrology, and that they consulted astrologers in regard to important decisions that Reagan made before becoming president and also during his presidency concerning both domestic and foreign policy (Roberts 1988; McDuffee 2017) It is also true that other people, such as some top executives in large businesses, are firm believers in astrology.

Yet, to my knowledge, no one has argued that it was essential for the Chinese to have an in-depth knowledge of astrology in order to better understand and deal with the United States, either on the level of foreign policy or trade, whether in the Reagan years or later. This fact points us back towards the origin of this East-West discourse in Western beliefs and values.

Thus, at least in the case of China, the reason that certain concepts emerge as 'key' is often in response to something in another culture, first European, then British, and now more and more, American. We have seen how it is only when filial piety comes to have negative associations in English that the term becomes of particular salience in explaining Chinese culture. Before then, they are merely good at it; afterwards, the Chinese become (dangerous) extremists. Likewise, it is only after the 1850s and British attempts to do away with local aristocratic power to bestow livings, and attempts to establish a meritocratic civil service, that corruption and nepotism becomes identified as a defining Chinese characteristic, which in the twentieth century morphs into the discourse on guanxi. The equating of 'yi' in Chinese with 'barbarian' in English is indicative as a marker of changes in British perceptions of China, including the gradual association of arrogance and self-aggrandisement with the Chinese. This later coalesces into the discourse on face in the late nineteenth century when, after almost a century of use in the treaty ports as a rather unremarkable term, it becomes a symbol of all that is wrong with the Chinese.

Yet at the same time, all four terms refer to phenomena that exist in the English-speaking world, either fairly directly, or with related but not exactly synonymous terms. Filial piety is an example of the former; as we have seen, the concept exists independently in English and initially there is thought to be a fairly close correspondence to the Chinese one, with the Chinese thus acting as exemplars. It is only later that the distinction develops, and even at its most extreme, there is a sense in which this must be a universal because it is rooted in 'natural' biological processes, to wit, the physical reliance of infants and young children on their parents leading to reverence. It is only when the Chinese are thought to have deviated from this natural impulse that Chinese filial piety becomes unique.

Although the other three concepts are all loans from Chinese, it is not difficult to see how face can be related to a range of pre-existing concepts in English that includes reputation, honour, prestige, social standing, name, stature, fame, prominence, and influence; phrases such as 'stand on ceremony' are available as well. Face has certainly successfully been integrated into the English language to an extent that neither fengshui nor guanxi has achieved. Guanxi is also caught up in a web of related English terms that overlap with it, ranging from relations, interpersonal relationships, ties, contacts, and bonds, to the more particular old boy's network, freemasonry, school ties, patronage, favour, and then through the more negative favouritism, nepotism, cronyism, clientelism, and corruption.

Of the four concepts, fengshui is probably the most specific to China, yet even here there are, if not the same concepts, at least similar ones. Astrology, mentioned above, is a good example of a system that posits a relation between the heavens and humanity, and involves a complex interlocking system of date of birth, movement of planets, stars, the moon and the sun, although it does not include the emphasis on physical location and spatial orientation of important objects such as houses and graves. Other folk practices such as hanging a horseshoe over a doorframe for good luck can be seen to be analogous; and finally, many magical practices posit a direct link between the human and the natural world, especially sympathetic magic. If we are willing to look back in time, there were many great builders of systems of correspondence between people and the natural world, including much of early Western medicine. Some might even argue that, to the extent that it builds a logical and internally coherent system, fengshui is akin to science. We have seen how fengshui is enmeshed in the discourse relating to science, religion, superstition, and magic.

All of this suggests that China and Chineseness continue to be used as a marker for difference in English discourse. This becomes part of subject construction, and therefore, even though these concepts are linked to China, they are also about Westerners. When two cultures share or exchange 'key concepts', not only is the process of influencing the meaning of those concepts mutual, but those concepts are part of how *both* cultures define themselves, whether they are thought to be peculiar to one culture or the other. In the end, it is just as much about one culture saying 'we are not *that*, we are the opposite'.[1]

The use of China as a marker for otherness is not limited to the geographic 'distant Cathay'; it is also a marker for the past. We might add another key concept to our list: 'old'. Since some of the earliest writings of the Catholic missionaries right down through the twenty-first century, China has been described as ancient and unchanging. In the early phase of contact, old was associated with stability and peace: the early missionaries held the Chinese state up as a model for a war-torn Europe. Later, old came to be associated with being backward, stagnant, and rotten. We have seen how late nineteenth- and early twentieth-century discourse around these characteristics portrayed them as holding China back from modernity. Thus Western modernity is also constructed upon the rejection of a set of characteristics associated with both distant countries and distant times. In the twentieth century, first Fei and then Hsu tried to rehabilitate this trait, again arguing that Chinese characteristics make for a stable and peaceful society. But they and the later neo-Confucianists who insist upon finding ancient precedents for current Chinese characteristics continue to reinforce this entrenched idea that whatever is Chinese is associated with antiquity and thus is not modern.

This means that any rehabilitation of these key concepts associated with China can also be an attack on Western modernity. We can see this clearly in the ways in which the Chinese government has also been busily rehabilitating the Chinese past, after Mao had sought to tear it all down, most obviously in the establishment of Confucius Institutes all over the world. Xi Jinping has also repeatedly made reference to the antiquity of Chinese civilisation in speeches while asserting China taking its own path, attributing 'China's great rejuvenation' to Chinese culture as passed down from 'forefathers' (the masculine pronoun crucially reinforcing the patriarchal nature of Confucianism) (Xi Jinping, quoted in 'Culture, Civilization, China and Xi Jinping' 2020). He has also said things like 'Traditional Chinese culture is broad and profound: learning and mastering its various essences helps people establish a correct view of the world, life, and values' (中國傳統文化博大精深, 學習和掌握其中的各種思想精華, 對樹立正確的世界觀, 人生觀, 價值觀很有益處; Xi 2013).[2]

Yet the reverse is also possible. We have seen how, in the May Fourth Movement, the equation between Chinese cultural concepts and the past led to intellectuals rejecting concepts such as fengshui, filial piety, face, and 'favour' (Lin Yutang's term for the type of connections that led to corruption, 'guanxi' not yet being widely used).

Translation and universals

I believe that the mass of evidence in this study also allows us to say something about the ongoing debate regarding universality, particularity, and the possibility of translation. The existence of universals is not a question of finding them 'out there' and convincing everyone of their truth value, but rather of constructing a paradigm that is acceptable to all scholars. In filial piety, we see an excellent example of what started out as a universal concept becoming culturally specific by its association with China, which then overshadows the implicit universality based on basic biological facts. In the case of face, which Goffman and then Brown and Levinson posited as a term for a universal of human social interaction, I would argue that they have not completely succeeded due to their failure to take into account certain cultural factors relating, not to the structure of Chinese and Japanese societies, but rather to the history of the terms face, lian, and mianzi.[3] It is the historical baggage that these terms carry with them that is the real problem. Guanxi is still resolutely Chinese, even though it is often tied to a more general term like 'networking', or similar phenomena in other countries. I would suggest first that it is too early to say whether guanxi will become a mainstream concept in the social sciences, business studies, or even popular usage. But the fact that researchers have chosen transliteration rather than translation points to a refusal of universality. In other words, if guanxi is truly universal, then it should exist in all cultures, and we might expect that there would be a term or terms for it that would be serviceable in the English-language literature. The refusal to translate is the refusal to establish equivalence, to insist upon its cultural specificity.

Fengshui is an interesting liminal case, where we have both equivalence (geomancy) and transliteration. Yet to the extent that fengshui has been able to travel into contemporary English, it has done so by being fairly radically altered. In mainstream English usage today, there is no connection to grave sites, burial practices, or ancestor worship.

Translation studies teaches us that perfect translation is impossible. We are left with the establishment and maintenance of equivalence, not as a scientific fact, but as a social fact. I will leave readers with a question, then, rather than a final conclusion. Is the quest for universal models in the social sciences a noble attempt to elevate these fields to the realm of truth, or is it as quixotic as the search for perfect equivalence in translation, doomed to fail because language can never completely escape cultural specificity?

Notes

1 I am grateful to the work of Holt (1995), whose discussion of race in America first drew my attention to the way in which subject construction often proceeds by opposition to some other group.

    In this regard, it might be instructive to pay attention to what concepts in Chinese are being used to explain the uniqueness of the United States, and what that discourse tells us about Chinese subject construction.

2 See also Xi's speech at the First Plenary Session of the Twelfth National People's Congress, 17 March 2013, 'The Chinese nation has a continuous history of civilisation of more than 5,000 years and has created a great and profound Chinese culture, which has made indelible contributions to the advancement of human civilization that cannot be effaced' (中華民族具有 5000 多年連續不斷的文明歷史, 創造了博大精深的中華文化, 為人類文明進步做出了不可磨滅的貢獻). Archived on 17 May 2017 at the Humanities Data Research Center's website: http://dataarchive.cafe24.com/习近平-在第十二届全国人民代表大会第一次会议-2/

3 Goffman's essay ends with a return to the notion of 'a universal human nature' comprised of various parameters *which each society may emphasise more or less*, but are constrained to take into account (1967, 44–45). His idea that you might come up with a list of parameters for something like 'face', and then look at how different cultures emphasise some of those parameters more or less in order to come up with a universal, does not seem to have been taken up by later researchers.

Bibliography

'A Chanson for Canton'. 1858. *London Punch*, 10 April, 151.

'Affairs in China'. 1866. *New York Times*, 26 August, 2.

'China, Ready or Not? Chinese Concepts'. 2013. Berkshire Publishing Group, last modified 12 March 2013, accessed 1 May 2013, https://attendee.gototraining. com/r/2266319213546731520

'Chinese "Face"'. 1898. *Chicago Daily Tribune*, 30 January, 30.

'Chinese Culture: Core Concepts'. Cultural Atlas, accessed 27 February 2022, https://culturalatlas.sbs.com.au/chinese-culture/chinese-culture-core-concepts.

'Chinese Internal Customs'. 1893. *The North-China Herald and Supreme Court and Consular Gazette*, 14 April, 536.

The Chinese Traveller. Containing a Geographical, Commercial, and Political History of China. with A Particular Account of their Customs, Manners, Religion, Agriculture, Government, Arts, Sciences, Ceremonies, Buildings, Language, Physick, Trade, Manufactures, Shipping, Plants, Trees, Beasts, Birds, &c. &c. to which is Prefixed the Life of Confucius, the Celebrated Chinese Philosopher. Collected from Du Halde, Le Compte, and Other Modern Travellers ... 2 vols. 1772. London: Printed for E. and C. Dilly.

'Culture, Civilization, China and Xi Jinping'. The Thar Review, last modified 30 October 2020, accessed 1 March 2022, https://tharreview.wordpress.com/2020/ 10/30/culture-civilization-china-and-xi-jinping/.

Hansard's Parliamentary Debates. Third Series 1829–1892. London: T. C. Hansard; G. Woodfall and Sons; Cornelius Buck.

'"管理學" 勝過 "關係學"' ['Management science' beats 'guanxi science']. 1983. 人民日報 [*People's Daily*] 23 November, 2nd edition.

A New Book for the Improvement of Young Gentlemen and Ladies. Filial Duty, Recommended and Enforc'd by a Variety of Instructive and Entertaining Stories ... 1785. London: Printed for E. Newbery.

'辦事只顧面子' [Prioritizing face when working]. 1904. 香港華字日報 [*The Chinese Mail*], 23 September, 3.

'說情面' [Speaking of face]. 1904. 香港華字日報 [*The Chinese Mail*], 6 June, 4.

Strange and Terrible Nevves from Cambridge: a True Relation of the Quakers Bewitching of Mary Philips Out of the Bed from Her Husband in the Night, and Transformed Her into the Shape of a Bay Mare, Riding Her from Dinton, Towards the University: With the Manner how She Became Visible again to the People in Her Own Likeness and Shape, with Her Sides all Rent and Torn, as if they had been Spur-Gal'd, Her Hands and Feet Worn as Black as a Coal, and Her Mouth Slit with the Bridle Bit: Likewise Her Speech to the Scholars and

Countrey-Men, upon this Great and Wonderful Change, Her Oath before the Judges and Justices, and the Names of the Quakers Brought to Tryal on Friday Last at the Assises Held at Cambridge, with the Judgment of the Court: As also the Devil's Snatching of One from His Company, and Hoisting of Him Up into the Air, with what Hapned Thereupon 1659. London: Printed for C. Brooks.

'SUPERSTITION FOE TO PROGRESS IN CHINA'. 1919. *The Statesman*, 16 November, A12.

'Tombs of Ancestors'. 1833. *The Chinese Repository*: 499–502.

'What Sort of Cultural Awareness Training Do You Need To Work in China?' Country Navigator, last modified 18 January 2022, accessed 27 February 2022, https://www.countrynavigator.com/blog/what-sort-of-cultural-awareness-training-do-you-need-to-work-in-china/

Abel, Clarke. 1818. *Narrative of a Journey in the Interior of China, and of a Voyage to and from That Country in the Years 1816 and 1817; Containing an Account of the Most Interesting Transactions of Lord Amherst's Embassy to the Court of Pekin, and Observations on the Countries Which It Visited.* London: Longman, Hurst, Rees, Orme, and Brown.

Abosch, David. 1964. 'Kato Hiroyuki and the Introduction of German Political Thought: 1868–1883'. Ph.D., University of California.

Adams, Thomas. 1675. *The Main Principles of Christian Religion in a 107 Short Articles Or Aphorisms, Generally Receiv'd as being Prov'd from Scripture: Now further Cleared and Confirm'd by the Consonant Doctrine Recorded in the Articles and Homilies of the Church of England ...* London: [s.n.].

Agrippa von Nettesheim, Heinrich Cornelius. 1655. *Henry Cornelius Agrippa His Fourth Book of Occult Philosophy. of Geomancy. Magical Elements of Peter De Abano. Astronomical Geomancy. the Nature of Spirits. Arbatel of Magick.* Translated into English by Robert Turner, Philomathes. London: Printed by J. C. for John Harrison.

Allom, Thomas and G. N. [George Newenham] Wright. 1858. *The Chinese Empire, Illustrated: Being a Series of Views from Original Sketches, Displaying the Scenery, Architecture, Social Habits, &c., of that Ancient and Exclusive Nation.* 2 vols. London: London Printing and Publishing Company.

Anderson, Eugene Newton. 1980. *Ecologies of the Heart: Emotion, Belief, and the Environment.* New York: Oxford University Press.

Andrews, Bridie. 2013. *The Making of Modern Chinese Medicine.* Vancouver: University of British Columbia.

Anson, George. 1748. *A Voyage Round the World in the Years MDCCXL, I, II, III, IV.* London: Printed for the author by J. and P. Knapton.

Arundale, Robert B. 2010. 'Constituting Face in Conversation: Face, Facework, and Interactional Achievement'. *Journal of Pragmatics* 42 (8): 2078–2105.

Austen, Jane. 1811. *Sense and Sensibility.* 3 vols. London: Printed for the author by C. Roworth.

———. 1813. *Pride and Prejudice.* 3 vols. London: T. Egerton.

Badeau, Adam. 1886. *Aristocracy in England.* New York: Harper and Brothers.

Baker, Richard, Sir. 1643. *A Chronicle of the Kings of England, from the Time of the Romans Goverment Unto the Raigne of our Soveraigne Lord, King Charles Containing all Passages of State Or Church, with all Other Observations Proper for a Chronicle. Faithfully Collected Out of Authours Ancient and Moderne, & Digested into a New Method.* London: Printed for Daniel Frere.

Bal, Mieke. 2002. *Travelling Concepts in the Humanities: A Rough Guide.* Toronto: University of Toronto Press.

Ball, J. Dyer 1904. *Things Chinese or Notes Connected with China*. New York: Charles Scribner's Sons.

——. 1911. *The Chinese at Home: Or, the Man of Tong and His Land.* London: Religious Tract Society.

Bargiela-Chiappini, Francesca and Michael Haugh, eds. 2010. *Face, Communication and Social Interaction*. London: Equinox.

Barmé, Jeremy. 2005. 'Towards a New Sinology'. *Chinese Studies Association of Australia* (31): 4–9.

Baron, Robert. 1647. *Mirza a Tragedie, Really Acted in Persia, in the Last Age: Illustrated with Historicall Annotations*. London: Printed for Humphrey Moseley ... and for T. Dring.

Barrow, Henry. 1591. *A Brief Discouerie of the False Church*. Dort?: s.n.

Barrow, John. 1751. *A New and Universal Dictionary of Arts and Sciences: ... with an Introductory Preface, ... and Illustrated with a Great Number of Copper-Plates, ...* London: Printed for the proprietors, and sold by John Hinton.

Bayle, Pierre. 1708. *Miscellaneous Reflections, Occasion'd by the Comet which Appear'd in December 1680. Chiefly Tending to Explode Popular Superstitions. Written to a Doctor of the Sorbon, by Mr. Bayle. Translated from the French. to which is Added, the author's Life.* 2 vol. London: Printed for J. Morphew near Stationers-Hall.

Beach, Narlan P. 1903. *Princely Men in the Heavenly Kingdom*. New York: The Young People's Missionary Movement.

Beasley, W. G. 2000. *The Rise of Modern Japan*. 3rd edition. New York: St. Martin's Press.

Beaumont, Joseph. 1648. *Psyche, Or, Loves Mysterie in XX Canto's, Displaying the Intercourse Betwixt Christ and the Soule*. London: Printed by John Dawson for George Boddington.

Benedict, Ruth. 1946. *the Chrysanthemum and the Sword: Patterns of Japanese Culture*. Cambridge, MA: Houghton Mifflin.

Benesch, Oleg. 2014. *Inventing the Way of the Samurai: Nationalism, Internationalism, and Bushido in Modern Japan*. Oxford: Oxford University Press.

Bennett, Steven J. 1978. 'Patterns of the Sky and Earth: A Chinese Science of Applied Cosmology'. *Chinese Science* 3: 1–26.

Bennett, Tony, Lawrence Grossberg, and Meaghan Morris, eds. 2005. *New Keywords: A Revised Vocabulary of Culture and Society*. Malden, MA: Blackwell.

Berlin, Isaiah. 1958. *Two Concepts of Liberty: An Inaugural Lecture Delivered before the University of Oxford on 31 October 1958*. Oxford: Oxford University Press.

Bian, Yanjie. 2019. *Guanxi: How China Works*. Cambridge: Polity Press.

Bielenstein, Hans. 1980. *The Bureaucracy of Han Times*. Cambridge: Cambridge University Press.

Binsbergen, Wim M. J. van. 2003. *Intercultural Encounters: African and Anthropological Lessons Towards a Philosophy of Interculturality*. Münster: Lit.

Bland, J. O. P. 1919. *Houseboat Days in China*. New York: Doubleday, Page and Company.

Boidin, Capucine. 2017. 'Traductions, Métissages, Doubles Malentendus Ou Co-Mensurations Dans Les Missions Jésuites Du Paraguay'. Paper presented at the conference Knowledge Translation on a Global Scale (Asia-Europe-the Americas, 16th–20th centuries), Institut d'études avancées, Paris, 12 January.

Bolton, Edmund. 1624. *Nero Caesar, or Monarchie Depraved. An Historicall Worke*. London: Printed by T. S. [Thomas Snodham] and Bernard Alsop for Thomas Walkley.

Bolton, Kingsley. 2003. *Chinese Englishes*. Cambridge: Cambridge University Press.

Botkin, R. A., ed. 1947. *A Treasury of New England Folklore: The Stories, Legends, Tall Tales, Traditions, Ballads and Songs of the Yankee People*. Revised edition. New York: Crown Publishers.

Bouvet, Joachim. 1699. *The History of Cang-Hy, the Present Emperour of China*. London: F. Coggan.

Boxer, Baruch. 1968. 'Space, Change and Feng-Shui in Tsuen Wan's Urbanization'. *Journal of Asian and African Studies* 3: 226–42.

Bramhall, John. 1656. *A Replication to the Bishop of Chalcedon His Survey of the Vindication of the Church of England from Criminous Schism Clearing the English Laws from the Aspertion of Cruelty: With an Appendix in Answer to the Exceptions of S. W.* London: Printed by R. H. for John Crook.

Brebner, Alexander. 1895. *A Little History of China, and a Chinese Story*. London: T. F. Unwin.

Bridgman, Elijah. C. 1835. '*Heaou King, Or Filial Duty*. Author and Age of the Work; its Character and Object; A Translation with Explanatory Notes'. *Chinese Repository* 4 (8): 345–53.

———. 1841. *A Chinese Chrestomathy in the Canton Dialect*. Macao: S. W. Williams.

Brignon, Thomas. 2017. 'De Madrid à Paracuaria En Passant Par Mexico Et Vice Versa: Le Naturalisme Salutaire De Juan Eusebio Nieremberg Traduit En Guarani Dans Les Missions Jésuites Du Paraguay'. Paper presented at the conference Knowledge Translation on a Global Scale (Asia-Europe-the Americas, 16th–20th centuries), Institut d'études avancées, Paris, 12 January.

Brine, Lindesay. 1862. *The Taeping Rebellion in China: A Narrative of Its Rise and Progress, Based upon Original Documents and Information Obtained in China*. London: John Murray.

Brome, Richard. 1659. *Five Nevv Playes, Viz. the English Moor, Or the Mock-Marriage. the Love-Sick Court, Or the Ambitious Politique: Covent Garden Weeded. the Nevv Academy, Or the Nevv Exchange. the Queen and Concubine*. London: Printed for A. Crook at the Green Dragon in Saint Pauls Church-yard, and for H. Brome at the Gunn in Ivy-Lane.

Brown, Penelope and Stephen C. Levinson. 1987. *Politeness: Some Universals in Language Usage*. Cambridge: Cambridge University Press.

Browne, Thomas, Sir. 1646. *Pseudodoxia Epidemica, or, Enquiries into very Many Received Tenents and Commonly Presumed Truths by Thomas Browne*. London: Printed by T. H. for E. Dod.

Brownell, Susan. 1995. *Training the Body for China: Sports in the Moral Order of the People's Republic*. Chicago: University of Chicago Press.

Bruun, Ole. 2003. *Fengshui in China: Geomantic Divination between State Orthodoxy and Popular Religion*. Singapore: Nordic Institute of Asian Studies.

Buck, Pearl S. 1931. *The Good Earth*. London: Methuen & Co., Ltd.

Buderi, Robert and Gregory T. Huang. 2006. *Guanxi (the Art of Relationships): Microsoft, China, and Bill Gates' Plan to Win the Road Ahead*. London: Random House Business Books.

Burke, Martin and Melvin Richter, eds. 2012. *Why Concepts Matter: Translating Social and Political Thought*. Leiden: Brill.

Burton, Henry. 1626. *A Plea to an Appeale Trauersed Dialogue Wise*. London: By W. I. [Jones].

Campbell, John. 1753. *The Travels of Edward Brown, Esq; Formerly a Merchant in London. Containing His Observations on France and Italy; His Voyage to the Levant; His Account of the Island of Malta; His Remarks in His Journies through the Lower and Upper Egypt; Together with a Brief Description of the Abyssinian Empire. Interspersed Throughout with Several Curious Historical Passages Relating to Our Own as Well as Foreign Nations; as also with Critical Disquisitions as to the Present State of the Sciences in Egypt, Particularly Physick and Chemistry*. 2 vols. London: Printed for Thomas Longman, Charles Hitch and Lacy Hawes, in Pater-Noster-Row; John Hinton, in Newgate-Street; and John and James Rivington, in St. Paul's Church-Yard.

Canada China Business Council. 2021. 'China Ready 2021 Series'. Canada China Business Council. Accessed 1 March 2022, https://ccbc.com/ccbc-past-events/the-power-of-language-in-business-communication/

Cao, Anran Nason. 2018. 'Resources and Tools for Corpus Compilation of Translated Literary Texts in Late Qing and Republican Period'. *Journal of Translation Studies* New Series 2 (1): 153–68.

Cardon, Peter W. 2005. 'A Qualitative Study of the Role of Face in Chinese Business Culture: Implications for American Businesspersons'. Ph.D., Utah State University.

Carlitz, Katherine. 2007. 'Genre and Justice in Late Qing China: Wu Woyao's *Strange Case of Nine Murders* and its Antecedents'. In *Writing and Law in Late Imperial China: Crime, Conflict, and Judgment*, edited by Robert Hegel and Katherine Carlitz, 234–57. Seattle: University of Washington Press.

Carpenter, Frank G. 1896. 'Li Hung Chang, French Gossip about the Famous Chinese Prince Who Will Visit America this Fall'. *Los Angeles Times*, 19 July, 25.

Cassin, Barbara. 2004. *Le Vocabulaire Européen des Philospohies: Dictionnaire des Intraduisibles*. Paris: Seuil.

Chambers, Ephraim. 1778–1788. *Cyclopædia: Or, an Universal Dictionary of Arts and Sciences. … by E. Chambers, F.R.S. with the Supplement, and Modern Improvements, Incorporated in One Alphabet …* London: Printed for W. Strahan, J. F. and C. Rivington, A. Hamilton, J. Hinton, T. Payne [and 31 others].

Chan, Alan K. L. and Sor-hoon Tan, eds. 2004. *Filial Piety in Chinese Thought and History*. London: Routledge Curzon.

Chan, Leo Tak-hung. 1998. 'Liberal Versions: Late Qing Approaches to Translating Aesop's Fables'. In *Translation and Creation: Readings of Western Literature in Early Modern China, 1840–1918*, edited by David E. Pollard, 57–78. Amsterdam: John Benjamins Publishing Company.

Chan, Mimi and Helen Kwok. 1985. *A Study of Lexical Borrowing from Chinese into English with Special Reference to Hong Kong*, edited by Helen Kwok. Hong Kong: Centre of Asian Studies, University of Hong Kong.

Chang, Chih Tung. 1900. *China's Only Hope. An Appeal by Her Greatest Viceroy*. Translated by Samuel Isett Woodbridge. New York: Fleming H. Revell Company.

Chang, Hui-ching and Richard G. Holt. 1994. 'A Chinese Perspective on Face as Inter-Relational Concern'. In *The Challenge of Face-Work: Cross-Cultural and Interpersonal Issues*, edited by Stella Ting-Toomey, 95–132. Albany: State University of New York Press.

Chang, Wei-Lin Melody and Michael Haugh. 2011. 'Strategic Embarrassment and Face Threatening in Business Interactions'. *Journal of Pragmatics* 43 (12): 2948–63.

Chapman, Richard A. 2004. *The Civil Service Commission, 1855–1991: A Bureau Biography*. London: Routledge.

Chen, Diexian. 1999. *The Money Demon*. Translated by Thomas O. Beebee. Honolulu: University of Hawai'i Press.

Chen, Ivan. 1908. *The Book of Filial Duty; Translated from the Chinese of the Hsiao Ching ... With the Twenty-Four Examples from the Chinese*. London: John Murray.

Chen, Pingyuan 陳平原. 1989. 二十世紀中國小說史. [A history of twentieth-century Chinese fiction]. Vol. 1. Beijing: Peking University Press.

Chen, Rong 陳融. 1986. '面子留面子丟面子----介紹 Brown 和 Levinson 的禮貌原則' [Face: saving it, losing it: An introduction to the politeness principles of Brown and Levinson]. 外國語 [*Journal of Foreign Languages*] (4): 19–23.

Chen, Yun 陳雲. 1981. '要講真理，不要講面子' [Speak the truth, not face talk]. 人民日報 [*People's Daily*], 31 December, 1st edition.

Chiao, Chien 喬健. (1980) 1989. '關係芻議' [Ruminations on guanxi]. In 中國人的心裡 [Psychology of the Chinese], edited by Kuo-shu Yang 楊國樞, 105–22. Taipei: Laureate Book Company Ltd.

Chow, Tse-Tsung. 1960. *The May Fourth Movement: Intellectual Revolution in Modern China*. Cambridge, MA: Harvard University Press.

Clayton, Nicola S., Timothy J. Bussey, and Anthony Dickinson. 2003. 'Can Animals Recall the Past and Plan for the Future?' *Nature Reviews Neuroscience* 4 (8): 685–91.

Clifford, James. 1992. 'Traveling Cultures'. In *Cultural Studies*, edited by Lawrence Grossberg, Cary Nelson and Paula Treichler, 96–116. New York: Routledge.

Coates, Austin. 1968. *Myself a Mandarin*. London: Frederick Muller.

Cockburn, George. 1896. *John Chinaman: His Ways and Notions*. London: J. Gardner Hitt.

Cohen, Paul. 1974. *Between Tradition and Modernity: Wang T'ao and Reform in Late Qing China*. Cambridge, MA: Harvard University Press.

Collie, David. 1828. *The Chinese Classical Works Commonly Called the Four Books. Translated, and Illustrated with Notes*. Malacca: Mission Press.

'Commercial Progress in China'. 1858. *Cincinnati Daily Enquirer*, 23 October, 3.

Confucius. 1724. *The Morals of Confucius. A Chinese Philosopher, Who Flourished above Five Hundred Years before the Coming of Our LORD and Saviour JESUS CHRIST. Being One of the Choicest Pieces of Learning Remaining of that Nation*. 2nd edition. London: Printed for F. Fayram.

Cooke, George Wingrove. 1859. *China: Being 'The Times' Special Correspondence from China in the Years 1857–58. Reprinted by Permission. with Corrections and Additions by the Author*. London: G. Routledge & Co.

Cook-Lynn, Elizabeth. 1999. *Aurelia: A Crow Creek Trilogy*. Niwot, CO: University Press of Colorado.

Cooper, James Fenimore. (1840) 1961. *The Pathfinder; Or, the Inland Sea*. New York: New American Library.

———. (1841) 1963. *The Deerslayer; Or, the First Warpath*. New York: New American Library.

Coryate, Thomas. 1618. *Mr Thomas Coriat to His Friends in England Sendeth Greeting from Agra the Capitall City of the Dominion of the Great Mogoll in the Easterne India, the Last of October, 1616. Thy Trauels and Thy Glory to Ennamell, with Fame We Mount Thee on the Lofty Cammell*. London: Printed by I. B. [Beale].

Couling, Samuel. 1917. *The Encyclopaedia Sinica*. Shanghai: Kelly and Walsh Limited.

Culler, Jonathan. 2002. 'Philosophy and Literature: The Fortunes of the Performative'. *Poetics Today* 21 (3): 48–67.

Culpeper, Jonathan and Dániel Z. Kádár. 2010. 'Historical (Im)Politeness: An Introduction'. In *Historical (Im)Politeness*, edited by Jonathan Culpeper and Dániel Z. Kádár, 9–36. Bern: Peter Lang.

Curzon, Henry. 1712. *The Universal Library: Or, Compleat Summary of Science. Containing Above Sixty Select Treatises.* 2 vols. London: Printed for George Sawbridge.

Davis, Sir John Francis. 1817. *Laou-Seng-Urh; Or, 'An Heir in His Old Age'. A Chinese Drama.* London: John Murray.

———. 1829. *The Fortunate Union, a Romance, Translated from the Chinese Original, with Notes and Illustrations. to which is Added, a Chinese Tragedy.* 2 vols. London: Printed for the Oriental Translation Fund, and sold by J. Murray.

———. 1836. *The Chinese: A General Description of the Empire of China and Its Inhabitants.* 2 vols. London: Charles Knight & Co.

de Groot, J. J. M. [Johan Jacob Maria]. 1892–1910. *The Religious System of China, its Ancient Forms, Evolution, History, and Present Aspect, Manners, Customs and Social Institutions Connected Therewith.* 6 vols. Leiden: E. J. Brill.

De 德. 1867. 'Fung Shuei'. *Notes and Queries on China and Japan* 1 (3): 29.

Defoe, Daniel. (1715–1718) 1800. *The Complete Family Instructor: In Five Parts. I. – --Relating to Fathers and Children. II. – --To Masters and Servants. III. – --To Husbands and Wives.* Liverpool: [s.n.].

———. 1719a. *The Farther Adventures of Robinson Crusoe: Being the Second and Last Part of His Life, and of the Strange Surprizing Accounts of His Travels Round Three Parts of the Globe. Written by Himself. To which is Added a Map ....* London: Printed for W. Taylor.

———. 1719b. *Robinson Crusoe.* 2nd edition. London: W. Taylor.

———. 1726. *The Political History of the Devil, as Well Ancient as Modern. in Two Parts.* London: printed for T. Warner.

Dennerline, Jerry. 1988. *Qian Mu and the World of Seven Mansions.* New Haven, CT: Yale University Press.

Dennys, N. B. [Nicholas Belfield]. 1876. *The Folk-lore of China, and Its Affinities with That of the Aryan Semitic Races.* London: Trübner.

Dodds, Eric R. 1951. *Greeks and the Irrational.* Berkeley, CA: University of California Press.

Dong, Fangzhi 東方智. 1998. 關係學全書 [Encyclopedia of guanxixue]. Beijing: National Library of China Publishing House.

Doolittle, Justus. 1865. *Social Life of the Chinese: With Some Account of their Religions, Governmental, Educational, and Business Customs and Opinions. With Special but Not Exclusive Reference to Fuhchau.* 2 vols. New York: Harper & Brothers, Publishers.

Doré, Henri. 1914–1938. *Researches into Chinese Superstitions. Translated from the French with Notes, Historical and Explanatory by M. Kennelly, S. J.* 13 vols. Shanghai: T'usewei Printing Press.

Douglas, Sir Robert Kennaway. 1899. *China.* New York: G. P. Putnam's Sons.

———. 1901. *Society in China: Illustrated from Photographs.* London: Ward Lock and Company.

Downing, Charles Toogood. 1838. *The Fan-Qui in China, 1836-7.* 3 vols. London: H. Colburn.

Du Halde, Jean Baptiste. 1736. *Description Géographique, Historique, Chronologique, Politique, Et Physique De l'Empire De La Chine Et De La*

Tartarie Chinoise, Enrichie Des Cartes Générales Et Particulieres De Ces Pays, De La Carte Générale Et Des Cartes Particulieres Du Thibet, & De La Corée; & Ornée d'Un Grand Nombre De Figures & De Vignettes Gravées En Tailledouce. 4 vols. La Haye: chez Henri Scheurleer.

———. 1738–41. *A Description of the Empire of China and Chinese-Tartary, Together with the Kingdoms of Korea, and Tibet: Containing the Geography and History (Natural as Well as Civil) of those Countries. Enrich'd with General and Particular Maps, and Adorned with a Great Number of Cuts. from the French of P.j.b. Du Halde, Jesuit: With Notes Geographical, Historical, and Critical; and Other Improvements, Particularly in the Maps, by the Translator.* 2 vols. London: Printed by T. Gardner in Bartholomew-Close, for Edward Cave, at St. John's Gate.

Duan Yucai 段玉裁, editor. 1988. 說文解字注 [Explaining depictions of reality and analyzing graphs of words]. Taipei: Li Ming Cultural Enterprise Co., Ltd.

DuBose, Hampden C. 1887. *The Dragon, Image, and Demon: Or, the Three Religions of China; Confucianism, Buddhism and Taoism. The Mythology, Idolatry, and Demonolatry of the Chinese.* New York: A. C. Armstrong and Son.

Dukes, Edwin Joshua. 1880. *Along River and Road in Fuh-Kien, China.* New York: American Tract Society.

———. 1885. *Everyday Life in China: Or, Scenes Along River and Road in Fuh-Kien.* London: Religious Tract Society.

———. 1912. 'Feng-Shui'. In *Encyclopedia of Religion and Ethics, Volume 5*, edited by James Hastings, 833–35. Edinburgh: T. & T. Clark.

Duns Scotus Bible Centre. 1968. 中文聖經合訂本. [*Duns Scotus Bible in One Volume*]. Hong Kong: Duns Scotus Bible Centre.

Eelen, Gino. 2001. *A Critique of Politeness Theories.* Manchester: St. Jerome Publishing.

Eitel, Ernest John. 1873. *Feng-Shui: Or, the Rudiments of Natural Science in China.* London: Trubner & Company.

———. 1895. *Europe in China: The History of Hongkong from the Beginning to the Year 1882.* London: Luzac and Company.

Emery, Nathan, Joanna Dally, and Nicola Clayton. 2004. 'Western Scrub-Jays (Aphelocoma Californica) Use Cognitive Strategies to Protect their Caches from Thieving Conspecifics'. *Animal Cognition* 7 (1): 37–43.

Epicurus. 1656. *Epicurus's Morals Collected Partly Out of His Owne Greek Text, in Diogenes Laertius, and Partly Out of the Rhapsodies of Marcus Antoninus, Plutarch, Cicero, & Seneca; and Faithfully Englished.* London: Printed by W. Wilson for Henry Herringman.

Fang, Yunyu. 2010. 'City to Honor 10,000 Stars of Filial Piety'. *Global Times*, 16 August 2010.

Faria e Sousa, Manuel de. 1695. *The Portugues Asia, Or, the History of the Discovery and Conquest of India by the Portugues Containing all their Discoveries from the Coast of Africk, to the Farthest Parts of China and Japan, all their Battels by Sea and Land, Sieges and Other Memorable Actions, a Description of those Countries, and Many Particulars of the Religion, Government and Customs of the Natives, &c.* 3 vols. London: Printed for C. Brome.

Fei, Xiaotong. 1992. *From The Soil: The Foundations of Chinese Society. A translation of Fei Xiaotong's Xiangtu Zhongguo, with an Introduction and Epilogue by Gary G. Hamilton and Wang Zheng.* Berkeley: University of California Press.

Feng, Menglong 馮夢龍. 1988. 警世通言 [Stories to Caution the World]. Taipei: Laureate Publications.

———. 2005. *Stories to Caution the World: A Ming Dynasty Collection*. Translated by Shuhui Yang and Yunqin Yang. Seattle: University of Washington Press.

Feuchtwang, Stephan. 2002. *An Anthropological Analysis of Chinese Geomancy*. Bangkok: White Lotus Press.

Fielding, Henry. 1749. *The History of Tom Jones: A Foundling*. London: A. Millar.

Fong, Vanessa. 2004. 'Filial Nationalism among Chinese Teenagers with Global Identities'. *American Ethnologist* 31 (4): 631–48.

Fortune, Robert. 1847. *Three Years' Wanderings in the Northern Provinces of China, Including a Visit to the Tea, Silk, and Cotton Countries; with an Account of the Agriculture and Horticulture of the Chinese, New Plants, etc.* London: John Murray.

———. 1857. *A Residence among the Chinese; Inland, on the Coast and at Sea; Being a Narrative of Scenes and Adventures during a Third Visit to China from 1853 to 1856, Including Notices of Many Natural Productions and Works of Art, the Culture of Silk, etc.* London: John Murray.

Foster, M. A. 1979. *The Day of the Klesh*. New York: DAW Books.

Foucault, Michel. 2003. *Society Must Be Defended: Lectures at the College De France, 1975–76*. Translated by David Macey, edited by Mauro Bertani, Alessandro Fontana. New York: Picador.

Fracchiolla, Béatrice. 2011. 'Politeness as a Strategy of Attack in a Gendered Political Debate—The Royal–Sarkozy Debate'. *Journal of Pragmatics* 43 (10): 2480–88.

Fraser, James. 1742. *The History of Nadir Shah, Formerly Called Thamas Kuli Khan, the Present Emperor of Persia. to which is Prefix'd a Short History of the Moghol Emperors. at the End is Inserted, a Catalogue of about Two Hundred Manuscripts in the Persic and Other Oriental Languages, Collected in the East.* 2nd edition. London: Printed for A. Millar, at Buchanan's Head, over against St. Clement's Church, in the Strand.

Freedman, F. M. 1908. 'PROBLEM FOR CHINESE: Far-Reaching Superstition is Great Bar to Progress'. *Washington Post*, 6 December, E12.

Friedman, Edward. 1994. 'Reconstructing China's National Identity: A Southern Alternative to Mao-Era Anti-Imperialist Nationalism'. *The Journal of Asian Studies* 53 (1): 67–91.

Fukada, Atsushi and Noriko Asato. 2004. 'Universal Politeness Theory: Application to the Use of Japanese Honorifics'. *Journal of Pragmatics* 36 (11): 1991–2002.

G. L. 1778. *The Honest Criminal: Or, Filial Piety. Translated from the French of M. Fenouillot De Falbaire*. London: Printed for the Translator.

Gallie, W. B. 1956. 'Essentially Contested Concepts'. *Proceedings of the Aristotelian Society* 56: 167–98.

Gao, Mingkai 高名凱 and Zhengtan Liu 劉正埮. 1958. 現代漢語外來詞研究 [Studies of loanwords in Modern Chinese]. Beijing: Wenzi gaige chubanshe.

García, César. 2014. 'Clientelism and Guanxi: Southern European and Chinese Public Relations in Comparative Perspective'. *Public Relations Review* 40 (5): 798–806.

Gentzler, Edwin. 2017. *Translation and Rewriting in the Age of Post-Translation Studies*. New York: Routledge.

Gerholm, Tove. 2011. 'Children's Development of Facework Practices—An Emotional Endeavor'. *Journal of Pragmatics* 43 (13): 3099–3110.

Gibbon, Charles. 1591. *A VVork VVorth the Reading VVherein is Contayned, Fiue Profitable and Pithy Questions, very Expedient, Aswell for Parents to Perceiue Howe to Bestowe their Children in Marriage, and to Dispose their Goods at their Death: As for all Other Persons to Receiue Great Profit by the Rest of the Matters Herein Expressed*. London: Imprinted by Thomas Orwin.

Gilbert, Rodney. 1932. *What's Wrong with China*. London: John Murray.

Giles, Herbert Allen. 1877. *From Swatow to Canton (Overland)*. London: Trubner.

Glosserman, Brad and Scott A. Snyder. 2015. *The Japan-South Korea Identity Clash: East Asian Security and the United States*. New York: Columbia University Press.

Goffman, Erving. 1967. *Interaction Ritual: Essays in Face-to-Face Behavior*. Chicago: Aldine Publishing.

Gold, Thomas, Douglas Guthrie, and David Wank, eds. 2002. *Social Connections in China: Institutions, Culture and the Changing Nature of Guanxi*. Cambridge: Cambridge University Press.

Golley, Jane, Linda Jaivin, Paul J. Farrelly, and Sharon Strange, eds. 2019. *China Story Yearbook 2018: Power*. Canberra: Australian National University Press.

Golley, Jane, Linda Jaivin, Ben Hillman, and Sharon Strange, eds. 2020. *China Story Yearbook: China Dreams*. Acton, Australia: Australian National University Press.

González de Mendoza, Juan. 1588. *The Historie of the Great and Mightie Kingdome of China, and the Situation Thereof: Togither with the Great Riches, Huge Cities, Politike Gouernement, and Rare Inuentions in the Same*. Translated Out of Spanish by R. Parke. London: Printed by I. Wolfe for Edward White.

Gordin, Michael D. 2015. *Scientific Babel: How Science Was Done Before and After Global English*. Chicago: University of Chicago Press.

Goslicki, Wawrzyniec. 1660. *The Sage Senator Delineated: Or, A Discourse of the Qualifications, Endowments, Parts, External and Internal, Office, Duty and Dignity of a Perfect Politician. with a Discourse of Kingdoms, Republiques, & States-Popular. as also, of Kings and Princes: To Which Is Annexed, the New Models of Modern Policy*. London: Printed by Ja: Cottrel, for Sam. Speed, at the signe of the Printing-Press in St. Paul's Church-yard.

Gove, Philip Babcock, ed. 1993. *Webster's Third New International Dictionary, Unabridged*. Worcester, MA: Merriam-Webster.

Graham, A. C. 1989. *Disputers of the Tao: Philosophical Argument in Ancient China*. La Salle, IL: Open Court.

Gray, J. H. [John Henry]. 1878. *China: A History of the Laws, Manners, and Customs of the People*. 2 vols. London: Macmillan and Co.

[Green, John?]. 1743–47. *A New General Collection of Voyages and Travels: Consisting of the most Esteemed Relations, which have Hitherto been Published in any Language …*. London: Thomas Astley.

Greville, Fulke, Baron Brooke. 1651. *The Tragedy of that Famous Roman Oratour Marcus Tullius Cicero*. London: Printed by Richard Cotes for John Sweeting.

Gu, Hua. 1996. *Virgin Widows*. Translated by Howard Goldblatt. Honolulu: University of Hawai'i Press.

Gu, Yueguo. 1990. 'Politeness Phenomena in Modern Chinese'. *Journal of Pragmatics* 14 (2): 237–57.

Guo, Qiyong 郭齊勇. 2004. 儒家倫理爭鳴集 [A collection of contention about Confucian ethics]. Wuhan: Hubei Jiaoyu Chubanshe.

———. 2007. 'Is Confucian Ethics a "Consanguinism"?' *Dao: A Journal of Comparative Philosophy* 6 (1): 21–37.

Guo, Wenchen, Shaosheng Sun and Rong Dai. 2017. 'Guanxi Deviant Behaviour in the Chinese Context'. *Qualitative Research in Organizations and Management: An International Journal* 13 (2): 162–82.

Gutzlaff, Charles (Karl Friedrich August). 1834a. *Journal of Three Voyages Along the Coast of China in 1831, 1832 and 1833: With Notices of Siam, Corea and the Loo-Choo Islands.* London: Frederick Westley & A. H. Davis.

———. 1834b. *A Sketch of Chinese History.* London: Smith and Elder.

———. 1838. *China Opened; Or, a Display of the Topography, History, Customs, Manners, Arts, Manufactures, Commerce, Literature, Religion, Jurisprudence, etc. of the Chinese Empire. Revised by the Rev. Andrew Reed.* 2 vols. London: Smith, Elder and Company.

Haines, William A. 2008. 'The Purloined Philosopher: Youzi on Learning by Virtue'. *Philosophy East and West* 58 (4): 470–91.

Hall, Joseph. 1608. *Pharisaisme and Christianity Compared and Set Forth in a Sermon at Pauls Crosse, May 1. 1608. by I.H. Vpon Matth. 5.20.* London: Printed by Melchisedech Bradwood for Samuel Macham.

———. 1654. *Cases of Conscience Practically Resolved Containing a Decision of the Principall Cases of Conscience of Daily Concernment and Continual Use Amongst Men: Very Necessary for their Information and Direction in these Evil Times.* London: Printed by R. H. and J. G. and are to be sold by Fr. Eglesfield.

Hambling-Jones, Oliver and Andrew John Merrison. 2012. 'Inequity in the Pursuit of Intimacy: An Analysis of British Pick-Up Artist Interactions'. *Journal of Pragmatics* 44 (9): 1115–27.

Hamilton, Gary G. 1990. 'Patriarchy, Patrimonialism, and Filial Piety: A Comparison of China and Western Europe'. *British Journal of Sociology* 41 (1): 77–104.

Hancock, Tom. 2015. 'What Filial Piety Means in China'. *The National* [UAE], 30 March 2015.

Hane, Mikiso. 1969. 'The Sources of English Liberal Concepts in Early Meiji Japan'. *Monumenta Nipponica* 24 (3): 259–72.

Hanks, William F. 2014. 'The Space of Translation'. *Hau: Journal of Ethnographic Theory* 4 (2): 17–39.

Hanyu Dazidian Bianji Weiyuanhui 漢語大字典編輯委員會. 1987. 漢語大字典 [Unabridged dictionary of Chinese characters]. Wuhan: Hubei Dictionary Publishing and Sichuan Dictionary Publishing.

Harrison, Lisa, Adrian Little, and Edward Lock, eds. 2015. *Politics: The Key Concepts.* Abingdon, Oxon: Routledge.

Hartmann, Franz. 1889. *The Principles of Astrological Geomancy: The Art of Divining by Punctuation, According to Cornelius Agrippa and Others.* London: Theosophical Publishing Company.

Haugh, Michael. 2007. 'Emic Conceptualisations of (Im)Politeness and Face in Japanese: Implications for the Discursive Negotiation of Second Language Learner Identities'. *Journal of Pragmatics* 39 (4): 657–80.

———. 2010. 'Face and Interaction'. In *Face, Communication and Social Interaction,* edited by Francesca Bargiela-Chiappini and Michael Haugh, 1–30. London: Equinox.

Hayes, James W. 1963. 'Movement of Villages on Lantau Island for *Fung Shui* Reasons'. *Journal of the Hong Kong Branch of the Royal Asiatic Society* 3: 143–44.

———. 1967. 'Geomancy and the Village'. In *Some Traditional Chinese Ideas and Conceptions in Hong Kong Social Life Today,* 22–30. Hong Kong: Hong Kong Branch of the Royal Asiatic Society.

———. 1980. 'Local Reactions to the Disturbance of "Fung Shui" on Tsingyi Island, Hong Kong, March 1978–December 1980'. *Journal of the Hong Kong Branch of the Royal Asiatic Society* 20: 155–56.

Hayford, Charles. 1985. 'Chinese and American Characteristics: Arthur Smith and His China Book'. In *Christianity in China*, edited by Susan Barnett and John Fairbank, 153–74. Cambridge, MA: Harvard University Press.

Haywood, Eliza Fowler. 1746. *The Female Spectator*. Dublin: Printed for George and Alexander Ewing at the Angel and Bible in Dame-street.

He, Beiren 河北仁. 1982. '共產黨人钓關係準則' [Guanxi guidelines for Communist Party members]. 人民日報 [*People's Daily*], 9 September, 8th edition.

He, Ming and Shao-jie Zhang. 2011. 'Re-Conceptualizing the Chinese Concept of Face from a Face-Sensitive Perspective: A Case Study of a Modern Chinese TV Drama'. *Journal of Pragmatics* 43 (9): 2360–72.

Hemyng, Bracebridge. 1904. *Jack Harkaway and His Son's Adventures in China*. Chicago: M. A. Donohue & Co.

Henderson, John B. 1984. *The Development and Decline of Chinese Cosmology*. New York: Columbia University Press.

Henry, Benjamin Couch. 1885. *The Cross and the Dragon: Or, Light in the Broad East*. New York: A. D. F. Randolph.

Herbert, Frank. 1965. *Dune*. New York: Berkeley Books.

Herbert, Thomas Sir. 1638. *Some Yeares Travels into Divers Parts of Asia and Afrique Describing Especially the Two Famous Empires, the Persian, and the Great Mogull: Weaved with the History of these Later Times as also, Many Rich and Spatious Kingdomes in the Orientall India, and Other Parts of Asia; Together with the Adjacent Iles. Severally Relating the Religion, Language, Qualities, Customes, Habit, Descent, Fashions, and Other Observations Touching them. with a Revivall of the First Discoverer of America. Revised and Enlarged by the Author*. London: Printed by R[ichard] Bi[sho]p. for Iacob Blome and Richard Bishop.

Heywood, Thomas. 1624. *Gynaikeion: Or, Nine Bookes of Various History. Concerninge Women Inscribed by Ye Names of Ye Nine Muses*. London: Printed by Adam Islip.

———. 1641. *The Life of Merlin, Sirnamed Ambrosius His Prophesies and Predictions Interpreted, and Their Truth made Good by Our English Annalls: Being a Chronographicall History of All the Kings, and Memorable Passages of This Kingdome, from Brute to the Reigne of Our Royall Soveraigne King Charles ....* London: Printed by J. Okes, and are to be sold by Jasper Emery.

Hill, Aaron. 1758. *The Insolvent: Or, Filial Piety*. London: Printed and Sold by W. Reeve.

Hill, Beverly, Sachiko Ide, Shoko Ikuta, Akiko Kawasaki, and Tsunao Ogino. 1986. 'Universals of Linguistic Politeness: Quantitative Evidence from Japanese and American English'. *Journal of Pragmatics* 10 (3): 347–71.

Hill, Justin. 2002. *The Drink and Dream Teahouse*. London: Orion Books.

Hill, Michael Gibbs. 2012. *Lin Shu Inc.: Translation and the Making of Modern Chinese Culture*. Oxford: Oxford University Press.

Ho, David Yau-fai. 1976. 'On the Concept of Face'. *The American Journal of Sociology* 81 (4): 867–84.

Ho, Yau Fai 何友暉, Shujuan Chen 陳淑娟, and Chi Yue Chiu 趙志裕. 1991. '關係取向：為中國社會心理方法論求答案' [Guanxi orientation: finding answers for Chinese social psychological methodology]. In 中國人的心裡與行為 [Psychology and behaviour of the Chinese], edited by Kuo-shu Yang 楊國樞 and Kwang-kuo Hwang 黃光國, 49–66. Taipei: Laureate Book Company Ltd.

Hobart, Alice Tisdale. 1936. *Yang and Yin: A Novel of an American Doctor in China*. New York: Bobbs-Merrill Company.

Hobbes, Thomas. 1651. *Leviathan, Or, the Matter, Forme, and Power of a Commonwealth, Ecclesiasticall and Civil*. London: Printed for Andrew Crooke.

Holt, Thomas C. 1995. 'Marking: Race, Race-Making, and the Writing of History'. *The American Historical Review* 100 (1): 1–20.

Hong, Pimo 洪丕謨. 1993. 中國風水研究 [Research into Chinese fengshui]. Wuhan: Hubei kexue jishu chubanshe.

Hoogenboom, Ari. 1961. 'Thomas A. Jenckes and Civil Service Reform'. *The Mississippi Valley Historical Review* 47 (4): 636–58.

Horak, Sven and Markus Taube. 2016. 'Same but Different? Similarities and Fundamental Differences of Informal Social Networks in China (*Guanxi*) and Korea (*Yongo*)'. *Asia Pacific Journal of Management* 33 (3): 595–616.

Horowitz, Maryanne Cline. 2004. *New Dictionary of the History of Ideas*. 6 vols. New York: Scribner.

House, Juliane. 1977. *A Model for Translation Quality Assessment*. Tübingen: Gunter Narr.

Howland, Douglas R. 2002. *Translating the West: Language and Political Reason in Nineteenth-Century Japan*. Honolulu: University of Hawai'i Press.

———. 2012. 'The Public Limits of Liberty: Nakamura Keiu's Translation of J. S. Mill'. In *Why Concepts Matter: Translating Social and Political Thought*, edited by Martin Burke and Melvin Richter, 177–92. Leiden: Brill.

Hsu, Francis L. K. 1948. *Under the Ancestor's Shadow: Chinese Culture and Personality*. New York: Columbia University Press.

———. 1955. *Americans and Chinese*. London: Cresset Press.

———. 1963. *Clan, Caste, and Club*. Princeton, NJ: Van Nostrand Company.

Hu, Hsien Chin. 1944. 'The Chinese Concepts of "Face"'. *American Anthropologist, New Series* 46 (1.1): 45–64.

Huang, Alexander C. Y. 2009. *Chinese Shakespeares: Two Centuries of Cultural Exchange*. New York: Columbia University Press.

Huang, Max Ko-wu. 2008. *The Meaning of Freedom: Yan Fu and the Origins of Chinese Liberalism*. Hong Kong: Chinese University Press.

Huc, M. 1854. *L'Empire chinois: faisant suite à l'ouvrage intitulé 'Souvenirs d'un voyage dans la Tartarie et le Thibet'*. Paris: L'imprimerie Impériale.

———. 1855. *the Chinese Empire. Forming a Sequel to the Work Entitled 'Recollections of a Journey through Tartary and Thibet'*. 2 vols. 2nd edition. London: Longman, Brown, Green and Longmans.

Hudson, Mutsuko Endo. 2011. 'Student Honorific's Usage in Conversations with Professors'. *Journal of Pragmatics* 43 (15): 3689–706.

Huters, Theodore. 1998. 'Review of *Translingual Practice: Literature, National Culture, and Translated Modernity-China, 1900–1937* by Lydia H. Liu'. *Harvard Journal of Asiatic Studies* 58 (2): 568–80.

Hwang, Kwang-kuo 黃光國. 1985. '人情與面子' [Renqing and face]. In 現代化與中國化論集 [Essays on modernization and sinicization], edited by Yih-Yuan Li 李亦園, Kuo-shu Yang 楊國樞 and Chung-i Wen 文崇一, 125–53. Taipei: Laureate Book Company Ltd.

———. 1987. 'Face and Favor: The Chinese Power Game'. *American Journal of Sociology* 92: 944–74.

I. C. 1619. *The Euer-Burning Lamps of Pietie and Deuotion Kindled by Many Excellent and Heauenly Prayers, Deuided into the Seuerall Dayes of the Weeke, and Other Occasions: To Auoide Which Weake Man Hath Continuall Cause to Retire into Himselfe, and Humbly Confer with Almightie God*. London: Printed by George Purslowe for Richard Hawkins.

Ide, Sachiko. 1989. 'Formal Forms and Discernment: Two Neglected Aspects of Universals of Linguistic Politeness'. *Multilingua* 8 (2–3): 223–48.

International Bible Society. 1979. 當代聖經: 中文聖經意譯本新舊約全書 [Chinese living Bible, containing both Old and New Testaments]. Hong Kong: Living Bibles International.

Iyenaga, Saburo. 1966. 'Problem of Accepting Foreign Ideas in the History of Japanese Thought'. *East Asian Cultural Studies* 5: 83–93.

J. B. 1616. *English Expositor Teaching the Interpretation of the Hardest Words Used in Our Language*. London: Printed by Iohn Legatt.

Jamieson, George. 1921. *Chinese Family and Commercial Law*. Shanghai: Kelly and Walsh.

Jiang, Caifen 姜彩芬. 2009. 面子與消費 [Face and consumption]. Beijing: Shehui kexue wenxian chubanshe.

Jin, Yuan. 1998. 'The Influence of Translated Fiction on Chinese Romantic Fiction'. In *Translation and Creation: Readings of Western Literature in Early Modern China, 1840–1918*, edited by David E. Pollard, 283–302. Amsterdam: John Benjamins Publishing Company.

Johnston, Reginald Fleming. 1910. *Lion and Dragon in Northern China*. London: John Murray.

Jones, Gwyn. 1968. *History of the Vikings*. London: Oxford University Press.

Jones, James. 1951. *From Here to Eternity*. New York: Charles Scribner's Sons.

Kádár, Dániel Z. 2010. 'Exploring the Historical Chinese Polite Denigration/ Elevation Phenomenon'. In *Historical (Im)Politeness*, edited by Jonathan Culpeper and Dániel Zoltán Kádár, 117–45. Bern: Peter Lang.

Karhunen, Päivi, Riitta Kosonen, Daniel J. McCarthy, and Sheila M. Puffer. 2018. 'The Darker Side of Social Networks in Transforming Economies: Corrupt Exchange in Chinese Guanxi and Russian Blat/Svyazi'. *Management and Organization Review* 14 (2): 395–419.

Keevak, Michael. 2022. *On Saving Face: A Brief History of Western Appropriation*. Hong Kong: Hong Kong University Press.

Kennett, White. 1689. *A Dialogue between Two Friends Occasioned by the Late Revolution of Affairs, and the Oath of Allegiance*. London: Printed for Ric. Chiswell.

Kidd, Samuel. 1841. *China: Or, Illustrations of the Symbols, Philosophy, Antiquities, Customs, Superstitions, Laws, Government, Education, and Literature of the Chinese. Derived from Original Sources, and Accompanied with Drawings from Native Works*. London: Printed for Taylor & Walton.

King, Ambrose Y. C. 1996. 'The Transformation of Confucianism in the Post-Confucian Era: The Emergence of Rationalistic Traditionalism in Hong Kong'. In *Confucian Traditions in East Asian Modernity*, edited by Wei-ming Tu, 264–76. Cambridge, MA: Harvard University Press.

King, Ambrose Yeo-chi 金耀基. (1980) 1989. '人際關係中人情之分析' [Analysis of emotions in interpersonal relationships]. In 中國人的心裡 [Psychology of the Chinese], edited by Kuo-shu Yang 楊國樞, 75–104. Taipei: Laureate Book Company Ltd.

———. 1994. 'Kuan-Hsi and Network Building: A Sociological Interpretation'. In *The Living Tree: The Changing Meaning of Being Chinese Today*, edited by Wei-ming Tu, 109–26. Stanford: Stanford University Press.

Kinney, Anne Behnke. 2004. *Representations of Childhood and Youth in Early China*. Stanford: Stanford University Press.

Kipnis, Andrew B. 1997. *Producing Guanxi: Sentiment, Self, and Subculture in a North China Village*. Durham, NC: Duke University Press.

Klaising Chen, Monica. 2017. 'Chinese Painting Mnemonics: Translating Practical Knowledge'. Paper presented at the conference Knowledge Translation on a Global Scale (Asia-Europe-the Americas, 16th–20th centuries), Institut d'études avancées, Paris, 13 January.

Knapp, Keith N. 1995. 'The *Ru* Reinterpretation of Xiao'. *Early China* 20: 195–222.

Koebner, Richard. 1951. 'Despot and Despotism: Vicissitudes of a Political Term'. *Journal of the Warburg and Courtauld Institutes* 14 (3/4): 275–302.

Koebner, Richard and Helmut Dan Schmidt. 1964. *Imperialism: The Story and Significance of a Political Word, 1840–1960*. Cambridge: Cambridge University Press.

Koh, Byong-ik. 1996. 'Confucianism in Contemporary Korea'. In *Confucian Traditions in East Asian Modernity*, edited by Wei-ming Tu, 191–201. Cambridge, MA: Harvard University Press.

Ku, Hung-ming. 1898. *The Discourses and Sayings of Confucius. A New Special Translation, Illustrated with Quotations from Goethe and Other Writers*. Shanghai: Kelly and Walsh, Limited.

———. 1915. *The Spirit of the Chinese People. With an Essay on 'The War and the Way Out'*. Peking: Peking Daily News.

Kuhn, Thomas S. 1962. *The Structure of Scientific Revolutions*. Chicago: University of Chicago Press.

Kuo, Eddie C. Y. 1996. 'Confucianism as Poltical Discourse in Singapore: The Case of an Incomplete Revitalization Movement'. In *Confucian Traditions in East Asian Modernity*, edited by Wei-ming Tu, 294–309. Cambridge, MA: Harvard University Press.

Kurtz, Joachim. 2012. 'Translating the Vocation of Man: Liang Qichao (1873–1929), J. G. Fichte, and the Body Politic in Early Republican China'. In *Why Concepts Matter: Translating Social and Political Thought*, edited by Martin Burke and Melvin Richter, 153–76. Leiden: Brill.

La Loubère, Simon de. 1693. *A New Historical Relation of the Kingdom of Siam*. 2 vols. Translated by A. P. London: Printed by F. L. for Thomas Horne, Francis Saunders, and Thomas Bennet.

Lackington, James. 1793. *Second Volume of Lackington's Catalogue for 1793. Consisting of Above Ninety Thousand Volumes, … Selling …*. London: s.n.

Lackner, Michael, Iwo Amelung, and Joachim Kurtz. 2001. *New Terms for New Ideas: Western Knowledge and Lexical Change in Late Imperial China*. Leiden: Brill.

Lake, Roseann. 2018. *Leftover in China: The Women Shaping the World's Next Superpower*. New York: W. W. Norton Company.

Langdon, William B. 1842. *Ten Thousand Things Relating to China and the Chinese: An Epitome of the Genius, Government, History, Literature, Agriculture, Arts, Trade, Manners, Customs, and Social Life of the People of the Celestial Empire, Together with a Synopsis of the Chinese Collection*. London: O. M'Kewan.

Langenberg, Eike A. 2007. *Guanxi and Business Strategy: Theory and Implications for Multinational Companies*. Heidelberg: Physcia-Verlag Heidelberg.

Lao She 老舍. 1999. 老舍全集 [Complete works of Lao She]. 19 vols. Beijing: Renmin wenxue chubanshe.

Laumer, Keith. 1973. *The Glory Game*. New York: Pocket Books.

Lay, G. [George] Tradescant. 1846. 'Outlines of a Natural History Calendar at Foo-Chow-Foo, the Capital of the Chinese Province of Fokien'. *Journal of the Royal Horticultural Society* 1: 119–26.

Le Comte, Louis. 1697. *Memoirs and Observations Topographical, Physical, Mathematical, Mechanical, Natural, Civil, and Ecclesiastical. Made in a Late Journey through the Empire of China, and Published in Several Letters. Particularly upon the Chinese Pottery and Varnishing; the Silk and Other Manufactures; the Pearl Fishing; the History of Plants and Animals. Description of their Cities and Publick Works; Number of People, their Language, Manners and Commerce; their Habits, Oeconomy, and Government. the Philosophy of Confucius. the State of Christianity, with Many Other Curious and Useful Remarks*. London: Benj. Tooke and Sam. Buckley.

Lean, Eugenia. 2007. *Public Passions: The Trial of Shi Jianqiao and the Rise of Popular Sympathy in Republican China*. Berkeley: University of California Press.

Lee, Cheuk Yin. 2004. 'Emperor Chengzu and Imperial Filial Piety of the Ming Dynasty: From the Classic of Filial Piety to the Biographical Accounts of Filial Piety'. In *Filial Piety in Chinese Thought and History*, edited by Alan K. L. Chan and Sor-hoon Tan, 141–53. London: RoutledgeCurzon.

Lefèvre, Corinne. 2017. 'The Transmission of Western Political Culture and History at the Mughal Court, Ca. 1600'. Speech presented at the conference Knowledge Translation on a Global Scale (Asia-Europe-the Americas, 16th–20th Centuries), Paris, January 12.

Legge, James. 1861. *The Chinese Classics: With a Translation, Critical and Exegetical Notes, Prologomena, and Copious Indexes. Volume One: Confucian Analects, the Great Learning, and the Doctrine of the Mean*. Hong Kong: At the Author's; London: Trübner.

———. 1893. *The Chinese Classics. in Seven Volumes. Second Edition, Revised. Volume One: Confucian Analects, the Great Learning, and the Doctrine of the Mean*. Oxford: The Clarendon Press.

———. 1895. *The Chinese Classics. in Seven Volumes. Second Edition, Revised. Volume Two: The Works of Mencius*. Oxford: The Clarendon Press.

Leland, Charles Godfrey. 1876. *Pidgin-English Sing-Song, Or, Songs and Stories in the China-English Dialect*. London: Trubner and Co.

Leong, Y. K. and L. K. Tao. 1915. *Village and Town Life in China*. London: George Allen & Unwin Ltd.

Lévi-Strauss, Claude. 1964. *Le cru et le cuit*. Paris: Plon.

Lewis, Charlton T. and Charles Short. 1879. *A Latin Dictionary Founded on Andrews' Edition of Freund's Latin Dictionary. Revised, Enlarged, and in Great Part Rewritten*. Oxford: Clarendon Press.

Li, Baojia 李寶嘉. 1956. 官場現形記 [Officialdom Unmasked]. Shanghai: Shanghai wenhua chubanshe.

Li, Fuqiang 李富強. 2019. '中國人日常生活中的 "耻" "臉" 與 "面子" –對近代以來國民性批判中的 "面子問題" 之省思' ['Shame', 'lian', and 'mianzi' in the daily life of Chinese people: reflections on the current 'face problem' in the national character]. 海南大學學報 (人文社會科學版) [*Journal of Hainan University* (Humanities and Social Sciences Edition)] 37 (5): 173–80.

Li, Ruzhen 李汝珍. 1991. 鏡花緣 [Flowers in the mirror]. Shanghai: Shanghai guji chubanshe.

Li, Wenrui. 2019. 'Chinese Teenagers Win National Award for Filial Piety'. *China Daily: English Edition*, 31 October 2019.

Li, Yih-Yuan 李亦園, Kuo-shu Yang 楊國樞, and Chung-I Wen 文崇一, eds. 1985. 現代化與中國化論集 [Essays on modernization and sinicization]. Taipei: Laureate Book Company Ltd.

Lin, Shu 林紓 and Wang Qingtong 王慶通 1918. 孝友鏡 [Mirror of filial friendship]. Translation of *Arme Edelman*, by Hendrik Conscience. Shanghai: The Commercial Press.

Lin, Shu 林紓 and Wang Shouchang 王壽昌. 1899. 巴黎茶花女遺事 [The Legacy of the Parisian Lady of the Camellias]. Translation of *La dame aux camélias*, by Alexandre Dumas Fils. Shanghai: Wei Cottage Editions.

Lin, Shu 林紓 and Wei Yi 魏易. 1905a. 英孝子火山報仇錄 [Record of a filial English son's revenge at the volcano]. Translation of *Montezuma's Daughter*, by H. Rider Haggard. Shanghai: Commercial Press.

———. 1905b. 迦茵小傳 [The story of Joan]. Translation of *Joan Haste*, by H. Rider Haggard. Shanghai: Commercial Press.

———. 1907a. 孝女耐兒傳 [Biography of Nell, a filial daughter]. Translation of *The Old Curiosity Shop*, by Charles Dickens. Shanghai: Commercial Press.

———. 1907b. 雙孝子噀血酬恩記 [Story of two filial sons returning gratitude with blood]. Translation of *The Martyred Fool*, by David Christie Murray. Shanghai: Commercial Press.

Lin, Yutang. 1935. *My Country and My People*. New York: Reynal & Hitchcock.

———. 1939a. *Moment in Peking*. New York: The John Day Company.

———. 1939b. *My Country and My People, New and Revised Edition*. London: William Heinemann.

———. 1948. *Chinatown Family*. New York: The John Day Company.

———. 1952. *The Widow Chuan*. New York: Reynal & Hitchcock.

———. 1954. *The Vermillion Gate*. New York: The John Day Company.

———. 1975. *The Red Peony*. New York: Mei Ya Publications.

Linschoten, Jan Huygen van. 1598. *His Discours of Voyages into Ye Easte & West Indies. Deuided into Foure Bookes*. London: [John Windet for] Iohn Wolfe printer to ye Honorable Cittie of London.

Lip, Evelyn. 1979. *Chinese Geomancy: A Layman's Guide to Feng Shui*. Singapore: Times Books International.

Liu, Lydia. 1995. *Translingual Practice: Literature, National Culture, and Translated Modernity—China, 1900–1937*. Stanford, CA: Stanford University Press.

Liu, Shide 劉世德 and Qing Zhu 竺青, eds. 2003. 警富新書; 九命奇冤 [New warning about wealth: A strange case of nine murders]. Beijing: Qunzhong Chubanshe.

Liu, Ts'un-yan. 1971. 'The Penetration of Taoism into the Ming Neo-Confucianist Elite'. *T'oung Pao* new series 57: 31–102.

Liu, Yongnuo 劉永諾. 1991. '把一切獻給祖國大地' [Giving everything to the fatherland]. *People's Daily*, 27 April, online.

Liu, Qingping. 2007. 'Confucianism and Corruption: An Analysis of Shun's Two Actions Described by Mencius'. *Dao: A Journal of Comparative Philosophy* 6 (1): 1–19.

Llerena, Laura León. 2017. 'Translating Stones: Dealing with Indigenous Material Culture in Colonial Peru'. Paper presented at the conference Knowledge Translation on a Global Scale (Asia-Europe-the Americas, 16th–20th centuries), Institut d'études avancées, Paris, 13 January.

Lloyd, David. 2011. *Irish Culture and Colonial Modernity, 1800–2000: The Transformation of Oral Space*. Cambridge: Cambridge University Press.

Lo. 1867. 'Fung shui—what is it?' *Notes and Queries on China and Japan* 1 (1): 6–7.

Lo, Yuet Keung. 2004. 'Filial Devotion for Women: A Buddhist Testimony from Third-Century China'. In *Filial Piety in Chinese Thought and History*, edited by Alan K. L. Chan and Sor-hoon Tan, 71–90. London: RoutledgeCurzon.

Locher, Miriam. 2008. 'Relational Work, Politeness, and Identity Construction'. In *Handbook of Interpersonal Communication*, edited by Gerd Antos and Eija Ventola, 509–40. Berlin: Mouton de Gruyter.

Longino, Helen E. 1990. *Science as Social Knowledge: Values and Objectivity in Scientific Inquiry*. Princeton, NJ: Princeton University Press.

Louis XIV, King of France. 1688. *The French King's Memorial to the Pope*. London: Printed for Joseph Hindmarsh.

Lu, Peijin 呂培進. 2019. '鄉村治理中的 "面子觀" --一種社區性貨幣的使用策略' ['Face outlook' in rural governance: a strategy using community currency]. 領導科學 [Leadership science] (19): 17–20.

Lu, Ping. 2006. *Love and Revolution*. Translated by Nancy Du. New York: Columbia University Press.

Lu, Xun 魯迅. 1926. 朝花夕拾 [*Dawn Blossoms Plucked at Dusk*]. Beijing: n.s.

———. 1976. *Dawn Blossoms Plucked at Dusk*. Translated by Xianyi Yang and Gladys Yang. Beijing: Peking Foreign Languages Press.

———. 1990. *Diary of a Madman and Other Stories*. Translated by William A. Lyell. Honolulu: University of Hawai'i Press.

———. 1994. '狂人日記' ['Diary of a Madman']. In 魯迅全集 [Complete works of Lu Xun] Vol. 1, 415–21. Beijing: Renmin wenxue chubanshe.

———. 1998. *Lu Xun Quan Ji* 魯迅全集 [Complete works of Lu Xun]. 16 Vols. Beijing: Renmin wenxue chubanshe.

———. 2006. *Lu Xun Zawen Quan Bian* 魯迅雜文全編 [Complete short essays of Lu Xun]. 7 Vols. Beijing: Renmin wenxue chubanshe.

Lü, Zhenzhong 呂振中. 1970. 聖經呂振中譯本 [The Holy Bible, translated by Lü Zhenzhong]. Hong Kong: Hong Kong Bible Society.

Luo, Yadong. 2020. *Guanxi and Business. Third Edition*. Singapore: World Scientific.

Ma, Dengge 馬登閣. 1995. '從語用學看語言交際中的禮貌原則及英語禮貌語言的表達方式' [Politeness principles in language communication and the expression of polite language in English from the perspective of pragmatics]. 北京第二外國語學院學報 [Journal of Beijing International Studies University] (2): 1–7.

Macgowan, John. 1907. *Sidelights on Chinese Life*. London: Kegan Paul, Trench, Trubner & Company, Ltd.

———. 1909. *Lights and Shadows of Chinese Life*. Shanghai: North China Daily News & Herald Ltd.

———. 1912. *Men and Manners in Modern China*. London: T. Fisher Unwin.

Machiavelli, Niccolò. 1663. *Machiavel's [Sic] Discourses upon the First Decade of T. Livius, Translated Out of the Italian. to which is Added His Prince. with some Marginal Animadversions Noting and Taxing His Errors. by E.D.* London: printed for G. Bedell, and T. Collins.

Mackaye, Steele. 1880. *Hazel Kirke, a Comedy Drama: Written Expressly for This Theatre*. New York: Penrose, Lowe and Company.

Mackenzie, George. 1713. *Essays Ut on Several Moral Subjects*. London: Printed for D. Brown, R. Sare, J. Churchill, J Nicholson, B. Tooke, and G. Strahan.

Mai, Jia. 2014. *Decoded*. Translated by Olivia Milburn and Christopher Payne. London: Allen Lane Press.

Malan, Rian. 1990. *My Traitor's Heart*. New York: Atlantic Monthly Press.

Malmkjaer, Kirsten. 2018. 'Key Cultural Texts in Translation'. Arts & Humanities
    Research Council, accessed 28 February 2018, http://translatingcultures.org.uk/
    awards/research-networking-awards/key-cultural-texts-in-translation/
Malmkjaer, Kirsten, Adriana Şerban, and Fransiska Louwagie, eds. 2018. *Key
    Cultural Texts in Translation.* Amsterdam: John Benjamins Publishing Company.
Mao, LuMing Robert. 1994. 'Beyond Politeness Theory: "Face" Revisited and
    Renewed'. *Journal of Pragmatics* 21 (5): 451–486.
Mao, Zedong 毛澤東. 1977. 毛澤東選集 [Selected works of Mao Zedong]. in Five
    Volumes. Beijing: People's Publishing House.
Margolis, Eric and Stephen Laurence. 2014. 'Concepts'. In *The Stanford
    Encyclopedia of Philosophy,* edited by Edward N. Zalta. Spring 2014 Edition.
    Stanford, CA: Stanford University Press.
Marshman, Joshua. 1809. *The Works of Confucius, Containing the Original Text,
    with a Translation.* Vol. 1. Serampore: Printed at the Mission Press.
Marshman, Joshua and Joannes Lassar. 1822. 聖經 [The Holy Bible].
    Serampore: Serampore Mission.
Martín de León, Celia. 2010. 'Metaphorical Models of Translation. Transfer Vs.
    Imitation and Action'. In *Thinking through Translation with Metaphors,* edited
    by James St. André, 75–108. Manchester: St. Jerome.
Martin, Helmut. 1986. 'Wu Wo-Yao'. In *The Indiana Companion to Traditional
    Chinese Literature, Second Revised Edition,* edited by Jr William H. Nienhauser,
    905–908. Bloomington: University of Indiana Press.
Masini, Federico. 1993. 'The Formation of Modern Chinese Lexicon and its
    Evolution Toward a National Language: The Period from 1840 to 1898'. *Journal
    of Chinese Linguistics, Monograph Series* 6: 1–295.
Matsumoto, Yoshiko. 1988. 'Reexamination of the Universality of Face: Politeness
    Phenomena in Japanese'. *Journal of Pragmatics* 12 (4): 403–426.
Maverick, Lewis. 1946. *China: A Model for Europe.* San Antonio: Paul Anderson
    Company.
Mayers, William F., N. B. [Nicholas Belfield] Dennys, and Charles King. 1867.
    *The Treaty Ports of China and Japan. A Complete Guide to the Open Ports of
    those Countries, Together with Peking, Yedo, Hongkong and Macao. Forming a
    Guide Book & Vade Mecum for Travellers, Merchants, and Residents in General.*
    London: Trubner and Company.
McCloskey, H. J. 1965. 'A Critique of the Ideals of Liberty'. *Mind* New Series 74
    (296): 483–508.
McDuffee, Allen. 'Ronald Reagan Actually used A San Francisco Astrologist to Make
    Presidential Decisions'. Timeline, last modified 30 May 2017, accessed 28 February,
    2022, https://timeline.com/ronald-reagan-astrology-quigley-aa81632662d9
Meadows, Thomas Taylor. 1847. *Desultory Notes on the Government and
    People of China, and on the Chinese Language; Illustrated with a Sketch of the
    Province of Kwang-Tung, Shewing Its Division into Departments and Districts.*
    London: William H. Allen and Company.
———. 1856. *The Chinese and Their Rebellions, Viewed in Connection with
    their National Philosophy, Ethics, Legislation, and Administration. To which
    is Added, an Essay on Civilization and Its Present State in the East and West.*
    London: Smith, Elder and Co.
Medhurst, Walter H. 1832. *Dictionary of the Hokëèn Dialect of the Chinese
    Language.* Macao: The Honorable East India Company's Press.
———. 1838. *China: Its State and Prospects.* London: John Snow.

——. 1842–1843. *Chinese and English Dictionary. Two Volumes.* Batavia: Parapattan.

Medhurst, Walter H., Elijah C. Bridgman, John Stronach, Walter M. Lowrie, and William Milne. 1852. 新約全書 [The New Testament in Chinese, translated by the committee of delegates]. Shanghai: London Missionary Society's Press.

Medhurst, Walter H., Elijah C. Bridgman, John Stronach, William Milne, and Jehu Lewis Shuck. 1854. 舊約全書 [The Old Testament in Chinese, translated by the committee of delegates]. Shanghai: British and Foreign Bible Society.

Medhurst, Walter H. jr. 1873. *Foreigner in Far Cathay.* New York: Scribner, Armstrong and Company.

Meuer, Johannes and Barbara Krug. 2011. 'The Current State of Research on Networks in China's Business System'. In *Institutional Variety in East Asia: Formal and Informal Patterns of Coordination*, edited by Werner Pascha, Cornelia Storz and Markus Taube, 145–67. Cheltenham, UK: Edward Elgar.

Mill, John Stuart. 1859. *On Liberty.* London: J. W. Parker.

Miller, J. Hillis. 1996. 'Border Crossings, Translating Theory: Ruth'. In *The Translatability of Cultures: Figurations of the Space between*, edited by Sanford Budick and Wolfgang Iser, 207–23. Stanford, CA: Stanford University Press.

Milne, William. 1817. *The Sacred Edict: Containing Sixteen Maxims of the Emperor Kang-He. Amplified by His Son, the Emperor Yoong-Ching Together with a Paraphrase on the Whole, by a Mandarin. Translated from the Chinese Original, and Illustrated with Notes.* London: Black, Kingsbury, Parbury and Allen.

Mirsky, Jonathan. 2013. 'How China Gets its Way'. *New York Review of Books* 60 (1): 52–53.

Missemer, George W. 1925. 'Handling Chinese Workers an Art to Be Studied if Profits Are to Be Made'. *The China Press*, 8 March, 18.

More, Thomas, Sir, Saint. 1533. *The Second Parte of the Co[N]Futacion of Tyndals Answere in Whyche Is also Confuted the Chyrche that Tyndale Deuyseth. And the Chyrche Also that Frere Barns Deuyseth.* London: Wyllyam Rastell.

Morisaki, Seiichi and William B. Gudykunst. 1994. 'Face in Japan and the United States'. In *The Challenge of Face-Work: Cross-Cultural and Interpersonal Issues*, edited by Stella Ting-Toomey. 47–93. Albany: State University of New York Press.

Morris, Rev T. M. 1892. *A Winter in North China.* London: Religious Tract Society.

Morrison, John Robert. 1834. *A Chinese Commercial Guide: Consisting of a Collection of Details and Regulations Respecting Foreign Trade with China.* Canton: Albion Press, and sold at the Canton Register Office.

Morrison, Robert. 1815–23. *A Dictionary of the Chinese Language.* Macao: Printed at the Honorable East India Company's Press, by P. P. Thoms.

——. 1828. *Vocabulary of the Canton Dialect.* Macao: Printed at the Honorable East India Company's Press.

Morrison, Robert and William Milne. 1823. 神天聖書. [The Holy Bible]. Malacca: British and Foreign Bible Society.

Morton, Thomas, of Berwick. 1596. *A Treatise of the Threefolde State of Man Wherein is Handled. 1 His Created Holinesse in His Innocencie. 2 His Sinfulnesse since the Fall of Adam. 3 His Renewed Holinesse in His Regeneration.* London: [By R. Robinson] for Robert Dexter and Raph Iackeson.

Moule, Arthur Evans. 1871. *Four Hundred Millions: Chapters on China and the Chinese.* London: Seeley, Jackson & Halliday.

——. 1878. *The Story of the Cheh-Kiang Mission of the Church Missionary Society.* London: Seeley, Jackson & Halliday.

———. 1891. *New China and Old: Personal Recollections and Observations of Thirty Years*. London: Seeley & Co., Ltd.

———. 1911. *Half a Century in China: Recollections and Observations*. London: Hodder and Stoughton.

———. 1914. *The Chinese People; a Handbook on China*. New York: E. S. Gorham.

Murakami, Haruki. 2011. 'Speaking as an Unrealistic Dreamer'. *Asia-Pacific Journal* 9 (29, no. 7): 1–8.

Murdock, Victor. 1920. *China: The Mysterious and Marvellous*. New York: Fleming H. Revell Company.

Nathan, Andrew J. and Andrew Scobell. 2012. *China's Search for Security*. New York: Columbia University Press.

Nathan, John. 2019. 'Night and Blood and Death'. *New York Review of Books* 66 (9): 29–31.

Needham, Joseph and Ling Wang. 1956. *Science and Civilization in China. Volume 2, History of Scientific Thought*. Cambridge: Cambridge University Press.

Neville, Robert. 2000. *Boston Confucianism: Portable Tradition in the Late-Modern World*. Albany: State University of New York Press.

Nevius, John. 1868. *China and the Chinese: A General Description of the Country and its Inhabitants; its Civilization and Form of Government; its Religious and Social Institutions; its Intercourse with Other Nations; and its Present Condition and Prospects*. New York: Harper and Brothers.

Ng, Guat Tin. 2008. 'The Essence and Elements of Chinese Culture: Implications for Cross-Cultural Competence in Social Work Practice'. *China Journal of Social Work* 1 (3): 205–7.

Ni, Dandan. 2018. 'Court Convicts Children for Abandoning Dying Father'. Sixth Tone, last modified 18 September 2018, accessed 12 December 2019, http://www.sixthtone.com/news/1002933/Court%20Convicts%20Children%20for%20 Abandoning%20Dying%20Father

Nida, Eugene. 1959. 'Principles of Translation as Exemplified by Bible Translating'. In *On Translation*, edited by Reuben Brower, 11–31. Cambridge, MA: Harvard University Press.

Nieuhof, Johannes. 1673. *An Embassy from the East-India Company of the United Provinces, to the Grand Tartar Cham, Emperor of China Deliver'd by their Excellencies, Peter De Goyer and Jacob De Keyzer, at His Imperial City of Peking: Wherein the Cities, Towns, Villages, Ports, Rivers, &c. in their Passages from Canton to Peking are Ingeniously Describ'd. By Mr. John Nieuhoff …; Also an Epistle of Father John Adams their Antagonist, Concerning the Whole Negotiation; With an Appendix of Several Remarks Taken Out of Father Athanasius Kircher; English'd, and Set Forth with their Several Sculptures*. London: Printed by the Author at his house in White-Friers.

Nitobe, Inazō. 1899. *Bushido: The Soul of Japan*. Philadelphia: Leeds & Biddle.

Northrop, Henry Davenport. 1894. *The Flowery Kingdom and the Land of the Mikado, Or, China, Japan, and Corea: Containing their Complete History Down to the Present Time*. Cleveland: American Book Concern.

———. 1903. *China; The Orient and the Yellow Man*. Kansas City, MO: S. D. Knapp.

Nylan, Michael. 1996. 'Confucian Piety and Individualism in Han China'. *Journal of the American Oriental Society* 116: 1–27.

O'Driscoll, Jim. 1996. 'About Face: A Defence and Elaboration of Universal Dualism'. *Journal of Pragmatics* 25 (1): 1–32.

————. 2011. 'Some Issues with the Concept of Face: When, What, How and How Much?' In *Politeness Across Cultures*, edited by Francesca Bargiela-Chiappini and Dániel Z. Kádár, 17–41. Basingstoke: Palgrave Macmillan.

Okamoto, Shigeko. 2011. 'The Use and Interpretation of Addressee Honorific's and Plain Forms in Japanese: Diversity, Multiplicity, and Ambiguity'. *Journal of Pragmatics* 43 (15): 3673–88.

Packard, Frank L. 1930. *Jimmie Dale and the Blue Envelope Murder*. Garden City, NY: Doubleday, Doran & Company, Inc.

Parker, Edward Harper. 1903. *China: Past and Present*. London: Chapman & Hall.

Parker, Henry. 1651. *Scotlands Holy VVar a Discourse Truly, and Plainly Remonstrating, how the Scots Out of a Corrupt Pretended Zeal to the Covenant have made the Same Scandalous, and Odious to all Good Men, and how by Religious Pretexts of Saving the Peace of Great Brittain they have Irreligiously Involved Us all in a most Pernitious Warre*. London: Printed by Fran. Neile.

Paterson, Samuel. 1773. *Bibliotheca Westiana: A Catalogue of the Curious and Truly Valuable Library of the Late James West, Esq; President of the Royal Society, Deceased: …* London: s.n.

Paton, Michael John. 2013. *Five Classics of Fengshui: Chinese Spiritual Geography in Historical and Environmental Perspective*. Leiden: E. J. Brill.

Philipps, Fabian. 1663. *The Antiquity, Legality, Reason, Duty and Necessity of Prae-Emption and Prourveyance, for the King, Or, Compositions for His Pourveyance as They Were Used and Taken for the Provisions of the Kings Household, the Small Charge and Burthen Thereof to the People, and the Many for the Author, Great Mischiefs and Inconveniences which Will Inevitably Follow the Taking of Them Away*. London: Printed by Richard Hodgkinson for the author, and are to be sold by Henry Marsh.

Phillips, John. 1695. *A Reflection on our Modern Poesy: An Essay*. Cambridge: Printed for W. Rogers in London and F. Hicks.

Picart, Bernard. 1741. *The Ceremonies and Religious Customs of the Various Nations of the Known World; with Additions and Remarks Omitted by the French Author: Whereby the Reader Will Be Informed (in a Concise, Clear and Intelligible Style) of the Customs and Ceremonies; in What Manner, and Under What Forms, Representations, Signs, &c. the Several Nations Under both Hemispheres Worship a Supreme Being. Written Originally in French and Now Faithfully Abridg'd from the French Original*. London: Printed and Sold for the Proprietor.

Piper, H. Beam. 1957. 'Omnilingual'. *Astounding Science Fiction* 58 (6): 8–46.

Pitkin, Hanna Fenichel. 1988. 'Are Freedom and Liberty Twins?' *Political Theory* 16 (4): 523–52.

Plath, Johann Heinrich. 1862. *Die Religion und der Cultus der Alten Chinesen*. 2 vols. Munich: Verlag der K. Akademie.

Pliny the Younger. 1645. *Pliny's Panegyricke: A Speech in Senate*. Oxford: [H. Hall].

Podger, Andrew and Hon Chan. 2015. 'The Concept of "Merit" in Australia, China and Taiwan'. *Australian Journal of Public Administration* 74 (3): 257–69.

Pratchett, Terry. 2011. *Snuff*. New York: Doubleday.

Pu, Songling. 1880. *Strange Stories from a Chinese Studio*. Translated by Herbert Allen Giles. London: Thos. De la Rue & Co.

Qiu, Xiaolong. 2000. *Death of a Red Heroine*. New York: Soho Press.

————. 2002. *A Loyal Character Dancer*. New York: Soho Press.

————. 2007. *Red Mandarin Dress*. New York: St. Martin's Minotaur.

Qu, Yaoxin 曲耀信. 1965. '向群眾承認錯誤並不丢面子' [Admitting mistakes in front of the masses is not a loss of face]'. 人民日報 [*People's Daily*], 8 November, 2nd edition.

Quesnay, François. (1767) 1888. 'Despotisme De La Chine'. In *Oeuvres economiques et philosophiques*, edited by Auguste Oncken. Paris: Joseph Baer & Compagnie.

Quincy, Josiah. 1847. *The Journals of Major Samuel Shaw*. Boston: William Crosby and H. P. Nichols.

Quine, Willard van Orman. 1959. 'Meaning and Translation'. In *On Translation*, edited by Reuben Brower, 148–72. Cambridge, MA: Harvard University Press.

Quinion, Michael B. 2004. *Port Out, Starboard Home: And Other Language Myths*. London: Penguin.

R. B. G. 1661. *Three Treatises Concerning the Scotish Discipline 1. A Fair Warning to Take Heed of the Same, by the Right Reverend Dr. Bramhall, Bishop of Derris: 2. A Review of Dr. Bramble, Late Bishop of London-Derry, His Fair Warning, &c. by R.B.G.: 3. A Second Fair Warning, in Vindication of the First, Against the Seditious Reviewer, by Ri. Watson, Chaplain to the Right Honorable the Lord Hopton: To which is Prefixed, a Letter Written by the Reverend Dean of St. Burien, Dr. Creyghton*. Hagh: Printed by Samuel Brown.

Radcliff, Ann. (1792) 1847. *Romance of the Forest*. London: Thomas Richardson and Son.

Raphals, Lisa. 2004. 'Reflections on Filiality, Nature, and Nurture'. In *Filial Piety in Chinese Thought and History*, edited by Alan K. L. Chan and Sor-hoon Tan, 215–25. London: RoutledgeCurzon.

Regardie, Israel. 1937–1940. *The Golden Dawn: An Account of the Teachings, Rites and Ceremonies of the Order of the Golden Dawn*. 4 vols. Chicago: The Aries Press.

Reichwein, Adolf. (1925) 1968. *China and Europe; Intellectual and Artistic Contacts in the Eighteenth Century*. New York: Barnes & Noble.

Richardson, Samuel. 1742a. *Clarissa: Or, the History of a Young Lady*. London: Printed for E. Newbery.

———. 1742b. *Pamela: Or, Virtue Rewarded. In a Series of Familiar Letters from a Beautiful Young Damsel to Her Parents ...* 4 vols. 3rd edition. London: Printed for S. Richardson.

———. 1753. *The History of Sir Charles Grandison. In a Series of Letters Published from the Originals, by the Editor of Pamela and Clarissa*. 7 vols. Dublin.

———. 1755. *A Collection of the Moral and Instructive Sentiments, Maxims, Cautions, and Reflexions, Contained in the Histories of Pamela, Clarissa, and Sir Charles Grandison*. London: printed for S. Richardson, and sold by C. Hitch and L. Hawes.

Richter, Melvin. 1986. 'Conceptual History (*Begriffsgeschichte*) and Political Theory'. *Political Theory* 14 (4): 604–37.

———. 1987. '*Begriffsgeschichte* and the History of Ideas'. *Journal of the History of Ideas* 48 (2): 247–63.

Roback, Charles W. 1854. *The Mysteries of Astrology, and the Wonders of Magic: Including a History of the Rise and Progress of Astrology, and the Various Branches of Necromancy: Together with Valuable Directions and Suggestions Relative to the Casting of Nativities, and Predictions by Geomancy, Chiromancy, Physiognomy, &c.: Also ... Narratives, Anecdotes, &c. Illustrative of the Marvels of Witchcraft, Spiritual Phenomena, and the Results of Supernatural Influence*. London: Sampson Low, Son.

Roberts, Steven V. 1988. 'White House Confirms Reagans Follow Astrology, Up to a Point'. *New York Times*, 4 May 1988, 1.

Rochon, Alexis. 1792. *A Voyage to Madagascar, and the East Indies. by the Abbe Rochon, Member of the Academies of Sciences of Paris and Petersburgh, Astronomer of the Marine, Keeper of the King's Philosophical Cabinet, Inspector of Machines, Money, &c. Translated from the French. Illustrated with an Accurate Map of the Island of Madagascar. to which is Added, a Memoir on the Chinese Trade*. London: Printed for G. G. J. and J. Robinson, Paternoster-Row.

Ropp, Paul S. 1981. *Dissent in Early Modern China: Ju-Lin Wai-Shih and Ch'ing Social Criticism*. Ann Arbor: The University of Michigan Press.

Rossbach, Sarah. 1983. *Feng Shui: the Chinese Art of Placement*. New York: Arkana.

Rossbach, Sarah. 1984. *Feng Shui: Ancient Wisdom for the Most Beneficial Way to Place and Arrange Furniture. Rooms and Buildings*. London: Rider and Company.

Ruhi, Sükriye and Hale Isik-Güler. 2007. 'Conceptualizing Face and Relational Work in (Im)Politeness: Revelations from Politeness Lexemes and Idioms in Turkish'. *Journal of Pragmatics* 39 (4): 681–711.

Rühle, Susanne. 2011. 'A Different Capitalism for China? the Role of *Guanxi* and the Family for Chinese Economic Development'. In *Institutional Variety in East Asia: Formal and Informal Patterns of Coordination*, edited by Werner Pascha, Cornelia Storz and Markus Taube, 168–99. Cheltenham, UK: Edward Elgar.

Russell, Bertrand. 1922. *The Problem of China*. London: George Allen & Unwin Ltd.

———. 1945. *A History of Western Philosophy: And Its Connection with Political and Social Circumstances from the Earliest Times to the Present Day*. New York: Simon and Schuster.

S., J. 1705. *Mathematical Ideas Delivered in Narratives Touching Mathematical Termes in the Way of Intellectual Vision: Or of Divine Contemplation, Together with Other Narratives of Divine Tendency also*. London: Printed for J. Nutt.

Saavedra Fjardo, Diego de. 1700. *The Royal Politician Represented in One Hundred Emblems*. Translated by Sir Ja Astry. London: Printed for Matt. Gylliflower and Luke Meredith.

Said, Edward. 1978. *Orientalism*. London: Routledge and Kegan Paul.

———. 1983. 'Traveling Theory'. In *The World, the Text and the Critic*, edited by Edward Said, 226–47. Cambridge, MA: Harvard University Press.

St. André, James. 1998. 'History, Mystery, Myth: A Comparative Study of Narrative Strategies in the *Baijia Gongan* and the *Complete Sherlock Holmes*'. Ph.D., The University of Chicago.

———. 2006. 'Travelling Toward True Translation: The First Generation of Sino-English Translators'. *The Translator* 12 (1): 189–210.

———. 2007. 'The Development of British Sinology and Changes in Translation Practice: The Case of Sir John Francis Davis (1795–1890)'. *Translating and Interpreting Studies* 2 (2): 3–42.

———. 2013. 'How the Chinese Lost "Face"'. *Journal of Pragmatics* 55: 68–85.

———. 2018a. 'Consequences of the Conflation of *Xiao* and Filial Piety in English'. *Translating and Interpreting Studies* 13 (2): 296–320.

———. 2018b. 'A Cost-Benefit Analysis of Using Online Corpora for Translation Research'. *Journal of Translation Studies* New Series 2 (1): 127–52.

———. 2018c. *Translating China as Cross-Identity Performance*. Honolulu: University of Hawai'i Press.

Sales, W. Sir. 1655. *Theophania, Or, Severall Modern Histories Represented by Way of Romance and Politickly Discours'd upon*. London: Printed by T. Newcomb for Thomas Heath.

Scarth, John. 1860. *Twelve Years in China: The People, the Rebels, and the Mandarins. by a British Resident*. Edinburgh: Thomas Constable and Co.

Scollon, Ron and Suzie Wong Scollon. 1994. 'Face Parameters in East-West Discourse'. In *The Challenge of Face-Work: Cross-Cultural and Interpersonal Issues*, edited by Stella Ting-Toomey, 133–57. Albany: State University of New York Press.

Selby, Thomas Gunn. 1900. *Chinamen at Home*. London: Hodder and Stoughton.

———. 1901. *As the Chinese See Us*. London: T. Fisher Unwin.

Semedo, Alvarez. 1655. *The History of that Great and Renowned Monarchy of China. Wherein all the Particular Privinces are Accurately Described: As also the Dispositions, Manners, Learning, Lawes, Militia, Goernment, and Religion of the People. Together with the Traffick and Commodities of that Countrey. Lately Written in Italian by F. Alvarez Semedo, a Portughess, After He had Resided Twenty Two Yeares at the Court, and Other Famous Cities of that Kingdom. Now Put into English by a Person of Quality, and Illustrated with several Mapps and Figures, to Satisfie the Curious, and Advance the Trade of Great Britain. to which is Added the History of the Late Invasion, and Conquest of that Flourishing Kingdom by the Tartars. with an Exact Account of the Other Affairs of China, Till these Present Times*. London: Printed by E. Tyler for John Crook.

Seneca, Lucius Annaeus. 1581. *Seneca His Tenne Tragedies, Translated into Englysh*. London: Thomas Marsh.

Shen. Tkin [He, Jinshan], translator. 1843. *The Rambles of the Emperor Ching Tih in Këang Nan: A Chinese Tale*. Translated by Tkin Shen, student of the Anglo-Chinese College, Malacca. With a preface by James Legge, D. D. President of the College. London: Longman, Brown, Green, & Longmans.

Shi, Zhen 史箴. 1995. '風水典故考略' [Textual research of the ancient codes and records of fengshui]. In 風水理論研究（二）[Research into fengshui theory (2)], edited by Qiheng Wang 王其亨, 13–30. Taipei: Lamper Enterprises Co. Ltd.

Shih, Kuo-heng. 1944. *China Enters the Machine Age: A Study of Labor in Chinese War Industry*. Translated by Hsiao-Tung Fei and Francis L. K. Hsu. Cambridge, MA: Harvard University Press.

Shih, Shu-mei. 2004. 'Global Literature and the Technologies of Recognition'. *Publication of the Modern Language Association* 119 (1): 16–30.

———. 2011. 'The Concept of the Sinophone'. *Publication of the Modern Language Association* 126 (3): 709–18.

Shirley, James. 1633. *The Bird in a Cage. A Comedie. as It Hath Beene Presented at the Phoenix in Drury-Lane*. London: Printed by B. Alsop. and T. Fawcet. for William Cooke.

———. 1640. *A Pastorall Called the Arcadia Acted by Her Majesties Servants at the Phaenix in Drury Lane*. London: Printed by J. D. for Iohn Williams, and F. Eglesfeild.

Sirr, Henry Charles. 1849. *China and the Chinese: Their Religion, Character, Customs, and Manufactures* ... 2 vols. London: William S. Orr & Company.

Sivin, Nathan. 1980. 'Science in China's Past'. In *Science in Contemporary China*, edited by Leo A. Orleans, 1–29. Stanford: Stanford University Press.

Skinner, Quentin. 1998. *Liberty Before Liberalism*. Cambridge: Cambridge University Press.

Smith, Adam. 1776. *An Inquiry into the Nature and Causes of the Wealth of Nations*. London: Printed for W. Strahan and T. Cadell.

Smith, Arthur Henderson. 1894. *Chinese Characteristics. Enlarged and Revised Edition with Marginal and New Illustrations*. New York: Fleming H. Revell Company.

———. 1899. *Village Life in China: A Study in Sociology*. New York: Fleming H. Revell Company.

———. 1901. *China in Convulsion*. 2 vols. Edinburgh: Oliphant, Anderson & Ferrier.

Smith, Richard J. 1991. *Fortune-Tellers and Philosophers: Divination in Traditional Chinese Society*. Boulder: Westview Press.

Smith, Robert J. 1996. 'The Japanese (Confucian) Family: The Tradition from the Bottom Up'. In *Confucian Traditions in East Asian Modernity*, edited by Wei-ming Tu, 155–74. Cambridge, MA: Harvard University Press.

Soong Chiang, May-ling 宋美齡. 1935a. '中華民族的再生（其七）— 七種致命的痼疾 [China Shall Rise again (no. 7) – Seven Deadly Sins]'. 中央日報 [*Central Daily News*], 26 February, 6.

———. 1935b. '中華民族的再生（其八）— 七種致命的痼疾 [China Shall Rise again (no. 8) – Seven Deadly Sins]'. 中央日報 [*Central Daily News*], 5 March, 6.

———. 1941. *China Shall Rise Again*. New York: Harper and Brothers Publishers.

Spedding, Patrick. 2011. ' "The New Machine": Discovering the Limits of ECCO'. *Eighteenth-Century Studies* 44 (4): 437–53.

Spencer-Oatey, Helen. 2007. 'Theories of Identity and the Analysis of Face'. *Journal of Pragmatics* 39 (4): 639–56.

Starkey, George. 1660. *Royal and Other Innocent Bloud Crying Aloud to Heaven for Due Vengeance. Humbly Represented to the Right Honourable the Lords and Commons Assembled in Parliament. and with all Humble Dutifull Submission Dedicated to the Two High and Mighty Princes, James Duke of York and Henry Duke of Gloucester, His Sacred Majestyes Royal Brethren. by George Starkey, a True Honourer and Faithfull Friend of His Country*. London: printed by A. Warren for Daniel White.

Staunton, George Thomas, Sir. 1810. *Ta Tsing Leu Lee; being the Fundamental Laws, and a Selection from the Supplementary Statutes of the Penal Code of China*. London: Cadell and Davies.

Steele, Richard and Joseph Addison. 1711a. *Spectator no. 123*, Saturday 21 July.

———. 1711b. *Spectator no. 202*, Monday 6 October.

———. 1712. *Spectator no. 472*, Monday 1 September.

Steiner, George. 1975. *After Babel: Aspects of Language and Translation*. London: Oxford University Press.

Stengers, Isabelle, ed. 1987. *D'une science à l'autre: des concepts nomades*. Paris: Seuil.

Su, Qing 蘇青. 1948. 歧途佳人 [Beauty gone astray]. Shanghai: Si hai chubanshe.

Sun, Lung-Kee 孫隆基. 1988. 中國文化的 '深層結構' [The deep structure of Chinese culture]. Hong Kong: Toisan Publishing. First published 1983.

Sydney, Philip Sir. 1590. *The Countesse of Pembrokes Arcadia*. London: Printed by Iohn Windet for William Ponsonbie.

Tambiah, Stanley Jeyaraja. 1990. *Magic, Science, Religion and the Scope of Rationality*. Cambridge: Cambridge University Press.

Tan, Sor-hoon. 2004. 'Filial Daughters-in-Law: Questioning Confucian Filiality'. In *Filial Piety in Chinese Thought and History*, edited by Alan K. L. Chan and Sor-hoon Tan, 226–40. London: RoutledgeCurzon.

Taylor, John. 1630. *All the VVorkes of Iohn Taylor the Water-Poet Beeing Sixty and Three in Number. Collected into One Volume by the Author: VVith Sundry New Additions Corrected, Reuised, and Newly Imprinted, 1630*. London: Printed by I[ohn] B[eale], Elizabeth Allde, Bernard Alsop, and Thomas F[awcet] for Iames Boler.

Taylor, Stephen. 1998. 'Robert Walpole, First Earl of Orford'. In *Biographical Dictionary of British Prime Ministers*, edited by Robert Eccleshall and Graham Walker, 1–13. New York: Routledge.

Teng, Ssu-yu. 1943. 'Chinese Influence on the Western Examination System'. *Harvard Journal of Asiatic Studies* 7 (4): 267–312.

Teon, Aris. 'Face, Filial Piety and Work Motivation in Chinese Culture'. The Greater China Journal, last modified 4 March 2017, accessed 27 February, 2022, https://china-journal.org/2017/03/04/face-filial-piety-and-work-motivation-in-chinese-culture/

Terkourafi, Marina. 2007. 'Toward a Universal Notion of Face for a Universal Notion of Cooperation'. In *Explorations in Pragmatics: Linguistic, Cognitive, and Intercultural Aspects*, edited by Istvan Kecskes and Laurence Horn, 307–38. Berlin: Mouton de Gruyter.

Teruo, Tarumoto. 1998. 'A Statistical Survey of Translated Fiction 1840–1920'. In *Translation and Creation: Readings of Western Literature in Early Modern China, 1840–1918*, edited by David E. Pollard, 37–42. Amsterdam: John Benjamins Publishing Company.

Thoms, P. P. 1853. *The Emperor of China v. the Queen of England: A Refutation of the Arguments Contained in the Seven Official Documents Transmitted by Her Majesty's Government at Hong Kong, Who Maintain that the Documents of the Chinese Government Contain Insulting Language*. London: P. P. Thoms.

Ting-Toomey, Stella, ed. 1994. *The Challenge of Facework: Cross-Cultural and Interpersonal Issues*. Albany: State University of New York Press.

Toll, Robert C. 1976. *On with the Show! The First Century of Show Business in America*. New York: Oxford University Press.

Tsui, Anne S. 2012. 'Contextualizing Research in a Modernizing China'. In *Handbook of Chinese Organizational Behaviour*, edited by Huang Xu and Michael Harris Bond, 29–47. Cheltenham, UK: Edward Elgar.

Tu, Wei-ming. 1976. *Neo-Confucian Thought in Action: Wang Yang-Ming's Youth*. Berkeley, CA: University of California Press.

———. 1984. *Confucian Ethics Today: The Singapore Challenge*. Singapore: Federal Publications.

———. 1985. *Confucian Thought: Selfhood as Creative Transformation*. Albany, NY: State University of New York Press.

———. 1994a. 'Cultural China: The Periphery as the Center'. In *The Living Tree: The Changing Meaning of Being Chinese Today*, edited by Wei-ming Tu, 1–34. Stanford, CA: Stanford University Press.

———. 1994b. 'Preface'. In *The Living Tree: The Changing Meaning of Being Chinese Today*, edited by Wei-ming Tu, v–x. Stanford, CA: Stanford University Press.

———. 1999. 'A Confucian Perspective on the Core Values of the Global Community'. *Review of Korean Studies* 2: 55–70.

———. 2000. 'Foreword'. In *Boston Confucianism: Portable Tradition in the Late-Modern World*, edited by Robert Neville, xi–xix. Albany, NY: State University of New York Press.

———. n.d. 'Biography'. About Tu Weiming, accessed 22 January 2022, http://tuweiming.net/about-tu/biography/

Turner, F. S. [Frederick Storrs]. 1874. 'Feng-shui'. *Cornhill Magazine* 29, no. 3 (March): 337–48.

Tylor, Edward Burnett. 1865. *Researches into the Early History of Mankind and the Development of Civilization*. London: John Murray.

———. 1871. *Primitive Culture: Researches into the Development of Mythology, Philosophy, Religion, Art, and Custom*. 2 vols. London: John Murray.

United Bible Association. (1919) 1988. 聖經: 新標點和合本 [The Holy Bible: Chinese Union Version with new punctuation]. Hong Kong: United Bible Association.

———. 1979. 聖經現代中文譯本 [The Holy Bible: modern Chinese translation]. Hong Kong: United Bible Association.

Usui, Emiko. 2019. 'Mothers of the State'. *New York Review of Books* 66 (11): 12, 14, 16.

Valensi, Lucette. 1990. 'The Making of a Political Paradigm: The Ottoman State and Oriental Despotism'. In *The Transmission of Culture in Early Modern Europe*, edited by Anthony Grafton and Ann Blair, 173–98. Philadelphia: University of Pennsylvania Press.

Virgil. 1660. *AEneas His Descent into Hell as it is Inimitably Described by the Prince of Poets in the Sixth of His AEneis. / made English by John Boys of Hode-Court, Esq; Together with an Ample and Learned Comment upon the Same, Wherein all Passages Criticall, Mythological, Philosophical and Historical, are Fully and Clearly Explained. to which are Added some Certain Pieces Relating to the Publick, Written by the Author*. London: Printed by R. Hodgkinsonne.

Wagstaff, George. 1776. *Wagstaff's Catalogue for 1776. of His Matchless Collection of Scarce Books, … which Will Begin to be Sold on Monday Next, …* London: s.n.

Walker, John. 1684. *The Antidote: Or, a Seasonable Discourse on Rom. 13. 1 Shewing the Necessity and Reasonableness of Subjection to the Higher Powers. with an Account of the Divine Right Or Original of Government*. London: printed by Thomas Hodgkin, for Anthony Stephens Bookseller.

Wan, Qingfeng 宛慶豐. 1989. '向上要錢竅門多向下撥錢看關係' [Seeking money from above, there are many doors; seeking money from below depends on guanxi]. 人民日報 [*People's Daily*], 14 January, 5th edition.

Wang, Lixiong. 2008. *China Tidal Wave*. Translated by Anton Platero. Folkestone, Kent: Global Oriental.

Wang, Peng. 2014. 'Extra-Legal Protection in China: How Guanxi Distorts China's Legal System and Facilitates the Rise of Unlawful Protectors'. *British Journal of Criminology* 54: 809–830.

Wang, Wenbin 王文斌, ed. 2012. 話說面子：關於面子的審視與反思 [Speaking of face: Review and reflection]. Kunming: Yunnan Renmin Chubanshe.

Wang, Wenxing. 1995. *Family Catastrophe*. Translated by Susan Wan Dolling. Honolulu: University of Hawai'i Press.

Wang, Yongdong, Liangliang Zhao, S. Arunmozhi, and N. Sri Madhava Raja. 2021. 'Understanding Chinese Cultural Values and Cultural Psychology'. *Aggression and Violent Behavior*: 101708. doi:https://doi.org/10.1016/j.avb.2021.101708.

Wanley, Nathaniel. 1673. *The Wonders of the Little World, Or, A General History of Man in Six Books: Wherein by Many Thousands of Examples is Shewed what*

Man Hath been from the First Ages of the World to these Times, in Respect of His Body, Senses, Passions, Affections, His Virtues and Perfections, His Vices and Defects, His Quality, Vocation and Profession, and Many Other Particulars Not Reducible to any of the Former Heads: Collected from the Writings of the Most Approved Historians, Philosophers, Physicians, Philologists and Others. London: Printed for T. Basset, R. Cheswel, J. Wright, and T. Sawbridge.

Waterhouse, Edward. 1663. *Fortescutus Illustratus, Or, A Commentary on that Nervous Treatise, De Laudibus Legum Angliae, Written by Sir John Fortescue, Knight.* London: Printed by Thomas Roycroft for Thomas Dicas.

Watts, Richard. (1992) 2005. 'Linguistic Politeness and Politic Verbal Behaviour: Reconsidering Claims for Universality'. In *Politeness in Language*, edited by Richard Watts, Sachiko Ide and Konrad Ehlich. 2nd edition, 43–69. Berlin: Mouton de Gruyter.

———. 2003. *Politeness*. Cambridge: Cambridge University Press.

Waugh, Evelyn. 1945. *Brideshead Revisited*. London: Chapman and Hall.

Webb, John. 1669. *An Historical Essay Endeavoring a Probability that the Language of the Empire of China is the Primitive Language*. London: Printed for Nathaniel Brook.

Wei, Yiqing 衞一清. 1958. '決心，面子和其他' [Determination, face and other matters]. 人民日報 [*People's Daily*], 13 March, 7th edition.

Weiner, Philip P., ed. 1973–74. *Dictionary of the History of Ideas: Studies of Selected Pivotal Ideas. in Five Volumes*. New York: Charles Scribner's Sons.

Wen, Hua 聞華. 1980. '面子與真理' [Face and truth]. 人民日報 [*People's Daily*], 21 October, 5th edition.

Weston, Stephen. 1814. *Fan-Hy-Cheu: A Tale, in Chinese and English, with Notes, and a Short Grammar of the Chinese Language*. London: Robert Baldwin.

Whorf, Benjamin. 1956. 'Languages and Logic'. In *Language, Thought, and Reality, Selected Writings of Benjamin Lee Whorf*, edited by John B. Carroll, 233–45. Cambridge, MA: MIT Press.

Wierzbicka, Anna. 1997. *Understanding Cultures through their Key Words: English, Russian, Polish, German, and Japanese*. New York: Oxford University Press.

Williams, Samuel Wells. 1848. *The Middle Kingdom: A Survey of the Geography, Government, Education, Social Life, Arts, Religion, &c., of the Chinese Empire and its Inhabitants. with a New Map of the Empire, and Illustrations Principally Engraved by J. W. Orb*. 2 vols. New York: Wiley and Putnam.

Williams, Raymond. 1985. *Keywords: A Vocabulary of Culture and Society. Revised Edition*. New York: Oxford University Press.

Wilson, Arthur. 1653. *The History of Great Britain. Being the Life and Reign of King James the First, Relating to What Passed from His First Access to the Crown, Till His Death*. London: Printed for Richard Lownds.

Wilson, Epiphanius. 1900. *The Wisdom of Confucius, with Critical and Biographical Sketches by Epiphanius Wilson*. New York: Colonial Press.

Wilson, Ernest Henry. 1913. *A Naturalist in Western China with Vasculum, Camera, and Gun*. 2 vols. London: Methuen & Co. Ltd.

Winterbotham, William. 1795. *An Historical, Geographical, and Philosophical View of the Chinese Empire: Comprehending a Description of the Fifteen Provinces of China, Chinese Tartary, Tributary States; Natural History of China; Government, Religion, Laws, Manners and Customs, Literature, Arts, Sciences, Manufactures, &c*. London: Printed for the editor; J. Ridgeway etc.

Woodbridge, Samuel Isett. 1919. *Fifty Years in China: Being an Account of the History and Conditions in China and of the Missions of the Presbyterian Church in the United States there from 1867 to the Present Day*. Richmond, VA: Presbyterian Committee of Publication.

Woolley, Hannah. 1673. *The Gentlewomans Companion; Or, A Guide to the Female Sex Containing Directions of Behaviour, in all Places, Companies, Relations, and Conditions, from their Childhood Down to Old Age: Viz. as, Children to Parents. Scholars to Governours. Single to Servants. Virgins to Suitors. Married to Husbands. Huswifes to the House Mistresses to Servants. Mothers to Children. Widows to the World Prudent to all. with Letters and Discourses upon all Occasions. Whereunto is Added, a Guide for Cook-Maids, Dairy-Maids, Chamber-Maids, and all Others that Go to Service. the Whole being an Exact Rule for the Female Sex in General*. London: printed by A. Maxwell for Dorman Newman at the Kings-Arms in the Poultry.

World Bible Association. 1976. 新約全書 (新譯本) [The New Chinese Bible (New Testament)]. Hong Kong: World Bible Association.

———. 1992. 舊約全書(新譯本) [The New Chinese Bible (Old Testament)]. Hong Kong: World Bible Association.

Wu, Yu 吳虞. 1917. '家族制度為專制主義之根據論' [On the family system as the root of despotism]. 新青年 [*New Youth*]: 1–4.

Wuyue, Sanren 五岳散人. 2013. 中國人的裡子與面子 [Substance and face of the Chinese]. Beijing: Jiuzhou Chubanshe.

Xi, Jinping 習近平. 2013. '在中央黨校建校80週年慶祝大會藍2013年春季學期開學典禮上的講話' [Speech given at the opening ceremony of the spring semester of 2013 to celebrate the 80th anniversary of the founding of the Central Party School]. 人民日報 [*People's Daily*], 1 March 2013.

Xi, Weiming 奚巍鳴. 1980. '要不得的 "關係學"' [Intolerable 'guanxixue']. 人民日報 [*People's Daily*], 17 March, 8th edition.

Xiao, Lu. 2010. *Dialogue*. Translated by Archibald McKenzie. Hong Kong: Hong Kong University Press.

Xu, Dongfeng. 2011. 'The Concept of Friendship and the Culture of Hospitality: The Encounter between the Jesuits and Late Ming China'. Ph.D., University of Chicago.

Yamashita, Samuel Hideo. 1996. 'Confucianism and the Japanese State, 1904–1945'. In *Confucian Traditions in East Asian Modernity*, edited by Wei-ming Tu, 132–54. Cambridge, MA: Harvard University Press.

Yan, Lianke. 2011. *Dream of Ding Village*. Translated by Cindy Carter. New York: Grove Press.

Yang, C. K. 1961. *Religion in Chinese Society: A Study of Contemporary Social Functions of Religion and Some of their Historical Factors*. Berkeley, CA: University of California Press.

Yang, Kuo-shu 楊國樞, ed. 1989. 中國人的心理 [Psychology of the Chinese]. Taipei: Laureate Book Company Ltd.

Yang, Kuo-shu 楊國樞 and Kwang-kuo Hwang 黃光國, eds. 1991. 中國人的心裡與行為 [Psychology and behaviour of the Chinese]. Taipei: Laureate Book Company Ltd.

Yang, Martin C. 1947. *A Chinese Village: Taitou, Shantung Province*. London: Kegan Paul, Trench, Trubner & Co., Ltd.

Yang, Mayfair Mei-hui. 1994. *Gifts, Favors and Banquets: The Art of Social Relationships in China*. Ithaca, NY: Cornell University Press.

———. 2002. 'The Resilience of Guanxi and its New Deployments: A Critique of Some New Guanxi Scholarship'. *The China Quarterly* 170 (June): 459–76.

Yang, Wesley. 2018. 'Paper Tigers'. In *The Souls of Yellow Folk*, 29–60. New York: W. W. Norton.

Yang, Yoon Sun. 2017. *From Domestic Women to Sensitive Young Men: Translating the Individual in Early Colonial Korea*. Cambridge, MA: Harvard University Press.

Yasuoka, Hideo 安岡秀夫. 1926. 小説から見た支那の民族性. [The ethnic character of the Chinese, as seen from their fiction]. Tokyo: Juhokaku.

Yates, M. T. 1868. 'Ancestral Worship and Fung-Shuy'. *The Chinese Recorder and Missionary Journal* 1 (2–3): 23–28; 37–43.

Ye, Ban. 1983. '講管理學, 不講 "關係學"' [Talk about management science, not 'guanxi science']. 人民日报 [*People's Daily*] 8 November, 3rd edition.

Yin, Zheng 尹筝. 1980. '同志關係' [Comradely guanxi]. 人民日報 [*People's Daily*], 4 February, 8th edition.

Yu, Bor-chuan 余伯泉 and Kwang-kuo Hwang 黃光國. 1991. '形式主義與人情關係對台灣地區國營企業發展的影響 [The influence of formalism and relations on the development of state-owned enterprises in Taiwan]'. In 中國人的心裡與行為 [Psychology and Behaviour of the Chinese], edited by Kuo-shu Yang 楊國樞 and Kwang-kuo Hwang 黃光國, 213–40. Taipei: Laureate Book Company Ltd.

Yu, Hua 余華. 1996. *The Past and Punishments*. Translated by Andrew Jones. Honolulu: University of Hawai'i Press.

———. 2010. 十個詞彙裡的中國. 台北市: 麥田出版.

———. 2011. *China in Ten Words*. Translated by Allan Hepburn Barr. New York: Pantheon Books.

———. 2013. 'When Filial Piety is the Law'. *New York Times*, 7 July 2013.

Zhai, Xuewei 翟學偉. 1995. 中國人的臉面觀：社會心理學的一項本土研究 [The face outlook of the Chinese: A social psychological indigenous study]. Taipei: Laureate Publishing.

Zhang, He 張賀. 2020. '餐飲浪費，不是有面子而是丟面子' [You don't gain face by wasting food and drink, you lose it]. 人民日報 [*People's Daily*], 14 September, 7th edition.

Zhang, Ren 張靭. 1994. '禮貌的概念及其它' [Politeness and other concepts]. 外語教學 [*Foreign Language Education*] (1): 10–16.

Zhang, Tao 張濤. 2006. 面子: 中國社會舞台上的面子藝術 [Face: The art of face on the Chinese stage]. Beijing: Dizhen Chubanshe.

Zhang, Zhidong 張之洞. 1990. *Quan Xue Pian* 勸學篇 [Learn!], edited by Shanbang Chen 陳山榜. Dalian: Dalian Chubanshe.

Zheng, Changgan 鄭昌淦. 1980. '封建的等級關係和特權制度' [Feudal hierarchy and the system of special privileges]. 人民日報 [*People's Daily*], 25 August, 5th edition.

Zhongshan Daxue Xixue Dongjian Wenxian Guan 中山大學西學東漸文獻館. 2016. '編者的話' [Editor's note]. In 西學東漸與儒家經典翻譯 [Dissemination of Western learning in China and translation of Confucianist classics], edited by Zhongshan Daxue Xixue Dongjian Wenxian Guan 中山大學西學東漸文獻館, 8. Beijing: The Commercial Press.

Zhu, Lin. 1998. *Snake's Pillow and Other Stories*. Translated by Richard King. Honolulu: University of Hawai'i Press.

Zhu, Wanjin 祝畹瑾. 1992. 社會語言學概論 [Sociolinguistics: An introduction]. Changsha: Hunan jiaoyu chubanshe.

Zhu, Wen. 2007. *I Love Dollars*. Translated by Julia Lovell. New York: Columbia University Press.

Zhuang, Zexuan 莊澤宣. 1938. 民族性與教育 [National character and education]. Shanghai: Commercial Press.

Index

Note: *literary works can be found under authors' names unless anonymous.*

EU authorised representative for GPSR:
Easy Access System Europe, Mustamäe tee 50,
10621 Tallinn, Estonia
gpsr.requests@easproject.com

www.ingramcontent.com/pod-product-compliance
Lightning Source LLC
Chambersburg PA
CBHW051957270326
41929CB00015B/2688